The GED®

FOR

DUMMIES®

2ND EDITION

The GED® FOR DUMMIES®

2ND EDITION

by Murray Shukyn and Dale E. Shuttleworth, PhD

WILEY

Wiley Publishing, Inc.

The GED® For Dummies®, 2nd Edition

Published by
Wiley Publishing, Inc.
111 River St.
Hoboken, NJ 07030-5774
www.wiley.com

Copyright © 2010 by Wiley Publishing, Inc., Indianapolis, Indiana

Published by Wiley Publishing, Inc., Indianapolis, Indiana

Published simultaneously in Canada

For general information on our other products and services, please contact our Customer Care Department within the U.S. at 877-762-2974, outside the U.S. at 317-572-3993, or fax 317-572-4002.

For technical support, please visit www.wiley.com/techsupport.

Wiley also publishes its books in a variety of electronic formats. Some content that appears in print may not be available in electronic books.

Library of Congress Control Number: 2010921248

ISBN: 978-0-470-57080-7

Manufactured in the United States of America

10 9 8 7 6

WILEY

About the Authors

Murray Shukyn, associate director of The Training Renewal Foundation, is a graduate of the University of Toronto with professional qualifications as a teacher at the elementary and secondary levels, including special education. During an extensive career spanning more than thirty years, he has taught at the elementary, secondary, and university levels. Murray has also taught professional development programs for teachers and training courses for adult learners. He is acknowledged as a Canadian leader in the field of alternative education through his work in the creation of such innovative programs for the Toronto Board of Education as SEED, Learnxs, Subway Academy, SOLE, and ACE. In 1995, he became associate director at The Training Renewal Foundation, which introduced the GED to the province of Ontario. Over the years, he has been a consultant to government, media, and public relations companies, as well as an author of textbooks and numerous articles in magazines and periodicals. He is a coauthor of the third and fourth Canadian editions of *How to Prepare for the GED,* published by Barron's Educational Series in the United States.

Dale E. Shuttleworth, PhD, is the executive director of The Training Renewal Foundation. Dale's career as a community educator has included experience as a teacher, school-community worker, consultant, principal, coordinator, superintendent, and university lecturer. In the fields of education and community economic development, he is a founder of the Learnxs Foundation, Inc., Youth Ventures Developments of Metropolitan Toronto, the Learning Enrichment Foundation, the York Business Opportunities Centre, the Centre for Community and Economic Renewal, and The Training Renewal Foundation. He is a coauthor of the third and fourth Canadian editions of *How to Prepare for the GED,* published by Barron's Educational Series in the United States, and the author of *School Management in Transition,* published by Routledge Falmer in 2003, *Enterprise Learning in Action,* published by Routledge in London and New York, and *Schooling for Life,* due to be published by the University of Toronto Press in 2010. He has been the recipient of the prestigious Dag Hammarskjold Gold Medal for Excellence in Education.

In 1995, Dale created the GED Preparation Centre pilot project, which brought the Hi School Equivalency Certificate to the Province of Ontario. In 2000, he was named le author/consultant for a study on "Innovations in School Management," conducted Organization for Economic Co-operation and Development (OECD) in Paris, Franc ing in the publishing of the book, *New School Management Approaches* in 2001.

Authors' Acknowledgments

We wish to express our appreciation to Marilyn Shuttleworth, who assisted us in the preparation of this manuscript; The Training Renewal Foundation for the opportunity to work in the world of the GED; and the late Peter Kilburn, former Canadian GED administrator, for his inspiration, friendship, and encouragement in introducing us to the potential of the GED to be a source of fulfillment and liberation in the lives and careers of so many adult learners who have dropped out of traditional schooling accreditation systems.

Publisher's Acknowledgments

We're proud of this book; please send us your comments at http://dummies.custhelp.com. For other comments, please contact our Customer Care Department within the U.S. at 877-762-2974, outside the U.S. at 317-572-3993, or fax 317-572-4002.

Some of the people who helped bring this book to market include the following:

Acquisitions, Editorial, and Media Development

Project Editor: Chad R. Sievers

        (Previous Edition: Tere Drenth)

Senior Acquisitions Editor: Lindsay Lefevere

        (Previous Edition: Kathy Cox)

Copy Editor: Amanda M. Langferman

Assistant Editor: Erin Calligan Mooney

Editorial Program Coordinator: Joe Niesen

Technical Editors: Betsy Delgado, Joan Borders

Editorial Manager: Michelle Hacker

Editorial Assistant: Jennette ElNaggar

Art Coordinator: Alicia B. South

Cover Photos: istock photography

Cartoons: Rich Tennant (www.the5thwave.com)

Composition Services

Project Coordinator: Sheree Montgomery

Layout and Graphics: Carl Byers, Carrie A. Cesavice, Christin Swinford, Ronald G. Terry

Special Art: Ricardo Checa

Proofreaders: Melissa D. Buddendeck, Lindsay Littrell

Indexer: Potomac Indexing, LLC

Publishing and Editorial for Consumer Dummies

    Diane Graves Steele, Vice President and Publisher, Consumer Dummies

    Kristin Ferguson-Wagstaffe, Product Development Director, Consumer Dummies

    Ensley Eikenburg, Associate Publisher, Travel

    Kelly Regan, Editorial Director, Travel

Publishing for Technology Dummies

    Andy Cummings, Vice President and Publisher, Dummies Technology/General User

Composition Services

    Debbie Stailey, Director of Composition Services

Contents at a Glance

Introduction 1

Part 1: Putting the GED into Perspective 5
Chapter 1: Taking a Quick Glance at the GED 7
Chapter 2: Navigating the GED Testing System 21
Chapter 3: Succeeding on the GED 31

Part II: Minding Your Ps and Qs:
The Language Arts, Writing Test 39
Chapter 4: The Write Stuff: Preparing for the Language Arts, Writing Test, Parts I and II 41
Chapter 5: Practice Test — Language Arts, Writing Test: Parts I and II 57
Chapter 6: Answers and Explanations for the Language Arts, Writing Test 81
Chapter 7: Another Practice Test — Language Arts, Writing Test: Parts I and II 89
Chapter 8: Answers and Explanations for the Language Arts, Writing Test 109

Part III: Finding Your Way: The Social Studies Test 115
Chapter 9: A Graph, a Map, and You: Getting Ready for the Social Studies Test 117
Chapter 10: Practice Test — Social Studies Test 129
Chapter 11: Answers and Explanations for the Social Studies Test 147
Chapter 12: Another Practice Test — Social Studies Test 151
Chapter 13: Answers and Explanations for the Social Studies Test 169

Part IV: Peering at Your Specimen: The Science Test 173
Chapter 14: From Aardvarks to Atoms: Confronting the Science Test 175
Chapter 15: Practice Test — Science Test 187
Chapter 16: Answers and Explanations for the Science Test 207
Chapter 17: Another Practice Test — Science Test 213
Chapter 18: Answers and Explanations for the Science Test 235

Part V: Checking Your Comprehension:
The Language Arts, Reading Test 241
Chapter 19: Reading between the Lines: Encountering The Language Arts, Reading Test 243
Chapter 20: Practice Test — Language Arts, Reading Test 251
Chapter 21: Answers and Explanations for the Language Arts, Reading Test 267
Chapter 22: Another Practice Test — Language Arts, Reading Test 271
Chapter 23: Answers and Explanations for the Language Arts, Reading Test 289

Part VI: Counting All the Possible Solutions:
The Mathematics Test 293
Chapter 24: Safety in Numbers: Facing the Mathematics Test, Parts I and II 295
Chapter 25: Practice Test — Mathematics Test: Parts I and II 321
Chapter 26: Answers and Explanations for the Mathematics Test 347
Chapter 27: Another Practice Test — Mathematics Test: Parts I and II 357
Chapter 28: Answers and Explanations for the Mathematics Test 379

Part VII: The Part of Tens 389

Chapter 29: Ten (Plus One) Surefire Ways to Maximize Your GED Test Scores 391
Chapter 30: Ten Ways to Be Successful on the GED Tests 399
Chapter 31: Ten Ways to Use Your GED After You Pass the Tests 403

Index 407

Table of Contents

Introduction 1

  About This Book 1
  Conventions Used in This Book 1
  Foolish Assumptions 2
  What You're Not to Read 2
  How This Book Is Organized 2
    Part I: Putting the GED into Perspective 2
    Part II: Minding Your Ps and Qs: The Language Arts, Writing Test 3
    Part III: Finding Your Way: The Social Studies Test 3
    Part IV: Peering at Your Specimen: The Science Test 3
    Part V: Checking Your Comprehension: The Language Arts, Reading Test 3
    Part VI: Counting All the Possible Solutions: The Mathematics Test 4
    Part VII: The Part of Tens 4
  Icons Used in This Book 4
  Where to Go from Here 4

Part 1: Putting the GED into Perspective 5

  Chapter 1: Taking a Quick Glance at the GED 7
    Reviewing the Test Sections 7
      Language Arts, Writing Test 7
        Language Arts, Writing Test, Part I 8
        Language Arts, Writing Test, Part II 9
      Social Studies Test 10
      Science Test 11
      Language Arts, Reading Test 12
      Mathematics Test, Parts I and II 13
    It's a Date: Scheduling the Test 16
      Discovering whether you're eligible 17
      Knowing when you can take the tests 17
      Signing up 18
      Working with unusual circumstances 18
    Taking the GED When English Is Your Second Language 18
    Eyeing What You Have to Score to Pass the GED 19
      Identifying how scores are determined 19
      Knowing what to do if you score poorly on one or more tests 20

  Chapter 2: Navigating the GED Testing System 21
    Identifying Who Takes the GED 21
      People who didn't finish high school 22
      Newcomers to the United States 22
    Opening Doors: Why People Take the GED 22
    Eyeing the Importance of Pretesting with the Practice Tests 23
      Using practice tests to prepare for the GED 23
      Working your way through a practice test 24
    Managing Your Time for the GED 26
      Before the tests 26
      During the tests 28

Chapter 3: Succeeding on the GED **31**

Leading Up to Test Time..31
Finding Out What to Take to the GED Tests 32
Knowing What to Expect When You Get There...........................33
Discovering Important Test-Taking Strategies 34
    Watching the clock 34
    Identifying different question types 35
        Analysis 35
        Application...35
        Comprehension 35
        Synthesis 36
        Evaluation 36
        Cognitive skills 36
    Addressing and answering questions 36
    Guess for success: Using intelligent guessing 37
    Leaving time for review...37
Keeping Your Head in the Game..38

**Part II: Minding Your Ps and Qs:
The Language Arts, Writing Test.................................. 39**

**Chapter 4: The Write Stuff: Preparing for the Language Arts,
Writing Test, Parts I and II** **41**

Understanding the Test Format..41
    Grasping what's on Part I..42
    Grasping what's on Part II...42
Passing Part I..42
    Looking at the skills Part I covers...42
    Identifying the types of passages in Part I............................44
    Preparing for Part I: Tactics that work.................................44
    Managing your time for Part I...45
    Practicing for Part I with some sample problems 46
    Revealing some helpful pointers for Part I 48
Passing Part II...49
    Looking at the writing skills Part II covers 49
    Preparing for Part II: Tactics that work 50
    Managing your time for Part II 51
        Planning..51
        Drafting...52
        Editing and revising 53
        Rewriting 54
    Practicing with some sample essays.....................................54
    Revealing some helpful pointers for Part II 55

Chapter 5: Practice Test — Language Arts, Writing Test: Parts I and II..................**57**

Chapter 6: Answers and Explanations for the Language Arts, Writing Test............**81**

Analysis of the Answers for Part I 81
Sample Essay for Part II 85
Answer Key for Part I 87

Chapter 7: Another Practice Test — Language Arts, Writing Test: Parts I and II 89

Chapter 8: Answers and Explanations for the Language Arts, Writing Test..........109
Analysis of the Answers for Part I 109
Sample Essay for Part II 113
Answer Key for Part I 114

Part III: Finding Your Way: The Social Studies Test...................... 115

Chapter 9: A Graph, a Map, and You: Getting Ready for the Social Studies Test...117
Looking at the Skills the Social Studies Test Covers 117
Understanding the Test Format..118
Identifying the Types of Questions and Knowing How to Prepare for Them 119
Questions about text passages 120
Questions about visual materials 121
Examining Preparation Strategies That Work..124
Managing Your Time for the Social Studies Test 125
Practicing with Sample Problems...125
Revealing Some Helpful Pointers 128

Chapter 10: Practice Test — Social Studies Test..129

Chapter 11: Answers and Explanations for the Social Studies Test 147
Analysis of the Answers..147
Answer Key...150

Chapter 12: Another Practice Test — Social Studies Test................................151

Chapter 13: Answers and Explanations for the Social Studies Test 169
Analysis of the Answers..169
Answer Key...172

Part IV: Peering at Your Specimen: The Science Test 173

Chapter 14: From Aardvarks to Atoms: Confronting the Science Test..........175
Looking at the Skills the Science Test Covers 175
Understanding the Test Format..176
Identifying the Types of Questions and Knowing How to Tackle Them 177
Questions about passages 178
Questions about visual materials 179
Tables 179
Graphs 179
Diagrams 180
Maps 181
Examining Preparation Strategies That Work..182
Managing Your Time for the Science Test 182
Practicing with Sample Problems...183
Revealing Some Helpful Pointers 184

Chapter 15: Practice Test — Science Test..187

Chapter 16: Answers and Explanations for the Science Test............................207

    Analysis of the Answers..207
    Answer Key...212

Chapter 17: Another Practice Test — Science Test............................213

Chapter 18: Answers and Explanations for the Science Test............................235

    Analysis of the Answers..235
    Answer Key...239

Part V: Checking Your Comprehension: The Language Arts, Reading Test.............................. **241**

Chapter 19: Reading between the Lines: Encountering the Language Arts, Reading Test............................243

    Looking at the Skills the Language Arts, Reading Test Covers....................243
    Understanding the Test Format..244
    Identifying the Types of Questions and Knowing How to Prepare for Them 245
        Literary passages..245
        Nonfiction passages..246
    Examining Preparation Strategies That Work...247
    Managing Your Time for the Language Arts, Reading Test.........................248
    Practicing with Sample Problems...248
    Revealing Some Helpful Pointers..250

Chapter 20: Practice Test — Language Arts, Reading Test............................251

Chapter 21: Answers and Explanations for the Language Arts, Reading Test........267

    Analysis of the Answers..267
    Answer Key...270

Chapter 22: Another Practice Test — Language Arts, Reading Test........................271

Chapter 23: Answers and Explanations for the Language Arts, Reading Test........289

    Analysis of the Answers..289
    Answer Key...292

Part VI: Counting All the Possible Solutions: The Mathematics Test **293**

Chapter 24: Safety in Numbers: Facing the Mathematics Test, Parts I and II........295

    Looking at the Skills the Math Test Covers..295
    Understanding the Test Format..296
    Identifying the Types of Questions and Knowing How to Tackle Them 297
        Multiple-choice questions 297
        Alternate-format questions...298
            Standard grid 298
            Coordinate-plane grid...299
        Questions with a calculator..299
        Questions without a calculator...300

Examining Preparation Strategies That Work..300
Managing Your Time for the Math Test...301
Practicing with Some Sample Problems 302
Number operations and number sense 302
Measurement and geometry..304
Data analysis, statistics, and probabilities...309
Algebra, functions, and patterns 314
A little pretest to help you prepare for the Mathematics Test.................318
Revealing Some Helpful Pointers...319

Chapter 25: Practice Test — Mathematics Test: Parts I and II.................321

Chapter 26: Answers and Explanations for the Mathematics Test..........347
Analysis of the Answers for Part I 347
Analysis of the Answers for Part II 352
Answer Key for Part I 355
Answer Key for Part II 356

Chapter 27: Another Practice Test — Mathematics Test: Parts I and II 357

Chapter 28: Answers and Explanations for the Mathematics Test..........379
Analysis of the Answers for Part I 379
Analysis of the Answers for Part II 384
Answer Key for Part I 387
Answer Key for Part II 388

Part VII: The Part of Tens.. 389

Chapter 29: Ten (Plus One) Surefire Ways to Maximize Your GED Test Scores 391
Studying Subject-Matter Books..391
Enrolling in a GED Preparation Class...393
Scheduling Time to Study..394
Preparing for the Test in Your Mind 394
Getting Good Rest the Week before the Test..394
Wearing Comfortable Clothes..395
Making Sure You Have Proper Identification...395
Practicing Your Route to the Test Site..395
Arriving Early 395
Starting with Easy Questions 396
Using Relaxation Techniques...396

Chapter 30: Ten Ways to Be Successful on the GED Tests.....................399
Selecting the Best-Possible Test Date..399
Preparing, Preparing, and Then Preparing Some More.............................399
Remaining Realistic 400
Being on Time for When the Tests Start..400
Keeping Your Comments to Yourself..400
Staying Focused on the Task at Hand 400
Looking at Only Your Test..401
Writing Clearly and Carefully...401
Thinking Positive 401
Doing Your Best, No Matter What 401

Chapter 31: Ten Ways to Use Your GED After You Pass the Tests **403**

Getting a Job...403
Being Promoted 403
Showing Others What You Can Achieve...404
Including Your GED in Your College Portfolio 404
Proving You're Ready for Further Education..404
Setting an Example for Your Kids...404
Enhancing Your Wall Décor 404
Making You Feel like Part of a Select Group 405
Motivating Yourself..405
Improving Your Self-Esteem..405

Index..*407*

Introduction

· ·

*P*erhaps you've applied for a job and have been refused an application because you don't have a high school diploma or a GED. Or maybe you were up for a promotion at work, but when your boss found out you didn't finish high school, he said you weren't eligible for the new job. Maybe you've always wanted to go to college but couldn't even apply because the college of your choice requires a high school diploma or equivalent (the GED) for admission. Or perhaps your kids are just about to graduate from high school, and you're motivated to finish, too.

Whatever your reasons are for wanting to earn a high school diploma — whether we've mentioned them here or not — this book is for you. It takes you through the process of preparing to take the GED tests — which, if you pass them, offer you the equivalent of a high school diploma without all the time-consuming bells and whistles of a high school education.

About This Book

If you want a high school diploma, you can always go back and finish high school the old-fashioned way. Of course, it may take you a few years, and you may have to quit your job to do it. Plus, you'd have to sit in a class with teenagers for eight or so hours a day (and probably be treated like one, too).

For most people, this situation doesn't sound too appealing. This book presents a different solution: to earn a high school diploma in the shortest time possible. If you don't mind preparing yourself for a series of challenging tests that determine whether you've mastered key skills, you can get a General Educational Development (GED) diploma that's the equivalent of a high school education — and you can do so in much less than four years.

If taking the GED tests to earn your diploma sounds like a great idea to you, this book is a necessary study tool because it's a fun-filled and friendly instruction manual for succeeding on the GED tests. It isn't a subject-matter preparation book — that is, it doesn't take you through the basics of math and then progress into algebra, geometry, and so on. It does, however, prepare you for the GED by giving you detailed information about each test, two sets of full-length practice tests, and plenty of easy-to-understand answers and explanations for those tests. Use this book as your first stop. We include numerous practice tests you can take to help you prepare for taking the GED tests. After taking the first set of practice tests and going through the answers and explanations, you can determine which subject areas you need to work on.

Conventions Used in This Book

To help you navigate your way around in this book, we use the following conventions:

- *Italics* to emphasize certain words and to point out new words or phrases that we define in the text
- **Boldface** to indicate key words in bulleted lists and action parts of numbered steps
- `Monofont` to set apart Web addresses from the rest of the text

Foolish Assumptions

Here's who we think you are:

- You meet your state's requirements regarding age, residency, and the length of time since leaving school that make you eligible to take the GED tests. (Check with your local GED administrator to find out your state's requirements.)
- You're serious about getting a high school diploma as quickly as you can.
- You're willing to put in the time to prepare, keeping in mind that you have a lot of other responsibilities, too.
- Getting a high school diploma is a priority in your life.
- You want a fun and friendly guide that helps you achieve your goal.
- You want to gain some insight from the experience of others.

If any of these descriptions sounds like you, welcome aboard. We've prepared an enjoyable tour of the GED.

What You're Not to Read

You probably have a very busy life with numerous responsibilities like children, a job or two, and social activities. You may not have the time to read every single word we write. The good news is you don't have to read everything. If you want to read just the essential information that can help you prepare for the GED, you can skip the sidebars. The sidebars are the areas of text on a gray background. They add a little background information, but they're not essential to your understanding of the subject.

How This Book Is Organized

This book has seven parts, each of which prepares you for the GED. We've organized this second edition a bit differently from the first: The first part gives you the ins and outs of the GED, each of the next five parts deals specifically with one of the five tests, and the last part includes some fun tips for maximizing your test scores and being successful on the GED tests. The following sections explain each part in a little more detail.

Part 1: Putting the GED into Perspective

If you've never heard of the GED tests, you can use Part I to find out everything you need to know about the GED as a whole, including what it covers and who can take it. If you have heard of the GED, turn to this part to find out some extra information and some handy tips for succeeding on all five of the GED tests. You also find out how to register for the tests and how to figure out your scores after you receive them.

Part II: Minding Your Ps and Qs: The Language Arts, Writing Test

This part tells you everything you ever wanted to know about the Language Arts, Writing Test and provides you with two practice tests (and the answers that go with them) to help you prepare for this test. Here, you get to test your ability to organize content, improve sentence structure, and correct grammatical mistakes. You also get to try your hand at writing an essay for Part II of this test. Don't panic! This essay isn't a full research essay — it's a short essay that uses your past experiences and knowledge as research. And, to help you do your best, this part offers you a handful of pointers and strategies to keep in mind as you take the test.

Part III: Finding Your Way: The Social Studies Test

This part is all about the Social Studies Test. Here, you get a chance to take inventory of your skills in understanding principles and concepts in history, geography, economics, and civics. You get to practice answering multiple-choice questions based on both textual and visual materials (these visual materials include maps, cartoons, and graphs). You also find some pointers and strategies to help you do your best on the test. Like the other test-specific parts of this book, this part offers you two full practice tests and the answers that go with them. Take some time to go through these tests and read their corresponding answer explanations as you prepare for the Social Studies Test.

Part IV: Peering at Your Specimen: The Science Test

For the Science Test, you're expected to know some scientific vocabulary and have a very basic understanding of scientific principles. Don't panic! You don't have to understand Beilstein's categorization of organic chemicals, but you do need to know basic concepts like the fact that carbon is present in many forms on earth. With a little bit of practice (**hint:** check out Part IV!) and some outside reading, you can become much more comfortable with the Science Test and amaze yourself with how much you already know about the topics it covers.

This part provides all the details you need to know about the Science Test, including the skills it tests you on, the test's format, and a few strategies to help you do your best on the real test. It also offers you a ton of practice answering questions about physics, chemistry, and earth sciences. And, then, to help you prepare for the real test, it provides all the answers and explanations you need to figure out which questions you got right and which ones you missed.

Part V: Checking Your Comprehension: The Language Arts, Reading Test

This part focuses on preparing you for the Language Arts, Reading Test by showing you the test's format, the skills it tests you on, and some strategies to help you do well on test day. As you may or may not know, this test tests your ability to understand literary passages. To help you get ready to answer the passages that appear on this test, take the two practice tests in this part. Then spend some time reading the answers and explanations that go with them to find out what you may need to practice a little more before you take the real test.

Part VI: Counting All the Possible Solutions: The Mathematics Test

For those of you who cringe at the words *mathematics, calculations,* and *problem solving* — or for those rare few of you who get excited about them — this part is for you. Here, you discover all the details about the Mathematics Test you need to know, including the skills it tests you on, the different answer formats it uses (and instructions on how to use them), and some strategies that can help you do well on the test. Take some time to go through the practice tests in this part, and then read all the answers and explanations to find out what you did right and what you did wrong (and why). If you're not great at math, don't worry! We're here to help you get familiar with the Mathematics Test so that you can feel calm and confident as you sit down to take the real test.

Part VII: The Part of Tens

This part is a treat to read — and you can review it in no time at all. Here you discover some key ways to prepare for the tests and improve your scores, ten ways to be successful on the GED, and ten ways to use your GED diploma after you pass the tests.

Icons Used in This Book

Icons — little pictures that you see in the margins of this book — highlight bits of text that you want to pay special attention to. Here's what they mean:

Whenever we want to tell you a special trick or technique that can help you succeed on the GED tests, we mark it with this icon. Keep an eye out for them.

This icon points out information you want to burn into your brain. Think of the text with this icon as the sort of stuff you'd tear out and put on a bulletin board or your refrigerator.

Take this icon seriously! Although the world won't end if you don't heed the advice next to these icons, the warnings are important to your success in preparing to take the GED tests.

We use this icon sparingly to point out additional technical information that you don't need to lose sleep over. When you see this icon, feel free to skip the material next to it if you're short on time.

Where to Go from Here

Some people like to read books from beginning to end. Others prefer to read only the chapters or sections that interest them. Still others look in the index or table of contents for specific information they need to know now. However you want to approach this book is fine with us — just don't peek at the practice tests until the moment you're ready to take them (and be sure not to look at the answers until *after* you take the tests that go with them!).

Part I
Putting the GED into Perspective

The 5ᵗʰ Wave   By Rich Tennant

"I always get a good night's sleep the day before a test so I'm relaxed and alert the next morning. Then I grab my pen, eat a banana, and I'm on my way."

In this part . . .

Okay, you want to earn your high school diploma but don't have time to attend classes eight or so hours a day for four years, so you've turned to the GED for help. And now you need help preparing for the GED! Lucky for you, this part of the book is here to help you get started in your test planning and preparation. It introduces you to the GED and gives you a brief look at each of the five tests. It gives you a chance to see what the GED expects you to know in order to receive your high school equivalency diploma, as well as what and how to prepare for the tests. It also offers some logistical help with how to schedule the test so you can make sure you're eligible to take it before you sign up. Plus, it gives you a peek inside how the tests are scored, which is definitely to your advantage.

Here you can also find plenty of tips for succeeding on the GED tests. You find out what to take with you and what to leave at home, what to do if you have special needs, and how to manage your time. Finally, this part explains the importance of practice tests. The more practice you get, the better prepared you'll be for what the test throws at you, so don't hesitate — turn the page and get ready to meet the GED head on!

Chapter 1

Taking a Quick Glance at the GED

In This Chapter

▶ Reviewing the different GED test sections and their questions

▶ Registering for the exam

▶ Knowing that you can take the GED when English is your second language

▶ Understanding what your scores mean and how they're determined

The GED tests measure whether you understand what high school seniors across the country are supposed to have learned before they graduate. When you pass these tests, you earn a high school equivalency diploma, which can open many doors for you — perhaps doors that you don't even know exist at this point.

Ready to get started? This chapter gives you the basics of the GED tests: what the tests look like, how to answer the questions on them, how to schedule the tests, and what to do after you get your scores back.

Reviewing the Test Sections

The GED tests include the following five tests, each of which you can take separately:

✔ Language Arts, Writing, Parts I and II

✔ Social Studies

✔ Science

✔ Language Arts, Reading

✔ Mathematics, Parts I and II

Note that although you can take each of the five tests separately, you must take both parts of the Language Arts, Writing or Mathematics Tests at the same time.

The following sections offer a closer look into what these tests cover and how they're set up.

Language Arts, Writing Test

The Language Arts, Writing Test is split into two parts (which we explain in further detail in the following sections):

✔ Part I asks you to rewrite and revise passages. This part focuses on your grammar, punctuation, and spelling skills.

✔ Part II asks you to write an essay on a given topic. This part examines your skills in organizing your thoughts and writing clearly.

You must pass both parts to get a score in this test. If you pass one part of the test but not the other, you must retake both parts the next time.

Language Arts, Writing Test, Part 1

The Language Arts, Writing Test, Part I, has 50 multiple-choice questions and a time limit of 75 minutes. In this test, you're asked to edit and revise material that's given to you. This material comes from the following sources:

- ✔ **Workplace materials:** Work-related letters, memos, and instructions that you may see on the job

- ✔ **How-to books:** Samples of all general reference books that are supposed to make you richer, stronger, and lighter or a better cook, driver, investor, or student (or anything else you want to become better at)

- ✔ **Informational works:** Documents that present you with information (often dry and boring information), such as the instructional manual that tells you how to set the clock on your DVD player

You find three question types in this part of the Language Arts, Writing Test:

- ✔ **Correction:** In these questions, you're asked to correct sentences presented to you.

- ✔ **Revision:** In these questions, you're presented with a sentence that has a word or phrase underlined. If the sentence needs a correction, one of the answer choices will be better than the words or phrase underlined. If no correction is needed, either one of the answer choices will be the same as the underlined portion, or one of the choices will be something like "no correction needed."

- ✔ **Construction shift:** In these questions, you have to correct a sentence by altering the sentence structure. The original sentence may not be completely wrong, but it can be improved with a little editing.

See Chapter 4 for the lowdown on this test, Chapters 5 and 7 for full-length practice Language Arts, Writing Tests, and Chapters 6 and 8 for answers and explanations to those tests.

To give you an idea of what the questions on this test look like, consider the following examples:

Questions 1 and 2 are based on the following business letter.

Dear Mr. Snyder:

(1) I have received your letter of February 3 and offer my apologi for the mistake in your account. (2) The charge for your checks should have been $16.20, not $1,620.00. (3) I have credited the entire amount, making your checks free. (4) I hope this settles the matter.

1. Sentence 1: **I have received your letter of February 3 and offer my apologi for the mistake in your account.**

   How can this sentence be improved?

   (1) insert a semicolon after <u>February 3</u>

   (2) change <u>February</u> to <u>Feb.</u>

   (3) insert a period after <u>February 3</u> and capitalize <u>and</u>

   (4) change <u>apologi</u> to <u>apology</u>

   (5) no correction needed

   The correct answer is Choice (4). The correct spelling is *apology*.

2. Sentence 3: **I have credited the entire amount, making your checks free.**

   How can this sentence be improved?

   (1) change <u>credited</u> to <u>credit</u>

   (2) change the comma after <u>amount</u> to a semicolon

   (3) change <u>free</u> to <u>freely</u>

   (4) change the comma after <u>amount</u> to a colon

   (5) no correction needed

   The correct answer is Choice (5). The sentence is correct in its current form.

Language Arts, Writing Test, Part II

In this part of the Language Arts, Writing Test, you write an essay in 45 minutes. Because the two parts of the Writing Test are given together, however, you can share time between the two parts. If you finish Part I in less than 75 minutes, you can use the extra time on Part II.

The topic you're given to write on may sound like a question you hear in a Miss America pageant. Here are two examples:

   ✔ What is the most important invention discovered in your lifetime?

   ✔ How have computers allowed you to accomplish everyday tasks more efficiently?

See Chapter 4 for more examples of essay topics, and take a stab at writing full-length essays in the practice tests in Chapters 5 and 7. Time the tests so that you're taking them under the same conditions as the real GED tests.

In your essay, you give your opinion or explain your viewpoint and then back it up with your own experiences and facts you may know from your life. This essay isn't a research paper. The information for the essay topics on this test is in your head — not in a research library.

When you write this essay, make sure it's a series of interconnected paragraphs on a single topic. Not only should the entire essay begin with an introduction and end with a conclusion, but each paragraph needs an introductory sentence and a concluding sentence, as well.

Write only on the assigned topic. To make sure you understand what the topic is about, read it several times. Essays written off topic don't receive scores (and if you don't receive a score on Part II of the Writing Test, you have to take both Parts I and II over again).

Two different people grade your essay, and, as they do, they look for the following:

   ✔ Material that's clearly organized

   ✔ Main points that are well focused

   ✔ Ideas that are well developed

   ✔ Words that are used properly

   ✔ Sentences that are well structured

   ✔ Sentences that use proper grammar, punctuation, and spelling

Note: Neat writing or printing makes grading easier for your real-life graders, so taking some time to practice writing neatly before the test isn't a bad idea.

Read the newspapers and watch television news for a few months before the tests. Doing so gives you some material with which to back up your opinions and viewpoints in your essay.

Social Studies Test

For the Social Studies Test, you have to answer 50 multiple-choice questions in 70 minutes. These questions deal with the following subject areas:

- ✔ American history (25 percent)
- ✔ World history (15 percent)
- ✔ Civics and government (25 percent)
- ✔ Economics (20 percent)
- ✔ Geography (15 percent)

The questions in this test are based on written texts, pictures, charts, tables, graphs, photographs, political cartoons, diagrams, or maps. These textual and pictorial excerpts come from a variety of sources, such as government documents, academic texts, material from work-related documents, and atlases.

See Chapter 9 for more information about the Social Studies Test, and be sure to take the full-length practice tests in Chapters 10 and 12. (Then check out Chapters 11 and 13 for the answers and explanations.)

You may see the following types of problems on the Social Studies Test.

Question 1 is based on the following table.

Type of Religion	Date Started (Approximate)	Sacred Texts
Buddhism	500 BC	None
Christianity	33 AD	Bible (Old Testament and New Testament)
Hinduism	4000 BC	Vedas; Upanishads
Islam	600 AD	Qur'an; Hadith
Judaism	2000 BC	Hebrew Bible; Talmud

1. According to the table, Hinduism

   (1) started in 600 AD

   (2) uses the Qur'an as one of its sacred texts

   (3) is the oldest religion

   (4) has no known sacred texts

   (5) has one known sacred text

The correct answer is Choice (3). The table shows that Hinduism is the oldest of the five religions listed because it began in 4000 BC.

Question 2 is based on the following excerpt from the diary of Christopher Columbus.

Monday, 6 August. The rudder of the caravel Pinta became loose, being broken or unshipped. It was believed that this happened by the contrivance of Gomez Rascon and Christopher Quintero, who were on board the caravel, because they disliked the voyage. The Admiral says he had found them in an unfavorable disposition before setting out. He was in much anxiety at not being able to afford any assistance in this case, but says that it somewhat quieted his apprehensions to know that Martin Alonzo Pinzon, Captain of the Pinta, was a man of courage and capacity. Made progress, day and night, of twenty-nine leagues.

2. Why would Rascon and Quintero have loosened the rudder?

    (1) They were trying to repair the rudder.

    (2) The Admiral found them in an unfavorable disposition.

    (3) The captain was very competent.

    (4) They wanted to stop to fish.

    (5) They did not want to be on the voyage.

The correct answer is Choice (5). This answer is the only one supported by the text. The others may be related to statements in the passage, but they don't answer the question.

Science Test

When you take the Science Test, you have to answer 50 multiple-choice science questions in 80 minutes. The questions deal with the following topics:

✔ Life science (45 percent)

✔ Physical science, including chemistry and physics (35 percent)

✔ Earth and space science (20 percent)

 Some of the information the questions refer to appears in passages that you read before answering the questions. Other information is presented in charts, figures, graphs, maps, or tables. Chapter 14 discusses these different formats in detail. Turn to Chapters 15 and 17 to take two full-length sample Science Tests that are similar to the real ones. (Don't forget to go to Chapters 16 and 18 to find the answers and explanations to those tests — after you finish taking them, of course!)

 Most of the information you need to answer the questions on the Science Test is given to you in the passages and other excerpts, although to get a perfect score, you're expected to have picked up a basic knowledge of science. However, even if you answer correctly only the questions based entirely on information presented, you should get a score high enough to pass.

Here are some sample problems that may be on the Science Test.

Questions 1 and 2 are based on the following excerpt from a press release.

A key feature of the Delta 4's operation is the use of a common booster core, or CBC, a rocket stage that measures some 150 feet long and 16 feet wide. By combining one or more CBCs with various upper stages or strap-on solid rocket boosters, the Delta 4 can handle an extreme range of satellite applications for military, civilian, and commercial customers.

1. The CBC in this context is a

    (1) Canadian broadcasting corporation

    (2) common booster core

    (3) cooperative boosters corps

    (4) civilian barbers cooperative

    (5) common ballistic cavalier

The correct answer is Choice (2). After all, it's the only answer choice mentioned in the passage.

2. How can the Delta 4 handle a wide range of applications?

    (1) using the Delta 4 with different names

    (2) developing a Delta 5

    (3) continuing research

    (4) using the CBC as the base of a rocket ship

    (5) creating a common core booster

The correct answer is Choice (4). The passage says that "By combining one or more CBCs with various upper stages or strap-on solid rocket boosters . . . ," so Choice (4) comes closest to answering the question.

Language Arts, Reading Test

The Language Arts, Reading Test includes 40 multiple-choice questions that you must answer in 65 minutes. Seventy-five percent of the questions are based on passages from literature and include at least one work from each of the following:

- Drama
- Poetry
- Prose fiction (that is, novels and short stories) written before 1920
- Prose fiction written between 1920 and 1960
- Prose fiction written after 1960

Twenty-five percent of the questions are based on nonfiction texts. These passages come from any of the following sources:

- **Critical reviews of visual and performing arts:** Most people go to the theater, movies, and concerts for entertainment, but if, after you leave, you tell other people your impression of what you saw, you're doing more than just watching for entertainment's sake — you're critically reviewing the performance. In this test, some of the questions may be based on excerpts from critical reviews.

- **Nonfiction prose:** *Prose* is any written words not written as poetry. Prose is divided into two main categories: fiction and nonfiction. If the story is made up by the author, it's usually referred to as *prose fiction*. If the words are based on facts, the work is considered *nonfiction prose*. A biography, an instruction manual, or a history text (even this book!) are all examples of nonfiction prose.

- **Workplace and community documents:** These documents are the types of materials you see on the job or in a community; they include workplace rules, employment contracts, wills, deeds, mortgage documents, instructions on how to use a voting machine, and income tax forms.

Chapter 19 gives you more information about the Language Arts, Reading Test, and Chapters 20 and 22 test your knowledge with full-length sample tests. (Don't forget to turn to Chapters 21 and 23 for the answers and explanations to those tests when you finish taking them.)

You may see questions like the following in the Language Arts, Reading Test.

Questions 1 and 2 are based on the following excerpt from a play.

Irvin and Mervin enter from stage left. Irvin is dressed sloppily in torn jeans, he wears a flannel shirt over a dirty T-shirt, and he has unkempt hair. Mervin is dressed more neatly in khakis, a blue buttondown shirt open at the neck, and loafers.

Irvin: What you want to do, man?

Mervin: *(laughing)* With you or to you?

Irvin: *(looking up)* What do you mean by that?

Mervin: What are you wearing?

Irvin: What's wrong with it?

Mervin: What's not wrong with it?

Irvin: So what? You don't want to go to the mall now?

Mervin: Why would I want to go to the mall with you, looking like that?

Irvin: Aren't I your best friend?

Mervin: Can't you dress a little better?

Irvin: Would I be a better friend if I dressed more like you?

Irvin and Mervin look at each other and shuffle off toward the mall.

1. What form of sentence does the author use to create this conversation?
   - (1) All of the dialogue is boring.
   - (2) All of the dialogue is in questions.
   - (3) Every sentence is in a different form.
   - (4) This is the way I talk to my friends.
   - (5) All of the dialogue is in exclamatory sentences.

   The correct answer is Choice (2). Each line of dialogue is a question.

2. According to the dialogue, why do Irvin and Mervin want to go to the mall?
   - (1) The latest *Harry Potter* movie is playing there.
   - (2) They are going to meet friends.
   - (3) Irvin wants to shop for clothes.
   - (4) Mervin works there.
   - (5) They are looking for something to do.

   The correct answer is Choice (5). According to the first line of dialogue, they're looking for something to do. In another scene, you may find out that they're going to see a movie, meeting friends, shopping for clothes, or going to work, but GED questions are based only on the dialogue presented.

Mathematics Test, Parts 1 and 11

The Mathematics Test has two parts: Part I allows you to use a calculator; Part II doesn't. Each part has 25 questions. You have 45 minutes to complete each part. In other words, you have to answer 50 questions in 90 minutes. Answer all the questions.

The Mathematics Test covers the following four major areas:

- ✔ Algebra, equations, and patterns (20 to 30 percent)

- ✔ Data analysis, statistics, and probability (20 to 30 percent)

- ✔ Measurement and geometry (20 to 30 percent)

- ✔ Number operations (20 to 30 percent)

Eighty percent of the questions are multiple choice; the other 20 percent require you to answer the question yourself in what is called an *alternate-format grid*.

An alternate-format grid is either a standard grid or a coordinate-plane grid. Instead of getting a set of multiple-choice answers to choose from, you figure an answer and enter it on whichever of these two grids you're given on the answer sheet. (Note that the coordinate-plane grid may require some practice — if you need help and reading through Chapter 24 isn't enough, contact a tutor to walk you through it.)

Chapter 24 gives you a lot more information about the Mathematics Test, including how to answer the different types of questions and how to prepare for the subject areas tested. Check out Chapters 25 and 27 for two full-length practice Mathematics Tests, and don't forget to turn to Chapters 26 and 28 for the answers and explanations.

Consider the following questions (one traditional multiple-choice question and two questions that you have to answer using alternate-format grids) that are similar to what you may see on the Mathematics Test.

1. A right-angle triangle has a hypotenuse of 5 feet and one side that's 36 inches long. What is the length of the other side in feet?

   (1) 3

   (2) 48

   (3) 243

   (4) 6

   (5) 4

The correct answer is Choice (5). Using the Pythagorean Relationship (a formula that's given to you on the Formula page of the test), you know that $a^2 + b^2 = c^2$, where c is the hypotenuse and a and b are either of the other two sides. Because you know the hypotenuse and one side, turn the equation around so that it reads $a^2 = c^2 - b^2$.

To get c^2, you square the hypotenuse: $5 \times 5 = 25$.

The other side is given in inches — to convert inches to feet, divide by 12: $36 \div 12 = 3$. To get b^2, square this side: $3 \times 3 = 9$.

Now solve the equation for a: $a^2 = 25 - 9$ or $a^2 = 16$. Take the square root of both sides, and you get: $a = 4$

The Mathematics Test presents real-life situations in the questions. So if you find yourself answering 37 feet to a question about the height of a room or $3.00 for an annual salary, recheck your answer because you're probably wrong.

2. Barb is counting the number of boxes in a warehouse. In the first storage area, she finds 24 boxes. The second area contains 30 boxes. The third area contains 28 boxes. If the warehouse has 6 storage areas where it stores boxes, and the areas have an average of 28 boxes, what is the total number of boxes in the last three areas? Record your answer on the standard grid by writing the number in the top boxes and shading in the bubbles below the boxes. You have to write the answer in both places.

	/	/	/	
.	.	.	.	.
0	0	0	0	0
1	1	1	1	1
2	2	2	2	2
3	3	3	3	3
4	4	4	4	4
5	5	5	5	5
6	6	6	6	6
7	7	7	7	7
8	8	8	8	8
9	9	9	9	9

The correct answer is 86 (which you record on the standard grid provided). If the warehouse has 6 storage areas and they have an average of 28 boxes in each, they have $6 \times 28 = 168$ boxes in the warehouse. The first three areas have $24 + 30 + 28 = 82$ boxes in them. The last three areas must have $168 - 82 = 86$ boxes in them.

8	6			
	/	/	/	
.	.	.	.	.
0	0	0	0	0
1	1	1	1	1
2	2	2	2	2
3	3	3	3	3
4	4	4	4	4
5	5	5	5	5
6	●	6	6	6
7	7	7	7	7
●	8	8	8	8
9	9	9	9	9

3. A rectangle has one corner on the origin. The base goes from the origin to the point (3,0). The right side goes from (3,0) to (3,4). Draw the missing point on the coordinate-plane grid.

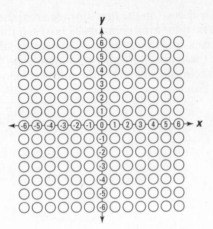

The correct answer is to shade the missing point at (0,4). If you shade the three points given on the coordinate-plane grid, you see that a fourth point at (0,4) creates the rectangle. Just be sure, however, that you don't draw on the GED test book as you're taking the test! Instead, draw the point as shown on the following coordinate-plane grid:

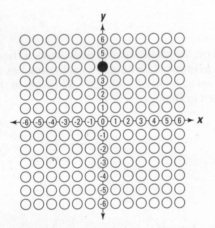

It's a Date: Scheduling the Test

To take the GED, you can't just drop in to the testing site and take the test whenever you please. You have to schedule it based on the available testing dates. Each state or local testing center sets its own schedule for the five GED tests, which means that your state decides how and when you take the five tests. Schedules for the tests vary by state or local testing center and may be offered as often as once every week or as seldom as once every couple of months. Your local GED administrator can give you all the information you need about scheduling the test. Locate the GED administrator in your area by logging on to www. gedtest.org or by calling 800-62-MYGED. In addition, local school districts and community colleges can provide information about local test centers in your area.

Taking all five of the GED tests together takes seven hours and five minutes, with breaks in between the tests. Depending on your local testing center, you may have to take all the tests in one sitting (a rare stipulation), or you may be able to break the tests up into two or more sittings. Some states allow you to take one test each time you go to the testing center, and some offer the tests in the evenings or on weekends.

The following sections answer some questions you may have before you schedule your test date.

Discovering whether you're eligible

Before you schedule your test, make sure you meet the requirements to take the GED. You're eligible to apply to take the GED tests only if

- **You're not currently enrolled in a high school.** If you're currently enrolled in a high school, you're expected to complete your diploma there. The purpose of the GED tests is to give people who aren't in high school a chance to get an equivalent high school diploma.

- **You're not a high school graduate.** If you're a high school graduate, you should have a diploma, which means you don't need to take the GED.

- **You meet state requirements regarding age, residency, and the length of time since leaving high school.** Check with your local GED administrator to determine your state's requirements concerning these criteria.

Knowing when you can take the tests

When can you take the GED tests? The simple answer is this: If you're eligible and prepared, you can apply to take the GED tests as soon as you want. Just contact your local testing center to get a test schedule, and then pick a day (or days) that works for you.

You can also apply to take the tests if you're not prepared, but if you do that, you don't stand a very good chance of passing. If you do need to retake any of the tests, use your time before your next test to get ready. You can retake the tests only a limited number of times, and, in most jurisdictions, taking the test costs money (check with your local testing center to find out how many times you can retake the test). To save time and money, prepare before you schedule the tests.

Are special accommodations available?

The GED testing centers make every effort to ensure that all qualified people have access to the tests. If you have a disability, you may not be able to register for the tests on Monday and take them on Friday, but, with some advanced planning, you can probably take the tests when you're ready. Here's what you need to do:

- Contact the GED Testing Service or your local GED center and explain your disability.

- Request any forms that you have to fill out for your special circumstances.

- Ensure that you have a recent diagnosis by a physician or other qualified professional.

- Complete all the proper forms and submit them with medical or professional diagnosis.

- Start planning early so that you're able to take the tests when you're ready.

Please note that, regardless of your disability, you still have to be able to handle the mental demands of the tests.

The GED Testing Service in Washington, D.C., defines specific disabilities, such as the following, for which it may make special accommodations, provided the disability severely limits your ability to perform essential skills required to pass the GED:

- Medical disabilities, such as cerebral palsy, epilepsy, or blindness

- Emotional disabilities, such as schizophrenia, major depression, attention deficit disorder, or Tourette's syndrome

- Specific learning disabilities, including perceptual handicaps, brain injury, minimal brain dysfunction, dyslexia, and developmental aphasia

Signing up

To sign up for the test, follow these steps:

1. **Contact your local GED administrator to make sure you're eligible.**

2. **Ask the office for an application (if needed) or an appointment.**

3. **Complete the application (if needed).**

4. **Return the application to the proper office, with payment, if necessary.**

   The fees vary state by state, so contact your local administrator or testing site to find out what you have to pay to take the tests. In some states, if you fall into a low-income bracket, you can have the fees paid for you.

Never send cash in an envelope to pay for the GED. Most local administrators have payment rules and don't accept cash.

Working with unusual circumstances

If you feel that you may have a special circumstance that prevents you from taking the GED tests, contact the GED administrator in your area. If, for example, the tests are going to be held on your Sabbath, the testing center may make special arrangements for you.

When applying for special circumstances, keep the following guidelines in mind:

✔ Document everything in your appeal for special consideration.

✔ Contact the GED administrator in your area as early as you can.

✔ Be patient. Special arrangements can't be made overnight. The administrator often has to wait for a group with similar issues to gather so he can make arrangements for the entire group.

✔ Ask questions. Allowances can be made if you ask. For example, special allowances include extended time for various disabilities, large print and Braille for visual impairments, and age (for those individuals older than 60 who feel they may have a learning disability).

Taking the GED When English Is Your Second Language

The good news is that English doesn't have to be your first language for you to take the GED. The GED tests are offered in English, Spanish, and French. If you want to take the test in Spanish or French, contact your local GED administrator so that you can apply.

If English, Spanish, or French isn't your first language, you must decide whether you read and write English as well as or better than 40 percent of high school graduates because you may be required to pass an English as a Second Language (ESL) Placement test. If you write and read English well, prepare for and take the tests (either in English or in Spanish or French). If you don't read or write English well, take additional classes to prepare yourself in English until you think you're ready. If you want or need more information about the language component of the GED tests, check out the "Your Language" section at www.acenet. edu/Content/NavigationMenu/ged/test/take/Take_GED.htm.

Web sites that can help you plan to take the GED

The Internet is a helpful and sometimes scary place. Some Web sites are there to help you in your GED preparation, while others just want to sell you something. You have to be on alert to separate the good from the bad. Here are a couple of essential ones:

✔ `www.acenet.edu/AM/Template.cfm? Section=GED_TS`: This Web site is the main site for the GED Testing Service. It contains all the essential information you may want to look up as you get ready for the GED. Look around at the various links on this site — you'll find a wealth of useful and relevant information here.

✔ `www.acenet.edu/Content/Navigation Menu/ged/test/admin.htm`: If you aren't sure who the GED administrator is in your area, go to this site for a list of all the administrators by location.

If you're curious and want to see what's out there, enter *GED* into any search engine and relax while you try to read about 22,000,000 entries ranging from the helpful to the helpless. We suggest leaving this last activity until after you've passed the tests. As useful as the Internet can be, it still provides the opportunity to waste vast amounts of time. And right now, you need to spend your time preparing for the tests — and leave the rest for after you get your diploma.

In many ways, the GED tests are like the TOEFL (the Test of English as a Foreign Language) comprehension tests. If you've completed the TOEFL tests with good grades, you're likely ready to take the GED. If you haven't taken the TOEFL tests, enroll in a GED preparation course to see whether you have difficulty understanding the subjects and skills assessed on the test. GED courses provide you not only with some insight into your comprehension ability, but also with a teacher to discuss your skills and struggles.

Eyeing What You Have to Score to Pass the GED

To pass the tests, you have to score at least 410 on each test and have an average score of 450 on the five tests. If you achieve a passing score, congratulate yourself: You've scored better than at least 40 percent of today's high school graduates, and you're now a graduate of the largest virtual school in the country.

The following sections address a few more points you may want to know about how the GED tests are scored and what you can do if you score poorly on some or all of the tests.

Identifying how scores are determined

Except for the essay, each correct answer is worth one point. No matter how hard or easy the question is, if you get it right, you get one point. In each test, the points you get are totaled, and the total converts to a standard score, ranging from 200 to 800 on each test.

Because you don't lose points for incorrect answers, make sure you answer all the questions on each test. After all, a guessed answer can get you a point. Leaving an answer blank, on the other hand, gives you only a zero.

Knowing what to do if you score poorly on one or more tests

If you discover that your average score is less than 450 on any of the tests, start planning to retake the test(s) — and make sure you leave plenty of time for additional studying and preparing.

As soon as possible after seeing your results, contact your local GED administrator to find out the rules for retaking tests. Some states may ask that you wait a certain amount of time. Some may ask that you attend a preparation course and show that you've completed it before you can take the GED tests again. Some may charge you an additional fee.

No matter what score you receive on your first round of tests, don't be afraid to retake any of them that you didn't pass. Now that you've taken them once, you know what you need to work on, and you know exactly what to expect on test day. Just take a deep breath, and get ready to prepare some more before you take your next round of tests.

Chapter 2

Navigating the GED Testing System

In This Chapter
▶ Figuring out who takes the GED
▶ Understanding why people take the test
▶ Using pretests to help you prepare for the GED
▶ Managing your time before and during the test

Y ou may be wondering why you should consider taking the GED, or, if you've already decided to take it, you may be curious about why you should spend a lot of time preparing for it. Well, the truth is that the GED is the best substitution for a high school diploma you can find in the United States today.

But why do you even need a high school diploma or its equivalent? To answer this question, take a serious look at the world today. In the United States, the number of people who have completed high school has increased sharply in the last few years. More and more people have completed college degrees, which brings us to the main problem. When you go to apply for a job, chances are good that the other people applying for that job will have more education than you. If you've been working for a while and you have recently been downsized, you probably entered the work force before education became one of the main applicant-screening tools. With the shifting of industries from place to place, your skills alone may no longer be valued. Thus, to make a living, you need to become more competitive. Lucky for you, the GED is one way to do just that.

Think of yourself as a product that people should want to buy. The ingredients of your product have to be interesting and enticing, and the marketing of those ingredients has to be superb. A high school diploma is one of the necessary ingredients, and it needs to appear prominently on your résumé for all potential employers to see.

This chapter gives you a clear idea of why you may want to take the GED and others who may be in a similar situation. This chapter also points out some general tidbits that can help you find your way through the GED test maze and come out ahead. Although preparing for the GED will definitely cut into your TV time and social life — and require some sacrifices and a real commitment from you — in the end, passing the test and receiving the GED will be worth all the effort and time.

Identifying Who Takes the GED

People who take the GED are people like you who want or need a high school diploma but, for one reason or another, don't have one. Check out the following sections to get a better picture of who takes the GED.

People who didn't finish high school

The majority of people who take the GED dropped out of high school for some reason before they finished and didn't receive a high school diploma. Perhaps you dropped out of school to help your family with living expenses. Perhaps school just wasn't right for you. Perhaps you had a baby and weren't able to take care of your newborn and go to school at the same time. The reason why you didn't finish high school is irrelevant.

If you're looking to take the GED, all that matters is

- ✔ You're not currently enrolled in school (and haven't been for a specified period of time).
- ✔ You've reached a certain minimum age.

The amount of time you've been out of school and the age you need to be to take the GED depend on your local school district. You can find out these qualifications and whether you qualify by contacting the GED administrator in your area. Check out www.acenet.edu/Content/NavigationMenu/ged/test/admin.htm to find your local administrator.

If you meet both qualifications, you're eligible to take the tests. If you choose to sign up and take the tests, making sure you're prepared is the next step, and that's where we can help. This book is chock-full of information and helpful hints to get you through the whole GED process.

Newcomers to the United States

If you've come to the United States from another country, you may have graduated from a school that is equivalent to a U.S. high school but have difficulty providing proof. Not all U.S. employers or schools immediately accept documents from another country, especially if they're in another language, which leaves you with a problem. Fortunately, the GED comes to the rescue. The GED is recognized across the United States and Canada; it's as close to a universal diploma as you can get. Passing the GED tests provides you a diploma that states you're the equivalent of a high school graduate, which is helpful for someone who's having difficulty proving her level of education.

If English isn't your first language and you have trouble reading it, you may need to beef up your English-speaking and reading skills before taking the GED. The GED tests are in English and require a level of English understanding equivalent to most senior high school students. We suggest you take some English classes to improve your reading skills before you take the GED. Although the GED test is available in French and Spanish as well as English, not all test centers offer the test in all languages, so you have to check first with your local test center. Some test centers also require that you prove you can read English and may require that you take an ESL test in addition to the GED test. Check all this out first with your local test administrator and avoid any last-minute surprises. To find out more about this test, visit www.acenet.edu and search for "GED Test of English as a Second Language." To find out if your jurisdiction requires the ESL test, contact your local testing center.

Opening Doors: Why People Take the GED

People take the GED because they want to increase their opportunities either in the workforce or in the world of education. In either case, the GED can open many doors for you. If you're considering taking the GED, you may find yourself in one of the following situations:

- ✔ **You want a better-paying job.** Most employers base their pay offer on your qualifications and experience. The GED diploma is a widely recognized credential and can help you climb up the rungs of the pay scale.

- ✔ **You want to gain admission to a college or other post-secondary institution.** Post-secondary institutions want to see that you have the ability to take their courses. Some may accept you if you're older than a certain age and ask that you pass certain courses or take certain exams before admitting you. Most accept a high school diploma or equivalent. The GED diploma is definitely an equivalent and is widely accepted for a high school diploma.

- ✔ **You want to enter a field in which a high school diploma is a necessity.** Many occupations and apprenticeships require a high school diploma or equivalent to enter. The GED diploma is the key to this lock.

- ✔ **You want to feel better about yourself.** People, in general, feel better about themselves when they have accomplished a challenging task. Passing the GED test is such a task, and, when you accomplish this one, you can spend some time patting yourself on the back as long as you don't strain anything while doing it. It may be better to tell your friends and relatives and let them pat you on the back. Then you can just enjoy all the attention.

No matter what your situation is, the GED offers you a way to reach your goals.

Eyeing the Importance of Pretesting with the Practice Tests

If you knew everything that would be on a particular test, you could probably just walk in and ace it, right? And suppose that you didn't pass, you could simply take it again and again until you passed it, couldn't you? Actually, you couldn't. The GED has strict rules about retaking it. You usually have to wait a period of time before retesting. Limits are set by the local authorities, so check with your local administrator. Because you can't retake the test whenever you want, you need to ensure you're prepared *before* you take the test so you pass it the first time.

The following sections discuss one of the best ways to prepare for the GED tests — pre-tests. A *pretest,* or *practice test* as we often call it, is an informal test that covers the same material that the real test covers. These tests help you get a feel for that material and the test format. Read on to find out how you can use pretests to your advantage in order to help you get ready for the GED.

Using practice tests to prepare for the GED

How you use the practice tests is key to how well you do when you take the real GED. You can take practice tests individually or in a group (depending on your preference) to give you an idea of how you may do on the real test. Essentially, practice tests assist you in preparing for the real GED by helping you find out what you don't know and what you do know. With this information, you can prepare for the test more efficiently.

Just because a practice test has the word *test* in it doesn't mean you have to panic. Repeat to yourself, "This practice test is my friend and only wants to help me." Doing so can help you relax and understand that the practice tests in this book are set up to do just that — help you relax and practice for the real tests. These practice tests also help you discover your weaknesses and strengths so you can concentrate on subject areas that you need to study, which can definitely improve your chances of success on the real tests.

We supply several practice tests throughout this book that help you get familiar with what to expect on test day. Before each set of tests in each part, we provide you with a chapter that outlines what's unique about that particular test. *Note:* Not all tests on the GED are the same, and knowing as much as you can about each test can help you pass it. (For example, the Language Arts Test has a different format than the Math Test.) After you read the initial chapter in each part, you're ready to take the ensuing practice tests.

Working your way through a practice test

To get the most out of the practice tests in this book, you need to know what to do when taking them. Set yourself up as if you were going to take the real test. Time yourself and don't take a break to check the answers. The closer you come to real test conditions, the better the result will be when you take the real test.

When taking any practice tests in this book, keep the following steps in mind to help you through the process:

1. **Carefully read the instructions at the beginning of each test.**

   Take a few minutes to read and understand them. Normally, the person giving the real test makes sure that everyone understands the instructions before going ahead with the test. If you have any questions about the directions for a particular practice test, ask. The best time to concern yourself about instructions is before the test. The instructions for the practice tests are as close as possible to the instructions for the real tests. You can find tons of info about the tests in this book as well as on the GED Web site at www.acenet.edu. If all else fails, ask your local administrator before the test about the instructions. He or she will tell you, if the answer is public knowledge. If the answer is to be revealed when you take the test, be patient.

2. **Know the time restrictions for the real test, and stick to them as you take the practice test.**

   Timing is very important during the GED tests. At the beginning of each test, the directions tell you how much time you have for the test. Make sure you stick to the allotted time. Use an alarm clock; have a friend keep an eye on the time; or do anything else you have to do to make sure you don't go over the time limit.

   During the real test, the person giving the test will remind you about the time allotment and what will happen at the end of the test. Usually, he tells you to put your writing instruments down and close your book. Whatever the test proctor says, make sure you do it. This is not the time to show how much of an individual you are. Be part of the crowd and follow instructions.

3. **Prepare for the practice test the way you would prepare for the real test.**

   Have your writing instruments ready and waiting. Have enough scrap paper to make notes. Make photocopies of the answer sheets or tear them out of this book so that you don't have to keep flipping back and forth in the book. Find an uncomfortable chair to sit on — test centers aren't famous for their comfortable seating. Concentrate on the test — not the chair — and you'll be fine. The other way around can be a recipe for disaster.

4. **Make a mental plan beforehand so you know how to answer the questions in the allotted time.**

   You know before you start taking the test how many questions are on it and how much time you have to answer them. You also know about how many minutes you can safely spend on each question. Make a mental plan of how you're going to use this information. Obviously, you can't time each question, but you may feel comfortable timing each set of five or ten questions to make sure you stay on track. You may want to set aside a few minutes at the beginning to scan over the material and pick out the easy questions. Or you may decide to read all the questions and start with the even-numbered ones and finish with the odd-numbered ones. Whatever you choose, make the decision ahead of time and stick to it.

5. **Skim the questions, answer the easy ones first, and then focus on the more difficult ones.**

   Be sure to record all your answers on your answer sheet. If possible, leave some time at the end of the test for review. Don't overthink the questions. You're looking for the best answer as stated or suggested by the question and any other material presented. If your previous knowledge tells you that the best answer according to the passage isn't the correct answer, play the multiple-choice game. Choose the best answer based on the material presented to you. In doing so, if your previous knowledge is flawed or if you forget something you should remember, you can still get the right answer and pass the test — which, of course, is the goal of this entire exercise.

6. **After you finish all the questions or run out of time, make some notes on your scrap paper about the difficulty of the test.**

   Make notes about which questions you found difficult to answer and which ones you found easy to answer. Make notes about how you felt as you took the test. Did you have enough time? Did specific sections cause you trouble? Make notes on everything you remember about the test — these notes will come in handy later.

7. **Check the answers to see how you did.**

   You can find the answers and their explanations in the chapter immediately following the practice test chapter. For each question, compare your answer to the correct answer. If you got it wrong, read the explanation to try to figure out why. If you're not sure why it's wrong, try reading the question and its answer's explanation again. If you're still not sure, ask for help. If you answered correctly, congratulate yourself, but read the explanation anyway. You may find out a bit more about doing a particular type of question, or you may just find out what you already know. If you don't read the explanation, you won't find out anything more.

8. **When you finish checking your answers, add up the number of questions you answered correctly.**

   On the real test, the scores are computed using a complex calculation that we can't do here. To be on the safe side, though, consider that getting 80 percent of the answers correct leaves you with a safe margin for error. If you scored more than 20 percent of the questions wrong, you still have work to do.

9. **Review the questions you missed, even if you missed only one, and read the notes you made right after you finished the test (see Step 6).**

   If your notes indicate that you knew you had problems with these questions when you answered them, compare those notes with the answers. For example, if you felt you had trouble with the questions about graphs and you got most of the graph-related questions wrong, you need more help with graphs. If you got them right, you may be worrying too much or you may just need a quick review of graphs. At this point, you can review your plan of action or make up one if you haven't already done so. That way, you have a plan for passing the test based on experience. Then decide for yourself what you want to do next to continue preparing.

In the introductory chapter for each test, we tell you what's being tested in that particular test. Go to the sections in the introductory chapter with headings that focus on the areas in which you need the most help (based on your analysis of your answers and posttest notes). If you made the most mistakes in one or more areas, spend most of your time working on that area as you prepare to take another practice test. And remember: Sometimes you have to take a slight detour to get to your goal. If you're having a lot of trouble with a particular test or section, consider looking into a course, asking a friend, or getting a tutor for that test or section. Whatever you decide to do, practice, practice, practice.

10. **Go on to the second practice test if you did well on the first one or if you've finished any extra preparation you wanted to do.**

Follow Steps 1 through 9 to complete that test the same way you did the first. If your score improves, congratulate yourself. If it doesn't and you get a less-than-perfect score, analyze your mistakes to find out your areas of weakness and concentrate on them. At this point, you may want to do some additional practice or consider joining a GED preparation class. You can also find some sample questions for the GED at www. acenet.edu/Content/NavigationMenu/ged/test/prep/sample_questions. htm. The important thing is to get some help and do more preparation. Whether you do well or not on the practice tests, the GED instructors can help you decide whether you're ready to take the real tests.

Managing Your Time for the GED

Time management becomes an important issue as soon as you decide you need a high school diploma equivalency. If you had all the time in the world, you could just meander through preparation and planning. Unfortunately, you have deadlines that you or others may have set for you, which means you have a limited time to do something. Managing your time means that you stand a very good chance of finishing on time. How well you figure out how to manage your time can make accomplishing your goals that much more possible in the time allotted.

In this section, we give you some hints about how to manage your time. To start, this section consists of about 800 words. Think about how long it takes you to read and understand an 800-word passage. Keep track of the time it actually takes to do this activity. You can use that information as you plan how to spend your time taking the test.

Before the tests

Prior to taking the GED, you have plenty of tasks to tend to, and you have to find time to take care of them. Before you start studying or doing any other preparation work, you need to have a firm grasp of what you need to do and how much time you need to devote to each task — which is where we come in to help you.

Before the test, make sure you do the following:

1. **Make a list of everything you need to do to prepare for the GED.**

We suggest you first look at the GED Web site at www.acenet.edu/AM/Template. cfm?Section=GED_TS, consult your local administrator, and review material such as this book to help you prepare. Create your own list based on your skills and the test areas where you need the most help. You can create a table like the one we provide you here to help you stay organized.

Step	Task	Estimated Time	Date Completed
1	Make sure that I can prove I'm eligible to take the GED test.		
	Get a copy of my birth certificate (if I don't already have it).		
	Get a copy of my high school transcript to prove when I left school (if I don't already have it).		
	Check with my local GED administrator to find out the actual requirements and if I presently meet them.		
2	Buy a copy of a good preparation book like this one.		
3	Contact my local GED administrator to get a schedule of tests.		
4	Figure out how much time I have to prepare for each test.		
5	Look at my high school transcript and make a list of the subject areas I had the most trouble with so I know where to spend most of my preparation time.		
6	Begin preparing for the practice tests by reading the appropriate sections of this book.		
7	Take the first practice tests, check my answers, and read the explanations.		
8	Make a list of the tests in order with my lowest scores at the top and my best scores at the bottom.		
9	Review the time I have for each test, and make any modifications I think would be in my best interest.		
10	If my test scores are low, consider a preparation class, a GED preparation group, or some form of additional help, and estimate how much time it will take.		
11	Begin to work on preparation, starting with my weakest area.		
12	Do regular reviews of all areas, spending the most time on my weakest areas.		
13	When I think I am better prepared, take the second practice test and repeat steps 7 to 12.		
14	Review and modify, if necessary, the time for the test.		
15	Register for the test.		
16	Read the sections in this book about what to expect on the test.		
17	Set up a review schedule, spending the most time on the weakest areas.		
18	Rehearse my route to the test.		

continued

continued

Step	Task	Estimated Time	Date Completed
19	Take the test.		
20	Wait for results while considering a realistic plan and schedule for retaking a test if any of the results are low.		

2. **After you have your list, approximate how much time you need to complete each task, indicating both when you'd like to have it done and leaving space to fill in the date you actually complete it.**

   Estimate how long you think it may take you to finish a task. Remember that some tasks will take longer than others. For example, getting a copy of your high school transcript may take only a couple of hours, while preparing for your weakest subject area may take 30 or 40 hours, depending on how much time you need. Make sure to take into consideration any lag time because you won't always get immediate answers to questions; sometimes you'll have to wait to see people or wait on the mail. Take a calendar and figure out when you should have the task completed.

Your plan for managing your time is written on paper, not carved in stone. As you work through the preparation process, you may realize that you need more time for one task, such as taking more math pretests, and less time for another task. If so, that's okay. You can simply revise your schedule to take your new needs into consideration. Sometimes a pencil and an eraser are a time manager's best friends. Make sure you write down the date when you've completed each task.

During the tests

After the GED starts, you're on strict timelines to finish each test. The best thing you can do to manage your time during the tests is simple: Relax. Many students get so psyched up right when they sit down to take the tests that they have trouble focusing and waste valuable time.

During the test, use the following time-management strategies to help keep yourself on track and to finish on time. We include specific time-management strategies for each test in the part of the book that deals with each particular test.

- ✔ **Take deep breaths, and do anything you can to relax and focus on the task at hand.** Some people like to meditate. Others like to visualize themselves doing well on the test. Still others like to close their eyes and say a little prayer. Whatever your preference, take a few minutes to relax, but remember you don't get extra time on the test to do so.

- ✔ **Skim the questions to spot the easy ones, and do those questions first.** After doing so, look at your watch and quickly calculate how many questions are left and how much time you have to do them. To determine how much time you can spend on each question, divide the time remaining by the number of questions you have left. Be sure to add in a little extra time at the end of the test for review (see the next bullet point for details). *Note:* In each part, we offer a chapter that outlines how many questions are on each test and how much time you have to answer them. Use these chapters to help you create a mental game plan before the test so you're better prepared to manage your time when you get to the real test.

- ✔ **Leave a few minutes at the end to review your answers.** You need a few minutes to make sure you answered everything correctly. Quickly look over your answers, but don't panic and change them because you think an answer is wrong at the last minute. Chances are that the answer you selected first is the right one. Try to realistically consider any changes you want to make.

After you pass the test: What you can do with your GED

After passing the GED and receiving that beautiful diploma, you're ready to think about your future. In addition to the obvious celebrations for your personal graduation, you have plenty more to do. Consider the following ways you can improve your life with your new GED in hand. Chapter 31 has some interesting ways your life can change with a GED.

✔ **You can qualify for a better job.** If you took the GED to get a better job, go for it. Having a GED may increase your chances of passing the initial screening process and getting an interview. During the interview, you can shine your way past the other qualified applicants. Make sure you let your prospective employer know that you passed a test that about 40 percent of high school graduates would have trouble passing. Furthermore, you've proved that you're a diligent worker by preparing and passing the GED after leaving school. You're dedicated, you know how to prepare, and you learn well — if you didn't, you couldn't have passed the test. Basically, you're worthy of being hired. With this attitude, you should do well in interviews and be on your way to getting a better job.

Take some information about the GED tests and diploma with you to your interview. Don't assume that every Human Resource person knows all about the GED. Go to the GED Home Page and download some information to strengthen your case. You can enter *GED ace* into a search engine or go to www.acenet.edu/AM/Template. cfm?Section=GED_TS.

If you get the job, you can earn a larger salary to help fund your future. If you're good at what you do and work your way up, you can fund your present and future needs.

✔ **You can go to college or some other post-secondary school.** With a GED, you can apply to and improve your chances of getting accepted at many post-secondary schools. Check with the school you want to apply to, and find out the admission requirements; review its deadlines for applying and the courses it offers. Consult with the financial aid office to find out about your options for payment.

Chapter 3

Succeeding on the GED

- -

In This Chapter

▶ Getting ready the night before and the day of the test

▶ Figuring out what to expect on test day

▶ Nailing down important test-taking strategies

▶ Staying calm and relaxed while you take the test

- -

*Y*ou may never have taken a standardized test before. Or if you have, you may wake up sweating in the middle of the night from nightmares about your past experiences. Whether you have or haven't experienced the joys or sorrows of standardized tests, to succeed on the GED, you have to know how to perform well on this type of test, which consists mostly of multiple-choice questions.

The good news is you've come to the right spot to find out more about this type of test. This chapter explains some important pointers for what you can do the days and nights before and the morning of the test and what you need to do during the test to be successful. It also explains some important test-taking strategies that can help you feel confident.

Leading Up to Test Time

Doing well on the GED involves more than walking into the test site and answering the questions. You need to be prepared for the challenges in the tests. To ensure you're ready to tackle the test head-on, make sure you do the following leading up to the test:

- ✔ **Get enough sleep.** We're sorry if we sound like your parents talking, but it's true — you shouldn't take tests when you're approaching exhaustion. Plan your time so that you can get a good night's sleep for several days before the test. If you prepare ahead of time, you'll be ready and sleep will come easier.

- ✔ **Eat a good breakfast.** A healthy breakfast fuels your mind and body. You have to spend several hours taking the test, and you definitely don't want to falter during that time. Eat some protein, such as eggs, bacon, or sausage with toast for breakfast. Avoid sugars (donuts, jelly, fruit) because they can cause you to tire easily. You don't want your empty stomach fighting with your full brain.

- ✔ **Take some deep breaths.** During your trip to the testing site, prepare yourself mentally for the test. Clear your head of all distractions, practice deep breathing, and imagine yourself acing the test. Don't panic.

- ✔ **Start at the beginning, not the end.** Remember that the day of the test is the end of a long journey of preparation and not the beginning. It takes time to build mental muscles.

- ✔ **Be on time.** Make sure you know what time the test begins and the exact location of your test site. Most examination centers don't let you enter if you're late. Don't take a chance — arrive early. If necessary, take a practice run to make sure you have enough time to get from your home or workplace to the testing center. You don't need the added pressure of worrying about whether you can make it to the test on time. In fact, this added pressure can create industrial-strength panic in the calmest of people.

Traffic happens. No one can plan for it, but you can leave extra time to make sure it doesn't ruin your day. Plan your route and practice it. Then leave extra time in case a meteor crashes into the street and the crowd that gathers around it stalls your progress. Examiners don't have a lot of sympathy for you if you show up late because you didn't check the starting time. They have even less sympathy if you show up on the wrong date.

Finding Out What to Take to the GED Tests

The GED may be the most important exam you ever take. Treat it seriously and come prepared. Make sure you bring the following items with you on test day:

- ✔ **You:** The most important thing to bring to the GED tests is you. If you enroll to take the tests, you have to show up; otherwise, you'll receive a big fat zero. If something unfortunate happens after you enroll, contact the test center and explain your situation to the test administrators.

- ✔ **Correct identification:** Before test officials let you into the room to take the test, they want to make sure you're you. Bring the approved photo ID — your state GED office can tell you what's an approved form of photo ID. Have your ID in a place where you can reach it easily. And when asked to identify yourself, don't pull out a mirror and say, "Yep, that's me."

- ✔ **Fees you still owe:** To take the GED, you must pay a registration fee, which varies from state to state. (Check with your local administrator to double-check when the fee has to be paid and how to pay it.) If you don't pay the fee, you can't take the exam. Bring your receipt in case of any misunderstanding at the door.

- ✔ **Registration confirmation:** The registration confirmation is your proof that you did register. If you're taking the tests in an area where everybody knows you and everything you do, you may not need the confirmation, but we still suggest you take it anyway. It's light and doesn't take up much room in your pocket.

- ✔ **Other miscellaneous items:** In the instructions you receive after you register for the tests, you get a list of what you need to bring with you. Besides yourself and the items we list previously, other items you want to bring or wear include the following:

  - Comfortable clothes

  - Comfortable shoes

  - Wristwatch with a second hand, if possible (If you haven't changed the battery lately, you may want to do so beforehand.)

  - Two No. 2 pencils or HB mechanical pencils; a pen for the essay (all of which may be provided for you at the testing center — but why take a chance?)

The rules about what enters the testing room are strict. Don't take any chances. If an item isn't on the list of acceptable items and isn't normal clothing, leave it at home. The last place on earth to discuss whether or not you can bring something into the test room is at the door on test day. If you have questions, contact the test center in advance. Check out www.acenet.edu/resources/GED/center_locator.cfm to find a list of sites close to your home with their addresses and phone numbers. You can also call 800-62-MYGED to ask your questions of real people. Whatever you do, be sure not to bring the following:

- ✔ Books

- ✔ Calculator (one is provided for you — see Chapter 24)

- ✔ Notes or scratch paper

- ✔ MP3 player

- ✔ Cell phone (leave it at home or in your car)

- ✔ Anything valuable, like a laptop computer or radio that you don't feel comfortable leaving outside the room while you take the exams

Knowing What to Expect When You Get There

Usually you take the GED in a large examination room with at least one official (sometimes called a *proctor* or *examiner*) who's in charge of the test. The proctor gives each test taker a booklet and an answer sheet when the test is scheduled to begin and then reads instructions to all the students. Listen carefully to these instructions so you know when and if you can take bathroom breaks, how much time you have to take the test, and other important information.

As soon as the proctor gives you permission to open the test booklet, start by skimming the questions. Don't spend a lot of time skimming — just enough to spot the questions you absolutely know and the ones you know you'll need more time to answer. Use your very own code to mark the easy ones in the test booklet. After you finish skimming, answer all the questions you know first; that way you leave yourself much more time for the difficult questions.

For each question — except for a few on the Mathematics Test (see Chapter 24) and the essay in Part II of the Language Arts, Writing Test (see Chapter 4) — you have five answers to choose from. Read each question carefully, keeping in mind that only one answer is correct. Choose the answer that's closest to the correct answer as presented to you in the question. If what you know is different from what the question says, go with the information in the question. A machine usually grades the tests, and the machine doesn't know what's in your head. Sometimes you have to choose the *best* answer, not the absolutely correct one.

You don't have to answer questions in order. Nobody except you will ever know in which order you answered the questions, so do the easiest questions first.

Because taking standardized tests probably isn't a usual situation for you, you may feel nervous. This is perfectly normal. Just try to focus on answering one question at a time, and push any other thoughts to the back of your mind. Sometimes taking a few deep breaths can clear your mind; just don't spend a lot of time focusing on your breath. After all, your main job is to pass the tests.

Throughout the test, keep your eyes on your test. If your eyes glance around the room, the GED examiner may wonder what you're doing. Never become the object of an examiner's attention during a test. In the worst-case scenario, he or she may think you're cheating and disqualify you.

Throughout the test, the examiner will periodically tell you how much time has elapsed or how much time is left. Listen to these reminders. When time is up, immediately stop writing, put down your pencil, and breathe a sigh of relief. When the test is over, hand in your answer sheet and test booklet. Listen for instructions on what to do or where to go next.

Discovering Important Test-Taking Strategies

You can increase your score by practicing — and mastering — a few smart test-taking strategies. To help you do so, we give you some tips in this section for planning your time, determining the question type, figuring out how to answer the different types of questions, guessing intelligently, and reviewing your work.

Watching the clock

You have only a certain amount of time for each test in the GED exam, so time management is an important part of succeeding on the test. You need to plan ahead and use your time wisely as you move through the tests.

 When the test begins, check your watch and write down the time you start and the time you have to finish. (Write these times near the top of your answer sheet in very light pencil marks that you can erase before handing it in.) This way, you don't have to waste time figuring out how much time you have left partway through the test. Don't try to remember the time; instead, write it down.

During the test, your proctor will probably warn you — perhaps more than once — about how much time remains. Check the times you're told against the times you write down at the beginning of the test. Table 3-1 shows you how much time you have, on average, for each question in each test.

Table 3-1	Time per Question for Each GED Test		
Test	Number of Questions	Time Limit (In Minutes)	Time per Question (In Minutes)
Language Arts, Writing, Part I	50	75	1.5
Language Arts, Writing, Part II	1 essay	45	45
Social Studies	50	70	1.4
Science	50	80	1.6
Language Arts, Reading	40	65	1.6
Mathematics, Parts I and II	50	90	1.8

As you can see from this table, if you take two minutes for each question, you won't have time to answer all the questions on the test. Keep in mind the following general time-management tips to help you complete each exam on time:

- **Measure the time you have to answer each question without spending more time on timing than answering.** Group questions together; for example, plan to do five questions in seven minutes. Doing so helps you complete all the questions and leaves you several minutes for review.

- **Keep calm and don't panic.** The time you spend panicking could be better spent answering questions.

- **Practice using the sample tests in this book.** The more you practice timed sample test questions, the easier managing a timed test becomes. You can become used to doing something in a limited amount of time if you practice.

Identifying different question types

Although you don't have to know too much about how the test makers developed the questions to answer them correctly, you do need some understanding of how they were constructed. Knowing the types of questions you're dealing with can make answering them easier — and you'll face fewer surprises. Some questions in math require a special form for the answer. Knowing the question type can shape the way you think about the answer. Some questions ask you to analyze material given in the passage, which means the information you need is in the passage. Others ask you to infer from the passage, which means that all the information may not be in the passage. Although none of the tests are labeled with the following titles, the GED test questions assess your skills in the following areas.

Analysis

Analysis questions require you to break down information and look at how the information bits are related to one another. Analyzing information in this way is part of reasoning and requires you to

- Separate facts from opinions.

- Realize that when an assumption isn't stated it may not necessarily be true. Assumptions stated in the passage or question help you find the best answer.

- Identify a cause-and-effect relationship. For example, you have to eat an ice cream cone quickly in hot weather. The cause is the hot weather and the effect is that the ice cream melts quickly.

- Infer. You may be asked to reach a conclusion based on evidence presented in the question. *Inferring* is a fancy way of saying that you'll reach a conclusion. In the preceding example, you can infer that you should stay in an air-conditioned space to eat your ice cream or eat it very quickly.

- Compare. If you consider the similarities between ideas or objects, you're *comparing* them. The world is like a basketball because both are round, for example.

- Contrast. If you consider the differences between ideas or objects, you're *contrasting* them. For example, the world isn't like a basketball because it is so much larger and has an irregular surface.

Relating to other people in social situations exposes most people to these skills. For example, in most sports-related conversations between friends (or rivals), you quickly figure out how to separate fact from opinion and how to infer, compare, contrast, and identify cause-and-effect relationships. In other social situations, you come to realize when an assumption isn't stated. For example, you likely assume that your best friend or significant other is going to join you for a late coffee the night before an important test, such as the GED, but, in reality, your friend may be planning on going to bed early. Unstated assumptions that you assume can get you into trouble in life and on the GED tests.

Application

Application questions require you to use the information presented to you in one situation to help you in a different situation. You've been applying information left and right for most of your life, but you probably don't realize it. For example, when you use the information from the morning newspaper to make a point in an argument in the afternoon, you use your application skills.

Comprehension

A *comprehension* question asks whether you understand written material. The GED test makers expect you to be able to state the info on the test in your own words, develop a summary of the ideas presented, discuss the implications of those ideas, and draw conclusions from those implications. You need to develop these comprehension skills to understand what the multiple-choice questions are asking you and to answer the questions successfully.

The best way to increase your comprehension is to read extensively and to ask another person to ask you questions about what you read. You can also use commercial books that specifically help you with your comprehension by presenting you with written material and asking you questions about it. One of those books is in your hands. All the other *For Dummies* test-preparation books, as well as *AP English Literature & Composition For Dummies* by Geraldine Woods (Wiley), have reading comprehension as a major focus, too. Feel free to check out these books to improve your comprehension if you still have difficulty after using this book.

Synthesis

Synthesis questions require you to take apart blocks of information presented to you and put the pieces back together to form a hypothesis, theory, or story. Doing so gives you a new understanding or twist on the information that you didn't have before. Have you ever discussed something that happened, giving it your own twist and explanation to create a brand new narrative? If so, you've already put your synthesis skills to use.

Evaluation

Any time someone presents you with information or opinion, you judge it to make sure it rings true in your mind. This *evaluation* helps you make decisions about the information presented before you decide to use it. If the clerk behind the ice cream counter suggests you get a raspberry cone instead of the flavor you wanted because everyone knows that raspberry melts slower than all the other flavors, you may be a bit suspicious. Especially if you notice that the clerk also has four containers of raspberry ice cream and only one of each other flavor, you may evaluate it as biased or even incorrect.

Cognitive skills

Mental skills that you use to get knowledge are called *cognitive skills* and include reasoning, perception, and intuition. They're particularly important in reading for understanding, which is what you're asked to do on the GED tests. You can increase your knowledge and comprehension by reading books, researching on the Web, or watching documentaries. After you read or watch something new, discuss it with others to make sure you understand it and can use it in conversation.

Addressing and answering questions

When you start the tests, you want to have a game plan in place for how to answer the questions. Keep the following tips in mind to help you address each multiple-choice question:

✔ **Whenever you read a question, ask yourself, "What am I being asked?"** Doing so helps you stay focused on what you need to find out to answer the question. You may even want to decide quickly what skills are required to answer the question (see the preceding section for more on these skills). Then try to answer it.

✔ **Try to eliminate some answers.** Because all the questions are straightforward, don't look for hidden or sneaky questions. The questions ask for an answer based on the information given. If you don't have enough information to answer the question, one of the answers will say so.

✔ **Find the best answer and quickly verify that it answers the question.** If it does, mark it on the answer sheet and go on. If it doesn't, mark the question in the test booklet and come back to it after you answer all the other questions, if you have time. Just remember to erase all marks in the test booklet before turning it in.

Guess for success: Using intelligent guessing

The multiple-choice questions provide you with five possible answers. You get one point for every correct answer, and nothing is subtracted for incorrect answers, which means you can guess on the questions you don't know for sure without fearing that you'll lose points. Make educated guesses by eliminating as many wrong choices as possible and choosing from just two or three answers.

When the question gives you five possible answers and you randomly choose one, you have a 20-percent chance of guessing the correct answer without even reading the question. Of course, we don't recommend using this method during the test.

If you know that one of the answers is definitely wrong, you now have just four answers to choose from and have a 25-percent chance (1 in 4) of choosing the correct answer. If you know that two of the answers are wrong, you leave yourself only three possible answers to choose from, giving you a 33-percent (1 in 3) chance of guessing right — much better than 20 percent! And, finally, if you know that three of the answers are wrong, your chances of choosing the correct answer move up to 50 percent, which is as good as a random choice gets!

If you don't know the answer to a particular question, try to spot the wrong choices by keeping in mind the following tips:

- **Make sure your answer really answers the question at hand.** Wrong choices usually don't answer the question; that is, they may sound good, but they answer a different question than the one the test asks.

- **When two answers seem very close, consider both answers carefully because they both can't be right — but they both *can* be wrong.** Answers that are very close are sometimes given to see whether you really understand the material.

- **Look for opposite answers in the hopes that you can eliminate one.** If two answers contradict each other, both can't be right, but both can be wrong.

- **Trust your instincts.** Some wrong choices may just strike you as wrong when you first read them. If you spend time preparing for these exams, you probably know more than you think.

Leaving time for review

Having a few minutes at the end of a test to check your work is a great way to set your mind at ease. These few minutes give you a chance to look at any questions that may be troubling. If you've chosen an answer for every question, enjoy the last few minutes before time is called — without any panic. Keep the following tips in mind as you review your answers:

- Although you technically have a minute and a half for each question, on average, try to do each question within a minute. The extra seconds you don't use the first time through the test add up for time at the end of the test to review. Some questions require more thought and decision making than others. Use your extra seconds to answer those questions.

- Do *not* try to change a lot of answers at the last minute. Second-guessing yourself can lead to trouble. If you have prepared well and done lots of sample questions, you have a good chance of getting the correct answers the first time. Ignoring all your preparation and knowledge to play a hunch isn't a good idea at the race track or on a test.

- Review is a good time to check that your answers are displayed properly. Make sure that the circles are filled and that you don't have any stray marks on the answer sheet. A machine may read your doodles as answers and miss a partially completed circle.

Keeping Your Head in the Game

To succeed in taking the GED, you need to be prepared. In addition to studying the content and skills needed for the five tests, you also want to be mentally prepared. Although you may be nervous, you can't let your nerves get the best of you. Stay calm and take a deep breath. Remember the following pointers to help you stay focused on the task at hand:

- **Take time to relax.** Passing the GED tests is an important milestone in life. Make sure you leave a bit of time to relax, both while you prepare for the tests and just before you take them. Relaxing has a place in preparing as long as it doesn't become your main activity.

- **Make sure you know the rules of the room before you begin.** If you have questions about using the bathroom during the test or what to do if you finish early, ask the proctor before you begin. If you don't want to ask these questions in public, call the GED office in your area before the test day, and ask your questions over the telephone. If you're a member of Facebook, send your questions to `www.facebook.com/group.php?gid=46193757671`, which is an easy way to go if you get caught in a jungle of unanswered voice mails. For general GED questions, call 800-62-MYGED or check out `www.gedtest.org`.

- **Keep your eyes on your paper.** Everybody knows not to look at other people's papers during the test, but, to be on the safe side, don't stretch, roll your eyes, or do anything else that may be mistaken for looking at another test.

- **Stay calm.** Your nerves can use up a lot of energy needed for the test. Concentrate on the job at hand. You can always be nervous or panicky some other time.

Part II
Minding Your Ps and Qs: The Language Arts, Writing Test

The 5th Wave   By Rich Tennant

YOUNG STEPHEN KING SUBMITS HIS GED WRITING SAMPLE.

"I finished my essay early, so I wrote essays on all the other questions, and then I had some time, so I wrote a few more essays on some spooky stuff I've been thinking about."

In this part . . .

This part takes you inside the Language Arts, Writing Test, giving you the lowdown on both Parts I and II. On this test, you get a chance to answer multiple-choice questions and write a short essay. Lucky you!

To keep yourself from panicking, all you have to do is prepare for these tasks — which is where this part comes in handy. Here you find out how the Language Arts, Writing Test is put together and on which skills it tests. With that information in hand, you can become familiar with what you're expected to know before taking the tests — and this familiarity will prove incredibly beneficial on test day. As an added bonus, we also offer you some strategies that can help you do your best on this test.

After cramming your head with test details, we give you a chance to test your skills and preparation on two full-length practice tests. Each of the tests has an answer chapter with explanations to help you understand why the answers are what they are, as well as suggestions for how to write a well-thought-out essay.

Chapter 4

The Write Stuff: Preparing for the Language Arts, Writing Test, Parts I and II

. . . .

In This Chapter

▶ Taking a look at the format of the Language Arts, Writing Test, Parts I and II

▶ Knowing what kinds of questions appear on Part I and figuring out how to prepare for them

▶ Preparing to write an essay for Part II and practicing with some sample prompts

. . . .

*T*he Language Arts, Writing Test evaluates your skills in comprehending and applying concepts in grammar and writing. In case you don't already know, *grammar* is the basic structure of language (you know — subjects, verbs, sentences, fragments, periods, commas, and all that). Most of what you're tested on (both in writing and grammar) is stuff you've picked up over the years, either in school or just by living and speaking and reading, but, to help you better prepare for this test, we give you some more skill-building tips in this chapter.

As you may have gathered from this chapter's title, the Language Arts, Writing Test comes in two parts. Much of Part I determines how well you know grammar by asking you 50 multiple-choice questions.

Part II of this test is different from all the other GED tests because you have to write an essay. Instead of coloring in circles, you write real words and sentences that connect to each other in some way or another and make sense to a reader. You have 45 minutes to produce a readable, coherent piece of work about a topic presented to you. In spite of its name, however, Part II doesn't consist of a real essay so much as a series of related paragraphs. You aren't expected to produce a book-length opus complete with documented research. Rather, you're expected to write a coherent series of interrelated paragraphs on a given topic and use the rules of grammar and correct spelling. Examiners look for a five-paragraph essay that is well organized and sticks to the topic given.

This chapter gives you the details on the Language Arts, Writing Test and offers you some helpful tips to assist you in succeeding.

Understanding the Test Format

As we mention earlier, the Language Arts, Writing Test breaks down into two parts, each of which has its own question type. Having a basic understanding of the two question types used in these two parts can help you avoid any surprises when you sit down to take the test. The following sections explain what types of questions you encounter on Part I and Part II and offer you some advice on how to prepare more effectively. We want you to feel at ease when you face these sections on the test.

Grasping what's on Part I

Part I of the Language Arts, Writing Test consists of 50 multiple-choice questions, which you have 75 minutes to complete. The questions ask you to read, revise, and edit documents that may include how-to info, informational texts, and workplace material. Don't worry — just because you haven't studied grammar for years doesn't mean you don't know the material. You probably know more than you think. And, lucky for you, all the questions in this part are multiple choice, which means you don't have to come up with the answers all on your own.

To answer the questions in this part, you need to carefully read the passage. Always read the entire document before answering the corresponding questions because the questions make more sense when you have a clear idea of the content. As you read each document, think to yourself, "Can I correct this passage? If so, how?"

Grasping what's on Part II

This 45-minute test has only one question, and it's a topic on which you have to write a short essay. You can add any time you have left after completing Part I of the Language Arts, Writing Test to your time for Part II.

For this part of the test, you're given one topic and a few instructions. Your task is to write approximately two pages (one front and one back) on that topic. Remember that you can't write about another topic or a similar topic — if you do, you'll receive zero points for your essay, and you'll have to retake the entire Language Arts, Writing Test.

The instructions that accompany your essay topic require that you use your personal observations, knowledge, and experience as you write about your given topic.

Passing Part I

The Language Arts, Writing Test, Part I requires you to draw on all your previous knowledge of grammar. To help you succeed on this test, we provide insightful information in the following sections that deals with what skills this part of the test covers, what types of questions you'll encounter, what you can do to prepare, how you can manage your time, and how the problems look on the actual test. With this information in hand, you can stare this test straight in the eyes on test day.

Looking at the skills Part I covers

Part I of the Language Arts, Writing Test evaluates you on the following types of skills related to grammar. Note that unlike the other GED tests, Part I of this test expects that you *know* or at least *are familiar with* the rules of grammar; looking at the passages provided won't do you much good if you don't understand the basics of these rules already.

✔ **Mechanics (25 percent; 12 or 13 questions):** You don't have to become a professional grammarian to pass this test, but you should know or review basic grammar. Check out *English Grammar For Dummies,* 2nd Edition, by Geraldine Woods (Wiley) to review what you should know or may have forgotten. The mechanics of writing include the following:

- **Capitalization:** You have to recognize which words start with a capital letter and which words don't. All sentences start with a capital letter, but so do titles, like "Miss," "President," and "Senator," when they're followed by a person's last name. Names of cities, states, and countries are also capitalized.

- **Punctuation:** This area of writing mechanics includes everyone's personal favorite — commas. (Actually, most people hate commas because they aren't sure how to use them, but the basic rules are simple to apply after you know them.) The more you read, the better you get at punctuation. If you're reading and don't understand why punctuation is or isn't used, check with your grammar guidebook or the Internet. A general rule: Don't use a comma unless the next group of words is a complete sentence. For example: "As agonizing as it was to leave her friends, college was what she wanted." *College was what she wanted* is a complete sentence and can stand alone. (Try `http://esl.about.com/od/englishgrammar/a/a_punctuation.htm` or `http://grammar.about.com/od/punctuationandmechanics/a/punctrules.htm` — just beware that these Web pages have advertising on them.)

- **Spelling:** You don't have to spot a lot of misspelled words, but you do have to know how to spell contractions and possessives and understand the different spellings of homonyms.

- **Contractions:** This area of writing mechanics has nothing to do with those painful moments before childbirth! Instead, *contractions* are formed when the English language shortens a word by leaving out a letter or a sound. For example, when you say or write *can't,* you're using a shortened form of *cannot.* In this example, *can't* is the contraction.

  The important thing to remember about contractions is that the *apostrophe* (that's a single quotation mark) takes the place of the letter or letters that are left out.

- **Possessives:** Do you know people who are possessive? They're all about ownership, right? So is the grammar form of possessives. *Possessives* are words that show ownership or possession, usually by adding an apostrophe to a person's or object's name. If Marcia owns a car, that car is *Marcia's* car. The word *Marcia's* is a possessive. Make sure you know the difference between singular and plural possessives. For example: "The girl's coat is torn." (*Coat* is singular, so the apostrophe goes before the *s.*) "The girls' coats are torn." (*Coats* is plural, so the apostrophe goes after the *s.*)

✔ **Organization (15 percent; 7 or 8 questions):** On the test, you're asked to correct passages by changing the order of sentences or leaving out certain sentences when they don't fit. You have to work with passages to turn them into logical, organized paragraphs. You may be asked to work with paragraphs to form a better composition by changing them around or editing them by improving or adding topic sentences or making sure that all the sentences are about the same topic. The important thing to remember is that the questions are all multiple choice, which means you have only a limited number of options for making the passages better. Read the questions carefully and you should have no problems.

✔ **Sentence structure (30 percent; 15 questions):** Every language has rules about the order in which words should appear in a sentence. You get a chance to improve sentences through your understanding of what makes a good sentence. Extensive reading before the test can give you a good idea of how good sentences are structured and put together. The advice here, as always, is read, read, and read some more.

✔ **Usage (30 percent; 15 questions):** Usage questions make up one of the largest portions of the test. Grammar has a wide variety of rules, and these questions test your knowledge and understanding. Subjects and verbs must agree. Verbs have tenses that must be consistent. Pronouns must refer back to nouns properly. If the last three sentences sound like Greek to you, make sure you review grammatical usage rules.

Having a firm grasp of these writing mechanics can help you get a more accurate picture of the types of questions you'll encounter on Part I of this test. The next section focuses more on the specific passage materials you'll face.

Identifying the types of passages in Part I

The passages that the questions in Part I are based on come in the following three forms:

- **How-to texts:** Each of these articles or excerpts consists of 200 to 300 words and deals with topics of interest to the reader, such as how to pass the GED tests, how to write a great résumé, how to build a fence, or how to do anything else that may be interesting to the general public.

- **Informational texts:** These articles or excerpts provide information or analysis on some topic. They may be position papers, support papers, or critical evaluations of some subject. Each of these documents consists of about 200 to 300 words and tries to convey information to the reader.

- **Workplace material:** These articles or excerpts are all around you; they include letters, meeting notes, executive summaries, and applications. Each of these documents consists of about 200 to 300 words and discusses the everyday topics that are familiar to you.

Regardless of what type of passage the questions in Part I are based on, your job is to correct the grammar. Grammar doesn't change with the type of passage, so, although you should be familiar with the various types of passages, you need to be most familiar with the rules of grammar so you can use them to improve the passages.

Preparing for Part I: Tactics that work

To succeed on Part I of the Language Arts, Writing Test, you can prepare in advance by reviewing rules of grammar, punctuation, and spelling and by familiarizing yourself with the format and subject matter of the Part I test. Here are some of the best ways you can prepare:

- **Read as often as you can.** This strategy is the best one for passing this test, and it's by far the simplest because reading exposes you to correct grammar.

  Keep in mind that what you read makes a difference. Reading catalogues may increase your product knowledge and improve your research skills, but reading literature is preferable because it introduces you to so many rules of grammar. Reading fiction exposes you to interesting words and sentences. It shows you how paragraphs tie into one another and how each paragraph has a topic and generally sticks to it. Reading historical fiction can give you some insight into what led up to today and can also help you with the Social Studies Test (see Chapter 9 for more on the Social Studies Test). Just because we didn't mention something here doesn't mean you shouldn't read it. Read everything you can get your hands on, including newspapers, textbooks, and much more.

- **Master the rules of basic grammar.** On this test, you don't have to define a gerund and give an example of one, but you do have to know about verb tenses, subject/verb agreement, pronoun/antecedent agreement, possessives, and the like. As your knowledge of grammar and punctuation improves, have a bit of fun by correcting what you read in small-town newspapers and low-budget novels — both sometimes have poor editing.

✔ **Practice grammar in everyday speaking.** As you review the rules of grammar, practice them every day as you talk to your friends, family, and co-workers. Although correct grammar usually "sounds" right to your ears, sometimes it doesn't because you and the people you talk to have become used to using incorrect grammar. If you see a rule that seems different from the way you talk, put it on a flashcard and practice it as you go through your day. Before long, you'll train your ears so that correct grammar sounds right.

Correcting other people's grammar out loud doesn't make you popular, but correcting it in your head can help you succeed on this test.

✔ **Understand punctuation.** Know how to use commas, semicolons, colons, and other forms of punctuation. To find out more about punctuation and when and why to use its different forms, check out a grammatical reference book like *English Grammar For Dummies*, 2nd Edition, by Geraldine Woods (Wiley).

✔ **Practice writing and reading.** Write as much and as often as you can, and then review it for errors. Look for and correct mistakes in punctuation, grammar, and spelling. If you can't find any, ask someone who knows grammar and punctuation for help.

✔ **Keep a journal or blog.** Journals and blogs are just notebooks (physical or virtual) in which you write a bit about your life every day. They both provide good practice for personal writing. Blogging or responding to blogs gives you practice in public writing because others see what you write. Whether you use a personal journal or a public blog, though, keep in mind that the writing is the important part. If public writing encourages you to write more and more often, do it. If not, consider the private writing of a journal or diary.

✔ **Improve your spelling.** As you practice writing, keep a good dictionary at hand. If you're not sure of the spelling of any word, look it up. We hear you. How do you look up a spelling word if you can't spell it? Try sounding out the word phonetically and look in an online dictionary. Type in the word and select the word that looks familiar and correct. If that doesn't work, ask someone for help. Add it to a spelling list that you keep and practice from. In addition, get a list of common *homonyms* (words that sound the same but are spelled differently and have different definitions), and review them every day. (You need to know, for example, the difference between *their, there,* and *they're.*) Many dictionaries contain a list of homonyms.

✔ **Keep in mind that these questions are multiple choice.** Multiple-choice questions always give you the correct answer. Of course, they also tell you four other answers that are incorrect, but all you have to do is find the correct one! As you practice speaking and writing, you tune your ears so that the correct answer sounds right, which, believe it or not, makes finding the correct answer easier on the test.

✔ **Take practice tests.** Take as many practice tests as you can. Be strict about time limitations, and check your answers when you're finished. Don't move on until you know and understand the correct answer. (Check out Chapters 5 and 7 for two sample tests and Chapters 6 and 8 for their answers.) The time you spend taking and reviewing these practice tests is well worth it.

Managing your time for Part 1

To complete Part I of the Language Arts, Writing Test, you have to answer 50 questions in 75 minutes, which breaks down to 1½ minutes per question. However, because the questions on this test are based on passages (of between 200 and 300 words), you have to give yourself enough time to read the passages, too. The upside is that you don't have to read a different passage for each question (because each passage is followed by a set of questions). The downside is that you have to remember the material you read about in each passage long enough to answer all the questions based on it.

You basically have two options for reading passages and answering questions in this part of the test. Before we explain these two options, imagine that you're faced with a passage of about 300 words followed by ten questions. You have 15 minutes to complete these ten questions (1½ minutes times ten). Here are your two options for moving through this passage and its corresponding questions:

- ✔ **Option No. 1:** For this option, you spend half a minute reading and understanding each question and the answer choices that follow, which takes about five minutes total. Then you spend about three minutes reading the passage, knowing what to look for, and you take the remaining seven minutes to answer the questions and review your answers. As you may recognize, we suggest using this option for managing your time on most of the GED tests (see Chapter 2).

- ✔ **Option No. 2:** Answering questions using Option No. 2 means taking a slightly different angle to managing your time than we discuss for most of the other tests on the GED. With this option, you begin by reading the passage as quickly as you can without sacrificing understanding. This option calls on your speed-reading skills, which allow you to spend less time reading the passage (and have more time left to choose and review your answers).

  Remember that speed-reading allows you to increase your reading speed *without* hurting your comprehension. If you want to try out speed-reading by yourself, pick up any reading material and try to train your eyes to read down a line in the middle of each page, allowing your peripheral vision to catch the words at each edge. You can use your finger to increase the speed at which you read by moving it along the same line you read along. You can also practice your speed-reading skills by setting a timer and decreasing the time you have to read a page each time you start reading a new page of a book. Try anything that helps you read faster. Developing your speed-reading skills improves your scores in all the GED tests, but especially this one because it uses longer passages. Check out *Speed Reading For Dummies* by Richard Sutz (Wiley) for more info.

Practicing for Part 1 with some sample problems

Before you take Part I of the Language Arts, Writing Test, make sure you take plenty of practice tests so you're well versed with the types of problems you'll face. Take the following sample problems to help you get started. When you finish these, move on to Chapters 5 and 7 to take the full-length practice tests.

Questions 1 through 4 refer to the following passage.

Project WKE

(1) **Referral:** Workers will refer dependent of WOW recipients to WKE.

(2) **Intake:** Intake process will involve a series of interviews and the use of transferable skills inventories combined with the evaluation of credentials.

(3) **Assessment:** A holistic asesment will be prepared and discussed with clients as preparation for additional experiences and training.

(4) **Pre-Employment Training:** Pre-employment training will include confidence building, interpersonal skills, goal setting, career path planning, problem-solving, résumé preparation, basic computer literacy, educational upgrading and child development and parenting skills as required.

(5) **Job Readiness Training:** Experiences, such as job-shadowing and mentoring will be provided as needed for clients ready to enter the work farce in a supportive environment. Other clients will be provided with additional skills in sectoral analysis, cold calling, budgeting, time management, development of job search strategies, preparation and presentation of Prior Learning Assessment and Recognition Portfolios, development and evaluation of transferable skills inventories, interview techniques and follow-up.

(6) **Referral:** Clients will be referred to appropriate community agencies, if required. If desired by the client, alternate career pathways will be investigated and career paths planned for these alternate careers.

(7) **Skill Enhancement:** Clients will have the opportunity to enhance the following skills: computer literacy, prior learning assessment and recognition, assistance in gaining additional certification, use of computers and Internet in job search and career research, and academic skills.

(8) **Supportive Job Search Activities (if unemployed):** Unemployed clients will be introduced to Supportive Job Search activities where they may volunteer for periods of time in positions congruent with their career plans to gain real world experience.

(9) **Employment Retention (if employed):** Employed clients will be able to call in to WKE to assist in the retention of clients in workplaces. Employers will be able to contact WKE if problems arise on the job and WKE will provide support, advice and mediation to try to maintain employment.

1. Section 1: **Workers will refer dependent of WOW recipients to WKE.**

   Which change should be made to Section 1?

   (1) omit <u>will</u>

   (2) change <u>dependent</u> to <u>dependent(s)</u>

   (3) place a comma after <u>Workers</u>

   (4) change <u>WOW</u> to <u>wow</u>

   (5) no changes necessary

   The correct answer is Choice (2). Because the sentence refers to the plural "recipients," you can't logically assume more than one dependent, but you need a word that allows for the possibility.

2. Section 3: **A holistic asesment will be prepared and discussed with clients as preparation for additional experiences and training.**

   Which change should be made to Section 3?

   (1) change <u>holistic</u> to <u>wholistic</u>

   (2) change <u>will be prepared</u> to <u>was prepared</u>

   (3) change <u>clients</u> to <u>patience</u>

   (4) change <u>asesment</u> to <u>assessment</u>

   (5) no changes necessary

   The correct answer is Choice (4). This question requires you to correct a spelling mistake. Always be careful of double letters. Many English words have double letters that are pronounced like single letters.

3. Section 5: **Experiences, such as job-shadowing and mentoring will be provided as needed for clients ready to enter the work farce in a supportive environment. Other clients will be provided with additional skills in sectoral analysis, cold calling, budgeting, time management, development of job search strategies, preparation and presentation of Prior Learning Assessment and Recognition Portfolios, development and evaluation of transferable skills inventories, interview techniques and follow-up.**

Which change should be made to Section 5?

(1) change <u>job-shadowing</u> to <u>jobshadowing</u>

(2) change <u>supportive</u> to <u>support</u>

(3) change <u>additional</u> to <u>a whole lot of</u>

(4) change <u>skills</u> to <u>skill</u>

(5) change <u>farce</u> to <u>force</u>

The correct answer is Choice (5). The word *farce* refers to a comic drama or film; this section is referring to a retraining program, which is definitely more serious.

4. Section 9: **Employed clients will be able to call in to WKE to assist in the retention of clients in workplaces. Employers will be able to contact WKE if problems arise on the job and WKE will provide support, advice and mediation to try to maintain employment.**

Which change should be made to Section 9?

(1) change <u>retention</u> to <u>resistence</u>

(2) rewrite the first sentence like this: <u>Employed clients will be able to call in to WKE if problems arise on the job.</u>

(3) omit <u>if problems arise</u>

(4) change <u>support, advice and mediation</u> to <u>supportive advice, and mediation</u>

(5) change <u>assist in the retention of clients</u> to <u>assist in the release of clients</u>

The correct answer is Choice (2). Of all the suggestions made, this one makes the most sense in the context of the passage. If you read the passage carefully, clients call in WKE if they have problems on the job. The original wording suggests otherwise.

As you practice doing these types of questions (here and in Chapters 5 and 7), remember to read the questions first; doing so gives you an idea of what you need to look for in the passage as you read it. Also, be sure to read the questions carefully — they aren't trick questions, but they do expect you to be a good reader.

Revealing some helpful pointers for Part 1

Remember the following tips as you move through Part I:

- ✔ **Read the questions quickly before you read the entire passage.** This way, you'll know what to look for in the passage.

- ✔ **Read carefully.** As you read the passages, look for errors and hard-to-read sentences. The more carefully you read the passages, the better chance you have of getting the right answers when you move on to the questions.

Passing Part II

Part II of the Language Arts, Writing Test asks you to write an essay on an assigned topic that will then be read by two essay graders (find out more about these graders and what they're looking for in the "Revealing some helpful pointers for Part II" section). You have 45 minutes to read the given topic and write your corresponding essay. This part of the test assesses your literacy and understanding. Even if you can understand the essay topic, you must thoroughly know the format of writing an essay and have a knowledge of the rules of grammar.

Keep in mind that writing this essay isn't that different from writing a letter or a blog — except that here you must explain or clarify the subject for the reader without rambling on until you run out of space.

If you don't pass this part of the Language Arts, Writing Test, you have to take both parts over again. That fact alone should be all the incentive you need to practice writing.

Looking at the writing skills Part II covers

Two trained essay readers grade your essay by focusing on five major criteria or skills. By having a clear understanding of the main skills covered in this part of the test, you can ensure that you address all of them when writing your essay — which will translate into success in terms of your essay score. The GED Testing Service defines the five essay criteria you need to address as follows:

- ✔ **Response to the prompt:** This criterion refers to how well you answer the topic, including whether or not the focus of the response shifts as you write.

- ✔ **Organization:** This criterion refers to whether or not you show the reader through your essay that you have a clear idea about what you're writing and that you're able to establish a definable plan for writing the essay.

- ✔ **Development and details:** This criterion refers to your ability to expand on initial concepts or statements through the use of examples and specific details instead of using generic lists or reiterating the same information.

- ✔ **Conventions of edited American English:** This criterion refers to your ability to appropriately use edited written English, including the application of the basic rules of grammar that you're tested on in Part I, such as sentence structure, mechanics, usage, and so forth.

- ✔ **Word choice:** This criterion refers to your ability to use appropriate words to express your ideas.

The evaluators grade your essay as inadequate, marginal, adequate, or effective, depending on your success in each of these five categories. You can check out www.acenet.edu/ Content/NavigationMenu/ged/etp/writing_2_test_descr.htm for a more in-depth breakdown of these five criteria and what the evaluators look for in an essay that receives a passing score. Read the sections on what constitutes a passing score very carefully. If you don't pass the essay, you have to retake the entire test.

Preparing for Part II: Tactics that work

As you prepare for the Language Arts, Writing Test, Part II, do the following:

✔ **Read and read some more.** Just like for Part I (and most other tests on the GED), reading is important. Reading exposes you to well-crafted sentences, which can help you improve your own writing. Reading also expands your horizons and provides you with little bits of information you can work into your essay.

As you read, make an outline of the paragraphs or chapters you read to see how the material ties together. Try rewriting some of the paragraphs from your outline, and compare what you write to the original. Yours may not be ready for prime time, but this little exercise gives you practice in writing organized, cohesive sentences and paragraphs, which can go a long way in this part of the test.

✔ **Practice writing neatly.** You can't take a computer and printer into the test for Part II, so you have to express your thoughts the old-fashioned way — with a pen and paper. Remember way back in grade school when you learned how to write neatly? Well, now's the time to call on all your good-handwriting skills (no matter how buried they may be). Graders have to read your essay to score it, so it's in your best interest to make reading your writing as easy as possible.

Really neat, beautiful penmanship is easy to read, but it takes a long time to write. You need something in between chicken scratch and calligraphy — legible writing that you can write quickly. Neat and quick are the important words to keep in mind here (after all, this is a timed test like all the others!).

✔ **Practice editing your own work.** After the test starts, the only person able to edit your essay is you. If that thought scares you, practice editing your own work. Take a writing workshop, or get help from someone who knows how to edit. Practice writing a lot of essays, and don't forget to review and edit them as soon as you're done writing.

✔ **Review how to plan an essay.** Few people can sit down, write a final draft of an essay the first time around, and receive a satisfactory grade. Instead, you have to plan what you're going to write. The best way to start is to jot down everything you know about a topic without worrying about the order. From there, you can organize your thoughts into groups. Check out the "Managing your time for Part II" section for more help on planning your essay.

✔ **Practice writing on a topic (and not going off topic!).** Your essay must relate to the given topic as closely as possible. If the test asks you to write about your personal goals, and you write about a hockey game you once played in, you can kiss your good score on this part of the test goodbye.

To help you practice staying on topic, read the newspaper and write a letter to the editor or a response to a columnist. Because you're responding to a very narrow topic that appeared in a particular newspaper article, you have to do so clearly and concisely — if you ever want to see it in print. (You can also practice staying on topic by picking a newspaper article's title and writing a short essay about it. Then read the actual story and see how yours compares.)

✔ **Think about and use related examples.** If you're writing about how machines make life harder, the difficult experience you had trying to get your toaster fixed under warranty makes for a great example. In contrast, a story about painting your bike fluorescent pink doesn't make such a hot example. Remember that examples can provide great support to your essay's main points, but, to do so, they have to relate to the topic.

✔ **Practice general writing.** If writing connected paragraphs isn't one of your fortes, practice doing so! Write long e-mails. Write long letters. Write to your member of

Congress. Write to your friends. Write articles for community newspapers. Write short stories. Write anything you want — whatever you do, just keep writing.

✔ **Write practice essays.** Check out the "Practicing with some sample essays" section later in this chapter for a sample essay you can read. Then see Chapters 5 and 7 for some more practice essay prompts (in actual test format). Write essays based on the topics given, and then ask a knowledgeable friend or former teacher to grade them for you. You can also turn to Chapters 6 and 8 to read a couple of sample essays based on the same topics you're given in Chapters 5 and 7. You may want to take a preparation class in which you're assigned practice topics to write about, too. When you're finished practicing, practice some more.

Managing your time for Part II

You have 45 minutes to finish your essay for Part II of the Language Arts, Writing Test, and, in that time, you have four main tasks:

✔ Plan

✔ Draft

✔ Edit and revise

✔ Rewrite

The following sections take a closer look at these tasks and explain how you can successfully complete each one in the time allotted for this test.

Taking 10 minutes to plan, 20 minutes to draft, 5 minutes to edit and revise, and 10 minutes to rewrite is a good plan for action. Keep in mind that this schedule is a tight one, though, so if it makes your writing too sloppy to read, consider allowing more time for rewriting. No one but you will see anything but the final version.

Planning

Before you begin writing your essay, read the topic carefully several times, and ask yourself what the topic means to you. Then, on scratch paper, write down everything you can think of that relates to the topic, no matter how silly it seems (this act of writing is called *brainstorming,* which is like dumping out the contents of a portion of your brain). Don't worry about the order in which you write your ideas or the ideas you think of. Just let everything you think of flow onto the paper. You can sort through all the information in the next phase.

For example, if the essay question asks you to discuss a major milestone in your life, you may choose to center your essay around the following topic: "Passing the GED will be a major milestone in my life." In your essay, you need to explain why passing the test is the major milestone for you at this moment and how you plan to use the GED for the betterment of your life. The planning stage of your essay writing is when you jot down everything you can think of about the GED and its effect on your life. The points you jot down here should include your personal observations, experience, and knowledge.

After you have these points written down, sit back for a moment to reflect. (Don't reflect too long, though, because you still have an essay to write. Just take a few minutes.) Look over your points and find an introduction, such as, "I have accomplished many things in my life, but my major milestone will be passing the GED tests." Write this sentence down beneath your brainstorming notes. Beneath this sentence, write down the points you came up with earlier that strongly back up your introduction.

Now write down a concluding sentence, such as, "Of all my accomplishments, passing the GED tests will be the most important because it will open doors that are closed to me now." Glancing at your introduction and the essay topic itself, select points that strengthen your conclusion. Some of these points may be the same ones you used in your introduction.

Next, plan a path from your introduction to your conclusion. The path may be several points long. Here's an example of an essay plan from introduction to conclusion:

- ✔ **Introduction:** "I have accomplished many things in my life, but my major milestone will be passing the GED tests."

- ✔ **Body:** Here's the path from your introduction to your conclusion:

  - • List my accomplishments.

  - • Discuss my goals.

  - • Discuss what's stopping me from reaching my goals.

  - • Tie in which of these things I may be able to eliminate by having a GED diploma.

  - • Discuss which goals are attainable with the GED diploma.

  - • Envision how my life will change as I accomplish those goals.

- ✔ **Conclusion:** "Of all my accomplishments, passing the GED tests will be the most important because it will open doors that are closed to me now."

Now reflect again. Can you add any more points to improve the essay? Don't just add points to have more points, though. This isn't a contest in which the one with the most points wins. This is an essay in which the one with the best points, logically written, gets the passing grade.

Look over your planning path and your points. Can you combine any parts of the path to make it tighter? For example

- ✔ **Introduction:** "I have accomplished many things in my life, but my major milestone will be passing the GED tests."

- ✔ **Body:** Here's the tightened path from your introduction to your conclusion:

  - • List my accomplishments.

  - • Discuss my goals and what's stopping me from reaching them.

  - • Tie in which of these things I may be able to eliminate by having a GED diploma, and discuss which goals are attainable with the GED diploma.

  - • Envision how my life will change as I accomplish those goals.

- ✔ **Conclusion:** "Of all my accomplishments, passing the GED tests will be the most important because it will open doors that are closed to me now."

Now that you have the outline, you're ready to go on to the next step — drafting your essay.

Drafting

During the drafting stage of writing your essay, you think in more detail about the main points you came up with in the planning stage. As you add new details (called *subpoints*) under each main point, you begin to see your essay taking shape.

Here's an example of what the drafting process may look like for the "major milestone in life" topic:

- ✔ **Introduction:** "I have accomplished many things in my life, but my major milestone will be passing the GED tests."

✔ **Body:** Here are all your main points and subpoints:

✔ List my accomplishments:

- I coach youth hockey.

- I have kept a job for four years.

- I got a small promotion.

- I got married.

✔ Discuss my goals and what's stopping me from reaching them:

- People expect more education from hockey coaches in the minor leagues.

- Many promotions are blocked to me because of my education.

- My children may be embarrassed to have an uneducated parent.

- My boss likes people with diplomas and certificates.

✔ Tie in which of these things I may be able to eliminate by having a GED diploma, and discuss which goals are attainable with the GED diploma:

- I may be able to coach in the minors.

- I can apply for more promotions.

- My boss may like me more.

- My children will be impressed by my accomplishment.

- I will have graduated from high school.

✔ Envision how my life will change as I accomplish those goals:

- As a minor-league coach, my picture will be in the papers.

- I could become a manager at my company.

- I may be invited to lunch by my boss to discuss ideas.

- I could be invited to my children's classes to talk about the importance of education.

- I will have a diploma to hang on the wall.

✔ **Conclusion:** "Of all my accomplishments, passing the GED tests will be the most important because it will open doors that are closed to me now. The doors are open — promotion, dreams, recognition — and that creates so many more possibilities."

Notice how each main point becomes a paragraph. The subpoints you come up with during the drafting process form the sentences in each paragraph.

Each paragraph starts with an *introductory sentence,* which hints at what is to come, and ends with a *transition sentence* that leads from the paragraph you're on to the next one. Your subpoints are your sentences within the paragraphs. If you put your sentences in a logical order from introduction to transition, you start to see paragraphs — as well as your essay — emerging.

Editing and revising

Now comes the hard part. You have to be your own editor. Turn off your ego and remember that every word is written on scratch paper, not carved in stone. Make your work better by editing and revising it. Make this the best piece of writing you've ever done — in a 45-minute time block, of course.

Rewriting

Neatly rewrite your edited work — in pen — in the proper place in the answer booklet. Two graders have to read this essay, so write neatly and clearly. Write large enough to be read. Leave some room between lines. Your essay has to be well written, but it also has to be readable. If you make a mistake, neatly cross it out and move on. Scratch-outs don't count against you.

Practicing with some sample essays

To help you get a feel for how the essay grader evaluates your essay, take a look at the sample essay that follows. The sample essay is based on this essay topic:

The Worst Traffic Control Idea — Ever

Write an essay explaining the positive and/or negative aspects of this idea. Use examples to support your point of view and be as specific as possible.

Use the five criteria we explain in the "Looking at the writing skills Part II covers" section to mark up the essay, pointing out its strengths and weaknesses. Also keep in mind the characteristics of a good essay that evaluators look for, which we list in the "Revealing some helpful pointers for Part II" section. (Check out www.acenet.edu/Content/NavigationMenu/ged/etp/writing_2_test_descr.htm for more details on how essays on this test are graded.)

Speed Bumps

We have all driven down a quiet residential street and without warning hit a bump in the road, so severe, that our teeth rattled. Well, we may have been going ever so slightly over the speed limit but needing dental work is not the usual punishment for speeding.

Living in a society where unenforced laws get ignored has presented a problem in many areas. Just look at all the Ponzi schemes being uncovered all around the world. Wherever there has been no enforcement, there has been an increase in crime but a little bit of speeding is not that serious a crime.

In Jamaica they call speed bumps, "Sleeping Policemen" because they do the job of speed control without the police being present. In St. Maarten, they have installed them on highways to keep the speed down in dangerous areas. But here, in the United States, do we need these ugly bumps in the road? We all know that these are just a political solution to calm down voters who do not want speeding traffic through their neighborhood. No one seems to care about the negative aspects of these devices.

Cars are most efficient at constant speed but speed bumps cause the driver to slow down and speed up all through the area, increasing pollution and wasting gas. Even bicyclists, the darlings of many city politicians, have trouble with speed bumps. If you go too fast over one of these bumps on a bicycle, you may become airborne and fly off your bicycle. That will do damage to your body.

Speed bumps are hard to see and force drivers to take their eyes off the road. This causes a dangerous situation. Who knows what could pass in front of a car while the driver is looking carefully for the next bump which will shatter teeth and probably destroy the car's suspension. Is there no justice for the driver on the roads?

Now that you have a sample essay to look at, try writing your essay that addresses the traffic control topic. When you're done, evaluate it using the same criteria you used to mark up the sample essay. Then write an essay on one of the following topics and mark it up in the same way (don't forget to use your personal experience and knowledge for support):

- ✔ Should the Government Bail Out Industries?
- ✔ Video Games Teach People Many Skills
- ✔ One Job the Guidance Department Forgot to Tell Me about
- ✔ Reality Television is the Most Unreal Programming Available

Revealing some helpful pointers for Part II

In addition to evaluating the main criteria or skills we list in the "Looking at the writing skills Part II covers" section, essay graders look for the following characteristics in your essay (if you have all these characteristics, your chances of receiving a high score are pretty good):

- ✔ Main points that focus on the topic
- ✔ Clear and organized main points and subpoints — both in the paragraphs and throughout the entire essay
- ✔ Logically and clearly developed ideas
- ✔ Transitions throughout the essay for a smooth flow between ideas
- ✔ Good vocabulary
- ✔ Proper punctuation
- ✔ Correct spelling

Knowing what essay graders are looking for in your essay can help you make sure you meet all their expectations. Here are a few other tips and ground rules you'd be wise to remember as you prepare for Part II of the Language Arts, Writing Test:

- ✔ **You have only 45 minutes to write an essay of about 250 words based on a single topic.** An essay usually consists of a number of paragraphs, each of which contains a topic sentence stating a main idea or thought. Be sure each paragraph relates to the overall topic of the essay. And, for the most part, make sure to place a topic sentence at the beginning of each paragraph to help readers focus on the main point you want them to understand.

- ✔ **You can prepare your essay by using the scratch paper provided.** You're given scratch paper at the test site. Use it to make notes and write down your rough work so that your final essay is well organized and neat. The graders don't look at it, so what you write on the scratch paper is just for you.

- ✔ **You must write about the topic and only about the topic.** You're graded for writing an essay on the topic, so make sure you really do write on the topic you're given. One of the easiest ways to fail this test is to write about something that isn't on topic.

  Keep in mind that the topic is always a brief one about an issue or situation that's familiar to you.

- ✔ **The essay tests your ability to write about an issue that has positive and/or negative implications but about which you have some general knowledge.** The essay doesn't test how much you know about a given topic; instead, it tests your ability to express yourself in writing.

✔ **You need to use stuff from your life to make your points stronger.** You're writing an essay about you, your life, and your experiences, so don't forget to use real examples to strengthen your main points. Specific examples and details support your point of view, so use them liberally.

✔ **Effective paragraphs use a variety of sentence types: statements, questions, commands, exclamations, and even quotations.** Vary your sentence structure and choice of words to spark the readers' interest. Some sentences may be short, and others may be long to catch the readers' attention.

✔ **Paragraphs create interest in several ways: by developing details, by using illustrations and examples, by presenting events in a time or space sequence, by providing definitions, by classifying persons or objects, by comparing and contrasting, and by demonstrating reasons and proof.** Organize your paragraphs and sentences in a way that both expresses your ideas and creates interest.

✔ **The readers want to see that you can express your ideas clearly and logically.** They're also reading to make sure that you stick to the topic given.

Chapter 5

Practice Test — Language Arts, Writing Test: Parts I and II

· ·

The Language Arts, Writing Test measures your ability to use clear and effective English. It is a test of English as it should be written, not as it may be spoken. This test includes both multiple-choice questions and an essay. The following directions apply only to the multiple-choice section; a separate set of directions is given for the essay.

The multiple-choice section consists of documents with lettered paragraphs and numbered sentences. Some of the sentences contain an error in sentence structure, usage, or mechanics (punctuation and capitalization). After reading the numbered sentences, answer the multiple-choice questions that follow. Some questions refer to sentences that are correct as written. The best answer for these questions is the one that leaves the sentence as originally written. The best answer for some questions is the one that produces a document that is consistent with the verb tense and point of view used throughout the text.

You have 120 minutes (2 hours) to complete both parts of the test. You can spend up to 75 minutes on the 50 multiple-choice questions, leaving the remaining time for the essay. Work carefully, but do not spend too much time on any one question. Answer every question. You will not be penalized for incorrect answers. You may begin working on the essay section of this test as soon as you complete the multiple-choice section.

Answer Sheet for Language Arts, Writing Test: Part 1

1 ① ② ③ ④ ⑤   26 ① ② ③ ④ ⑤

2 ① ② ③ ④ ⑤   27 ① ② ③ ④ ⑤

3 ① ② ③ ④ ⑤   28 ① ② ③ ④ ⑤

4 ① ② ③ ④ ⑤   29 ① ② ③ ④ ⑤

5 ① ② ③ ④ ⑤   30 ① ② ③ ④ ⑤

6 ① ② ③ ④ ⑤   31 ① ② ③ ④ ⑤

7 ① ② ③ ④ ⑤   32 ① ② ③ ④ ⑤

8 ① ② ③ ④ ⑤   33 ① ② ③ ④ ⑤

9 ① ② ③ ④ ⑤   34 ① ② ③ ④ ⑤

10 ① ② ③ ④ ⑤   35 ① ② ③ ④ ⑤

11 ① ② ③ ④ ⑤   36 ① ② ③ ④ ⑤

12 ① ② ③ ④ ⑤   37 ① ② ③ ④ ⑤

13 ① ② ③ ④ ⑤   38 ① ② ③ ④ ⑤

14 ① ② ③ ④ ⑤   39 ① ② ③ ④ ⑤

15 ① ② ③ ④ ⑤   40 ① ② ③ ④ ⑤

16 ① ② ③ ④ ⑤   41 ① ② ③ ④ ⑤

17 ① ② ③ ④ ⑤   42 ① ② ③ ④ ⑤

18 ① ② ③ ④ ⑤   43 ① ② ③ ④ ⑤

19 ① ② ③ ④ ⑤   44 ① ② ③ ④ ⑤

20 ① ② ③ ④ ⑤   45 ① ② ③ ④ ⑤

21 ① ② ③ ④ ⑤   46 ① ② ③ ④ ⑤

22 ① ② ③ ④ ⑤   47 ① ② ③ ④ ⑤

23 ① ② ③ ④ ⑤   48 ① ② ③ ④ ⑤

24 ① ② ③ ④ ⑤   49 ① ② ③ ④ ⑤

25 ① ② ③ ④ ⑤   50 ① ② ③ ④ ⑤

Language Arts, Writing Test: Part 1

Do not mark in this test booklet. Record your answers on the separate answer sheet provided. To record your answers, fill in the numbered circle on the answer sheet that corresponds to the answer you select for each question in the test booklet.

EXAMPLE:

Sentence 1: **We were all honored to meet governor Phillips and his staff.**

Which correction should be made to sentence 1?

(1) change <u>were</u> to <u>was</u>

(2) insert a comma after <u>honored</u>

(3) change <u>governor</u> to <u>Governor</u>

(4) insert a comma after <u>Phillips</u>

(5) no correction is necessary

(On Answer Sheet)

① ② ● ④ ⑤

In this example, the word "governor" should be capitalized; therefore, answer space 3 would be marked on the answer sheet.

Do not rest the point of your pencil on the answer sheet while you are considering your answer. Make no stray or unnecessary marks. If you change an answer, erase your first mark completely. Mark only one answer space for each question; multiple answers will be scored as incorrect. Do not fold or crease your answer sheet. All test materials must be returned to the test administrator.

Note: Refer to Chapter 6 for the answers for Parts I and II of this practice test.

DO NOT BEGIN TAKING THIS TEST UNTIL TOLD TO DO SO

Directions: Choose the <u>one best answer</u> to each question.

Questions 1 through 10 refer to the following business letter.

BETA Café Equipment, Inc.
700 Millway Avenue, Unit 6
Concord, MA 12345

John Charles
Executive Director
American Specialty Coffee Association
425 Pacific Drive, Suite 301
San Diego, CA 56789

Dear Mr. Charles:

(A)

(1) Thank you for you're interest in our new company, which serves the rapidly expanding specialty coffee industry. (2) BETA Café Equipment, Inc. were formed in 2002 to provide an affordable source of reconditioned Italian espresso/cappuccino machines for new businesses entering the industry.

(B)

(3) During our first year of operation BETA plans to repair and recondition 500 machines for use in restaurants and cafés. (4) This will generate revenue of more then $1,000,000.
(5) Almost half a million dollars will be created for returning thirteen jobs to the local economy.

(C)

(6) BETA will purchase used equipement, which will be shipped to our centralized repair and reconditioning depot. (7) After total rebuilding, equipment will be forwarded to regional sales offices to be sold to local restaurants and cafés at a much lower price than comparable new equipment. (8) Entrepreneurs wishing to start new specialty coffee businesses particularly should be interested in our products.

(D)

(9) To learn more about BETA please consult our Web site at www.betace.com or give us a call at our toll-free number, 1-800-TRY-BETA. (10) Any assistence you can provide in sharing this information with your membership will be very much appreciated.

Yours truly,

Edwin Dale, President

Go on to next page

1. Sentence 1: **Thank you for you're interest in our new company, which serves the rapidly expanding specialty coffee industry.**

   Which correction should be made to sentence 1?

   (1) change you're to your
   (2) place a comma after serves
   (3) change interest to concern
   (4) insert but after rapidly
   (5) place expanding before rapidly

2. Sentence 2: **BETA Café Equipment, Inc. were formed in 2002 to provide an affordable source of reconditioned Italian espresso/cappuccino machines for new businesses entering the industry.**

   What is the best way to write the underlined portion of this sentence?

   (1) was being formed
   (2) had formed
   (3) was formed
   (4) is formed
   (5) have been formed

3. Sentence 3: **During our first year of operation BETA plans to repair and recondition 500 machines for use in restaurants and cafés.**

   What correction should be made to sentence 3?

   (1) insert a colon after operation
   (2) insert a comma after operation
   (3) insert a comma after recondition
   (4) insert a semicolon after machines
   (5) place a question mark after cafés

4. Sentence 4: **This will generate revenue of more then $1,000,000.**

   What correction should be made to sentence 4?

   (1) change $1,000,000 to $100,000
   (2) change generate to genarate
   (3) insert about after will
   (4) replace will with may
   (5) change then to than

5. Sentence 5: **Almost half a million dollars will be created for returning thirteen new jobs to the local economy.**

   The most effective revision of sentence 5 would begin with which group of words?

   (1) Thirteen new jobs will be created, returning
   (2) Half a million dollars will be created almost
   (3) Created will be thirteen new jobs almost
   (4) Almost half a million jobs will be created
   (5) no correction required

6. Sentence 6: **BETA will purchase used equipement, which will be shipped to our centralized repair and reconditioning depot.**

   What correction should be made to sentence 6?

   (1) change repair to repare
   (2) insert a colon after purchase
   (3) change equipement to equipment
   (4) replace depot with depote
   (5) insert a comma after repair

7. Sentence 7: **After total rebuilding, equipment will be forwarded to regional sales offices to be sold to local restaurants and cafés at a much lower price than comparable new equipment.**

   Which is the best way to rewrite the underlined portion of this sentence?

   (1) will forward
   (2) be forwarded
   (3) forwarded
   (4) will be
   (5) no correction required

Go on to next page

8. Sentence 8: **Entrepreneurs wishing to start new specialty coffee <u>businesses particularly should be interested</u> in our products.**

What correction should be made to the underlined portion?

(1) businesses should particularly be interested

(2) businesses should be particularly interested

(3) businesses particularly should be interested

(4) businesses should be interested particularly

(5) particularly businesses should be interested

9. Sentence 9: **To learn more about BETA please consult our Web site at www. betace.com or give us a call at our toll-free number, 1-800-TRY-BETA.**

Which addition should be made to sentence 9?

(1) no addition required

(2) insert a colon after <u>Web site</u>

(3) insert a comma after <u>please</u>

(4) insert a comma after <u>BETA</u>

(5) insert a period after <u>www.betace.com</u>

10. Sentence 10: **Any assistence you can provide in sharing this information with your membership will be very much appreciated.**

Which correction should be made to sentence 10?

(1) change <u>membership</u> to <u>member</u>

(2) insert a comma after <u>provide</u>

(3) change <u>appreciated</u> to <u>appreciate</u>

(4) change <u>assistence</u> to <u>assistance</u>

(5) change <u>you</u> to <u>I</u>

Go on to next page

> *Questions 11 through 20 refer to the following prospectus.*

Marketing

(A)

(1) BETAs product is reconditioned Italian café equipment.

(2) The initial's priority will be espresso/cappuccino machines.

(3) There are four ways of marketing the reconditioned machines (a) direct sales (b) sales through a network of distributors (c) leasing directly (d) leasing through a network of distributors.

(4) Direct sales and leasing will take time, because establishing a network of distributors will be the priority in year one.

(5) In order for BETA to be successful, a trained workforce are essential.

(6) A secondary business will be reconditioning machines too order.

Sales

(B)

(7) All estimates for potential units reconditioned and soled or leased are conservative.

(8) The initial mix of leasing and sales is estimated to be 20 percent leasing and 80 percent sales for the first year.

Raw Material

(C)

(9) The average trade-in for an espresso machine will be $75, while the average price paid for used machines will be $250.

(10) Twenty percent of the machines acquired will be trade-ins, the balance will be purchased.

Go on to next page

11. Sentence 1: **BETAs product is reconditioned Italian café equipment.**

    Which correction should be made to sentence 1?

    (1) insert an apostrophe before the *s* in BETAs

    (2) change <u>Italian</u> to <u>italian</u>

    (3) replace <u>is</u> with <u>are</u>

    (4) insert a comma after <u>reconditioned</u>

    (5) change <u>reconditioned</u> to <u>recondition.</u>

12. Sentence 2: **The initial's priority will be espresso/cappuccino machines.**

    Which change should be made to sentence 2?

    (1) insert <u>to</u> after <u>will</u>

    (2) replace <u>will</u> with <u>may</u>

    (3) change <u>priority</u> to <u>prior</u>

    (4) change <u>initial's</u> to <u>initial</u>

    (5) no correction required

13. Sentence 3: **There are four ways of marketing the reconditioned machines (a) direct sales (b) sales through a network of distributors (c) leasing directly (d) leasing through a network of distributors.**

    Which punctuation should be added to sentence 3?

    (1) add a colon after <u>machines</u>

    (2) add a semicolon after <u>ways</u>

    (3) add a comma after <u>directly</u>

    (4) add a comma after <u>ways</u>

    (5) add a colon after <u>marketing</u>

14. Sentence 4: **Direct sales and marketing will take time, because establishing a network of distributors will be the priority in year one.**

    The most effective revision of sentence 5 would begin with?

    (1) Because establishing a network of distributors will be the priority in year one,

    (2) Direct sales and marketing since establishing a network,

    (3) The priority in year one will take time,

    (4) A network of distributors will take time,

    (5) Because direct sales and marketing will take time,

15. Sentence 5: **In order for BETA to be successful, a trained workforce are essential.**

    Which correction should be made to sentence 5?

    (1) replace <u>to be</u> with <u>being</u>

    (2) remove the comma after <u>successful</u>

    (3) change <u>are</u> to <u>is</u>

    (4) change <u>for</u> to <u>four</u>

    (5) replace <u>trained</u> with <u>train</u>

16. Sentence 6: **A secondary business will be reconditioning machines too order.**

    Which change should be made to sentence 6?

    (1) change <u>will be</u> to <u>would be</u>

    (2) change <u>reconditioning</u> to <u>recondition</u>

    (3) change <u>machines</u> to <u>machine</u>

    (4) replace <u>too</u> with <u>to</u>

    (5) change <u>secondary</u> to <u>second</u>

17. Sentence 7: **All estimates for potential units reconditioned and soled or leased are conservative.**

    Which correction should be made to sentence 7?

    (1) change <u>for</u> to <u>four</u>

    (2) change <u>soled</u> to <u>sold</u>

    (3) replace <u>are</u> with <u>is</u>

    (4) change <u>estimates</u> to <u>estimate</u>

    (5) place a comma after <u>reconditioned</u>

18. Sentence 8: **The initial mix of leasing and sales is estimated to be 20 percent leasing and 80 percent sales for the first year.**

    Which revision should be made to sentence 8?

    (1) move <u>for the first year</u> between <u>sales</u> and <u>is</u>

    (2) change <u>is</u> to <u>are</u>

    (3) change <u>sales</u> to <u>sails</u>

    (4) move <u>is estimated to</u> between <u>mix</u> and <u>of</u>

    (5) change <u>first</u> to <u>1st</u>

Go on to next page ⟹

19. Sentence 9: **The average trade-in for an espresso machine will be $75, while the average price paid for used machines will be $250.**

    Which revision should be made to sentence 9?

    (1) remove the comma after $75
    (2) change an to a
    (3) change will be to should be
    (4) change paid to payed
    (5) insert price after trade-in

20. Sentence 10: **Twenty percent of the machines acquired will be trade-ins, the balance will be purchased.**

    Which is the best way to improve the underlined portion of sentence 10?

    (1) remove the comma after trade-ins
    (2) change to trade-ins, while the balance
    (3) change to traded, the balance
    (4) change to trade-ins the balance
    (5) no correction required

Go on to next page

Questions 21 through 30 refer to the following executive summary.

Marketing

Drycleaning and Laundering Industry Adjustment Committee
Report on the Local Labor Market Partnership Project
April 2007 – August 2009

Executive Summary

(A)

(1) Over the past two years, the Drycleaning and Laundering Industry Adjustment Committee has worked hard to become a cohesive group focused on assessing and addressing the human resource implications associated with changes in the fabricare industry. (2) As of August 2009, the Committee has an active membership of over 15 individuals involved in all aspects of the project. (3) The Committee, which has great difficulty speaking with one voice, has taken responsibility for undertaking actions that will benefit this large, highly fragmented industry.

(B)

(4) During the initial period that the Committee was in existence, its work focused on outreaching to and building a relationship with key individuals within the industry. (5) One of its first steps was to undertake a Needs Assessment Survey within the industry.

(C)

(6) During the first year, the Committee explored ways of meeting the needs identified in the Needs Assessment Survey, including raising the profile of the industry and offering on-site training programs, particularly in the areas of spotting and pressing. (7) A great deal of feasibility work was undertaken during this phase yet each possible training solution proved to be extremely difficult and costly to implement.

(D)

(8) As the Committee moved into its second year, it officially established a joint project with the National Fabricare Association to achieve goals in two priority areas: mentorship, training, and profile building.

(E)

(9) During this passed year, much effort and vision has gone into achieving the goals established by the Industry Adjustment Committee and the Association. (10) The new priority areas have provided an opportunity for the industry to do the following

- Introduce technology

- Build capacity and knowledge

- Enhance skills

- Build partnerships and networks

Go on to next page

21. Sentence 1: **Over the past two years, the Drycleaning and Laundering Industry Adjustment Committee has worked hard to become a cohesive group focused on assessing and addressing the human resource implications associated with changes in the fabricare industry.**

    Which is the best way to improve sentence 1?

    (1) remove the comma after <u>years</u>

    (2) place a period after <u>group</u> and start a new sentence beginning with <u>It has focused on</u>

    (3) place a comma after <u>group</u>

    (4) change <u>focused</u> to <u>focussed</u>

    (5) place a period after <u>group</u> and start a new sentence beginning with <u>To become focused</u>

22. Sentence 2: **As of August 2009, the Committee has an active membership of over 15 individuals involved in all aspects of the project.**

    Which revision should be made to sentence 2?

    (1) change <u>has</u> to <u>have</u>

    (2) remove the comma after <u>2009</u>

    (3) change <u>individuals</u> to <u>individual's</u>

    (4) change <u>aspects</u> to <u>aspect</u>

    (5) remove <u>over</u>

23. Sentence 3: **The Committee, which has great difficulty speaking with one voice, has taken responsibility for undertaking actions that will benefit this large, highly fragmented industry.**

    Which revision is required to improve sentence 3?

    (1) remove the comma after <u>large</u>

    (2) change <u>Committee</u> to <u>committee</u>

    (3) move <u>,which has great difficulty speaking with one voice,</u> to the end of the sentence after <u>industry</u>

    (4) change <u>has taken</u> to <u>have taken</u>

    (5) no correction required

24. Sentence 4: **During the initial period that the Committee was in existence, its work focused on outreaching to and building a relationship with key individuals within the industry.**

    Which correction should be made to sentence 4?

    (1) change <u>its</u> to <u>it's</u>

    (2) change <u>outreaching to</u> to <u>reaching out to</u>

    (3) place a comma after <u>period</u>

    (4) change <u>outreaching</u> to <u>out-reaching</u>

    (5) change <u>within</u> to <u>between</u>

25. Sentence 5: **One of its first steps was to undertake a Needs Assessment Survey within the industry.**

    Which change should be made to sentence 5?

    (1) change <u>its</u> to <u>it's</u>

    (2) change <u>first</u> to <u>1st</u>

    (3) change <u>within</u> to <u>with</u>

    (4) change <u>was</u> to <u>were</u>

    (5) no correction required

26. Sentence 6: **During the first year, the Committee explored ways of meeting the needs identified in the Needs Assessment Survey, including raising the profile of the industry and offering on-site training programs, particularly in the areas of spotting and pressing.**

    Which is the best way to improve sentence 6?

    (1) insert a comma after <u>including</u>

    (2) place a period after <u>Survey</u> and start a new sentence with <u>These included</u>

    (3) place a period after <u>industry</u> and start a new sentence with <u>Offering on-site</u>

    (4) remove the comma after <u>programs</u>

    (5) no correction required

Go on to next page

27. Sentence 7: **A great deal of feasibility work was undertaken during this phase yet each possible training solution proved to be extremely difficult and costly to implement.**

    Which correction should be made to sentence 7?

    (1) change <u>was</u> to <u>were</u>

    (2) change <u>proved</u> to <u>prove</u>

    (3) insert a comma after <u>undertaken</u>

    (4) insert a comma after <u>phase</u>

    (5) change <u>difficult</u> to <u>difficulty</u>

28. Sentence 8: **As the Committee moved into its second year, it officially established a joint project with the National Fabricare Association to achieve goals in two priority areas: mentorship, training, and profile building.**

    What correction should be made to sentence 8?

    (1) change <u>its</u> to <u>it's</u>

    (2) change <u>Association</u> to <u>association</u>

    (3) change <u>with</u> to <u>between</u>

    (4) change <u>two</u> to <u>three</u>

    (5) no correction required

29. Sentence 9: **During this passed year, much effort and vision has gone into achieving the goals established by the Industry Adjustment Committee and the Association.**

    What correction should be made to sentence 9?

    (1) insert a comma after <u>Committee</u>

    (2) change <u>passed</u> to <u>past</u>

    (3) change <u>into</u> to <u>in</u>

    (4) change <u>goals</u> to <u>goal</u>

    (5) remove the comma after <u>year</u>

30. Sentence 10: **The new priority areas have provided an opportunity for the industry to do the following**

    • **Introduce technology**

    • **Build capacity and knowledge**

    • **Enhance skills**

    • **Build partnerships and networks**

    What punctuation should be added to sentence 10?

    (1) place a semicolon after <u>technology</u>

    (2) place a semicolon after <u>knowledge</u>

    (3) place a semicolon after <u>skills</u>

    (4) place a semicolon after <u>following</u>

    (5) place a colon after <u>following</u>

Go on to next page

Questions 31 through 40 refer to the following information piece.

Prior Learning Assessment and Recognition

Introduction

(A)

(1) This course is based on a Prior Learning Assessment and Recognition (PLAR) model, as a component of the PLAR, which utilizes preparation for a standardized challenge examination. (2) In addition candidates are guided through the creation of a portfolio, which can be evaluated by a college for admission or advanced standing. (3) This is an opportunity for adults, who have learned in non-formal as well as formal venues to document and assess there prior learning. (4) The course is intents and concentrated and is not meant for every applicant.

(B)

(5) Candidates, who score low in the pre-test, should be directed to remedial programs before beginning such a rigorous course. (6) Those who extremely score well in a pre-test may be advised to arrange immediately to take a challenging test, such as one of the GED tests. (7) This course is meant for candidates who will gain from review and re-mediation but do not require extensive teaching.

Rationale

(C)

(8) This course is designed to help adult learners gain acknowledgement and accreditation of their prior learning in preparation for post secondary study. (9) Students will learn methods for documenting prior knowledge and will develop skills while becoming reacquainted with educational environments and developing the skills needed to succeed in such environments. (10) Through the use of assessment tools and counciling, students will gain a realistic understanding of their levels of competence, personal strengths, weaknesses, and learning styles.

Go on to next page

31. Sentence 1: **This course is based on a Prior Learning Assessment and Recognition (PLAR) model, as a component of the PLAR, which utilizes preparation for a standardized challenge examination.**

    Which is the best way to improve sentence 1?

    (1) no improvement required

    (2) delete <u>, as a component of the PLAR,</u>

    (3) change <u>is</u> to <u>has</u>

    (4) change <u>utilizes</u> to <u>utilized</u>

    (5) place a comma after <u>Assessment</u>

32. Sentence 2: **In addition candidates are guided through the creation of a portfolio, which can be evaluated by a college for admission or advanced standing.**

    Which correction should be made to sentence 2?

    (1) insert a comma after <u>candidates</u>

    (2) change <u>are guided</u> to <u>is guided</u>

    (3) change <u>by</u> to <u>through</u>

    (4) insert a comma after <u>addition</u>

    (5) change <u>portfolio</u> to <u>port-folio</u>

33. Sentence 3: **This is an opportunity for adults, who have learned in non-formal as well as formal venues to document and assess there prior learning.**

    Which correction should be made to sentence 3?

    (1) change <u>there</u> to <u>their</u>

    (2) remove the comma after <u>adults</u>

    (3) change <u>an</u> to <u>a</u>

    (4) change <u>venues</u> to <u>venue</u>

    (5) no correction required

34. Sentence 4: **The course is intents and concentrated and is not meant for every applicant.**

    Which correction should be made to sentence 4?

    (1) change <u>is not</u> to <u>are not</u>

    (2) change <u>not</u> to <u>only</u>

    (3) change <u>meant</u> to <u>mend</u>

    (4) place a comma after <u>concentrated</u>

    (5) change <u>intents</u> to <u>intense</u>

35. Sentence 5: **Candidates, who score low in the pre-test, should be directed to remedial programs before beginning such a rigorous course.**

    Which improvement should be made to Sentence 5?

    (1) remove the comma after <u>candidates</u>

    (2) remove the comma after <u>pre-test</u>

    (3) remove both the comma after <u>candidates</u> and the comma after <u>pre-test</u>

    (4) change <u>before</u> to <u>after</u>

    (5) change <u>pre-test</u> to <u>post-test</u>

36. Sentence 6: **<u>Those who extremely score well</u> in a pre-test may be advised to arrange immediately to take a challenging test, such as one of the GED tests.**

    Which is the best way to write the underlined portion of this sentence?

    (1) Extremely those who score well

    (2) Those who score well extremely

    (3) Those who score extremely well

    (4) Those extremely who score well

    (5) no correction required

37. Sentence 7: **This course is meant for candidates who will gain from review and re-mediation but do not require extensive teaching.**

    Which correction should be made to sentence 7?

    (1) change <u>review</u> to <u>revue</u>

    (2) place a comma after <u>candidates</u>

    (3) place a comma after <u>re-mediation</u>

    (4) change <u>re-mediation</u> to <u>remediation</u>

    (5) no correction required

Go on to next page

38. Sentence 8: **This course is designed to help adult learners gain acknowledgement and accreditation of their prior learning in preparation for post secondary study.**

   Which change should be made to sentence 8?

   (1) change <u>post secondary</u> to <u>post-secondary</u>

   (2) change <u>acknowledgement</u> to <u>acknowledge</u>

   (3) change <u>prior learning</u> to <u>prior-learning</u>

   (4) change <u>their</u> to <u>there</u>

   (5) no correction required

39. Sentence 9: **Students will learn methods for documenting prior knowledge and will develop skills while becoming reacquainted with educational environments and developing the skills needed to succeed in such environments.**

   Which is the best way to improve sentence 9?

   (1) remove <u>for documenting</u>

   (2) remove <u>and developing the skills needed to succeed in such environments</u>

   (3) remove <u>prior knowledge</u>

   (4) remove <u>with educational environments</u>

   (5) no correction required

40. Sentence 10: **Through the use of assessment tools and counciling, students will gain a realistic understanding of their levels of competence, personal strengths, weaknesses, and learning styles.**

   Which correction should be made to sentence 10?

   (1) change <u>realistic</u> to <u>real</u>

   (2) change <u>levels</u> to <u>level</u>

   (3) change <u>weaknesses</u> to <u>weeknesses</u>

   (4) change <u>students</u> to <u>students'</u>

   (5) change <u>counciling</u> to <u>counseling</u>

Go on to next page

Questions 41 through 50 refer to the following business letter.

CanLearn Study Tours, Inc.
2500 Big Beaver Road
Troy, MI 70523

Dr. Dale Worth, Ph.D.
Registrar
BEST Institute of Technology
75 Ingram Drive
Concord, MA 51234

Dear Dr. Worth:

(A)

(1) Our rapidly changing economic climate has meant both challenges never before known. (2) It has been said that only those organizations who can maintain loyalty and commitment among their employees, members, and customers will continue to survive and prosper in this age of continuous learning and globalization.

(B)

(3) Since 1974, CanLearn Study Tours, Inc. have been working with universities, colleges, school districts, voluntary organizations, and businesses to address the unique learning needs of their staff and clientele. (4) These have included educational travel programs that explore the following, artistic and cultural interests, historic and archeological themes, environmental and wellness experiences, and new service patterns. (5) Professional development strategies have been organized to enhance international understanding and boost creativity. (6) Some organizations' have used study tours to build and maintain their membership or consumer base. (7) Other organizations discover a new soarce of revenue in these difficult economic times.

(C)

(8) The formats has varied from a series of local seminars to incentive conferences or sales promotion meetings. (9) Our professional services, including the best possible transportation and accommodation at the most reasonable rates, have insured the success of these programs.

(D)

(10) We would appreciate the opportunity to share our experiences in educational travel and discuss the ways we may be of service to your organization.

Yours sincerely,

Todd Croft, M.A., President
CanLearn Study Tours, Inc.

Go on to next page

41. Sentence 1: **Our rapidly changing economic climate has meant both challenges never before known.**

    Which improvement should be made to sentence 1?

    (1) insert <u>and opportunities</u> between <u>challenges</u> and <u>never</u>

    (2) change <u>has meant</u> to <u>have meant</u>

    (3) change <u>known</u> to <u>none</u>

    (4) change <u>challenges</u> to <u>challenge</u>

    (5) no correction required

42. Sentence 2: **It has been said that only those organizations who can maintain loyalty and commitment among their employees, members, and customers will continue to survive and prosper in this age of continuous learning and globalization.**

    Which change should be made to sentence 2?

    (1) insert a comma after <u>commitment</u>

    (2) change <u>has been</u> to <u>had been</u>

    (3) change <u>who</u> to <u>that</u>

    (4) change <u>those</u> to <u>these</u>

    (5) no correction required

43. Sentence 3: **Since 1974, CanLearn Study Tours, Inc. <u>have been working</u> with universities, colleges, school districts, voluntary organizations, and businesses to address the unique learning needs of their staff and clientele.**

    Which is the best way to write the underlined portion of sentence 3?

    (1) had been working

    (2) has been working

    (3) will be working

    (4) shall be working

    (5) no correction required

44. Sentence 4: **These have included educational travel programs that explore the following, artistic and cultural interests, historic and archeological themes, environmental and wellness experiences, and new service patterns.**

    Which correction should be made to sentence 4?

    (1) insert a comma after <u>have included</u>

    (2) change the comma after <u>following</u> to a colon

    (3) change the comma after <u>interests</u> to a colon

    (4) change the comma after <u>themes</u> to a colon

    (5) change the comma after <u>experiences</u> to a colon

45. Sentence 5: **Professional development strategies have been organized to enhance international understanding and boost creativity.**

    Which change should be made to sentence 5?

    (1) change <u>strategies</u> to <u>strategy</u>

    (2) change <u>boost</u> to <u>boast</u>

    (3) change <u>have been organized</u> to <u>has been organized</u>

    (4) change <u>enhance</u> to <u>enhancing</u>

    (5) no correction required

46. Sentence 6: **Some organizations' have used study tours to build and maintain their membership and consumer base.**

    Which correction should be made to sentence 6?

    (1) change <u>Some</u> to <u>All</u>

    (2) change <u>their</u> to <u>there</u>

    (3) change <u>have used</u> to <u>has used</u>

    (4) change <u>organizations'</u> to <u>organizations</u>

    (5) change <u>base</u> to <u>bays</u>

Go on to next page

47. Sentence 7: **Other organizations discover a new soarce of revenue in these difficult economic times.**

    Which change should be made to sentence 7?

    (1) change <u>organizations</u> to <u>organization's</u>

    (2) change <u>soarce</u> to <u>source</u>

    (3) change <u>these</u> to <u>this</u>

    (4) change <u>discover</u> to <u>discovering</u>

    (5) no correction required

48. Sentence 8: **The formats has varied from a series of local seminars to incentive conferences or sales promotion meetings.**

    Which revision should be made to sentence 8?

    (1) add a comma after <u>seminars</u>

    (2) add an apostrophe after <u>sales</u>

    (3) change <u>formats</u> to <u>format</u>

    (4) add a period after <u>seminars</u>

    (5) no correction required

49. Sentence 9: **Our professional services, including the best possible transportation and accommodation at the most reasonable rates, have insured the success of these programs.**

    Which correction should be made to sentence 9?

    (1) change <u>services</u> to <u>service</u>

    (2) replace <u>insured</u> with <u>ensured</u>

    (3) remove the comma after <u>services</u>

    (4) remove the comma after <u>rates</u>

    (5) no correction required

50. Sentence 10: **We would appreciate the opportunity to share our experiences in educational travel and discuss the ways we may be of service to your organization.**

    Which revision should be made to sentence 10?

    (1) change <u>would appreciate</u> to <u>appreciate</u>

    (2) insert a comma after <u>share</u>

    (3) insert a comma after <u>ways</u>

    (4) change <u>may</u> to <u>will</u>

    (5) no correction required

Go on to next page

Language Arts, Writing Test: Part II

Look at the box on the following page. In the box, you find your assigned topic and the letter of that topic.

You must write on the assigned topic **ONLY**.

Mark the letter of your assigned topic in the appropriate space on your answer sheet booklet.

You have 45 minutes to write on your assigned essay topic. If you have time remaining in this test period after you complete your essay, you may return to the multiple-choice section. Do not return the Language Arts, Writing Test booklet until you finish both Parts I and II of the Language Arts, Writing Test.

Two evaluators will score your essay according to its overall effectiveness. Their evaluation will be based on the following features:

- ✔ Well-focused main points
- ✔ Clear organization
- ✔ Specific development of your ideas
- ✔ Control of sentence structure, punctuation, grammar, word choice, and spelling

REMEMBER, YOU MUST COMPLETE BOTH THE MULTIPLE-CHOICE QUESTIONS (PART I) AND THE ESSAY (PART II) TO RECEIVE A SCORE ON THE LANGUAGE ARTS, WRITING TEST.

To avoid having to repeat both parts of the test, be sure to observe the following rules:

- ✔ Before you begin writing, jot notes or outline your essay on the sheets provided.
- ✔ For your final copy, write legibly in ink so that the evaluators will be able to read your writing.
- ✔ Write on the assigned topic. If you write on a topic other than the one assigned, you will not receive a score for the Language Arts, Writing Test.
- ✔ Write your essay on the lined pages of the separate answer sheet booklet. Only the writing on these pages will be scored.

Note that if you do not pass one portion of the test, you must take both parts over again.

Go on to next page

Topic C

Many people enjoy a hobby or special interest in their spare time.

Write an essay that encourages someone else to enjoy a hobby or special interest. Use your personal experiences, knowledge gained, relationships formed, and so on to develop your ideas.

Part II is a test to determine how well you can use written language to explain your ideas.

In preparing for your essay, you should take the following steps:

- ✔ Read the DIRECTIONS and the TOPIC carefully.
- ✔ Plan your essay before you write. Use the scratch paper provided to make any notes. These notes will be collected but not scored.
- ✔ Before you turn in your essay, reread what you have written and make any changes that will improve your essay.

Your essay should be long enough to develop the topic adequately.

Note: Refer to Chapter 6 for the answers for Parts I and II of this practice test.

END OF TEST

Answer Sheet for Language Arts, Writing Test: Part II

Use a No. 2 pencil to write the letter of your essay topic in the box,
then fill in the corresponding circle.

TOPIC ☐ Ⓐ Ⓑ Ⓒ Ⓓ Ⓔ Ⓕ Ⓖ Ⓗ Ⓘ Ⓙ Ⓚ Ⓛ Ⓜ Ⓝ Ⓞ Ⓟ Ⓠ Ⓡ Ⓢ Ⓣ Ⓤ Ⓥ Ⓦ Ⓧ Ⓨ Ⓩ

Chapter 6

Answers and Explanations for the Language Arts, Writing Test

. . . .

After taking the Language Arts, Writing Test in Chapter 5, use this chapter to check your answers. Take your time as you move through the explanations of the answers for Part I that we provide in the first section. They can help you understand why you missed the answers you did. You may also want to read the explanations for the questions you answered correctly because doing so can give you a better understanding of the thought process that helped you choose the correct answers.

Be sure to take a look at the sample essay we provide in the "Sample Essay for Part II" section of this chapter. Compare your essay to the sample to get an idea of what score your essay may have received on the real test.

If you're short on time, turn to the end of the chapter for an abbreviated answer key for Part I of the Language Arts, Writing Test.

Analysis of the Answers for Part 1

1. **1.** Change *you're* (which means "you are") to *your*. *Your* indicates ownership of the new company, which is the meaning you want. The other choices are either grammatically incorrect or do nothing to make the sentence clearer.

2. **3.** The verb tense must be the singular *was,* not the plural *were.* Singular subjects always take singular verbs.

3. **2.** The sentence needs a comma after *operation* to separate the introductory adverb clause.

4. **5.** Homonyms are words that sound alike but are spelled differently and have different meanings, such as *then* and *than.* The correct word to use in this sentence is *than. Than* is used for comparisons, while *then* refers to time sequences. Because this sentence needs a word that indicates a comparison, *than* is the correct answer.

5. **1.** Although you can revise this sentence in many ways, the answer that makes the most sense is "Thirteen new jobs will be created, returning half a million dollars to the local economy." This change improves the organization of the sentence.

6. **3.** *Equipment* is the correct spelling.

To improve your spelling skills, read as much as you can before you take the GED Language Arts, Writing Test, Part I. Seeing words spelled correctly (as you do when you read published works) is a great way to help you recognize when words are misspelled on this test.

7. **5.** The sentence is correct. No changes are needed, so the answer is *no correction required*.

   Some sentences on the test are correct. Don't correct grammar and punctuation if the sentence looks right to you.

8. **2.** To improve the sentence structure, insert *particularly* (an adverb modifying *interested*) before *interested*. This change makes the sentence easier to read and understand.

9. **4.** You need a comma after *BETA* to separate the introductory adverb phrase from the rest of the sentence.

10. **4.** Correct the spelling error: Change *assistence* to *assistance*.

11. **1.** Apostrophes have two uses: to take the place of a missing letter or to indicate possession. You need to add an apostrophe before the *s* in *BETA* because it's a singular possessive. The text indicates that the product belonging to BETA is reconditioned Italian café equipment, which means you need the apostrophe to show this relationship.

12. **4.** You need to eliminate the extra apostrophe in this sentence. The correct form of the word is *initial*.

13. **1.** You need a colon after *machines* to indicate to readers that a list is coming.

14. **1.** The sentence "Direct sales and marketing will take time, because establishing a network of distributors will be the priority in year one" isn't easy to understand, and it doesn't flow easily off the tongue. Phrases starting with *because* usually make more sense at the beginning of the sentence. You can then write, "Because establishing a network of distributors will be the priority in year one, direct sales and marketing will take time." Because the meaning of the second section flows from the meaning of the first section, this sentence is an improvement from the original.

15. **3.** The singular noun *workforce* doesn't belong with the plural verb *are*. The subject and verb in a sentence must always agree, so you need to use the singular verb *is* rather than the plural *are*.

16. **4.** *Too* means "also," which isn't what you need in this sentence. Replace *too* with *to*.

   Before taking the GED Language Arts, Writing Test, Part I, study a list of *homonyms* — words that sound the same but are spelled differently and have different meanings. Several incorrect homonyms are thrown into the test to assess your ability to differentiate between them.

17. **2.** Correct the homonym spelling error from *soled* to *sold*. *Sold*, the word you want to use, is the past tense of *sell*.

18. **1.** The sentence "The initial mix of leasing and sales is estimated to be 20 percent leasing and 80 percent sales for the first year" has a problem because it could be misunderstood. The best way to correct this sentence is to change it around to read, "The initial mix of leasing and sales for the first year is estimated to be 20 percent leasing and 80 percent sales." When you read a sentence and words are out of order or make reading awkward, go back and correct them.

19. **5.** Because the sentence is talking about price, add the word *price* to clarify the meaning.

20. **2.** Changing the sentence to read *trade-ins, while the balance* improves the sentence structure. Another way to correct the original sentence is to replace the comma with a semicolon; however, because that's not an answer given, you must pick Choice (2).

21. **2.** Avoid the overly long and complex sentence, "Over the past two years, the Drycleaning and Laundering Industry Adjustment Committee has worked hard to become a cohesive group focused on assessing and addressing the human resource implications in the fabricare industry." To improve it, create two new sentences, such as the following: "Over

the past two years, the Drycleaning and Laundering Industry Adjustment Committee has worked hard to become a cohesive group. It has focused on assessing and addressing the human resource implications in the fabricare industry."

22. **5.** Remove *over* to clarify the meaning of the sentence. If you know that the group has 29 members (or however many it has over 15), say so.

23. **3.** The sentence in question says that the *committee* has great difficulty speaking in one voice, which may be true. However, a more accurate statement is that the *industry* has great difficulty speaking in one voice. You know this statement is true because the sentence given describes the industry as *fragmented*. A better organization for the sentence is, "The Committee has taken responsibility for undertaking actions that will benefit this large, highly fragmented industry, which has great difficulty speaking with one voice."

24. **2.** *Outreaching* isn't a verb; *reaching out* is.

25. **5.** No correction is required because none of the other options improves the sentence.

Are you thinking that we made a mistake in the sentence just above? Well, we didn't; it's correct. The noun *none* goes with the verb *improves*. The prepositional phrase *of the other options* doesn't determine how the noun and verb agree. *None* is a singular noun and, therefore, goes with *improves,* not *improve.* If this situation comes up on your test, replace *none* with *not one* (in your head), ignore any prepositional phrases between *none* and the verb, and see whether *not one* agrees with the verb given.

26. **2.** The sentence "During the first year, the Committee explored ways of meeting the needs identified in the Needs Assessment Survey including raising the profile of the industry and offering on-site training programs, particularly in the areas of spotting and pressing" is simply too long to be understood. Find a logical place to break it into two sentences. The first part of the sentence discusses the uses of the Needs Assessment Survey; the second discusses the type of training. You can split the sentence into two smaller, more easily understood, sentences, as follows: "During the first year, the Committee explored ways of meeting the needs identified in the Needs Assessment Survey. These included raising the profile of the industry and offering on-site training programs, particularly in the areas of spotting and pressing."

27. **4.** Insert a comma after *phase* to improve the sentence structure because this compound sentence is joined by the conjunction *yet* and needs the comma to ensure that the two thoughts remain separate.

A *compound sentence* contains two independent clauses or thoughts. The clauses have to be separated by a conjunction like *but* or *yet,* and the conjunction needs a comma before it.

28. **4.** This answer is a gimme: Three priority areas are listed, not two.

29. **2.** Correct the homonym spelling error from *passed* to *past.*

30. **5.** The introductory clause needs a colon at the end.

If you thought the items in the list needed semicolons, they can have them or not, depending on *house style* (the style used and followed religiously by the company or publishing house writing or editing the text). However, if you use semicolons, you need to use them at the end of each component in the list, which isn't an answer choice.

31. **2.** The phrase *as a component of the PLAR* is unnecessary.

32. **4.** You need a comma after *in addition.*

Not sure about commas? Check out *English Grammar For Dummies,* 2nd Edition, by Geraldine Woods (Wiley) for the lowdown on this sometimes tricky form of punctuation.

33. **1.** *Their* is possessive (showing belonging) and is the correct choice in this sentence. Correct the spelling error from *there* to *their*.

The homonyms, *there, their,* and *they're* probably trip up more high school and college students than any other homonyms. Before heading into the GED Language Arts, Writing Test, Part I, know the differences between these three words!

34. **5.** *Intense* and *concentrated* are synonyms used in this sentence for emphasis, but *intense* is misspelled as *intents. Intents* is where you sleep on a camping trip.

35. **3.** The clause *who score low in the pre-test* is a *restrictive clause,* which means it refers to a specific noun — *candidates* in this case — and specifies something about the noun that the sentence needs to make sense to readers. Restrictive clauses aren't separated by commas because they're an integral part of the sentence.

Contrast the restrictive clause with the *nonrestrictive clause,* which adds information about the noun that isn't essential to the meaning of the sentence. If you remove a nonrestrictive clause from the sentence, you can still fully understand the meaning of the sentence. Nonrestrictive clauses require commas to separate them from the sentence.

36. **3.** *Those who score extremely well* is the best order of the words. *Extremely,* an adverb, is best placed next to the word it modifies, which is *well.*

37. **4.** Correct the error in the spelling of *re-mediation.*

Although exceptions exist, when a prefix that ends in a vowel (as *re-* does) precedes a consonant, no hyphen is used. In many (but not all) cases, when a prefix that ends in a vowel precedes another vowel, a hyphen is used.

38. **1.** When two adjectives (like *post* and *secondary* in the example) combine to modify one noun, they're almost always hyphenated. Keep in mind, however, that when an adverb and adjective (such as newly formed) combine to modify a noun, they're usually not hyphenated.

If you have trouble remembering this rule, keep in mind that words ending in *–ly* and forming two-word adjectives are almost never hyphenated. As you probably already know, English usage can be strange and irrational. There are many exceptions to rules and probably just as many rules about exceptions. Style manuals can help you write correctly in particular areas of writing.

39. **2.** The sentence "Students will learn methods for documenting prior knowledge and will develop skills while becoming reacquainted with educational environments and developing skills needed to succeed in such environments" is complex and redundant. Delete the entire phrase *and developing skills needed to succeed in such environments.*

Unless you're being paid by the word, always try to say what you mean in as few words as possible.

40. **5.** This sentence contains a spelling error. Correct the spelling error by changing *counciling* to *counseling.*

41. **1.** Although the word *both* refers to two options, here, you're given only one option — *challenges.* If you insert *and opportunities* between *challenges* and *never,* you include a second option and correct the sentence.

42. **3.** An organization is never a *who;* only people can be referred to as *who.* An organization is a collective noun made up of people, but the collective noun itself is an impersonal entity and doesn't qualify as a *who.*

Although the sentence may appear long and, therefore, may benefit from rewriting, the sentence isn't technically incorrect. Although commas do serve to make sentences clearer, you don't want to insert them unless punctuation rules make them correct.

43. **2.** CanLearn Study Tours is a single entity because it's one company. Therefore, it's a singular noun and needs the singular verb *has* instead of the plural *have.*

People like to refer to companies as *them* when, in fact, a company is always an *it*. Even though a company is made up of a lot of people, it's still a singular entity.

44. **2.** You need to insert a colon before the list to introduce it.

45. **5.** The options presented either make the sentence difficult to understand or introduce errors, so the correct answer is *no correction required.*

46. **4.** A stray apostrophe has landed on this sentence. The one after *organizations'* is unnecessary because you're not trying to show possession here.

Get comfortable with the uses of apostrophes — especially those used for possession — before taking the GED Language Arts, Writing Test, Part I. See Chapter 3 for more info.

47. **2.** Correct the spelling error by changing *soarce* to *source.*

48. **3.** *Formats* is plural, but *has* is a singular verb. Verbs and their subjects must agree.

Study both subject-verb agreement and pronoun-antecedent agreement before taking the Language Arts, Writing Test.

49. **2.** Correct the spelling error by changing *insured* to *ensured.*

Using *insure* is a common error. Use *insure* only when you mean the thing you buy to protect your car, house, health, life, and so on. This example has nothing to do with insurance, so use *ensure,* instead.

50. **5.** No correction is required. The other choices don't improve or correct the sentence.

Sample Essay for Part 11

The essay topic for the practice test in Chapter 5 is as follows:

> Many people enjoy a hobby or special interest in their spare time.
>
> Write an essay that encourages someone else to enjoy a hobby or special interest. Use personal experiences, knowledge gained, relationships formed, and so on to develop your ideas.

As the test graders read and evaluate your essay, they look for the following:

- ✔ Well-focused main points
- ✔ Evidence of clear organization
- ✔ Specific development of your ideas
- ✔ Proper sentence structure
- ✔ Correct grammar
- ✔ Necessary punctuation
- ✔ Appropriate use of words
- ✔ Correct spelling

Although every essay will be unique, we provide a sample here to give you a better idea of what the test graders expect to see in your essay. Compare the structure of this essay to yours.

Hiking is a hobby I can recommend to anyone. Being outdoors, getting exercise, and spending quiet time alone are all facets of hiking that make it unique in today's mostly indoor, sedentary — and yet overly busy — life. Many areas — even large cities — offer parks with dirt or grass paths that are perfect for a daily hike.

Hiking gets me outdoors, away from potentially harmful indoor air. Too much time indoors cuts humans off from the sun, which is vital to mental health, and can also lead to allergies or other illnesses from too much exposure to chemicals and other products that are trapped indoors. Just an hour per day of hiking can counteract many of the effects of spending too much time indoors.

Hiking is also great exercise, because it works the heart, lungs, and leg muscles without adding stress to the knees and other joints. You can hike in your street clothes (although a good pair of hiking boots is a good idea), so hiking does not require the investment in gear that many forms of exercise do.

Perhaps the best — and most unique — feature of hiking, however, is that it provides solace from our loud, fast-paced, materialistic world. When hiking — even in or near a large, metropolitan area — I see deer, listen to birdsongs, and watch squirrels busy with their work. Without the constant sound of a TV or radio in the background, I can focus on my own thoughts instead of on what is expected by society and promoted by advertisers. While on the trail, I can focus on the natural beauty around me instead of worrying about bills or comparing myself to others. This quiet disconnection from society helps me remember what is important in life.

In short, hiking helps me break free of the work-a-day world by getting me outside to appreciate nature, encouraging me to exercise, and giving me long periods of restful silence. I recommend hiking to anyone.

After reading through the sample essay once, reread it and answer the following questions about it:

✔ Is there a series of main points in this essay that clearly relate to the topic? (Underline the main points to check.)

✔ Does each paragraph have an introductory sentence or thought?

✔ Does each paragraph have a concluding sentence or thought?

✔ Are the sentences within each paragraph well organized?

✔ Are the paragraphs organized in a natural flow from beginning to end? In other words, does each paragraph build on the previous one and lead to the next one?

✔ Have the ideas in the given topic and the first paragraph been developed throughout the essay?

✔ Are all the sentences grammatically correct?

✔ Are all the sentences properly structured?

✔ Are all the sentences correctly punctuated?

✔ Are all the words used correctly?

✔ Are all the words spelled correctly?

As far as this particular sample essay is concerned, a test evaluator would probably have given it a high score because it has all the attributes of a good essay that we list earlier in this section. It isn't perfect, but no one's asking you to write a perfect essay. Look over the list of characteristics the readers are looking for, and try to determine whether your practice essay satisfies those requirements. If you can impose on a friend, ask him or her to answer the questions we list here about your essay. If you or your friend answers no to any questions, rewrite your essay until you and your friend can answer yes.

Your essay shouldn't be just a collection of grammatically correct sentences that flow from beginning to end. Rather, your essay needs to be interesting and even entertaining to read. After all, no one — not even professional test graders — wants to read a boring essay!

The evaluators don't know you, so make sure you wow them when you write the essay, especially your conclusion. When you're finished writing your essay, read it over to ensure it makes sense and you use correct spelling and grammar.

Note: Check out Chapter 4 for tips and ideas on mastering the Language Arts, Writing Test, Part II.

Answer Key for Part 1

1. **1**	18. **1**	35. **3**
2. **3**	19. **5**	36. **3**
3. **2**	20. **2**	37. **4**
4. **5**	21. **2**	38. **1**
5. **1**	22. **5**	39. **2**
6. **3**	23. **3**	40. **5**
7. **5**	24. **2**	41. **1**
8. **2**	25. **5**	42. **3**
9. **4**	26. **2**	43. **2**
10. **4**	27. **4**	44. **2**
11. **1**	28. **4**	45. **5**
12. **4**	29. **2**	46. **4**
13. **1**	30. **5**	47. **2**
14. **1**	31. **2**	48. **3**
15. **3**	32. **4**	49. **2**
16. **4**	33. **1**	50. **5**
17. **2**	34. **5**	

Chapter 7

Another Practice Test — Language Arts, Writing Test: Parts I and II

The Language Arts, Writing Test measures your ability to use clear and effective English. It is a test of English as it should be written, not as it may be spoken. This test includes both multiple-choice questions and an essay. The following directions apply only to the multiple-choice section; a separate set of directions is given for the essay.

The multiple-choice section consists of documents with lettered paragraphs and numbered sentences. Some of the sentences contain an error in sentence structure, usage, or mechanics (punctuation and capitalization). After reading the numbered sentences, answer the multiple-choice questions that follow. Some questions refer to sentences that are correct as written. The best answer for these questions is the one that leaves the sentence as originally written. The best answer for some questions is the one that produces a document that is consistent with the verb tense and point of view used throughout the text.

You have 120 minutes (2 hours) to complete both parts of the test. You can spend up to 75 minutes on the 50 multiple-choice questions, leaving the remaining time for the essay. Work carefully, but do not spend too much time on any one question. Answer every question. You will not be penalized for incorrect answers. You may begin working on the essay section of this test as soon as you complete the multiple-choice section.

Answer Sheet for Language Arts, Writing Test: Part 1

1 ① ② ③ ④ ⑤	26 ① ② ③ ④ ⑤
2 ① ② ③ ④ ⑤	27 ① ② ③ ④ ⑤
3 ① ② ③ ④ ⑤	28 ① ② ③ ④ ⑤
4 ① ② ③ ④ ⑤	29 ① ② ③ ④ ⑤
5 ① ② ③ ④ ⑤	30 ① ② ③ ④ ⑤
6 ① ② ③ ④ ⑤	31 ① ② ③ ④ ⑤
7 ① ② ③ ④ ⑤	32 ① ② ③ ④ ⑤
8 ① ② ③ ④ ⑤	33 ① ② ③ ④ ⑤
9 ① ② ③ ④ ⑤	34 ① ② ③ ④ ⑤
10 ① ② ③ ④ ⑤	35 ① ② ③ ④ ⑤
11 ① ② ③ ④ ⑤	36 ① ② ③ ④ ⑤
12 ① ② ③ ④ ⑤	37 ① ② ③ ④ ⑤
13 ① ② ③ ④ ⑤	38 ① ② ③ ④ ⑤
14 ① ② ③ ④ ⑤	39 ① ② ③ ④ ⑤
15 ① ② ③ ④ ⑤	40 ① ② ③ ④ ⑤
16 ① ② ③ ④ ⑤	41 ① ② ③ ④ ⑤
17 ① ② ③ ④ ⑤	42 ① ② ③ ④ ⑤
18 ① ② ③ ④ ⑤	43 ① ② ③ ④ ⑤
19 ① ② ③ ④ ⑤	44 ① ② ③ ④ ⑤
20 ① ② ③ ④ ⑤	45 ① ② ③ ④ ⑤
21 ① ② ③ ④ ⑤	46 ① ② ③ ④ ⑤
22 ① ② ③ ④ ⑤	47 ① ② ③ ④ ⑤
23 ① ② ③ ④ ⑤	48 ① ② ③ ④ ⑤
24 ① ② ③ ④ ⑤	49 ① ② ③ ④ ⑤
25 ① ② ③ ④ ⑤	50 ① ② ③ ④ ⑤

Language Arts, Writing Test: Part 1

Do not mark in this test booklet. Record your answers on the separate answer sheet provided. To record your answers, fill in the numbered circle on the answer sheet that corresponds to the answer you select for each question in the test booklet.

EXAMPLE:

Sentence 1: **We were all honored to meet governor Phillips and his staff.**

Which correction should be made to sentence 1?

(1) change <u>were</u> to <u>was</u>

(2) insert a comma after <u>honored</u>

(3) change <u>governor</u> to <u>Governor</u>

(4) insert a comma after <u>Phillips</u>

(5) no correction is necessary

(On Answer Sheet)

① ② ● ④ ⑤

In this example, the word "governor" should be capitalized; therefore, answer space 3 would be marked on the answer sheet.

Do not rest the point of your pencil on the answer sheet while you are considering your answer. Make no stray or unnecessary marks. If you change an answer, erase your first mark completely. Mark only one answer space for each question; multiple answers will be scored as incorrect. Do not fold or crease your answer sheet. All test materials must be returned to the test administrator.

Note: Refer to Chapter 8 for the answers for Parts I and II of this practice test.

DO NOT BEGIN TAKING THIS TEST UNTIL TOLD TO DO SO

Directions: Choose the <u>one best answer</u> to each question.

Questions 1 through 10 refer to the following excerpt, which is adapted from Customer Service For Dummies *by Karen Leland and Keith Bailey (Wiley).*

Fix the Problem

(1) This step requires you to listen to each customers assessment of the problem. (2) Your job when she explains the situation from her perspective is to fully absorb what she is saying about her unique set of circumstances. (3) After you identify the customer's problem, the next step, obviously, is to fix it. (4) Sometimes, you can easily remedy the situation by changing an invoice, redoing an order, waving or refunding charges, or replacing a defective product. (5) At other times fixing the problem is more complex because the damage or mistake cannot be repaired simply. (6) In these instances, mutually exceptable compromises need to be reached.

(7) Whatever the problem, this step begins to remedy the situation and gives the customer what she needs to resolve the source of the conflict. (8) Don't waste time and effort by putting the horse before the cart and trying to fix the wrong problem. (9) Its easy to jump the gun and think that you know what the customer is about to say because you've heard it all a hundred times before. (10) Doing so loses you ground on the recovery front and farther annoys the customer. (11) More often than not, what you think the problem is at first glance, is different from what it becomes upon closer examination.

1. Sentence 1: **This step requires you to listen to each customers assessment of the problem.**

   Which correction should be made to sentence 1?

   (1) change <u>requires</u> to <u>required</u>
   (2) change <u>customers</u> to <u>customers'</u>
   (3) change <u>assessment</u> to <u>assessing</u>
   (4) change <u>customers</u> to <u>customer's</u>
   (5) no correction required

2. Sentence 2: **Your job when she explains the situation from her perspective is to fully absorb what she is saying about her unique set of circumstances.**

   The most effective revision of sentence 2 would begin with which group of words?

   (1) When she explains the situation from her perspective,
   (2) Your job when she explains,
   (3) What she is saying about,
   (4) Her unique set of circumstances,
   (5) no correction required

3. Sentence 4: **Sometimes, you can easily remedy the situation by changing an invoice, redoing an order, waving or refunding charges, or replacing a defective product.**

   Which correction should be made to sentence 4?

   (1) change <u>redoing</u> to <u>re-doing</u>
   (2) change <u>invoice</u> to <u>invoise</u>
   (3) change <u>waving</u> to <u>waiving</u>
   (4) change <u>defective</u> to <u>defected</u>
   (5) no correction required

4. Sentence 5: **At other times fixing the problem is more complex because the damage or mistake cannot be repaired simply.**

   Which is the best way to improve this sentence?

   (1) add a comma after <u>because</u>
   (2) add a semicolon after <u>times</u>
   (3) add a comma after <u>times</u>
   (4) add a comma after <u>mistake</u>
   (5) add a semicolon after <u>mistake</u>

Go on to next page

5. Sentence 6: **In these instances, mutually exceptable compromises need to be reached.**

   Which correction should be made to sentence 6?

   (1) remove the comma after <u>instances</u>

   (2) change <u>these</u> to <u>those</u>

   (3) change <u>need</u> to <u>needed</u>

   (4) change <u>exceptable</u> to <u>acceptable</u>

   (5) no correction required

6. Sentence 7: **Whatever the problem, this step begins to remedy the situation and gives the customer what she needs to resolve the source of the conflict.**

   Which is the best way to begin sentence 7? If the original is the best way, choose option (1).

   (1) Whatever the problem,

   (2) This step begins to remedy,

   (3) What she needs to resolve,

   (4) To resolve the source of the conflict,

   (5) To remedy the situation,

7. Sentence 8: **Don't waste time and effort by putting the horse before the cart and trying to fix the wrong problem.**

   Which change should be made to sentence 8?

   (1) change <u>waste</u> to <u>waist</u>

   (2) revise to read <u>the cart before the horse</u>

   (3) change <u>trying</u> to <u>try</u>

   (4) change <u>Don't</u> to <u>Doesn't</u>

   (5) no correction required

8. Sentence 9: **Its easy to jump the gun and think that you know what the customer is about to say because you've heard it all a hundred times before.**

   What correction should be made to sentence 9?

   (1) replace <u>is</u> with <u>was</u>

   (2) change <u>heard</u> to <u>herd</u>

   (3) replace <u>you've</u> with <u>you had</u>

   (4) change <u>Its</u> to <u>It's</u>

   (5) no correction required

9. Sentence 10: **Doing so loses you ground on the recovery front and farther annoys the customer.**

   Which change should be made to sentence 10?

   (1) replace <u>loses</u> with <u>looses</u>

   (2) change <u>recovery</u> to <u>recover</u>

   (3) replace <u>farther</u> with <u>further</u>

   (4) change <u>you</u> to <u>your</u>

   (5) no correction required

10. Sentence 11: **More often than not, what you think the problem is at first glance, is different from what it becomes upon closer examination.**

    Which correction should be made to sentence 11?

    (1) remove the comma after <u>not</u>

    (2) remove the comma after <u>glance</u>

    (3) insert a comma after <u>different</u>

    (4) insert a comma after <u>from</u>

    (5) no correction required

Go on to next page

> *Questions 11 through 17 refer to the following business letter.*

BEST Institute of Technology
75 Ingram Drive
Concord, MA 51234

To whom it may concern:

(1) I am pleased to comment on the relationship of our organization to Peta Jackson of the York Square Employment resource Center. (2) The BEST Institute of Technology has partnered with the York Square ERC in recruiting candidates for our Café Technician and Operator training programs since April 2002.

(3) In support of the partnership, Peta provided the following services to our programs

- Set up information **presentations as part** of her job readiness seminars

- Distributed print materials

- Counseled applicants

- Expedited meetings with potential candidates

- Arranged five graduating ceremonies held at York Square ERC

(4) Peta has always been a strong advocate for our program, which has trained more than 50 technicians and operators during the past 18 months. (5) The fact that York Square was our primary source of referrals are a tribute to Peta's efforts. (6) She has, with a high degree of professional competence and efficiency, pursued her responsibilities. (7) On a personal level, it has been a joy to work with Peta and I wish her the very best in her future endeavors.

Dale Worth, Ph.D., Registrar

11. Sentence 1: **I am pleased to comment on the relationship of our organization to Peta Jackson of the York Square Employment resource Center.**

Which revision should be made to sentence 1?

(1) change <u>to Peta Jackson</u> to <u>of Peta Jackson</u>

(2) change <u>pleased</u> to <u>please</u>

(3) change <u>resource</u> to <u>Resource</u>

(4) change <u>Center</u> to <u>Centre</u>

(5) no correction required

12. Sentence 2: **The BEST Institute of Technology has partnered with the York Square ERC in recruiting candidates for our Café Technician and Operator training programs since April 2002.**

Which is the best way to improve sentence 2?

(1) move <u>since April 2002</u> to the start of the sentence

(2) change <u>has partnered</u> to <u>have partnered</u>

(3) change <u>with</u> to <u>between</u>

(4) change <u>in recruiting</u> to <u>while recruiting</u>

(5) no correction required

Go on to next page ⟹

13. Sentence 3: **In support of the partnership, Peta provided the following services to our programs**

    - **Set up information presentations as part of her job readiness seminars**
    - **Distributed print materials**
    - **Counseled applicants**
    - **Expedited meetings with potential candidates**
    - **Arranged five graduating ceremonies held at York Square ERC**

    Which correction should be made to sentence 3?

    (1) remove the comma after <u>partnership</u>

    (2) add a semicolon after <u>seminars</u>

    (3) add a semicolon after <u>materials</u>

    (4) insert a colon after <u>programs</u>

    (5) insert a comma after <u>services</u>

14. Sentence 4: **Peta <u>has always been</u> a strong advocate for our program, which has trained more than 50 technicians and operators during the past 18 months.**

    Which is the best way to write the underlined portion of this sentence? If the original is the best way, choose option (1).

    (1) has always been

    (2) always has been

    (3) has been always

    (4) have always been

    (5) always have been

15. Sentence 5: **The fact that York Square was our primary source of referrals are a tribute to Peta's efforts.**

    Which correction should be made to sentence 5?

    (1) change <u>Peta's</u> to <u>Petas'</u>

    (2) change <u>are</u> to <u>is</u>

    (3) change <u>was</u> to <u>were</u>

    (4) change <u>our</u> to <u>her</u>

    (5) no correction required

16. Sentence 6: **She has, with a high degree of professional competence and efficiency, pursued her responsibilities.**

    Which revision should be made to sentence 6?

    (1) move <u>with a high degree of professional competence and efficiency,</u> after <u>She</u>

    (2) move <u>, with a high degree of professional competence and efficiency,</u> after <u>pursued</u>

    (3) move <u>, with a high degree of professional competence and efficiency</u> to the end of sentence after <u>responsibilities</u>

    (4) place <u>With a high degree of professional competence and efficiency,</u> at the front of the sentence before <u>She</u>

    (5) no correction required

17. Sentence 7: **On a personal level, it has been a joy to work with Peta and I wish her the very best in her future endeavors.**

    Which improvement should be made to sentence 7?

    (1) add a comma after <u>Peta</u>

    (2) change <u>endeavors</u> to <u>endeavours</u>

    (3) change <u>has been</u> to <u>have been</u>

    (4) move <u>on a personal level</u> to come after <u>Peta</u>

    (5) no correction required

Go on to next page

> Questions 18 through 28 refer to the following excerpt, which is adapted from Customer Service For Dummies by Karen Leland and Keith Bailey (Wiley).

The Care Token Coupon

(1) A new copy shoppe recently opened near our office. (2) Modern and full of new, streamlined, state-of-the-art copiers. (3) The store was just what I needed. (4) The first time I went over I waited 45 minutes to get served because of a shortage of trained staff. (5) They bounced back by apologizing, explaining the situation, and gave me a care token coupon that was worth 100 free copies. (6) Okay, I thought, fair enough, they're new and getting their act together, no big deal. (7) A week later, I went back and waited 30 minutes for service. (8) They apologised, explained the situation, and gave me a coupon for 100 free copies. (9) This time I was a little less understanding. (10) Two weeks later, I went back and the same thing happened again. (11) I didn't want another free coupon — they had bounced back just once too often. (12) My opinion of their services were so soured that I began looking for another copy shop.

18. Sentence 1: **A new copy shoppe recently opened near our office.**

    Which correction should be made to sentence 1?

    (1) change <u>copy</u> to <u>copie</u>
    (2) change <u>shoppe</u> to <u>shop</u>
    (3) change <u>opened</u> to <u>is opening</u>
    (4) change <u>a</u> to <u>an</u>
    (5) no correction required

19. Sentences 2 and 3: **Modern and full of new, streamlined, state-of-the-art copiers. The store was just what I needed.**

    Which improvement should be made to sentences 2 and 3?

    (1) combine the two sentences by changing <u>The</u> to <u>the</u> and replacing the period after <u>copiers</u> with a comma
    (2) remove the hyphens from <u>state-of-the-art</u>
    (3) change <u>streamlined</u> to <u>streamlining</u>
    (4) change <u>store was</u> to <u>the copiers were</u>
    (5) no correction required

20. Sentence 4: **The first time I went over I waited 45 minutes to get served because of a shortage of trained staff.**

    Which is the best way to begin sentence 4?

    (1) Because to get served
    (2) I waited 45 minutes
    (3) To get served because
    (4) Because of a shortage
    (5) no correction required

21. Sentence 5: **They bounced back by apologizing, explaining the situation, and gave me a care token coupon that was worth 100 free copies.**

    Which correction should be made to sentence 5?

    (1) change <u>apologizing</u> to <u>apologized</u>
    (2) replace <u>explaining</u> with <u>explained</u>
    (3) change <u>gave</u> to <u>giving</u>
    (4) replace <u>was</u> with <u>were</u>
    (5) no correction required

22. Sentence 6: **Okay, I thought, fair enough, they're new and getting their act together, no big deal.**

    Which revision should be made to sentence 6?

    (1) change <u>thought</u> to <u>am thinking</u>
    (2) change the one sentence into three sentences
    (3) change <u>no</u> to <u>know</u>
    (4) change <u>getting</u> to <u>got</u>
    (5) change the first <u>they're</u> to <u>their</u>

Go on to next page

23. Sentence 7: **A week later I went back and waited 30 minutes for service.**

    Which addition should be made to sentence 7?

    (1) add a comma after <u>later</u>

    (2) add a comma after <u>back</u>

    (3) add a colon after <u>back</u>

    (4) add <u>more</u> after <u>minutes</u>

    (5) no correction required

24. Sentence 8: **They apologised, explained the situation, and gave me a coupon for 100 free copies.**

    Which correction is required for sentence 8?

    (1) change <u>apologised</u> to <u>apologising</u>

    (2) change <u>explained</u> to <u>explaining</u>

    (3) change <u>apologised</u> to <u>apologized</u>

    (4) change <u>copies</u> to <u>copys</u>

    (5) no correction required

25. Sentence 9: **This time I was a little less understanding.**

    Which correction should be made to sentence 9?

    (1) insert a comma after <u>time</u>

    (2) change <u>was</u> to <u>am</u>

    (3) change <u>less</u> to <u>least</u>

    (4) change <u>understanding</u> to <u>understood</u>

    (5) no correction required

26. Sentence 10: **Two weeks <u>later, I went back</u> and the same thing happened again.**

    Which is the best way to write the underlined portion of the sentence?

    (1) later, back I went,

    (2) back, later I went

    (3) later, I went back,

    (4) I, later, went back,

    (5) I went back later

27. Sentence 11: **I didn't want another free coupon — they had bounced back just once too often.**

    Which is the best way to revise sentence 11?

    (1) remove <u>once</u>

    (2) insert a period after <u>coupon</u>

    (3) change <u>had</u> to <u>have</u>

    (4) change <u>another</u> to <u>no</u>

    (5) no correction required

28. Sentence 12: **My opinion of their services were so soured that I began looking for another copy shop.**

    Which correction should be made to sentence 12?

    (1) change <u>began</u> to <u>begun</u>

    (2) insert a comma after <u>soured</u>

    (3) replace <u>my</u> with <u>our</u>

    (4) change <u>were</u> to <u>was</u>

    (5) no correction required

Go on to next page

Questions 29 through 41 refer to the following executive summary.

Executive Summary
KWIK Stop Auto Center

The correct approach for the 21st century

(1) Back in 1978, Morris James, President and Founder of KWIK Stop Auto Center, foresaw changes necessary for the automotive-service industry. (2) The market was becoming much more sophisticated. (3) Combined with 5 years' experience as a licensed mechanic and owner/operator of a repair facility, this knowledge, led to the opening of KWIK Stop Auto Center's first location.

(4) Morris James analyzed the "fast food" concept of providing high quality merchandize at affordable prices. (5) This concept combined with speedy service helped the industry grow every year. (6) Morris decided that the same principals should be applied to the automotive industry, and he started KWIK Stop as the first logical step.

(7) In 1987, Morris was relocated to Woodbridge and began searching for a new shop site to begin franchising. (8) The opening of a concord franchise became very profitable and proved Morris's theory to be correct. (9) He then opened the corporate store having established the validity of the concept in Wellesley, in 1991.

(10) Now the challenge is to develop the corporate store in a way that it can not only function in its capacity as a profit center but also be used as a hands-on training center for future franchise owners.

(11) The start up costs will require some initial investment, but will be regained within the first three years. (12) We will look at this situation more in-depth within the plan. (13) The addition of a wide selection of accessories, for the customer, will broaden the impact of this new concept.

29. Sentence 1: **Back in 1978, Morris James, President and Founder of KWIK Stop Auto Center, foresaw changes necessary for the automotive-service industry.**

Which change should be made to sentence 1?

(1) change <u>foresaw</u> to <u>forseen</u>

(2) remove the comma after <u>1978</u>

(3) remove the comma after <u>Center</u> and add one after <u>changes</u>

(4) move <u>necessary</u> to between <u>foresaw</u> and <u>changes</u>

(5) no correction required

30. Sentence 2: **The market <u>was becoming</u> much more sophisticated.**

Which is the best way to write the underlined portion of this sentence? If the original is the best way, choose option (1).

(1) was becoming

(2) will becoming

(3) were becoming

(4) is becoming

(5) would becoming

Go on to next page ⟹

31. Sentence 3: **Combined with 5 years' experience as a licensed mechanic and owner/operator of a repair facility, this knowledge, led to the opening of KWIK Stop Auto Center's first location.**

Which improvement should be made to sentence 3?

(1) change years' to year's
(2) remove the comma after knowledge
(3) change licensed to licenced
(4) move This knowledge, to the beginning of the sentence
(5) change Center's to Centers

32. Sentence 4: **Morris James analyzed the "fast food" concept of providing high quality merchandize at affordable prices.**

What correction should be made to sentence 4?

(1) change analyzed to analysed
(2) change merchandize to merchandise
(3) change concept to consept
(4) delete of
(5) no correction required

33. Sentence 5: **This concept combined with speedy service helped the industry grow every year.**

Which change should be made to sentence 5?

(1) add commas after concept and service
(2) change helped to has helped
(3) change grow to growing
(4) change service to servicing
(5) no correction required

34. Sentence 6: **Morris decided that the same principals should be applied to the automotive industry, and he started KWIK Stop as the first logical step.**

Which correction should be made to sentence 6?

(1) change principals to principles
(2) change decided to had decided
(3) change should be to shouldn't be
(4) change industry to industries
(5) no correction required

35. Sentence 7: **In 1987, Morris <u>was relocated</u> to Woodbridge and began searching for a new shop site to begin franchising.**

Which is the best way to write the underlined portion of this sentence? If the original is the best way, choose option (1).

(1) was located
(2) is located
(3) has located
(4) relocated
(5) will locate

36. Sentence 8: **The opening of a concord franchise became very profitable and proved Morris's theory to be correct.**

Which revision should be made to sentence 8?

(1) change concord to Concord
(2) change franchise to franchize
(3) change Morris's to Morris'
(4) change profitable to profiting
(5) no correction required

37. Sentence 9: **He then opened the corporate store having established the validity of the concept in Wellesley, in 1991.**

Which is the best way to begin this sentence? If the original is the best way, choose option (1).

(1) He then opened the corporate store
(2) Having established the validity of the concept
(3) In Wellesley, in 1991, he then opened
(4) In 1991, he then opened
(5) The validity of the concept having established

Go on to next page

38. Sentence 10: **Now the challenge is to develop the corporate store in a way that it can not only function in its capacity as a profit center but can also be used as a hands-on training center for future franchise owners.**

    Which is the best way to improve sentence 10?

    (1) insert , as a profit center, between store and in

    (2) change can not only to only can not

    (3) place a comma after capacity

    (4) change challenge is to challenges are

    (5) no correction required

39. Sentence 11: **The start up costs will require some initial investment but will be regained within the first three years.**

    Which correction should be made to sentence 11?

    (1) change some to any

    (2) change start up to start-up

    (3) add a comma after investment

    (4) change within to between

    (5) no correction required

40. Sentence 12: **We will look at this situation more in-depth within the plan.**

    Which is the best way to improve the underlined portion of this sentence? If the original is the best way, choose option (1).

    (1) situation more in-depth

    (2) more situation in-depth

    (3) situation in more depth

    (4) more in-depth situation

    (5) in-depth more situation

41. Sentence 13: **The addition of a wide selection of accessories, for the customer, will broaden the impact of this new concept.**

    Which revision should be made to sentence 13?

    (1) move for the customer to the end of the sentence and eliminate the commas

    (2) change will broaden to broaden

    (3) begin the sentence with The impact of this new concept

    (4) begin the sentence with The customer will broaden

    (5) change the commas after accessories and customer to semicolons

Go on to next page

> Questions 42 through 50 refer to the following passage, which is adapted from Customer Service For Dummies *by Karen Leland and Keith Bailey (Wiley).*

The Customer Chain

(1) The relationship among internal customers and external customers is what forms the customer chain. (2) If you have a back room kind of job where you see the light of day, rarely, you can easily begin to feel that your work has little or no impact on external customers. (3) But if you look at the bigger picture, you can see that everyone in a company plays some part in fulfilling the customers needs. (4) Barely an hour goes by during the day when you are not, in some form or another, providing somebody for something. (5) Each interaction with an internal customer is an important link in a chain of events that always end up at the external customer's feet.

(6) About two years ago, *The Wall Street Journal* ran an article entitled, Poorly treated employees treat the customer just as poorly. (7) We had dealt with a frightening percentage of managers who do not realize that their staffs are their internal customers. (8) That the quality of service that a company provides to its customers — we are convinced — is a direct reflection of how the staff of the company are treated by their managers. (9) View your staff members as some of your most important customers and treat them accordingly.

42. Sentence 1: **The relationship among internal customers and external customers is what forms the customer chain.**

Which correction should be made to sentence 1?

(1) replace <u>among</u> with <u>between</u>

(2) change <u>relationship</u> to <u>relations</u>

(3) replace <u>is what</u> with <u>was what</u>

(4) change <u>customer</u> to <u>customers'</u>

(5) no correction required

43. Sentence 2: **If you have a back room kind of job <u>where you see the light of day, rarely,</u> you can easily begin to feel that your work has little or no impact on external customers.**

Which is the best way to write the underlined portion of this sentence? If the original is the best way, choose option (1).

(1) where you see the light of day, rarely

(2) where the light of day you see rarely

(3) where you rarely see the light of day

(4) where you see rarely the light of day

(5) where rarely you see the light of day

44. Sentence 3: **But if you look at the bigger picture, you can see that everyone in a company plays some part in fulfilling the customers needs.**

Which correction should be made to sentence 3?

(1) replace <u>customers</u> with <u>customers'</u>

(2) change <u>bigger</u> to <u>biggest</u>

(3) replace <u>everyone</u> with <u>everybody</u>

(4) change <u>fulfilling</u> to <u>fulfiling</u>

(5) no correction required

45. Sentence 4: **Barely an hour goes by during the day when you are not, in some form or another, providing somebody for something.**

Which revision should be made to sentence 4?

(1) replace <u>barely</u> with <u>about</u>

(2) change <u>somebody for something</u> to <u>something for somebody</u>

(3) replace <u>during</u> with <u>over</u>

(4) change <u>providing</u> to <u>provided</u>

(5) no correction required

Go on to next page

46. Sentence 5: **Each interaction with an internal customer is an important link in a chain of events that always end up at the external customer's feet.**

    Which correction should be made to sentence 5?

    (1) replace <u>customer's</u> with <u>customers</u>

    (2) change <u>is</u> to <u>are</u>

    (3) change <u>with</u> to <u>between</u>

    (4) change <u>end</u> to <u>ends</u>

    (5) no correction required

47. Sentence 6: **About two years ago, *The Wall Street Journal* ran an article entitled, Poorly treated employees treat the customer just as poorly.**

    Which addition should be made to sentence 6?

    (1) place quotation marks before <u>Poorly</u> and after <u>poorly</u>

    (2) remove the comma after <u>ago</u>

    (3) remove the comma after <u>entitled</u>

    (4) remove italics from *The Wall Street Journal*

    (5) no correction required

48. Sentence 7: **We had dealt with a frightening percentage of managers who do not realize that their staffs are their internal customers.**

    Which correction should be made to sentence 7?

    (1) replace <u>frightening</u> with <u>frightened</u>

    (2) change <u>staffs</u> to <u>staff</u>

    (3) change <u>had dealt</u> to <u>have dealt</u>

    (4) place an apostrophe after <u>managers</u>

    (5) no correction required

49. Sentence 8: **That the quality of service that a company provides to its customers — we are convinced — is a direct reflection of how the staff of the company are treated by their managers.**

    Which is the best way to begin sentence 8? If the original is best, choose option (1).

    (1) That the quality of service

    (2) We are convinced

    (3) How the staff of the company

    (4) That a company provides

    (5) A direct reflection of how

50. Sentence 9: **View your staff members as some of your most important customers and <u>treat them accordingly</u>.**

    Which is the best way to revise the underlined portion of the sentence?

    (1) accordingly treat them

    (2) treat accordingly them

    (3) them treat accordingly

    (4) remove <u>them</u>

    (5) no correction required

Go on to next page ⟹

Language Arts, Writing Test: Part II

Look at the box on the following page. In the box, you find your assigned topic and the letter of that topic.

You must write on the assigned topic **ONLY**.

Mark the letter of your assigned topic in the appropriate space on your answer sheet booklet.

You have 45 minutes to write on your assigned essay topic. If you have time remaining in this test period after you complete your essay, you may return to the multiple-choice section. Do not return the Language Arts, Writing Test booklet until you finish both Parts I and II of the Language Arts, Writing Test.

Two evaluators will score your essay according to its overall effectiveness. Their evaluation will be based on the following features:

- ✔ Well-focused main points
- ✔ Clear organization
- ✔ Specific development of your ideas
- ✔ Control of sentence structure, punctuation, grammar, word choice, and spelling

REMEMBER, YOU MUST COMPLETE BOTH THE MULTIPLE-CHOICE QUESTIONS (PART I) AND THE ESSAY (PART II) TO RECEIVE A SCORE ON THE LANGUAGE ARTS, WRITING TEST.

To avoid having to repeat both parts of the test, be sure to observe the following rules:

- ✔ Before you begin writing, jot notes or outline your essay on the sheets provided.
- ✔ For your final copy, write legibly in ink so that the evaluators will be able to read your writing.
- ✔ Write on the assigned topic. If you write on a topic other than the one assigned, you will not receive a score for the Language Arts, Writing Test.
- ✔ Write your essay on the lined pages of the separate answer sheet booklet. Only the writing on these pages will be scored.

Note that if you do not pass one portion of the test, you must take both parts over again.

Go on to next page

Topic B

Cellphones have certainly made a difference in our lives. You may own and use one or have put up with other people who use them while driving or at the movies. Cellphones have made our lives better, more difficult, or both.

Write an essay explaining the positive or negative effects — or both — of this innovation in communication. Use examples to support your point of view and be as specific as possible.

Part II is a test to determine how well you can use written language to explain your ideas.

In preparing for your essay, you should take the following steps:

- ✔ Read the DIRECTIONS and the TOPIC carefully.

- ✔ Plan your essay before you write. Use the scratch paper provided to make any notes. These notes will be collected but not scored.

- ✔ Before you turn in your essay, reread what you have written and make any changes that will improve your essay.

Your essay should be long enough to develop the topic adequately.

Note: Refer to Chapter 8 for the answers for Parts I and II of this practice test.

END OF TEST

Answer Sheet for Language Arts, Writing Test: Part II

Use a No. 2 pencil to write the letter of your essay topic in the box, then fill in the corresponding circle.

TOPIC | Ⓐ Ⓑ Ⓒ Ⓓ Ⓔ Ⓕ Ⓖ Ⓗ Ⓘ Ⓙ Ⓚ Ⓛ Ⓜ Ⓝ Ⓞ Ⓟ Ⓠ Ⓡ Ⓢ Ⓣ Ⓤ Ⓥ Ⓦ Ⓧ Ⓨ Ⓩ

Chapter 8

Answers and Explanations for the Language Arts, Writing Test

· ·

After taking the Language Arts, Writing Test in Chapter 7, use this chapter to check your answers. Take your time as you move through the explanations of the answers for Part I that we provide in the first section. They can help you understand why you missed the answers you did. You may also want to read the explanations for the questions you answered correctly because doing so can give you a better understanding of the thought process that helped you choose the correct answers.

Be sure to take a look at the sample essay we provide in the "Sample Essay for Part II" section of this chapter. Compare your essay to the sample to get an idea of what score your essay may have received on the real test.

If you're short on time, turn to the end of the chapter for an abbreviated answer key for Part I of the Language Arts, Writing Test.

Analysis of the Answers for Part 1

1. **4.** The *assessment* belongs to each customer and requires a possessive form of customer: *customer's.* The other answers are neither correct nor do they improve the sentence.

2. **1.** The meaning of this sentence is that the clerk should listen to the customer, so put the most important information first. The best way to start this sentence is with the *When she explains the situation from her perspective* phrase.

3. **3.** *Waving* means to motion with the hand, while *waive* means to dismiss. It may be interesting to wave at a charge, but the proper meaning of the sentence is to dismiss (or not collect) the charge. These two words are *homonyms* (words that sound the same but have different spellings and meanings). You are expected to understand most homonyms for this test.

4. **3.** The only place you can use a comma in this sentence is after the introductory phrase *At other times.*

5. **4.** *Exceptable* may sound like a word, but it's not. The correct word to use is *acceptable.*

    The more reading you do as you prepare for the test, the better your chances are for recognizing misspellings.

6. **1.** A gift for you: No correction is required.

     If you chose Choice (5), keep in mind that this sentence has one subject and two verbs. These types of sentences don't require a comma between the two verbs. Not sure about subjects and verbs? Here, the subject is *step* and the two verbs are *begins* and *gives*. If the sentence had a second subject before the second verb, it would need a comma.

7. **2.** If you live anywhere near Amish country, you know that the horse comes before the cart. Or you may have heard the idiomatic expression, "Don't put the cart before the horse." In either case, the proper correction is to reverse the order of *horse* and *cart.*

8. **4.** *Its* is possessive (meaning that it shows that something belongs to *it*), while *it's* stands for "it is." Here, the sentence clearly means "it is."

Confusing these two words is a common error that's usually tested in some way. Master the difference between *its* and *it's*. *It's* means "it is" and is often confused with the possessive form of other words that use the apostrophe.

9. **3.** *Farther* always refers to distance. *Further* is a matter of degree. Here, you want degree, not distance.

If you didn't know the answer, this question is a good example of one that you could answer by intelligent guessing. Choice (1) isn't correct because *looses* isn't a word. Choice (2) doesn't make sense in the context of the sentence. Choice (4) isn't right because the person losing ground is you, and because you don't own the ground, you don't want to use a possessive. Now you just have to guess between Choices (3) and (5).

10. **2.** Commas used in moderation help sentences. Extra commas hurt sentences. A comma is never used to separate a subject from a verb.

11. **3.** In the letter, the *York Square Employment Resource Center* is a title; as such, all words (except prepositions and articles) are capitalized.

12. **1.** Moving *since April 2002* is the only good answer here. The current sentence sounds as though the training programs have been in existence since April 2002 when, in fact, the partnership has been in existence since that time.

13. **4.** Most (although not all) lists begin with a colon. You don't need semicolons after the items in the list (the bullets serve as separators). You need a comma after the introductory phrase, which eliminates Choice (1), and you don't separate a direct object from an indirect object with a comma, which eliminates Choice (5).

14. **1.** No correction is required.

15. **2.** The subject of the sentence is *fact,* which is singular, but the verb is *are,* which is plural. Verbs must agree with their subjects.

16. **3.** In its current form, this sentence forces the reader to pause too long and remember too much. Rewriting it as "She has pursued her responsibilities with a high degree of professional competence and efficiency" is far more straightforward.

17. **1.** As is, this sentence is a run-on sentence. To make it a compound sentence, all you have to do is add a comma after *Peta.*

18. **2.** The word *shoppe* is quaint, but it isn't common usage. If you were living in Williamsburg 200 years ago, the answer would be different. Today, people use the shorter and more common *shop.*

19. **1.** Before the change, the first sentence is missing a verb, making it an incomplete sentence. Choice (2) is incorrect because *state-of-the-art* is acting as a single adjective to *copiers,* and multiword adjectives are nearly always hyphenated. Choice (4) is incorrect because the first sentence is clearly describing the store, not the copiers.

20. **5.** No change is required in this sentence. The copy shop may want to consider changing the way it hires and trains its staff, but that's another matter altogether.

21. **3.** Lists have to be parallel. In this case, you have *apologizing, explaining,* and *gave,* which aren't parallel (all three are verbs, but the first two are gerunds, while the second is an infinitive). Changing *gave* to *giving* makes the list parallel.

22. **2.** This is a classic run-on sentence, so you need to break it apart into separate sentences (in this case, three separate sentences). A good change is as follows: "Okay, I thought, fair enough. They're new and getting their act together. No big deal." (Note that the third sentence doesn't appear to have a verb, but the implied subject and verb are *it is,* as in "It is no big deal.")

23. **1.** The correct answer is to add a comma after *later.* Most of the time, you want to set off an introductory clause with a comma; however, be aware that when the introductory clause is very short, the convention isn't always clear: Some people use the comma and others don't. On this test, however, you're always better off putting a comma after any introductory clause.

24. **3.** Change *apologised* to *apologized,* which is the correct spelling. The other answer choices do nothing to improve the sentence.

25. **1.** Add a comma after the introductory phrase. See the answer explanation to Question 23 for further details.

26. **3.** Whenever a sentence has two clauses, each with a subject and a verb, a comma has to separate them. In this sentence, *I went back* is a clause that has both a subject *(I)* and a verb *(went)*. The clause *and the same thing happened again* also has a subject *(thing)* and a verb *(happened)*. *Two weeks later* is an introductory phrase that requires a comma after *later.*

27. **5.** This answer is a gift. The sentence is correct as is.

A point of interest with this sentence is that it uses one of the dreaded *two/to/too* words. These words are all *homonyms*: words that sound the same but have different spellings and meanings. Here, the use of *too* is correct, but be sure you put these three words on your list of homonyms to study.

28. **4.** *My opinion* is a singular subject that needs a singular verb. *Were* is a plural verb and must be changed to the singular form *was.* Don't let that prepositional phrase *of their services* throw you off track. Just act as if that part of the sentence weren't there.

If you have trouble with singular and plural verbs and subject-verb agreement, try changing the subject into a pronoun. This sentence would become *It were,* which sounds wrong. Changing it to *It was* sounds right. Trust your ears.

One exception to the "it sounds right" rule is the *subjunctive form* of verbs. Whenever something is contrary to fact, you use *were* with singular subjects. For example, "If I were taller" is correct. Look for terms and phrases like *if, I wish,* and *if only:* These words are usually followed by the subjunctive form of the verb.

29. **4.** This question is a good example of when using elimination can help you get the right answer. Choice (1) introduces the wrong verb tense. Choice (2) introduces a punctuation error because the comma is needed. Choice (3) introduces another punctuation error: This comma is also needed. When you plug in Choice (4), the sentence reads more smoothly, so you know you have a winner.

30. **1.** Choice (1) is the only option of all the ones presented that is correct in terms of both verb form and meaning. Choices (2), (3), and (5) all introduce errors in verb form; Choice (4) changes the sentence to present tense, which then changes its meaning.

31. **4.** The words *this knowledge* are out of place, but they're necessary to the sentence because they add to the meaning of the sentence. You can improve the sentence by moving *This knowledge* to the front of the sentence and changing *Combined* to *combined.* Another way to change the sentence is to simply remove the comma after *knowledge* (because subjects and verbs are never separated by commas), but that option isn't an answer choice.

32. **2.** This sentence contains a spelling mistake. Change *merchandize* to *merchandise.*

33. **1.** This sentence is badly in need of a comma transfusion. It should read "This concept, combined with speedy service, helped the industry grow every year." These two little commas help the sentence by separating the phrase *combined with speedy service* from the rest of the sentence.

34. **1.** This sentence is fairly long and seems to ramble, but none of the options offers a way to split it into two. However, the sentence does have an error: Schools have *principals;* people and businesses (you hope!) have *principles.* These two words are *homonyms,* meaning that they sound alike but have different meanings and spellings.

35. **4.** You should change the underlined phrase to *relocated.* The other answer choices introduce new errors.

36. **1.** From the context of the passage, you can assume Concord is a town or city and deserves a capital letter at the beginning of the word.

37. **2.** The sentence is supposed to say that he (Morris James) had established the validity of the concept before (in 1991) and then (later) he wanted to establish a corporate store. Rewriting the sentence like this is clearer: "Having established the validity of the concept in Wellesley in 1991, he then opened the corporate store." The other answer choices don't maintain this meaning.

Choice (4) may look good, but it changes the meaning of the sentence. He didn't open the corporate store in 1991; he established the validity of the concept in 1991.

38. **5.** Okay, this sentence is really long, but, technically, nothing is wrong with it. If you had the option of splitting it into two sentences, you'd want to do so. But because you're not given that option and all the other options are incorrect, leave it as is.

39. **2.** Here, *start up* is acting as an adjective for *costs*. Most multiword adjectives are hyphenated.

If you chose Choice (3), you must've thought that the second half of the sentence had a second subject. If so, reread that part of the sentence to try to find the subject. It's not there. This is a sentence with one subject *(cost)* and two verbs *(will require* and *will be regained)*. A sentence like this one, with only one subject and two verbs, doesn't require a comma. If it had a second subject before the second verb, it would need a comma.

40. **3.** Changing the phrase to *in more depth* improves the sentence structure. The other answer choices don't really make much sense when you plug them into the sentence.

41. **1.** Moving *on the customer* to the end of the sentence improves the sentence organization by placing the direct object *(the impact)* closer to the second indirect object *(the customer)*. (What's the first indirect object? *This new concept.*)

If you chose Choice (5), you essentially said that the customer would have a wide selection of accessories added to him or her.

42. **1.** *Among* is used when comparing three or more entities; *between* is used to compare only two things. Here, you have two types of customers, so *between* is correct.

43. **3.** *Where you rarely see the light of day* is an improved word order because you want the adverb (in this case, *rarely*) to be as close as possible to the verb it modifies (in this case, *see*).

44. **1.** The needs belong to the customers, so you need to make *customers* possessive by making it *customers'*.

45. **2.** *Providing somebody for something* doesn't make sense. You don't provide people for things; rather, you provide things for people.

46. **4.** Examine the phrase *that always end up.* What's the phrase referring to? *Important link,* right? Yes, but *link* is singular, so you don't say, *link . . . end.* Instead, you say *link . . . ends.*

47. **1.** "Poorly treated employees treat the customer just as poorly" is the title of a newspaper article and must be in quotation marks. Names of newspapers are in italics, while the stories that are run in them are placed in quotes.

The idea of the entire work (the newspaper) being in italics, while the inner works (the articles) are in quotes extends to other situations, as well. For example, a book title is in italics, while the name of each chapter is in quotes. A TV series is in italics, while the name of each episode is in quotes.

48. **3.** This sentence has two related problems. First, the past tense of *deal* is *dealt,* not *dealed.* Second, according to the context in the passage, you know that this action began in the past and continues in the present. You can indicate that timeline by using *have.* On the other hand, using *had* means that the action began in the past and also stopped in the past — in other words, that it isn't continuing today.

49. **2.** Putting *we are convinced* in the middle of the sentence interrupts the main point of the sentence — to point out a specific cause-and-effect relationship.

50. **5.** A final gift for you — no correction is needed, and all the other answer choices make the sentence worse.

Sample Essay for Part II

The essay topic for the practice test in Chapter 7 is as follows:

> Cellphones have certainly made a difference in our lives. You may own and use one or have put up with other people who use them while driving or at the movies. Cellphones have made our lives better, more difficult, or both.

> Write an essay explaining the positive or negative effects — or both — of this innovation in communication. Use examples to support your point of view and be as specific as possible.

As the test graders read and evaluate your essay, they look for the following:

- ✔ Well-focused main points
- ✔ Evidence of clear organization
- ✔ Specific development of your ideas
- ✔ Proper sentence structure
- ✔ Correct grammar
- ✔ Necessary punctuation
- ✔ Appropriate use of words
- ✔ Correct spelling

Although every essay will be unique, we provide a sample here to give you a better idea of what the test graders expect to see in your essay. Compare the structure of this essay to yours.

Cellphones make life easier

My children and I recently signed up for a family-rate calling plan—complete with four separate phones and phone numbers—so that we could communicate more easily. Although I put off the purchase for several years, thinking that having a cellphone would make me so accessible to others that I would never get any time to myself, the truth is, the phones have made all of our lives easier.

My three children attend three different schools. The youngest, Doug, is in the 4th grade and takes a free acting class year-round at the local playhouse. His lessons run from 4:00 to 5:00 three days per week, but he can sometimes catch rides home with other children in the class. Because I work until 5:30, my oldest daughter, Sydney, who is a junior in high school, waits for him to call to tell her whether he needs a ride. Before we had cellphones, Doug always had to find a working pay phone, and Sydney had to wait by the phone at home.

The middle child, Maggie, is in eighth grade and plays three sports: soccer, basketball, and track. I can usually pick her up from practice on my way home from work, but her practices end at different times every day. While she, too, used to have to hunt down a pay phone and call me at work, now she just calls and lets me know where she'll be waiting. I can run errands while I wait for her call instead of waiting at work or by the curb at her school.

The best part of the phones, though, is that whenever people want to reach any of the four of us, they call the number for the individual, not the entire family. I no longer answer the phone for all of Doug's, Maggie's, and Sydney's friends, and people trying to reach me no longer get a busy signal.

For us, cellphones are the ultimate convenience. In fact, we like our cellphones so much that we no longer have regular phone service in our home.

Note: To evaluate this sample essay, as well as your own, turn to Chapter 6 for a list of questions to ask yourself about both essays. For tips and ideas on mastering the Language Arts, Writing Test, Part II, check out Chapter 4.

Answer Key for Part 1

1. **4**	18. **2**	35. **4**
2. **1**	19. **1**	36. **1**
3. **3**	20. **5**	37. **2**
4. **3**	21. **3**	38. **5**
5. **4**	22. **2**	39. **2**
6. **1**	23. **1**	40. **3**
7. **2**	24. **3**	41. **1**
8. **4**	25. **1**	42. **1**
9. **3**	26. **3**	43. **3**
10. **2**	27. **5**	44. **1**
11. **3**	28. **4**	45. **2**
12. **1**	29. **4**	46. **4**
13. **4**	30. **1**	47. **1**
14. **1**	31. **4**	48. **3**
15. **2**	32. **2**	49. **2**
16. **3**	33. **1**	50. **5**
17. **1**	34. **1**	

Part III
Finding Your Way: The Social Studies Test

The 5th Wave   By Rich Tennant

©RICHTENNANT

Well, this should help me ace the DANDRUFF section of the test.

SOCIAL STUDY

In this part . . .

In this part, you find questions, questions, and more questions about social studies in the form of sample test questions — but, lucky for you, you also get the answers and explanations. In addition, this part explains what skills the Social Studies Test expects you to know, what subject areas the test covers, and how the test is laid out so you get a better idea of what you need to do to get good marks on the test. It also offers you some helpful strategies you can use to do your best on the test.

Before taking the actual Social Studies Test, take the two practice tests in this part to determine how well you've mastered the required skills in social studies. Pretend they're real tests by timing yourself, following the instructions, and asking someone to act as the test administrator to keep you honest (if you can find someone willing to help). The closer you come to mimicking the real test conditions, the more you get out of practicing here and in all the other tests.

Chapter 9

A Graph, a Map, and You: Getting Ready for the Social Studies Test

· ·

In This Chapter

▶ Figuring out what the Social Studies Test covers and how it's formatted

▶ Surveying the types of questions on this test and knowing how to prepare for them

▶ Using strategies that achieve the best results

▶ Managing your time for this test and looking at sample problems

· ·

Do you enjoy knowing about how events in the past may help you foretell the future? Do the lives of people in faraway places interest you? Are politics something you care about? If you answered yes to any of these questions, you're going to like social studies! After all, social studies helps you discover how humans relate to their environment and to other people. This overarching area of study includes subjects like history, government, geography, and economics.

The GED Social Studies Test assesses your skills in understanding and interpreting concepts and principles in history, geography, economics, and civics. Consider this test as a kind of crash course in where you've been, where you are, and how you can continue living there. You can apply the types of skills tested in the Social Studies Test to your experience in visual, academic, and workplace situations as a citizen, a consumer, or an employee. This test includes questions drawn from a variety of written and visual passages taken from academic and workplace materials, as well as from primary and secondary sources. The passages in this test are like the ones you read or see in most daily newspapers and news magazines. Reading either or both of these news sources regularly can help you become familiar with the style and vocabulary of the passages you find here.

The information in this chapter helps you prepare for the Social Studies Test.

Looking at the Skills the Social Studies Test Covers

The GED Social Studies Test requires you to draw on your previous knowledge of events, ideas, terms, and situations that may be related to social studies. From a big-picture perspective, the Social Studies Test and the skills it measures break down like this:

✔ **20 percent:** Relates to your ability to identify information and ideas and interpret their meaning.

✔ **20 percent:** Assesses your ability to use the information and ideas in different ways to explore their meanings or solve a problem.

✔ **40 percent:** Measures your ability to use the information or ideas to do the following:

- Determine the difference between facts and opinions.

- Arrive at conclusions using material.

- Influence other people's attitudes.

- Find other meanings or mistakes in logic.

- Identify causes and their effects.

- Recognize a writer's historical point of view.

- Compare and contrast differing views and opinions.

- Determine what impact these views and opinions may have both at this time and in the future.

✔ **20 percent:** Measures your ability to make judgments about the material's appropriateness, accuracy, and differences of opinion, as well as the role information and ideas play in influencing current and future decision making. These questions ask you to think about issues and events that affect you every day. That fact alone is interesting and has the potential to make you a more informed citizen of the modern world. What a bonus for a test!

Being aware of what skills the Social Studies Test covers can help you get a more accurate picture of the types of questions you'll encounter. The next section focuses more on the specific subject materials you'll face in this test.

Understanding the Test Format

The Social Studies Test contains 50 multiple-choice questions that you must answer in 70 minutes, which means you have less than 1½ minutes per question. These 50 questions check your knowledge in the following subject areas:

✔ **American history (25 percent; 12 or 13 questions):** You may have to read passages about the American Revolution, the Civil War, colonization, reconstruction, settlement, industrial development, or the Great Depression — and answer questions about them, of course. If you didn't have to answer questions, reading these passages would be a dream assignment because American history can be a lot of fun.

To practice for this section of the test, read articles and books about historical events and trends. Remember that 60 percent of these questions are based on visual passages, including illustrations, maps, and charts, so take a look at those, too. With practice, you can learn to read visual passages as well as you read text.

✔ **World history (15 percent; 7 or 8 questions):** The types of questions and potential sources of information you encounter for the world history questions are identical to those you find in the American history questions, except that they deal with history from around the world, which means they go back much further than U.S. history does.

✔ **Civics and government (25 percent; 12 or 13 questions):** These passages are all about civic life, government, politics (especially the American political system), Americans' relationships with other countries, and America's role in the world. Your job, if you wish to accept it, is to read and understand the passages and answer questions about them. You can find a lot of material about civics and government in newspapers and news magazines. If you don't read these types of publications regularly and want to look at old issues, visit your public library (or go to your doctor's waiting room). Try to get a sense of what's going on by pretending you want to explain the issue to a friend. (Don't actually explain all the current issues to your friends, though, because you'll probably run out of friends before you run out of issues.)

✔ **Economics (20 percent; 10 questions):** Economics is the study of how the earth's resources are used to create wealth, which is then distributed and used to satisfy the needs of mankind. It involves the worlds of banking and finance in both small businesses and large corporations. It includes workers and owners who import and export manufactured goods and natural resources and services. You can find sources of economic articles on the Internet and in newspapers, magazines, textbooks, and software programs.

✔ **Geography (15 percent; 7 or 8 questions):** Geography passages usually read like a list of places you want to go. Geography deals with the world and what's going on in it, including the impact of weather and environmental conditions and the political divisions of land and its use by living creatures. For geography questions, you often have to read maps and then answer questions about them. Although reading maps is a different kind of reading, with a little practice, it can be a fun and wonderful way to daydream about where you'd like to go on your next vacation.

To help you prepare for the geography questions, you can read several good geographic magazines with fascinating articles and beautiful photographs. Plus, you can find Internet sites and library books about every place on earth. The important thing is to read, read, and read some more just to become comfortable with the language of geography.

The passages in the Social Studies Test are taken from the following two types of sources:

✔ **Academic material:** The type of material you find in a school — textbooks, maps, newspapers, magazines, software, and Internet material

✔ **Workplace material:** The type of material found on the job — manuals, documents, business plans, advertising and marketing materials, correspondence, and so on

The material may be from primary or secondary sources, which means the following:

✔ **Primary sources:** The original documents, such as the Declaration of Independence

✔ **Secondary sources:** Material written about an event or person, sometimes long after the event takes place or the person dies

Identifying the Types of Questions and Knowing How to Prepare for Them

The Social Studies Test contains two main types of questions. Having a basic understanding of these two types can help you prepare and avoid any surprises when you sit down to the take the test.

As you read the passages to get ready to answer the questions about them, you're expected to use the following skills:

✔ Comprehension

✔ Application

✔ Analysis

✔ Evaluation

These skills are considered higher-level thinking skills and are the ones most adults use regularly. To better understand these skills, consider the following three examples:

✔ When you buy something new, you likely have to read the users' manual that came with it to figure out how to use what you bought. As you read the manual and follow its instructions, you use the skills of *comprehension* and *application.* You first have to understand what the manual says and then use that information to make the thing you bought work. Without the skills of comprehension and application, the clock on your electronic devices might blink *12:00* forever.

✔ If you were in the checkout line of your favorite grocery store and saw a magazine that said the president was born on Mars, you probably wouldn't run directly to your friends screaming about this amazing development. Instead, you'd likely first want to decide whether this new "fact" could possibly be true by doing some further research and clarifying your thinking. When you read or hear something and you take time to think about it before using the information in a discussion with your friends, you use the skills of *evaluation* and *application.*

✔ If someone said to you, "The United States is a dictatorship with occasional outbreaks of democracy," you'd need to use the skill of *analysis* to either agree or disagree with that statement. Do the "occasional outbreaks of democracy" refer to the elections? In this case, what happens between elections? Can the president make decisions without consulting the public or the elected representatives? Can an elected representative vote however he or she wants without considering the needs of his or her constituents? The answers to these questions are what you get when you analyze the initial statement.

The following sections explain the two types of questions you encounter on this test and offer you advice on how to prepare for them so that you can solve them with ease when you face them on test day.

Questions about text passages

The first type of question you have to answer on the Social Studies Test is based on text passages. You read a textual excerpt or passage and then answer questions about it.

The best way to prepare for these types of questions is to read, read, read. In particular, these questions require you to read excerpts from documents such as the following:

✔ Declaration of Independence

✔ U.S. Constitution

✔ Landmark Supreme Court cases

✔ Consumer information guides

✔ Voters' guides

✔ Atlases

✔ Tax forms

✔ Budget graphs

✔ Political speeches

✔ Almanacs

✔ Statistical abstracts

The more you read these types of documents, the more you think about what you read, and the more you think about what you read, the better prepared you'll be for the text-based questions on this test. You can find examples of each of these possible sources in libraries and on the Internet.

When you're preparing for the test and then again when you're reading these passages on the test, read between the lines and look at the implications and assumptions in the passages. An *implication* is something you can understand from what's written even though it isn't directly stated. An *assumption* is something you can accept as the truth even though proof isn't presented in the text.

When you take the test, be sure to read each question carefully so you know exactly what it's asking for. If you're being asked for facts, they're presented to you in the passage. If you're asked for opinions, they may be either stated or implied in the passages (and they may disagree with your own opinions — but you still have to answer with the best choice based on the material presented). Keep in mind that you usually find opinions in textual passages, political cartoons, and works of art.

If a question doesn't specifically tell you to use additional information that isn't presented in the passage, use *only* the information that is presented. An answer may be incorrect in your opinion, but according to the information presented, it's correct (or vice versa). Go with the information presented unless a question tells you to do otherwise.

Questions about visual materials

To make sure you don't get bored taking this test, only 40 percent of the questions are based on textual material. Another 40 percent are based on maps, graphs, tables, political cartoons, diagrams, photographs, and artistic works. The remaining 20 percent of the questions are based on a combination of visual material and text.

Although the fact that 40 percent of the questions deal with visual material may seem overwhelming when you think about it, consider the following:

✔ **You're probably already familiar with maps.** Travel maps (see Figure 9-1) help you get from place to place. Weather maps help you see what the weather has in store for your area. To help you prepare for the map-based questions on the test, study the maps you see on TV or in newspapers or magazines; try to figure out what they're showing you.

✔ **Every time you turn around, someone in the media is trying to make a point with a graph.** The real reason people use graphs to explain themselves so often is because a graph can clearly show trends and relationships between different sets of information. The next time you see a graph, such as the one in Figure 9-2, study it carefully to see whether you understand what the information in the graph is telling you. (Keep in mind that graphs are also called *charts*.)

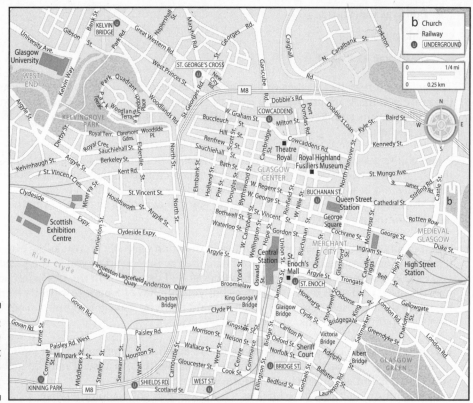

Figure 9-1:
Peruse
different
maps like
this one.

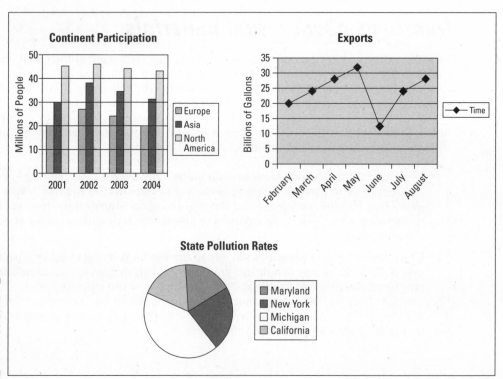

Figure 9-2:
Check out
different
graphs like
these.

✔ **Tables are everywhere.** If you've ever looked at the nutrition label on a food product, you've read a table. Study any table you can find, whether in a newspaper or on the back of a can of tuna. See Figure 9-3 for an example of a table that could appear on the Social Studies Test. (Note that tables are also sometimes called *charts,* which can be a little confusing. The thing to remember is that it doesn't matter whether a visual passage is a table, a cartoon, a drawing, or a graph — as long as you know how to read it.)

✔ **Political cartoons appear in the newspapers every day.** If you don't read political cartoons in the daily newspaper (usually located on the Editorial or Op-Ed pages), give them a try. Some days, they're the best entertainment in the paper. Political cartoons in the newspaper are usually based on an event in the last day or week. If you want to get the most out of political cartoons, look for small details, facial expressions, and background clues. The cartoons on the test are obviously older than the ones in daily newspapers, so you may not get the context unless you've been reading the newspapers or watching the news for the past several weeks or months.

✔ **You've no doubt seen countless photographs in your day.** Photos are all around you. All you need to do to prepare for the photograph-based questions on the test is to begin getting information from the photographs you see. Start with the newspapers or magazines, where photos are chosen to provide information that connects directly to a story. See if you can determine what message the photograph carries with it and how it relates to the story it supports.

✔ **You probably like to look at works of art.** On the Social Studies Test, you have a chance to "read" works of art. You look at a work of art and gather information you can use to answer the question. To get yourself ready to gather information from works of art on the test, take a look at art galleries, the Internet, and library books. Lucky for you, some books even give some background or other explanation for these works.

Impact on the Environment

Figure 9-3:
See if you can understand the basic information in tables like this one.

Type of Vehicle	MPG	Cost of Resources
SUV	12.8	$3,900
Sedan	19.6	$2,400
2-door	19.5	$2,700
All-wheel drive	17.2	$3,100
Sports car	18.6	$3,300

If you're unsure of how to read a map, go to any search engine and search for *Map reading help* to find sites that explain how to read a map. If any of the other types of visual materials cause you concern, do the same thing — with the exception of political cartoons. If you try to follow the same procedure for political cartoons, you'll get a lot of actual cartoons but not a lot of explanations about them. Instead, look at some examples of political cartoons (either in the newspaper or online) to try to understand what the cartoonist is saying to you. Then look up the topic of the cartoon and the date to read some of the news stories it refers to. Talk about the cartoon with your friends. If you can explain a cartoon or carry on a logical discussion about the topic, you probably understand its contents.

All the visual items you have to review on this test are familiar. Now all you have to do is practice until your skills in reading and understanding them increase. Then you, too, can discuss the latest political cartoon or pontificate about a work of art.

Examining Preparation Strategies That Work

To improve your skills and get better results, we suggest you try the following strategies when taking the Social Studies Test:

✔ **Take as many practice tests as you can get your hands on.** The best way to prepare is to answer all the sample social studies questions you can find. Do practice tests (see Chapters 10 and 12), practice questions (see the "Practicing with Sample Problems" section later in this chapter), and examples, such as those on the GED site (www.acenet. edu/Content/NavigationMenu/ged/test/prep/sample_questions.htm).

Consider taking a preparation class to get your hands on even more sample Social Studies Test questions, but remember that your task is to pass the test — not to collect every question ever written.

✔ **Practice reading a variety of different documents.** As we mention in the previous section, read, read, and read some more. The documents you need to focus on include historic passages from original sources (such as the Declaration of Independence, U.S. Constitution, and so on), as well as practical information for consumers (such as voters' guides, atlases, budget graphs, political speeches, almanacs, and tax forms).

✔ **Prepare summaries of the passages you read in your own words.** After you read these passages, summarize what you've read. Doing so can help you identify the main points of the passages, which is an important part of succeeding on the Social Studies Test. Ask yourself the following two questions when you read a passage or something more visual like a graph:

- **What's the passage about?** When reading passages of text, ask yourself what the passage is about. The answer is usually in the first or last sentence of the passage. If you don't see the answer there, you may have to look carefully through the rest of the passage.

- **What's the visual material about?** When reading maps, charts, graphs, political cartoons, diagrams, photographs, and artistic works, ask yourself what the visual material is about. Look for the answer in the title, labels, captions, and any other information that's included.

After you get an initial grasp of the main idea, determine what to do with it. Some questions ask you to use information you gain from one situation in another similar situation. If you know the main idea of the passage, you'll have an easier time applying it to another situation.

✔ **Draft a series of your own test questions that draw on the information contained in the passages you read.** Doing so can help you become familiar with social studies–based questions. Look in newspapers and magazines for articles that fit into the general passage types that appear on the Social Studies Test. Find a good summary paragraph, and develop a question that gets to the point of the summary.

✔ **Compose answers for each of your test questions.** Write out five answers to each of your test questions, only one of which is correct based on the passage. Creating your own questions and answers helps reduce your stress level by showing you how answers are related to questions. It also encourages you to read and think about material that could be on the test. Finally, it gives you some idea of where to look for answers in a passage.

✔ **Discuss questions and answers with friends and family to make sure you've achieved an understanding and proper use of the material.** If your friends and family understand the question, you know it's a good question. Discussing your questions and answers with others gives you a chance to discuss and explain social studies topics and concepts, which is an important skill to have as you get ready to take this test.

Managing Your Time for the Social Studies Test

Remember that you have to answer 50 questions in 70 minutes to complete this test, which means you have less than 1½ minutes to spend on each question. Because you don't have a lot of time, you want to make sure you plan accordingly to give yourself enough time to answer every question and to quickly review your answers.

As we mention earlier in this chapter, the questions on the Social Studies Test are based on both regular textual passages and visual materials like maps and charts, so, when you plan your time for answering the questions, you have to consider the amount of time it takes to read both types of passages. (See the "Questions about visual materials" section for advice on how you can get more comfortable with questions based on graphs, charts, and the like.)

When you come to a prose passage, read the questions first and then skim the passage looking for sections that answer the questions. If this method doesn't work, read the passage carefully, looking for the answers. This way, you take more time only when needed.

Because you have such little time to gather all the information you can from a visual material and answer questions about it, you can't study the map, chart, or cartoon all afternoon. You have to skim it the way you skim a paragraph. Reading the questions that relate to a particular visual passage first helps you figure out what you need to look for as you skim the material. The practice tests in Chapters 10 and 12 contain examples of questions based on visual materials, and so do the sample problems in the "Practicing with Sample Problems" section in this chapter.

If you're unsure of how quickly you can answer questions based on visual materials, time yourself on a few and see. If your time comes out to be more than 1½ minutes, you need more practice.

Realistically, you have about 20 seconds to read the question and the possible answers, 40 seconds to look for the answer in the cartoon, and 10 seconds to fill in the circle for the answer. Dividing your time in this way leaves you less than 20 seconds for review or for time at the end of the test to spend on difficult questions. To finish the Social Studies Test completely, you really have to be organized and watch the clock. Check out Chapter 2 for more general time-management tips.

Practicing with Sample Problems

The sample problems in this section give you a taste of what to expect in the practice tests in Chapters 10 and 12 of this book.

Remember that the Social Studies Test doesn't measure your ability to recall information, such as dates, facts, or events. It requires you to read a passage, analyze the information, evaluate its accuracy, and draw conclusions according to the printed text or visual materials contained in the passage. You then choose the one best answer to each question.

Questions 1 through 5 are based on the following passage.

Bridging both temperate and tropical regions, Mexico's terrain includes mountains, plains, valleys, and plateaus. Snow-capped volcanoes slope down to pine forests, deserts, and balmy tropical beaches. This diverse topography supports a variety of industries, including manufacturing, mining, petroleum, and agricultural production. As a member of the North American Free Trade Agreement (NAFTA), Mexico has the United States and Canada as main trading partners. In economic terms, Mexico boasts a GDP (gross domestic product) of $370 billion ($8,100 per person), which ranks it thirteenth in the world. Mexico currently enjoys an annual growth rate of over 6 percent. Beginning in 1985, Mexico began a process of trade liberalization and privatization. From 1982 to 1992, government-controlled enterprises were reduced from 1,155 to 217.

1. Which of the following are not part of Mexico's terrain?

   (1) plateaus

   (2) polar ice caps

   (3) mountains

   (4) valleys

   (5) plains

   The correct answer is Choice (2) because the country doesn't lie either at the North or South Pole, where polar ice caps are found. The passage mentions the other answer choices — plateaus, mountains, valleys, and plains — but this question asks for what isn't mentioned.

2. Which adjectives demonstrate that the Mexican climate represents extremes in temperature?

   (1) sunny and rainy

   (2) dark and misty

   (3) plains and valleys

   (4) snow-capped and balmy

   (5) forests and deserts

   The correct answer is Choice (4). Snow-capped volcanoes represent an extremely low temperature, while balmy beaches refer to the higher temperatures found in a tropical climate. Other adjectives — such as sunny and rainy or dark and misty — don't refer to changes in temperature. Plains and valleys and forests and deserts are nouns that refer to terrain, not temperature.

3. What does "diverse topography" refer to?

   (1) differences in terrain

   (2) uniqueness in manufacturing

   (3) differences in agriculture

   (4) diversity of tropical beaches

   (5) abundance of petroleum production

   The correct answer is Choice (1). *Topography* is another word for terrain. *Diverse* means different. Manufacturing, agriculture, and petroleum production are types of industries. Tropical beaches are just one type of terrain.

4. Which countries are Mexico's trading partners in NAFTA?

   (1) the United States and the United Kingdom

   (2) France and Germany

   (3) North America

   (4) Canada and the United Kingdom

   (5) the United States and Canada

The correct answer is Choice (5). The text states that the United States and Canada joined with Mexico to form the North American Free Trade Agreement. The United Kingdom, France, and Germany aren't partners in NAFTA.

5. What happened in Mexico between 1982 and 1992?

    (1) Government control of enterprises increased.

    (2) The government controlled fewer enterprises.

    (3) Mexico achieved the highest GDP in the world.

    (4) Mexico's growth rate was less than 6 percent.

    (5) Mexico won the World Cup.

The correct answer is Choice (2). According to the passage, during the decade from 1982 to 1992, Mexico's government reduced its control of enterprises from 1,155 to 217. It didn't increase enterprise control, nor did Mexico achieve the highest GDP in the world — 12 countries were higher. The country's growth rate was more than 6 percent. And although Mexico would love to win the World Cup in soccer, the passage doesn't say it did so during the mentioned decade.

Questions 6 and 7 are based on the following graph:

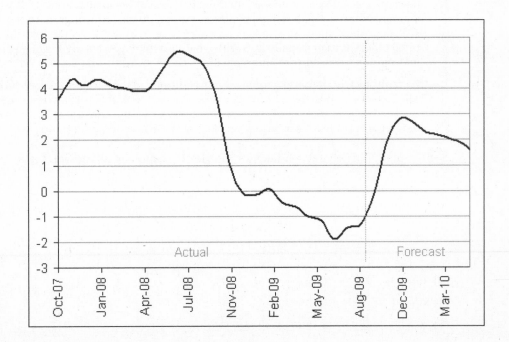

6. In what period was the inflation rate the highest?

    (1) January to April 2008

    (2) April to August 2008

    (3) August to November 2008

    (4) November 2008 to February 2009

    (5) February to May 2009

The correct answer is Choice (2). The highest point on the graph occurs in the period represented by April to August 2008. If there were finer divisions on the x-axis (horizontal axis) of the graph, you could be more accurate in the timing, but, as it is, the graph indicates this level of accuracy.

7. In what period did the inflation rate first dip below zero?

    (1) January to April 2008

    (2) April to August 2008

    (3) August to November 2008

    (4) November 2008 to February 2009

    (5) February to May 2009

The correct answer is Choice (4). The first time that the line on this graph passes through the horizontal line labeled *0* on the vertical axis is during the period November 2008 to February 2009. The numbers below this horizontal line are negative.

Revealing Some Helpful Pointers

The following additional tips can serve you well in this test:

✔ **Don't assume.** Be extra careful with visual material and read it carefully. You want to be able to read visual material as accurately as you read text material, and doing so takes practice. Don't assume something is true just because it looks that way in a diagram, chart, or map. Visual materials can be precise drawings, with legends and scales, or they can be drawn in such a way that, at first glance, the information appears to be different than it really is. Verify what you think you see by making sure the information looks correct and realistic.

✔ **Be familiar with general graphical conventions.** Maps and graphs have conventions. The top of a map is almost always north. The horizontal axis is always the *x*-axis, and the vertical axis (the *y*-axis) is dependent on the *x*-axis. Looking at the horizontal axis first usually makes the information clearer and easier to understand.

See Chapter 3 for general test-taking strategies that apply to all the GED tests.

Chapter 10

Practice Test — Social Studies Test

• •

*T*he Social Studies Test consists of multiple-choice questions that measure general social studies concepts. The questions are based on short readings that often include a map, graph, chart, cartoon, or figure. Study the information given and then answer the question(s) following it. Refer to the information as often as necessary in answering the questions.

You have 70 minutes to answer the 50 questions in this booklet. Work carefully, but do not spend too much time on any one question. Be sure you answer every question.

Answer Sheet for Social Studies Test

1 ① ② ③ ④ ⑤   26 ① ② ③ ④ ⑤
2 ① ② ③ ④ ⑤   27 ① ② ③ ④ ⑤
3 ① ② ③ ④ ⑤   28 ① ② ③ ④ ⑤
4 ① ② ③ ④ ⑤   29 ① ② ③ ④ ⑤
5 ① ② ③ ④ ⑤   30 ① ② ③ ④ ⑤
6 ① ② ③ ④ ⑤   31 ① ② ③ ④ ⑤
7 ① ② ③ ④ ⑤   32 ① ② ③ ④ ⑤
8 ① ② ③ ④ ⑤   33 ① ② ③ ④ ⑤
9 ① ② ③ ④ ⑤   34 ① ② ③ ④ ⑤
10 ① ② ③ ④ ⑤   35 ① ② ③ ④ ⑤
11 ① ② ③ ④ ⑤   36 ① ② ③ ④ ⑤
12 ① ② ③ ④ ⑤   37 ① ② ③ ④ ⑤
13 ① ② ③ ④ ⑤   38 ① ② ③ ④ ⑤
14 ① ② ③ ④ ⑤   39 ① ② ③ ④ ⑤
15 ① ② ③ ④ ⑤   40 ① ② ③ ④ ⑤
16 ① ② ③ ④ ⑤   41 ① ② ③ ④ ⑤
17 ① ② ③ ④ ⑤   42 ① ② ③ ④ ⑤
18 ① ② ③ ④ ⑤   43 ① ② ③ ④ ⑤
19 ① ② ③ ④ ⑤   44 ① ② ③ ④ ⑤
20 ① ② ③ ④ ⑤   45 ① ② ③ ④ ⑤
21 ① ② ③ ④ ⑤   46 ① ② ③ ④ ⑤
22 ① ② ③ ④ ⑤   47 ① ② ③ ④ ⑤
23 ① ② ③ ④ ⑤   48 ① ② ③ ④ ⑤
24 ① ② ③ ④ ⑤   49 ① ② ③ ④ ⑤
25 ① ② ③ ④ ⑤   50 ① ② ③ ④ ⑤

Social Studies Test

Do not mark in this test booklet. Record your answers on the separate answer sheet provided. Be sure that all requested information is properly recorded on the answer sheet.

To record your answers, fill in the numbered circle on the answer sheet that corresponds to the answer you select for each question in the test booklet.

EXAMPLE:

Early colonists of North America looked for settlement sites with adequate water supplies and access by ship. For this reason, many early towns were built near

(1) mountains

(2) prairies

(3) rivers

(4) glaciers

(5) plateaus

(On Answer Sheet)

① ② ● ④ ⑤

The correct answer is "rivers"; therefore, answer space 3 would be marked on the answer sheet.

Do not rest the point of your pencil on the answer sheet while you are considering your answer. Make no stray or unnecessary marks. If you change an answer, erase your first mark completely. Mark only one answer space for each question; multiple answers will be scored as incorrect. Do not fold or crease your answer sheet. All test materials must be returned to the test administrator.

Note: Refer to Chapter 11 for the answers for this practice test.

DO NOT BEGIN TAKING THIS TEST UNTIL TOLD TO DO SO

Directions: Choose the one best answer to each question.

Questions 1 through 4 refer to the following passage, which is excerpted from CliffsQuickReview U.S. History I by P. Soifer and A. Hoffman (Wiley).

The First Inhabitants of the Western Hemisphere

In telling the history of the United States and also of the nations of the Western Hemisphere in general, historians have wrestled with the problem of what to call the hemisphere's first inhabitants. Under the mistaken impression he had reached the "Indies," explorer Christopher Columbus called the people he met "Indians." This was an error in identification that has persisted for more than five hundred years, for the inhabitants of North and South America had no collective name by which they called themselves.

Historians, anthropologists, and political activists have offered various names, none fully satisfactory. Anthropologists have used "aborigine," but the term suggests a primitive level of existence inconsistent with the cultural level of many tribes. Another term, "Amerindian," which combines Columbus's error with the name of another Italian explorer, Amerigo Vespucci (whose name was the source of "America"), lacks any historical context. Since the 1960s, "Native American" has come into popular favor, though some activists prefer "American Indian." In the absence of a truly representative term, descriptive references such as "native peoples" or "indigenous peoples," though vague, avoid European influence. In recent years, some argument has developed over whether to refer to tribes in the singular or plural — Apache or Apaches — with supporters on both sides demanding political correctness.

1. Why did Columbus call the native inhabitants "Indians"?

    (1) They were in the Western Hemisphere.

    (2) He thought he'd reached the Indies.

    (3) North and South America had not been discovered.

    (4) They were the hemisphere's first inhabitants.

    (5) He liked the sound of the name.

2. Who used the term "aborigine"?

    (1) historians

    (2) political activists

    (3) Columbus

    (4) anthropologists

    (5) explorers

3. What name has been favored since 1960?

    (1) Amerindian

    (2) Native American

    (3) native peoples

    (4) indigenous peoples

    (5) Indian

4. How was America named?

    (1) after an Italian explorer

    (2) after its first inhabitants

    (3) because of the European influence

    (4) after the native peoples

    (5) because of political correctness

Go on to next page

Questions 5 through 9 refer to the following passage, which is excerpted from
CliffsQuickReview U.S. History I *by P. Soifer and A. Hoffman (Wiley).*

The Voyages of Christopher Columbus

Christopher Columbus, a Genoese sailor, believed that sailing west across the Atlantic
Ocean was the shortest sea route to Asia. Ignorant of the fact that the Western Hemisphere
lay between Europe and Asia and assuming the earth's circumference to be a third less than
it actually is, he was convinced that Japan would appear on the horizon just three thousand
miles to the west. Like other seafarers of his day, Columbus was untroubled by political allegiances; he was ready to sail for whatever country would pay for his voyage. Either because
of his arrogance (he wanted ships and crews to be provided at no expense to himself) or
ambition (he insisted on governing the lands he discovered), he found it difficult to find a
patron. The Portuguese rejected his plan twice, and the rulers of England and France were
not interested. With influential supporters at court, Columbus convinced King Ferdinand
and Queen Isabella of Spain to partially underwrite his expedition. In 1492, Granada, the last
Muslim stronghold on the Iberian Peninsula, had fallen to the forces of the Spanish monarchs.
With the Reconquista complete and Spain a unified country, Ferdinand and Isabella could
turn their attention to overseas exploration.

5. Which direction did Columbus sail to reach
   Asia?

   (1) east

   (2) south

   (3) north

   (4) west

   (5) northwest

6. What did he assume the earth's circumference to be?

   (1) three thousand miles

   (2) between Europe and Asia

   (3) a third less than it was

   (4) shortest sea route to Asia

   (5) across the Atlantic Ocean

7. How did Columbus feel about politics?

   (1) He was not troubled.

   (2) He was troubled.

   (3) He was ready to sail.

   (4) He was arrogant.

   (5) He was ambitious.

8. Which country finally agreed to provide
   funds for his plan?

   (1) Portugal

   (2) England

   (3) France

   (4) Japan

   (5) Spain

9. How were Ferdinand and Isabella convinced by Columbus?

   (1) They now had a unified country.

   (2) The Muslims were defeated.

   (3) The English and French were not
       interested.

   (4) They were convinced by influential
       supporters at court.

   (5) They were ready for overseas
       exploration.

Go on to next page

Questions 10 through 15 refer to the following passage, which is excerpted from CliffsQuickReview U.S. History I *by P. Soifer and A. Hoffman (Wiley).*

Social Structure of the Thirteen Colonies

At the bottom of the social ladder were slaves and indentured servants; successful planters in the south and wealthy merchants in the north were the colonial elite. In the Chesapeake area, the signs of prosperity were visible in brick and mortar. The rather modest houses of even the most prosperous farmers of the seventeenth century had given way to spacious mansions in the eighteenth century. South Carolina planters often owned townhouses in Charleston and would probably have gone to someplace like Newport to escape the heat in summer. Both in their lifestyles and social pursuits (such as horse racing), the southern gentry emulated the English country squire.

Large landholders were not confined just to the southern colonies. The descendants of the Dutch patrons and the men who received lands from the English royal governors controlled estates in the middle colonies. Their farms were worked by tenant farmers, who received a share of the crop for their labor. In the northern cities, wealth was increasingly concentrated in the hands of the merchants; below them was the middle class of skilled craftsmen and shopkeepers. Craftsmen learned their trade as apprentices and became journeymen when their term of apprenticeship (as long as seven years) was completed. Even as wage earner, a journeyman often still lived with his former master and ate at his table. Saving enough money to go into business for himself was the dream of every journeyman.

10. Who were the elite at the top of the social ladder in the Colonies?

    (1) slaves and servants
    (2) apprentices and journeymen
    (3) horse racers
    (4) tenant farmers
    (5) planters and merchants

11. What were the South Carolina planters?

    (1) prosperous farmers
    (2) wealthy merchants
    (3) indentured servants
    (4) spacious mansions
    (5) city squires

12. Why would they go to Newport?

    (1) for horse racing
    (2) to find modest houses
    (3) to be near the sea
    (4) to escape the heat
    (5) for social pursuits

13. Who were the tenant farmers?

    (1) large landholders
    (2) those who worked for a share of the crops
    (3) royal governors who were appointed
    (4) Dutch patrons
    (5) southern colonials who inherited wealth

14. Who comprised the middle class?

    (1) noblemen
    (2) squires
    (3) merchants
    (4) patrons
    (5) shopkeepers and skilled craftsmen

15. What did a journeyman dream of?

    (1) seven years of apprenticeship
    (2) eating at the master's table
    (3) going into business himself
    (4) becoming a wage earner
    (5) saving his money

Go on to next page

Questions 16 through 20 refer to the following passage, which is excerpted from The Declaration of Independence, 1776.

Declaration of Independence

We hold these truths to be self-evident: that all men are created equal; that they are endowed by their Creator with certain inalienable rights; that among these are life, liberty, and the pursuit of happiness. That to secure these rights, governments are instituted among men, deriving their just powers from the consent of the governed; that whenever any form of government becomes destructive of these ends it is the right of the people to alter or to abolish it, and to institute a new government, laying its foundation on such principles, and organizing its powers in such form, as to them shall seem most likely to effect their safety and happiness. Prudence, indeed, will dictate that governments long established should not be changed for light and transient causes; and accordingly, all experience hath shown, that mankind are more disposed to suffer, while evils are sufferable, than to right themselves by abolishing the forms to which they are accustomed. But when a long train of abuses and usurpations, pursuing invariably the same object, evinces a design to reduce them under absolute despotism, it is their right, it is their duty, to throw off such government, and to provide new guards for their future security. Such has been the patient sufferance of these colonies; and such is now the necessity which constrains them to alter their former system of government. The history of the present king of Great Britain is a history of repeated injuries and usurpations, all having in direct object the establishment of an absolute tyranny over these states. To prove this, let facts be submitted to a candid world.

16. What truths were self-evident?

    (1) that all men are not created equal

    (2) that men don't have rights

    (3) that men are suffering

    (4) that men must exercise prudence

    (5) that men have certain rights

17. From where do governments get their power?

    (1) from the people

    (2) from the Creator

    (3) among men

    (4) from a new foundation

    (5) from the king

18. Why should a new government be instituted?

    (1) There were light and transient reasons.

    (2) It was long established.

    (3) The people were suffering.

    (4) There was concern for safety and happiness.

    (5) They needed to abolish the accustomed forms.

19. How does the Declaration of Independence describe the thirteen colonies?

    (1) king's injuries and usurpations

    (2) suffering patiently

    (3) absolute despotism

    (4) pursuing the same object

    (5) providing new guards

20. How does the Declaration of Independence describe the king of Great Britain?

    (1) He caused injuries.

    (2) He was a kindly ruler.

    (3) He was an absolute tyrant.

    (4) He was a friend of the people.

    (5) He guarded the people securely.

Go on to next page

Questions 21 through 23 refer to the following political cartoon.

21. How does the cartoon depict the use of cellphones?

    (1) wonderful invention

    (2) aid to communication

    (3) medical breakthrough

    (4) useful appliance

    (5) injurious to health

22. How would you best describe the cellphone user in the cartoon?

    (1) foolhardy

    (2) talkative

    (3) considerate

    (4) courageous

    (5) cowardly

23. How do we know that cellphones may represent a risk to health?

    (1) going to the movies

    (2) scientific research

    (3) urban legends

    (4) popular opinion

    (5) crime reports

Go on to next page

Questions 24 through 26 refer to the following passage, which is excerpted from CliffsQuickReview U.S. History I by P. Soifer and A. Hoffman (Wiley).

Resistance to Slavery

Resistance to slavery took several forms. Slaves would pretend to be ill, refuse to work, do their jobs poorly, destroy farm equipment, set fire to buildings, and steal food. These were all individual acts rather than part of an organized plan for revolt, but the objective was to upset the routine of the plantation in any way possible. On some plantations, slaves could bring grievances about harsh treatment from an overseer to their master and hope that he would intercede on their behalf. Although many slaves tried to run away, few succeeded for more than a few days, and they often returned on their own. Such escapes were more a protest — a demonstration that it could be done — than a dash for freedom. As advertisements in southern newspapers seeking the return of runaway slaves made clear, the goal of most runaways was to find their wives or children who had been sold to another planter. The fabled underground railroad, a series of safe houses for runaways organized by abolitionists and run by former slaves like Harriet Tubman, actually helped only about a thousand slaves reach the North.

24. Why did the slaves refuse to work?

    (1) They were ill.

    (2) They did their jobs poorly.

    (3) They destroyed farm equipment.

    (4) They longed to be free.

    (5) They stole food.

25. What did running away represent?

    (1) a form of protest

    (2) a grievance about ill treatment

    (3) an upset to the routines

    (4) an appeal to the master

    (5) being sold to another planter

26. Who organized the underground railroad?

    (1) Harriet Tubman

    (2) former slaves

    (3) abolitionists

    (4) runaways

    (5) southern newspapers

Go on to next page

Questions 27 through 30 refer to the following report.

Weather and Traffic Report

Good morning and welcome to America's weather and traffic on WAWT, the voice of the world in the ear of the nation. Today is going to be hot. That's H-O-T, and we all know what that means. The big "P" is coming back for a visit. We are going to have pollution today for sure. With our record heat today on each coast, there is a problem. If you think that it's hot here, it's even hotter up higher. And that means unhealthy air leading to unhealthy people. I can hear the coughs and sneezes coast to coast. I think I hear a whole series of gasps from our nation's capital, good ol' Washington D.C., and it's not Congress that is producing all that hot air. And out in western California, it's just as bad. Just the other day, I looked up "poor air quality" in the dictionary, and it said "see California." Lots of luck breathing out there.

This morning, once again, there's a layer of hot air just above ground level. That's where we live — ground level. This air acts like a closed gate, and it keeps the surface air from going up and mixing. Of course, we are all going to drive our cars all day in heavy traffic, and some of us will go to work in factories. And, surprise — by afternoon, all those pollutants from the cars mix with the emissions from the factories and get trapped by the layer of hot air, and it's try-to-catch-your-breath time. Unhealthy air is here again. Tomorrow and every day after, we'll probably have more of the same until we learn to take care of our environment.

Well, I'll see you tomorrow, if the air's not too thick to see through.

27. When is the worst time for pollution?
    (1) in the morning
    (2) in the afternoon
    (3) late at night
    (4) before breakfast
    (5) after dinner

28. What are the main sources of pollution?
    (1) record heat
    (2) air rising and mixing
    (3) unhealthy air quality
    (4) exhausts and emissions
    (5) warmer air aloft

29. Where will pollution be most serious?
    (1) the Midwest
    (2) the Deep South
    (3) up north
    (4) the East and West coasts
    (5) near the Great Lakes

30. What is the best way to prevent pollution?
    (1) Change the temperature.
    (2) Reduce emissions.
    (3) Get rid of the hot air layer.
    (4) Prevent air from rising.
    (5) Keep warmer temperatures aloft.

Go on to next page

> Questions 31 through 35 refer to the following passage, which is excerpted from
> CliffsQuickReview U.S. History II *by P. Soifer and A. Hoffman (Wiley).*

The End of the Cold War

In July 1989, Gorbachev repudiated the Brezhnev Doctrine, which had justified the intervention of the Soviet Union in the affairs of communist countries. Within a few months of his statement, the Communist regimes in Eastern Europe collapsed — Poland, Hungary, and Czechoslovakia, followed by Bulgaria and Romania. The Berlin Wall came down in November 1989, and East and West Germany were reunited within the year. Czechoslovakia eventually split into the Czech Republic and Slovakia with little trouble, but the end of the Yugoslav Federation in 1991 led to years of violence and ethnic cleansing (the expulsion of an ethnic population from a geographic area), particularly in Bosnia-Herzegovina. The Soviet Union also broke up, not long after an attempted coup against Gorbachev in August 1991, and the Baltic states of Latvia, Estonia, and Lithuania were the first to gain their independence. That December, Gorbachev stepped down, and the old Soviet Union became the Commonwealth of Independent States (CIS). The CIS quickly disappeared, and the republics that had once made up the Soviet Union were recognized as sovereign nations. The end of the Cold War led directly to major nuclear weapons reduction agreements between President Bush and the Russian leaders, as well as significant cutbacks in the number of troops the United States committed to the defense of NATO.

31. Who or what caused the end of the Cold War?

    (1) the Soviet Union

    (2) Communist regimes

    (3) Gorbachev

    (4) Brezhnev

    (5) Eastern Europe

32. How were East and West Germany reunited?

    (1) the fall of the Berlin Wall

    (2) intervention of the Soviet Union

    (3) the Brezhnev Doctrine

    (4) the collapse of regimes

    (5) intervention of the United States

33. What is ethnic cleansing?

    (1) years of violence

    (2) the end of the Yugoslav Federation

    (3) expelling populations

    (4) the split of Czechoslovakia

    (5) the breakup of the Soviet Union

34. What happened to the republics of the Soviet Union?

    (1) They quickly disappeared.

    (2) They joined NATO.

    (3) They became the CNS.

    (4) They joined the Baltic states.

    (5) They became sovereign nations.

35. What was one of the results of the end of the Cold War?

    (1) more nuclear weapons

    (2) more tension between the United States and the former Soviet Union

    (3) no agreements between leaders

    (4) an increase in U.S. troops

    (5) cutbacks in U.S. troops

Go on to next page

> *Questions 36 through 40 refer to the following passage, which is excerpted from*
> CliffsQuickReview U.S. History I *by P. Soifer and A. Hoffman (Wiley).*

The Panic of 1873

During his second term, Grant was still unable to curb the graft in his administration, Secretary of War William Belknap was impeached by the House, and he resigned in disgrace for taking bribes from dishonest Indian agents. The president's personal secretary was involved with the Whiskey Ring, a group of distillers who evaded paying internal revenue taxes. A much more pressing concern though was the state of the economy.

In 1873, over-speculation in railroad stocks led to a major economic panic. The failure of Jay Cooke's investment bank was followed by the collapse of the stock market and the bankruptcy of thousands of businesses; crop prices plummeted and unemployment soared. Much of the problem was related to the use of greenbacks for currency. Hard-money advocates insisted that paper money had to be backed by gold to curb inflation and level price fluctuations, but farmers and manufacturers, who needed easy credit, wanted even more greenbacks put in circulation, a policy that Grant ultimately opposed. He recommended and the Congress enacted legislation in 1875 providing for the redemption of greenbacks in gold. Because the Treasury needed time to build up its gold reserves, redemption did not go into effect for another four years, by which time the longest depression in American history had come to an end.

36. What were the main problems President Grant had in his second term with his government?

    (1) problems with his administration

    (2) problems with whiskey

    (3) problems with the IRS

    (4) problems with personal bankruptcy

    (5) problems with his wife

37. What was the cause of the Panic of 1873?

    (1) investment failure

    (2) bankruptcy

    (3) over-speculation

    (4) tax evasion

    (5) economic panic

38. What type of money was used for investment?

    (1) British pounds

    (2) silver

    (3) gold

    (4) inflation

    (5) greenbacks

39. What followed the failure of Jay Cooke's bank?

    (1) collapse of the stock market

    (2) increase in market value

    (3) business profitability

    (4) rising crop prices

    (5) soaring employment

40. How did Congress end the depression?

    (1) It provided easy credit.

    (2) It leveled prices.

    (3) It built up gold reserves.

    (4) It hoarded greenbacks.

    (5) It curbed inflation.

Go on to next page

Questions 41 through 45 refer to the following tables.

Comparison of Gross Domestic Product

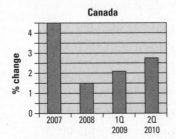

Canada

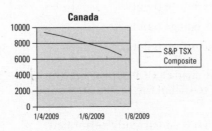

Comparison of Major Indexes

Canada

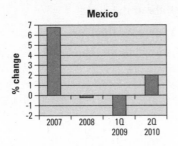

Mexico

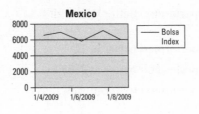

Mexico

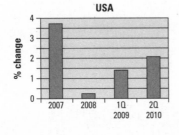

USA

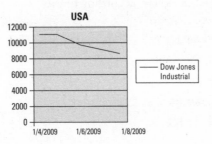

USA

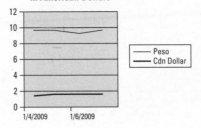

Comparison of Value of Canadian Dollar and Mexican Peso in American Dollars

Go on to next page

41. By how much did the Mexican gross domestic product (GDP) outperform the U.S. GDP in the year 2007?

    (1) 8.4 percentage points

    (2) 2.8 percentage points

    (3) 0.7 percentage points

    (4) 5.9 percentage points

    (5) 1.3 percentage points

42. Why does Canada's GDP appear healthy as compared to that of the United States and Mexico?

    (1) Canada has consistently performed well.

    (2) Canada performed better than it did in 2Q.

    (3) Canada performed better in 1Q.

    (4) Canada performed better in 2008.

    (5) Canada performed better in 2007.

43. How did the Canadian dollar perform against the U.S. dollar, according to the graph?

    (1) moved higher

    (2) stayed the same

    (3) lost ground

    (4) finished even

    (5) changed a lot

44. How did the S&P TSX Composite Index compare on 1/4/2009 and 1/8/2009?

    (1) down almost 2,000

    (2) up about 1,000

    (3) about the same

    (4) up less than 300

    (5) down more than 3,000

45. According to the graph, how did the Dow Jones compare on 1/4/2009 and 1/8/2009?

    (1) down more than 5,000

    (2) up more than 1,000

    (3) about the same

    (4) up more than 300

    (5) down more than 2,000

Go on to next page

Questions 46 through 50 refer to the following political cartoon.

46. What is the setting for the cartoon?

    (1) living room
    (2) laboratory
    (3) playroom
    (4) library
    (5) kitchen

47. What problem has the researcher been studying?

    (1) the common cold
    (2) a rare blood disease
    (3) vision
    (4) hair loss
    (5) limited patents for medicines

48. How does the cartoonist depict drug companies?

    (1) caring
    (2) religious
    (3) greedy
    (4) generous
    (5) curious

49. Why is this solution important for the drug companies?

    (1) to share with all people
    (2) to make their employees famous
    (3) for good public relations
    (4) to make them look good to their customers
    (5) to increase their profits

50. What is the theme of the cartoon?

    (1) greed
    (2) inventing
    (3) curiosity
    (4) diligence
    (5) patience

END OF TEST

Chapter 11

Answers and Explanations for the Social Studies Test

· ·

*A*fter taking the Social Studies Test in Chapter 10, use this chapter to check your answers. Take your time as you move through the explanations of the answers that we provide in the first section. They can help you understand why you missed the answers you did. You may also want to read the explanations for the questions you answered correctly because doing so can give you a better understanding of the thought process that helped you choose the correct answers.

If you're short on time, turn to the end of the chapter for an abbreviated answer key.

Analysis of the Answers

1. **2.** Columbus thought he had reached the Indies when he landed in North America, so he called the natives "Indians." The other answers — the natives' being in the Western Hemisphere, the fact that the Americas hadn't been discovered yet, the natives' being the hemisphere's first inhabitants, or Columbus's liking the sound of the name — just don't make sense as reasons.

2. **4.** Anthropologists coined the term *aborigine*. Historians, activists, Columbus, or explorers may also have used the term, but according to the passage, *anthropologists* is the correct answer.

3. **2.** In the 1960s, after much debate, *Native American* was chosen as the name for the indigenous peoples. Other terms, such as Indian, Amerindian, native peoples, and indigenous peoples, were discarded.

4. **1.** According to the passage, America was named after Italian explorer Amerigo Vespucci rather than Christopher Columbus, who discovered the lands.

5. **4.** According to the passage, Columbus sailed west to cross the Atlantic Ocean in search of Asia.

6. **3.** Columbus thought the circumference was a third less than it really was. The other answers are incorrect, according to the passage.

7. **1.** Columbus was not troubled about political allegiances. He would sail for any country that was willing to pay for the trip. The other choices — that he was troubled, arrogant, ready to sail, or ambitious — don't refer to political allegiances.

8. **5.** Columbus finally got partial funding from the king and queen of Spain. Portugal, England, France, and Japan didn't provide any funding.

9. **4.** Columbus convinced Ferdinand and Isabella to fund the voyage by using influential supporters at court. The other answers — that they had a unified country, the Muslims were defeated, the English and French weren't interested, and they were ready for exploration — aren't the best answers.

10. **5.** The passage states that planters and merchants were the colonial elite. Slaves, servants, apprentices, journeymen, and tenant farmers were lower on the ladder. Horse racers aren't mentioned in the passage.

11. **1.** South Carolina planters were prosperous farmers. The term *planters* refers to farming as a way of making a living, so they weren't merchants or servants, which are other occupations. City squires aren't mentioned in the passage. Mansions are buildings, not people.

12. **4.** They went to Newport to escape the summer's heat. Other possible choices, such as horse racing, to find modest houses, to be near the sea, or social pursuits, may make sense (and may even be true), but the passage doesn't describe them as the best reason.

13. **2.** Tenant farmers worked for a share of the crops they produced. They weren't landholders, governors, patrons, or colonials, none of whom are involved with actual farming.

14. **5.** You must read the passage slowly and carefully to determine that shopkeepers and skilled craftsmen were in the middle class. (Note that the passage then breaks down the group of skilled craftsmen into two categories: *apprentices,* who worked with another skilled craftsman for as many as seven years, and *journeymen,* who had completed their apprenticeships.) The passage doesn't mention noblemen, squires, merchants, or patrons.

15. **3.** Each journeyman dreamed of having his own business someday. Other choices, such as having a seven-year apprenticeship, eating at the master's table, becoming a wage earner, and saving money, may have some validity, but according to the passage, they aren't the best answers.

16. **5.** The passage lists two self-evident truths: that all men are created equal and that the Creator endowed men with certain rights. (*Self-evident* means evident without need of explanation or proof.)

17. **1.** According to the passage, governments were to get their power from the people. Getting power from the Creator, among men, from a new foundation, and from the king are incorrect answers, according to the passage.

18. **3.** The people were suffering because of evils of the old government, which was the main reason why they sought a new government. The other answers may have some truth to them, but they aren't the main reason, according to the passage.

19. **2.** The colonies had been suffering patiently. The other choices — king's injuries, despotism, same object, and new guards — don't refer directly to the colonies.

20. **3.** George III had become an absolute tyrant. He was neither a kindly ruler nor a friend of the people. Having caused injuries and guarded securely aren't the best answers.

21. **5.** Some researchers believe cellphones are injurious to your health, particularly if they damage the brain or cause accidents while driving. The other answers — wonderful invention, aid to communication, medical breakthrough, and useful appliance — are all factors, but they aren't the ones depicted in the cartoon.

22. **1.** The cellphone user is foolhardy in that he's driving dangerously by not paying enough attention to the road. Other choices, such as considerate and courageous, are incorrect. Talkative and cowardly aren't the best answers, according to the cartoon.

23. **2.** Some scientific research indicates that cellphones may represent a risk to health (radiation and brain tumors, for example). Movies, legends, opinion, and reports aren't correct choices, according to the cartoon.

24. **4.** Refusing to work was the main way slaves showed that they longed to be free. Illness, poor jobs, destroyed equipment, and stolen food may have been other ways they showed their frustration, but, according to the passage, those answers aren't as important.

25. **1.** Running away represented a form of protest. Other factors, including taking out grievances, upsetting routines, appealing to the master, or being sold, weren't nearly as strong as protesting.

26. **3.** The underground railroad was organized by the abolitionists. Other possible players, such as Harriet Tubman, former slaves, runaways, and Southern newspapers, may have been involved, but, according to the passage, they weren't the organizers.

27. **2.** Pollution tends to be at its worst in the afternoon when exhausts and emissions are trapped. According to the passage, other times of day don't have as much pollution.

28. **4.** Exhausts and emissions are the main sources of pollution. Other answers, such as record heat, air rising, unhealthy air, and warmer air, are factors, but they aren't the most important ones.

29. **4.** Pollution tends to be most serious on the East and West coasts. The passage doesn't mention the other locations — Midwest, Deep South, up north, and near the Great Lakes.

30. **2.** Pollution can best be prevented by reducing emissions. The other choices (changing the temperature, eliminating the hot air layer, preventing air from rising, and keeping warmer temperatures aloft) may contribute, but they aren't the best answers.

31. **3.** Gorbachev ended the Cold War when he repudiated the Brezhnev Doctrine. Communist regimes, Brezhnev, Eastern Europe, and the Soviet Union are incorrect answers.

32. **1.** When the Berlin Wall fell, East and West Germany were once again united. Soviet intervention, the Brezhnev Doctrine, regimes collapsing, and U.S. intervention may have existed, but they aren't the best answers according to the passage.

33. **3.** According to the passage, *ethnic cleansing* refers to the expulsion of minority ethnic populations. The other answers are incorrect because they don't refer specifically to how people were expelled.

34. **5.** The former Soviet republics became sovereign nations. According to the passage, the Soviet republics didn't disappear, weren't invited to join NATO, and didn't become the Baltic States. The passage doesn't mention anything called CNS.

35. **5.** All the factors except Choice (5) are the opposite of what the last sentence of the passage states, so Choice (5) is the only correct answer.

36. **1.** The main problems President Grant faced involved grafts in his administration, which means that members of his administration faced all sorts of problems and left their jobs under pressure. The other answers are incorrect, based on the passage.

37. **3.** Over-speculation in railroad stocks led to the Panic of 1873. Other factors, such as investment failure, bankruptcy, tax evasion, and economic panic may have also occurred, but they didn't directly cause the Panic of 1873.

38. **5.** Greenbacks — not British pounds, gold, or silver — were used as a source of investment capital. Inflation has nothing to do with the question.

39. **1.** The failure of Cooke's bank was followed by a collapse of the stock market. The other answers are the opposite of what happened, according to the passage.

40. **3.** The main way Congress ended the depression was to build up its gold reserves. Credit, prices, greenbacks, and inflation didn't have as much to do with the end of the depression.

41. **2.** The Mexican GDP was 2.8 percentage points higher than the U.S. GDP. The other answers are simply incorrect, according to the graphs.

42. **1.** According to the GDP graphs, Canada's economy has consistently performed well when compared to the economies of the United States and Mexico.

43. **2.** The value of the Canadian dollar is a straight line, which means its value stayed the same.

44. **5.** On 1/4/2009, the index was just under 10,000, and on 1/8/2009, it was above 6,000. Thus, Choice (5) is the most correct.

45. **5.** The Dow Jones was down by more than 2,000 points, from around 11,000 to around 9,000, which makes Choice (5) the correct answer.

46. **2.** The setting for the cartoon is a laboratory, not a living room, playroom, library, or kitchen.

47. **5.** The researcher has been studying limited patents for medicines. You can tell this from the phrase *perpetual patents*.

48. **3.** The cartoonist depicts drug companies as greedy. Drug companies may also be caring or generous, but the cartoon doesn't suggest this. Drug companies certainly aren't religious, and the term *curious* just doesn't make sense in this context.

49. **5.** The solution is important for the drug companies because it will increase their profits. Other potential effects — sharing with people, making employees famous, improving public relations, and looking good — may all be important to people, but they aren't the primary reason for wanting the solution.

50. **1.** The overall theme of the cartoon is the greed of the drug companies.

Answer Key

1. **2**	18. **3**	35. **5**
2. **4**	19. **2**	36. **1**
3. **2**	20. **3**	37. **3**
4. **1**	21. **5**	38. **5**
5. **4**	22. **1**	39. **1**
6. **3**	23. **2**	40. **3**
7. **1**	24. **4**	41. **2**
8. **5**	25. **1**	42. **1**
9. **4**	26. **3**	43. **2**
10. **5**	27. **2**	44. **5**
11. **1**	28. **4**	45. **5**
12. **4**	29. **4**	46. **2**
13. **2**	30. **2**	47. **5**
14. **5**	31. **3**	48. **3**
15. **3**	32. **1**	49. **5**
16. **5**	33. **3**	50. **1**
17. **1**	34. **5**	

Chapter 12

Another Practice Test — Social Studies Test

. . . .

*T*he Social Studies Test consists of multiple-choice questions that measure general social studies concepts. The questions are based on short readings that often include a map, graph, chart, political cartoon, or figure. Study the information given and then answer the question(s) following it. Refer to the information as often as necessary in answering the questions.

You have 70 minutes to answer the 50 questions in this test. Work carefully, but do not spend too much time on any one question. Be sure you answer every question.

Answer Sheet for Social Studies Test

1 ① ② ③ ④ ⑤
2 ① ② ③ ④ ⑤
3 ① ② ③ ④ ⑤
4 ① ② ③ ④ ⑤
5 ① ② ③ ④ ⑤
6 ① ② ③ ④ ⑤
7 ① ② ③ ④ ⑤
8 ① ② ③ ④ ⑤
9 ① ② ③ ④ ⑤
10 ① ② ③ ④ ⑤
11 ① ② ③ ④ ⑤
12 ① ② ③ ④ ⑤
13 ① ② ③ ④ ⑤
14 ① ② ③ ④ ⑤
15 ① ② ③ ④ ⑤
16 ① ② ③ ④ ⑤
17 ① ② ③ ④ ⑤
18 ① ② ③ ④ ⑤
19 ① ② ③ ④ ⑤
20 ① ② ③ ④ ⑤
21 ① ② ③ ④ ⑤
22 ① ② ③ ④ ⑤
23 ① ② ③ ④ ⑤
24 ① ② ③ ④ ⑤
25 ① ② ③ ④ ⑤

26 ① ② ③ ④ ⑤
27 ① ② ③ ④ ⑤
28 ① ② ③ ④ ⑤
29 ① ② ③ ④ ⑤
30 ① ② ③ ④ ⑤
31 ① ② ③ ④ ⑤
32 ① ② ③ ④ ⑤
33 ① ② ③ ④ ⑤
34 ① ② ③ ④ ⑤
35 ① ② ③ ④ ⑤
36 ① ② ③ ④ ⑤
37 ① ② ③ ④ ⑤
38 ① ② ③ ④ ⑤
39 ① ② ③ ④ ⑤
40 ① ② ③ ④ ⑤
41 ① ② ③ ④ ⑤
42 ① ② ③ ④ ⑤
43 ① ② ③ ④ ⑤
44 ① ② ③ ④ ⑤
45 ① ② ③ ④ ⑤
46 ① ② ③ ④ ⑤
47 ① ② ③ ④ ⑤
48 ① ② ③ ④ ⑤
49 ① ② ③ ④ ⑤
50 ① ② ③ ④ ⑤

Social Studies Test

Do not mark in this test booklet. Record your answers on the separate answer sheet provided. Be sure that all requested information is properly recorded on the answer sheet.

To record your answers, fill in the numbered circle on the answer sheet that corresponds to the answer you select for each question in the test booklet.

EXAMPLE:

Early colonists of North America looked for settlement sites with adequate water supplies and access by ship. For this reason, many early towns were built near

(1) mountains

(2) prairies

(3) rivers

(4) glaciers

(5) plateaus

(On Answer Sheet)

① ② ● ④ ⑤

The correct answer is "rivers"; therefore, answer space 3 would be marked on the answer sheet.

Do not rest the point of your pencil on the answer sheet while you are considering your answer. Make no stray or unnecessary marks. If you change an answer, erase your first mark completely. Mark only one answer space for each question; multiple answers will be scored as incorrect. Do not fold or crease your answer sheet. All test materials must be returned to the test administrator.

Note: Refer to Chapter 13 for the answers for this practice test.

DO NOT BEGIN TAKING THIS TEST UNTIL TOLD TO DO SO

Directions: Choose the <u>one best answer</u> to each question.

Questions 1 through 5 refer to the following passage, which is excerpted from CliffsQuickReview U.S. History I *by P. Soifer and A. Hoffman (Wiley).*

Industry and Trade in the Thirteen Colonies

The colonies were part of an Atlantic trading network that linked them with England, Africa, and the West Indies. The pattern of commerce, not too accurately called the Triangular Trade, involved the exchange of products from colonial farms, plantations, fisheries, and forests with England for manufactured goods and the West Indies for slaves, molasses, and sugar. In New England, molasses and sugar were distilled into rum, which was used to buy African slaves. Southern Europe was also a valuable market for colonial foodstuffs.

Colonial industry was closely associated with trade. A significant percentage of Atlantic shipping was on vessels built in the colonies, and shipbuilding stimulated other crafts, such as the sewing of sails, milling of lumber, and manufacturing of naval stores. Mercantile theory encouraged the colonies to provide raw materials for England's industrializing economy; pig iron and coal became important exports. Concurrently, restrictions were placed on finished goods. For example, Parliament, concerned about possible competition from colonial hatters, prohibited the export of hats from one colony to another and limited the number of apprentices in each hatmaker's shop.

1. What did England, Africa, and the West Indies have in common?

    (1) They all had fisheries.

    (2) They all bought slaves.

    (3) They all distilled rum.

    (4) They all had forests.

    (5) They all exchanged products.

2. What was rum used for?

    (1) colonial farms

    (2) milling of lumber

    (3) purchase of slaves

    (4) molasses and sugar

    (5) manufactured goods

3. Why were the colonies important to Atlantic trade?

    (1) They built the ships.

    (2) They sewed sails.

    (3) They had naval stores.

    (4) They milled lumber.

    (5) They stimulated other crafts.

4. How did the colonies support British industry?

    (1) They took part in sewing.

    (2) They produced finished goods.

    (3) They developed mercantile theory.

    (4) They provided raw materials.

    (5) They set up restrictions.

5. What product was threatened by colonial competition?

    (1) coal

    (2) pig iron

    (3) hats

    (4) lumber

    (5) cotton

Go on to next page ⟹

Questions 6 through 11 refer to the following passage, which is excerpted from The Declaration of Independence, 1776.

Charges against the King

He has forbidden his governors to pass laws of immediate and pressing importance, unless suspended in their operation till his assent should be obtained; and when so suspended, he has utterly neglected to attend to them.

He has refused to pass other laws for the accommodation of large districts of people, unless those people would relinquish the right of representation in the legislature — a right inestimable to them, and formidable to tyrants only.

He has called together legislative bodies at places unusual, uncomfortable, and distant from the depository of their public records, for the sole purpose of fatiguing them into compliance with his measures.

He has dissolved representative houses repeatedly, for opposing, with manly firmness, his invasions on the rights of the people.

He has refused, for a long time after such dissolutions, to cause others to be elected; whereby the legislative powers, incapable of annihilation, have returned to the people at large, for their exercise, the state remaining in the meantime exposed to all the dangers of invasion from without, and convulsions within.

He has endeavored to prevent the population of these states; for that purpose obstructing the laws for naturalization of foreigners; refusing to pass others to encourage their migration hither, and raising the conditions of new appropriations of lands.

He has obstructed the administration of justice, by refusing his assent to laws for establishing judiciary powers.

He has made judges dependent on his will alone, for the tenure of their offices, and the amount and payment of their salaries.

He has erected a multitude of new offices, and sent hither swarms of officers, to harass our people, and eat out their substance.

He has kept among us, in times of peace, standing armies, without the consent of our legislature.

He has affected to render the military independent of, and superior to, the civil power.

Go on to next page

6. What is one way that the king neglected the colonies?

    (1) lacked money

    (2) failed to pass laws

    (3) removed their right of condemnation

    (4) gave power to his governors

    (5) didn't visit the colonies

7. How did the king treat the legislative bodies?

    (1) He never called them together.

    (2) He made them comfortable.

    (3) He made sure they were well rested.

    (4) He made them comply with his wishes.

    (5) He deposited their records.

8. How did the king threaten the rights of the people?

    (1) He dissolved representative houses.

    (2) He abdicated the throne.

    (3) He annihilated them.

    (4) He returned them to the people.

    (5) He was ambitious.

9. How did the king feel about adding to the population of the colonies?

    (1) He gave away free land to people willing to settle.

    (2) He encouraged people to settle.

    (3) He settled there himself.

    (4) He sent his son over to settle.

    (5) He discouraged people from settling.

10. How did the king obstruct the judicial system?

    (1) He made it independent of his authority.

    (2) He erected new offices.

    (3) He refused to enact certain laws.

    (4) He harassed the people.

    (5) He paid for houses.

11. What was one way the freedom of the people was threatened?

    (1) a dependent military

    (2) an independent military

    (3) civil authority

    (4) a tea party

    (5) friendly officers

Go on to next page

> *Questions 12 through 17 refer to the following passage, which is excerpted from* CliffsQuickReview U.S. History I *by P. Soifer and A. Hoffman (Wiley).*

The War of 1812

For the United States, the most obvious British target was Canada. Its population was small, many Canadians were actually Americans by birth, and a quick victory there would stop British plans to ruin American trade. The military facts painted a different picture, however. Thousands of Native Americans in the northwestern territories sided with the British when the war began, bolstering their strength, while the small U.S. army was composed of poorly trained state militiamen led by elderly and incompetent generals.

In July 1812, an American army led by General William Hull moved from Detroit into Canada. Almost immediately the Shawnee cut his supply lines, forcing him back to Detroit. Although Hull commanded two thousand men, he surrendered to a considerably smaller British and Native American force. Other embarrassments followed as the United States suffered defeat at Queenston Heights in western New York and the militia under General Henry Dearborn refused to march to Montreal from northeastern New York.

The United States fared better on Lake Erie in 1813. The Royal Navy could not reach the lake from the St. Lawrence River, so both the British and Americans raced to build ships on opposite sides of the lake. On September 10, 1813, the small American fleet under Oliver Hazard Perry defeated the British in the Battle of Lake Erie. "We have met the enemy, and they are ours," he reported, a victory statement that became legendary.

Less than three weeks later, on October 5, William Henry Harrison (a general by then) defeated a combined British and Native American force at the Battle of the Thames. Tecumseh was killed in this battle, ending Native Americans' hopes for a coalition that could stand against the advance of U.S. settlement. Despite these victories, U.S. efforts to capture Canada ended in a stalemate.

Go on to next page

12. Why was Canada a target for the United States?

    (1) Its citizens were American by birth.

    (2) It had a large population.

    (3) It was a British possession.

    (4) Americans had visited Canada many times.

    (5) It would protect American trade.

13. Whom did Native Americans support in the conflict?

    (1) the British

    (2) the Canadians

    (3) the Americans

    (4) the U.S. army

    (5) the French

14. Why did General Hull surrender?

    (1) He was forced back to Detroit.

    (2) He commanded only two thousand men.

    (3) He couldn't cross the Thames.

    (4) The British force was too strong.

    (5) His supply lines were cut.

15. What did Queenston Heights represent for the United States?

    (1) a victory

    (2) an embarrassment

    (3) a proposal

    (4) a refusal to march

    (5) a lot of suffering

16. What kept the Royal Navy fleet from Lake Erie?

    (1) the St. Lawrence River

    (2) the Detroit River

    (3) Lake Ontario

    (4) Lake St. Clair

    (5) not enough information given

17. What was the result of the War of 1812?

    (1) The Americans won.

    (2) The British won.

    (3) It ended in a stalemate.

    (4) The Native Americans won.

    (5) Tecumseh was killed.

Go on to next page

Questions 18 through 23 refer to the following passage, which is excerpted from Lincoln's Gettysburg Address, November 19, 1863.

Gettysburg Address

Four score and seven years ago our fathers brought forth upon this continent a new nation, conceived in liberty and dedicated to the proposition that all men are created equal. Now we are engaged in a great civil war, testing whether that nation or any nation so conceived and so dedicated can long endure. We are met on a great battle-field of that war. We have come to dedicate a portion of that field as a final resting place for those who here gave their lives that that nation might live. It is altogether fitting and proper that we should do this. But, in a larger sense, we cannot dedicate, we cannot consecrate, we cannot hallow this ground. The brave men, living and dead, who struggled here have consecrated it far above our poor power to add or detract. The world will little note nor long remember what we say here, but it can never forget what they did here . . . .

18. What issues were of primary importance in a great civil war?

    (1) happiness and friendship

    (2) safety and security

    (3) liberty and equality

    (4) wealth and greed

    (5) peace and prosperity

19. Where was President Lincoln's speech delivered?

    (1) on a train

    (2) at the White House

    (3) in a playground

    (4) on a battlefield

    (5) on the radio

20. What does "little note nor long remember" mean?

    (1) The audience is not taking notes.

    (2) The TV crews are getting in the way.

    (3) Lincoln has a bad memory.

    (4) The soldiers are not there to hear the speech.

    (5) People around the world will not remember the speech.

21. What will a portion of the battlefield be used for?

    (1) burial ground

    (2) athletic field

    (3) cow pasture

    (4) shopping area

    (5) farming

22. Who has "hallow[ed] this ground"?

    (1) President Lincoln

    (2) the U.S. government

    (3) the Confederate government

    (4) the Union government

    (5) those who fought there

23. What does "four score and seven" probably refer to?

    (1) soldiers

    (2) consecration

    (3) time

    (4) the war

    (5) speeches

Go on to next page

> Questions *24 through 29 refer to the following passage, which is excerpted from* CliffsQuickReview U.S. History II *by P. Soifer and A. Hoffman (Wiley).*

Causes of World War I

On June 28, 1914, a Serbian nationalist assassinated the Archduke Franz Ferdinand, the heir to the throne of Austria-Hungary. Austria demanded indemnities from Serbia for the assassination. The Serbian government denied any involvement with the murder and, when Austria issued an ultimatum, turned to its ally, Russia, for help. When Russia began to mobilize its army, Europe's alliance system, ironically intended to maintain the balance of power on the continent, drew one country after another into war. Austria's ally, Germany, declared war on Russia on August 1 and on France (which was allied with Russia) two days later. Great Britain entered the war on August 4, following Germany's invasion of neutral Belgium. By the end of August 1914, most of Europe had chosen sides: the Central Powers — Germany, Austria-Hungary, Bulgaria, and the Ottoman Empire (Turkey) — were up against the Allied Powers — principally Great Britain, France, Russia, and Serbia. Japan joined the Allied cause in August 1914, in hopes of seizing German possessions in the Pacific and expanding Japanese influence in China. This action threatened the Open Door Policy and led to increased tensions with the United States. Originally an ally of Germany and Austria-Hungary, Italy entered the war in 1915 on the side of Britain and France because they had agreed to Italian territorial demands in a secret treaty (the Treaty of London).

24. Where did the assassin of Archduke Ferdinand originate?

    (1) Great Britain

    (2) France

    (3) Russia

    (4) Serbia

    (5) Germany

25. How did Austria initially react to the assassination?

    (1) denied any involvement

    (2) demanded indemnities

    (3) turned to its ally

    (4) declared war

    (5) mobilized its army

26. Which countries were not allies?

    (1) Serbia and Russia

    (2) Austria and Hungary

    (3) Germany and France

    (4) France and Great Britain

    (5) Germany and Austria

27. What caused Great Britain to enter the war?

    (1) Germany invaded Belgium

    (2) Russia attacked Serbia

    (3) France invaded Russia

    (4) Austria invaded Hungary

    (5) Germany attacked Russia

28. Which country was not an Allied Power?

    (1) Great Britain

    (2) France

    (3) Germany

    (4) Russia

    (5) Serbia

29. Why did Italy join the Allies?

    (1) the Open Door Policy

    (2) increased tensions

    (3) business demands

    (4) the expanding Japanese influence

    (5) the Treaty of London

Go on to next page

Questions 30 through 33 refer to the following political cartoon.

30. How is President Barack Obama portrayed in the cartoon?

    (1) stand-up comedian

    (2) inspiring teacher

    (3) stern disciplinarian

    (4) fashion model

    (5) super salesman

31. How are most of the young people being portrayed?

    (1) bored

    (2) disruptive

    (3) lazy

    (4) inattentive

    (5) eager to learn

32. What is the main message the cartoonist wishes to convey?

    (1) America faces many problems.

    (2) Schools aren't very effective.

    (3) Barack Obama has a nice smile.

    (4) The president has all the answers.

    (5) Classroom behavior is a concern.

33. What problems are the students facing in the future?

    (1) unemployment

    (2) shortage of energy

    (3) escalating debt

    (4) conflict in the Middle East

    (5) all of the above

Go on to next page

Questions 34 through 37 refer to the following passage, which is excerpted from CliffsQuickReview U.S. History I *by P. Soifer and A. Hoffman (Wiley).*

Farm Production and Declining Prices

Bringing new lands under cultivation and the widespread use of machinery led to a tremendous increase in farm production. The wheat crop, which became an export staple, grew from 170 million bushels at the end of the Civil War to more than 700 million bushels by the close of the century. Overproduction in the United States and expanded crop production in Argentina, Australia, Canada, and Russia drove agricultural prices down during the same period. Unfortunately, American farmers did not seem to understand how the market operated. When prices fell, the inclination was to plant more, which added to the worldwide surplus and pushed prices still lower.

The promise of wealth through agriculture failed to materialize for most settlers in the West. They had borrowed heavily to buy their land and equipment and, as prices continued to fall, were unable to pay their debts. Foreclosures and the number of tenant farmers steadily increased in the late nineteenth century, particularly on the Great Plains. Farmers typically blamed their plight on others: the railroads for charging exorbitant shipping rates; the federal government for keeping the supply of money tight by adhering to the gold standard; and middlemen, such as grain elevator operators, for not paying the full value for their crops. Although organizations such as the Patrons of Husbandry, or the Grange, (which was founded in 1867 and grew quickly to more than a million members) brought redress of some grievances, discontent among the farmers continued to grow at the end of the nineteenth century.

34. What did new land and the use of machinery do to farm production?

(1) curtailed it

(2) expanded it

(3) encouraged it

(4) discouraged it

(5) destroyed it

35. What impact did these changes have on the market?

(1) drove prices up

(2) caused underproduction

(3) led to less protection

(4) drove prices down

(5) created a deficit

36. How did American farmers initially respond to falling prices?

(1) planted more grain

(2) sold their land

(3) had larger families

(4) went deeper in debt

(5) lost their farms

37. What was the purpose of the Grange?

(1) to invent new machinery

(2) to plant more crops

(3) to buy and sell farm land

(4) to charge exorbitant shipping rates

(5) to help farmers settle their disputes with others

Go on to next page

Questions 38 through 42 refer to the following timeline.

Timeline of Major Events in U.S. History

1900: Gold standard for currency adopted by United States

1914: World War I begins

1918: World War I ends

1929: Stock market crashes; Great Depression begins

1933: Gold exports banned; daily price established; U.S. citizens ordered to turn in all gold

1934: Price of gold fixed at $35 per troy ounce

1939: World War II begins

1945: World War II ends

1950: Korean Conflict begins

1953: Korean Conflict ends

1965: Vietnam War begins

1973: Vietnam War ends; gold prices allowed to float; U.S. currency removed from gold standard

1974: U.S. citizens allowed to own gold again

1979: Soviet Union invades Afghanistan; U.S. hostages seized in Iran

1980: Historic high prices for gold

1987: Stock market crashes

1989: Berlin Wall falls

1990: Gulf War begins

1991: Gulf War ends

2001: Terrorist attacks on the United States

2002: Invasion of Afghanistan and Iraq

2008: United States elects first Black president

2009: United States slips into a recession

Go on to next page

38. On what did the United States base the value of its currency in 1900?

    (1) stock market

    (2) value of gold

    (3) value of silver

    (4) trade surplus

    (5) interest rates

39. What caused the Great Depression in 1929?

    (1) price of gold

    (2) weak currency

    (3) stock market crash

    (4) World War I

    (5) President Roosevelt

40. What does "U.S. citizens ordered to turn in all gold" mean?

    (1) Citizens turned into gold.

    (2) Citizens got to keep their gold.

    (3) Citizens had to tell the government about their gold.

    (4) Citizens could buy gold from each other, for profit.

    (5) Citizens had to take all their gold to government offices.

41. When was U.S. currency removed from the gold standard?

    (1) 1934

    (2) 1945

    (3) 1969

    (4) 1973

    (5) 1974

42. Based on what you see in the timeline, what likely caused the price of gold to reach an historic high?

    (1) Citizens were allowed to hold bullion.

    (2) Gold stocks were sold.

    (3) The Soviet Union invaded Afghanistan.

    (4) The stock market crashed.

    (5) The Gulf War began.

Go on to next page

Questions 43 through 46 refer to the following newscast.

World Environmental News

Good evening and welcome to World Environmental News.

Our stories this evening: cyclones in Korea, hurricane near Mexico, flooding in Europe and India, volcanic eruptions in New Guinea, drought in Australia, tornadoes in the United States, hailstorms in Italy, earthquakes in Iran, and locusts in Denmark.

Now, let's look at our top stories.

Drought in Australia: The wheat fields west of Canberra, New South Wales, are in great danger today because of the ongoing drought. In the next week, farmers may have to write off this year's crop, and this will likely lead to financial ruin for many of them. To add to the misery, hundreds of thousands of sheep had to be sold because there was not enough water for them to drink.

Locusts in Denmark: The unseasonably warm weather in Denmark is proving to be inviting to the lowly locust. Normally found along the Mediterranean coast, the locust has been found far from its normal habitat. These discoveries in southwest Denmark are causing concern because locusts have not been seen in Denmark for over 50 years.

Hurricane near Mexico: Hurricane Herman is losing force off the Pacific coast of Mexico. The country is giving a sigh of relief as the hurricane winds down.

For wine drinkers: And a last note for you wine drinkers. The recent violent hailstorms in Italy are expected to cause a poor grape harvest. This means lower wine production and, consequently, higher prices.

There's more as nature lashes out. Tune in again for World Environmental News.

43. In which ocean is the tropical storm called Hurricane Herman located?

   (1) Pacific

   (2) Arctic

   (3) Atlantic

   (4) Indian

   (5) Antarctic

44. According to the newscast, where is the extreme drought causing major loss of wheat crops?

   (1) India

   (2) China

   (3) Saudi Arabia

   (4) Death Valley

   (5) Australia

45. Why have locusts been found in Denmark?

   (1) unseasonably warm weather

   (2) prevailing winds

   (3) foreign ships

   (4) wild birds

   (5) Mediterranean climate

46. What will be the impact of hailstorms in Italy?

   (1) lower olive oil prices

   (2) devastating floods

   (3) damaged cars

   (4) higher wine prices

   (5) more insurance coverage

Go on to next page

Questions 47 through 50 refer to the following political cartoon.

47. What happens if oil prices rise?

(1) SUV sales decrease.

(2) People stop traveling.

(3) Oil companies make less profit.

(4) Gas stations close.

(5) Gasoline prices rise.

48. How does a rise in oil prices affect the cost of living?

(1) has no impact

(2) raises the cost of living

(3) doesn't really matter

(4) forces rich nations to pay more

(5) protects the oil companies

49. What adjective best describes the characters in the cartoon?

(1) smug

(2) arrogant

(3) wasteful

(4) thoughtful

(5) angry

50. What phrase does not describe the SUV or its occupants?

(1) pollution creator

(2) road warrior

(3) energy saver

(4) gas guzzler

(5) monster truck

END OF TEST

Chapter 13

Answers and Explanations for the Social Studies Test

• •

Afterterms taking the Social Studies Test in Chapter 12, use this chapter to check your answers. Take your time as you move through the explanations of the answers that we provide in the first section. They can help you understand why you missed the answers you did. You may also want to read the explanations for the questions you answered correctly because doing so can give you a better understanding of the thought process that helped you choose the correct answers.

If you're short on time, turn to the end of the chapter for an abbreviated answer key.

Analysis of the Answers

1. **5.** England, Africa, and the West Indies all traded products: The West Indies traded molasses, sugar, and slaves with England for food and wood. England (via the New England colonies) then made the molasses and sugar into rum and traded it with Africa for more slaves.

2. **3.** Rum was used to purchase slaves for use in the colonies. The other answer choices — colonial farms, milling of lumber, molasses and sugar, and manufactured goods — were all patterns of commerce but were not uses of rum.

3. **1.** Ships were built in the colonies to increase Atlantic trade. Sewing sails, naval stores, milled lumber, and other crafts were products of the colonies that shipbuilding stimulated, but ships were the primary reason why the colonies were important to the Atlantic trade — the other choices were secondary.

4. **4.** The colonies provided raw materials for British manufacturing industries. According to the passage, "Mercantile theory encouraged the colonies to provide raw materials for England's industrializing economy . . . ."

5. **3.** The export of hats — a finished good — from the colonies was prohibited because it threatened British manufacturing. Coal, pig iron, lumber, and cotton were all raw materials, which didn't threaten English manufacturing.

6. **2.** According to the first paragraph of the passage, the king neglected the colonies in a number of ways. Of the ways listed here, only failing to pass laws (ones that would alleviate grievances) is correct. Although the other choices are grievances, they can't be alleviated until the appropriate laws are passed.

7. **4.** According to the third paragraph of the passage, the legislative bodies were forced to comply with the king's rule (". . . for the sole purpose of fatiguing them into compliance with his measures. . .").

8. **1.** According to the fourth paragraph of the passage, when the king dissolved the representative houses, he threatened the rights of the people.

9. **5.** The sixth paragraph of the passage says, "He has endeavored to prevent the population of these states." In other words, he has discouraged newcomers from settling.

10. **3.** The seventh paragraph of the passage states that the king didn't give his approval to laws that would've created a local judicial system.

11. **2.** The king made sure the military was independent from the colonists (last paragraph). This independence meant the colonists didn't have any authority over when to hire or fire soldiers, how large the military was, or who the officers were. Only the king made those kinds of decisions.

12. **3.** Canada was a target for the United States because it was a British possession with a small population (refer to the first sentence of the passage).

13. **1.** The first paragraph states that Native Americans were loyal to the British in the war.

14. **5.** Hull surrendered because the Shawnee cut his supply lines (refer to the second paragraph of the passage).

15. **2.** The battle of Queenston Heights was a defeat for the United States — so it represented an embarrassment, not a victory. Refusal to march and suffering are also incorrect answers. A battle isn't ever likely to be considered a proposal, so that answer choice is wrong, too.

16. **5.** Although you may know that Niagara Falls kept the Royal Navy from sailing from the St. Lawrence River into Lake Erie, the passage doesn't tell you so. For this reason, "not enough information given" is the best answer here.

17. **3.** The last sentence of the passage states that the War of 1812 ended in a stalemate, with neither side claiming victory. The death of Tecumseh was also an outcome, but it wasn't the *overall* result of the war, which is why stalemate is the best answer.

18. **3.** As stated in the first two sentences of the passage, the issues of prime importance in the Civil War were liberty and equality. Happiness and friendship, safety and security, wealth and greed, and peace and prosperity aren't the best answers.

19. **4.** You know from the passage that President Lincoln was delivering his speech on a battlefield at Gettysburg. This fact rules out every answer choice except "on a battlefield" and "on the radio" (he could've recorded his speech, and it could've been broadcast by radio at the battlefield). However, Lincoln gave this speech in 1863, and radios hadn't yet been invented.

20. **5.** Lincoln was saying that the world would remember the soldiers who died but would not remember his speech. (He was wrong, given that the Gettysburg Address is one of the most famous speeches in American history.)

21. **1.** Some of the battlefield was to become a burial ground for the fallen. Athletic field, cow pasture, shopping area, and farming aren't relevant answer choices.

22. **5.** The ground was hallowed by those who fought there. Lincoln doesn't believe the people involved in the dedication of the battlefield can make the place holy or important; only the people who fought on the battlefield can do so.

23. **3.** The word "years" follows "four score and seven," so you can assume that phrase relates to time. (By the way, a score is 20 years, so four score and seven is 87 years.)

24. **4.** Archduke Ferdinand was assassinated by a Serbian nationalist, so the correct answer is Serbia. Great Britain, France, Russia, and Germany are incorrect.

25. **2.** Austria demanded indemnities in response to the assassination. This answer comes directly from the passage.

26. **3.** Germany and France weren't allies in the war. Although the list of allies is rather confusing, the passage does sum up who was on which side.

27. **1.** You know that Great Britain entered the war when Germany invaded Belgium from the sentence that states, "Great Britain entered the war on August 4, following Germany's invasion of neutral Belgium."

28. **3.** Germany was not an Allied power. About halfway through the passage is a list of the Central powers (on one side of the war) and the Allied powers (on the other side).

29. **5.** Italy joined the Allies because of the Treaty of London. The Open Door Policy, increased tensions, territorial demands, and the expanding Japanese influence may have played a part, but, according to the passage, they aren't the best answers.

30. **2.** In the cartoon, Barack Obama is portrayed in front of a chalkboard in a classroom setting. Most of the students are seen as receptive to his role as an inspiring teacher. The other choices — comedian, disciplinarian, fashion model, or salesman — don't go with the cartoon.

31. **5.** Most of the young people are portrayed as *eager to learn* except for one at the back who's trying to make an important point. In general, they aren't portrayed as being bored, disruptive, lazy, or inattentive.

32. **1.** Each of the students in the cartoon represents a different problem facing America, so the correct answer is Choice (1). The other answers don't specifically answer the question.

33. **5.** *All of the above* is the only correct choice because each of the students represents one of the problems facing America.

34. **2.** New land and use of machinery have expanded farm production. The first sentence of the passage tells you so.

35. **4.** Improved production drove prices down. Rising prices, underproduction, and the creation of a deficit are the opposite of what the passage states. The choice "led to less protection" is nonsense — it doesn't have anything to do with the passage.

36. **1.** Farmers responded to falling prices by planting more grain. Although this answer may go against your instinct, which may be to say that they sold their land, went deeper into debt, or lost their farms, the passage clearly states that they planted more grain. The word *initially* in the question is important.

37. **5.** The phrase *redress of some grievances* is used to describe the Grange. *Redress* means "to set right," and *grievances* means "complaints" or "disputes."

38. **2.** The timeline shows that, in 1900, the gold standard was adopted for U.S. currency.

39. **3.** The Great Depression was caused by the crash of the stock market. The other answers — gold prices, weak currency, World War I, and President Roosevelt — may or may not have had some influence on the crash, but they weren't the cause.

40. **5.** U.S. citizens had to take all their gold to U.S. offices and not keep any in their own homes. The timeline and graph don't tell you why they had to do so, just that they did. *Turn in* is the key phrase here.

41. **4.** The U.S. currency was removed from the gold standard in 1973, not in the other dates listed.

42. **3.** The best answer is that gold reached a historic high when the Soviets invaded Afghanistan. You have to read the timeline to answer this question.

43. **1.** According to the newscast, Hurricane Herman is located off Mexico's Pacific coast.

44. **5.** Extreme drought conditions exist in Australia because of a lack of rainfall.

45. **1.** Because of unseasonably warm weather, locusts were found in Denmark. Locusts are drawn to warm weather, so they're leaving the warm Mediterranean for usually chilly Denmark.

46. **4.** The hailstorms will ruin many of the grapes that are on the vines when the storms hit, which will result in a reduced grape harvest and higher wine prices in Italy. One principle of economics is the law of supply and demand: The less supply of something you have, the greater the demand is for that something, so the more you can charge for it. When something is in low supply, the price usually goes up.

47. **5.** If oil prices rise, gasoline prices will rise — this answer is best according to the cartoon. Although you can guess that SUV sales may decrease and people may travel less as a result of higher oil prices, you don't have evidence of either of these results in the cartoon.

48. **2.** Because oil is used to fuel cars and some homes, if oil prices rise, the cost of living (which includes paying for gas and home heating) will also rise.

49. **3.** The characters in the cartoon are willing to waste gasoline to drive their SUV. When you waste gasoline, not only do you waste money, but you also waste all the natural resources and energy that went into getting the oil out of the ground and turning it into gasoline.

50. **3.** The SUV isn't an energy saver: That's the point of the cartoon.

Answer Key

1. **5**	18. **3**	35. **4**
2. **3**	19. **4**	36. **1**
3. **1**	20. **5**	37. **5**
4. **4**	21. **1**	38. **2**
5. **3**	22. **5**	39. **3**
6. **2**	23. **3**	40. **5**
7. **4**	24. **4**	41. **4**
8. **1**	25. **2**	42. **3**
9. **5**	26. **3**	43. **1**
10. **3**	27. **1**	44. **5**
11. **2**	28. **3**	45. **1**
12. **3**	29. **5**	46. **4**
13. **1**	30. **2**	47. **5**
14. **5**	31. **5**	48. **2**
15. **3**	32. **1**	49. **3**
16. **5**	33. **5**	50. **3**
17. **3**	34. **2**	

Part IV
Peering at Your Specimen: The Science Test

In this part . . .

How is the Science Test different from the other GED tests, and what do you have to know to pass it? The secrets lie within this part, which tells you all about what you need to know for the Science Test and how to be prepared. Here we also show you how the Science Test is set up and give you some strategies to follow to do your best.

Like in the other parts about the specific tests, we provide you with two practice tests to get your feet wet. You can see how you did on those tests by perusing the answers and explanations — take the time to congratulate yourself when you're right and figure out what went wrong when you aren't. We recommend that you take these practice tests after you've studied and brushed up on your skills and science vocabulary. Mastering this set of practice tests tells you that you're ready to take the real GED tests. If you don't do as well as you'd hoped on these tests, you know you have a bit more preparation to do before you're ready for the real deal.

Chapter 14

From Aardvarks to Atoms: Confronting the Science Test

- -

In This Chapter

▶ Eyeing the skills you need to succeed on the Science Test

▶ Getting a feel for the test format

▶ Figuring out how to tackle the different question types

▶ Managing your time carefully

▶ Mastering effective preparation strategies and looking at sample problems

- -

The Science Test shares some of the same features as the other tests; however, there are some differences. Although the questions are multiple choice (like the other tests), they're based on scientific text passages or visual images, including diagrams, graphs, maps, and tables. To do well on the Science Test, you're expected to have a passing knowledge of scientific vocabulary, and one of the best ways to improve your scientific vocabulary is to read scientific material and look up any words you don't know. Rest easy that you aren't expected to know the difference between terms like *fission* and *fusion* — just being slightly familiar with them can help you on the test.

The Science Test covers material from life science, physical science (chemistry and physics), and earth and space science. Don't panic — you don't need to memorize material from those subjects. You just need to be able to read and understand the material and correctly answer questions. The hardest part of this test is understanding science vocabulary; to help you out, we offer you more than one chance to improve your science vocabulary as you work through this chapter. In this chapter, we also help you get a feel for the Science Test's format. We lift the fog from the different types of questions that may appear on your test. Finally, we try to help you stay awake for what may be some of the driest material on any of the GED tests. After you understand the words on this test, along with its basic format and subject areas, you can try out the practice tests in Chapters 15 and 17.

Looking at the Skills the Science Test Covers

The Science Test doesn't test you on your knowledge of science, and you're not expected to memorize any scientific information to do well on this test. Instead, this test assesses your ability to ferret out information presented in passages or visual materials.

If you're totally unfamiliar with science and its vocabulary, you'll likely have trouble with the questions on this test. You're expected to have some basic knowledge about how the physical world works, how plants and animals live, and how the universe operates. This material tests you on ideas that you observe and develop throughout your life, both in and out of school. You probably know a little about traction, for example, from driving and walking in slippery weather. On the other hand, you may not know a lot about equilibrium aside from what you read in school.

As you take the Science Test, you're expected to understand that science is all about inquiry. In fact, inquiry forms the basis of the *scientific method* — which is the process every good scientist follows when faced with an unknown. The steps of the scientific method are

1. **Ask questions.**
2. **Gather information.**
3. **Do experiments.**
4. **Think objectively about what you find.**
5. **Look at other possible explanations.**
6. **Draw one or more possible conclusions.**
7. **Test the conclusion(s).**
8. **Tell others what you found.**

Look at your studying for the Science Test as a scientific problem. The question you're trying to answer is, "How can I increase my scientific knowledge?" Follow the scientific method to come up with a procedure to fix the problem. Hopefully, your solution includes reading, reading, and more reading! A high school science book is a great tool to use, as is a GED preparation book or course that teaches the basics of high school science. (Go to your local library to get your hands on a copy of one of these books, and check with your local school board to find basic science courses in your area.)

Understanding the Test Format

The Science Test contains 50 multiple-choice questions, which you have 80 minutes to answer. As with the other tests, the information and questions on the Science Test are straightforward — no one is trying to trick you. To answer the questions, you have to read and interpret the passages or other visual materials provided with the questions (and you need a basic understanding of science and the words scientists use when they communicate).

In terms of format, the 50 questions are grouped as sets. All the questions in a particular set refer to a given passage, chart, diagram, graph, map, or table. Your job is to read or review the material and decide on the best answer for each question based on the given material.

In terms of subject matter, the questions on the Science Test check your knowledge in the following areas:

✔ **Physical science (35 percent; 17 or 18 questions):** *Physical science* is the study of atoms, chemical reactions, forces, and what happens when energy and matter get together. As a basic review, keep the following in mind:

• Everything is composed of atoms. (The paper this book is printed on is composed of atoms, for example.)

• When chemicals get together, they have a reaction — unless they're *inert* (which means they don't react with other chemicals; inert chemicals are sort of like antisocial chemicals).

• You're surrounded by forces and their effects. (If the floor didn't exert a force up on you when you stepped down, you would go through the floor.)

For more information about physical science (which includes basic chemistry and basic physics), read and review a basic science textbook. You can borrow one from your local library (or from your local high school, if you call the office in advance and ask whether the school has any extras). You can also find one on the Internet. When reading this material, you may need definitions for some of the words or terms to make understanding the concepts easier. Use a good dictionary or the Internet to find these definitions. (If you use the Internet, enter any of the topics into a search engine and add "definition" after it. Become amazed at the number of hits produced, but don't spend time reading them all.)

✔ **Life science (45 percent; 22 or 23 questions):** *Life science* is the study of cells, heredity, evolution, and other processes that occur in living systems. All life is composed of *cells,* which you can see under a microscope. If you don't have access to a microscope and a set of slides with cells on them, most life science–related books and the Internet have photographs of cells that you can look at. When someone tells you that you look like your parents or that you remind them of another relative, they're talking about *heredity.* Reading a bit about heredity in biology-related books can help you practice answering some of the questions on the Science Test.

Use a biology textbook to help you review for this portion of the test. (Get your hands on a copy of one at your local library or high school.)

✔ **Earth and space science (20 percent; 10 questions):** This area of science looks at the earth and the universe, specifically weather, astronomy, geology, rocks, erosion, and water.

When you look down at the ground as you walk, you're interacting with earth sciences. When you look up at the stars on a clear night and wonder what's really up there, you're thinking about earth sciences. When you complain about the weather, you're complaining about earth sciences. In a nutshell, you're surrounded by earth sciences, so you shouldn't have a problem finding materials to read on this subject.

You don't have to memorize everything you read about science before you take the test. All the answers to the test questions are based on information provided in the passages or on the basic knowledge you've acquired over the years about science. Any science reading you do prior to the test not only helps you increase your basic knowledge but also improves your vocabulary. An improved science vocabulary increases your chances of being able to read the passages and answer the related questions on the test quickly.

As the basis for its questions, the Science Test uses the National Science Education Standards (NSES) content standards, which are based on content developed by science educators from across the country.

Identifying the Types of Questions and Knowing How to Tackle Them

Like the Social Studies Test, the Science Test has two main types of questions — questions about textual passages and questions about visual materials (see Chapter 9 for details on the Social Studies Test). Having a basic understanding of these two question types can help you avoid any surprises when you sit down to take the test. In general, you can prepare for these questions similarly to how you prepare for the Social Studies Test. The following sections break down the two types of questions you encounter and offer you advice on how to answer them.

Like with all the other GED tests, make sure you read every word and symbol that appears on the Science Test, including every chart, diagram, graph, map, table, passage, and question. Information — both relevant and irrelevant — is all over the test, and you never know where you'll find what you need to answer the questions quickly and correctly. Don't skip something because it doesn't immediately look important. (Check out the "Examining Preparation Strategies That Work" section for more tips on how you can handle problems that may arise on this test.)

Questions about passages

The first question type on the Science Test is based on passages you have to read and understand. The written passages on this test — and the questions that accompany them — are very similar to a reading-comprehension test: You're given textual material, and you have to answer questions about it. The passages present everything you need to answer the questions — but you usually have to understand all the words used in those passages to figure out what they're telling you (which is why we recommend that you read as much science information as you can prior to the test).

The difference between this test and other reading-comprehension tests is that the terminology and examples are all about science. Thus, the more you read about science, the more science words you'll know, understand, and be comfortable seeing on the test — which, as you may imagine, can greatly improve your chances of success.

Keep the following tips and tricks in mind when answering questions about passages:

✔ **Read each passage and question carefully.** Some of the questions on the Science Test assume that you know a little bit from past experience. For example, you may be expected to know that a rocket is propelled forward by an engine firing backward. (On the other hand, you won't have to know the definition of *nuclear fission* — thank goodness!)

Regardless of whether a question assumes some basic science knowledge or asks for an answer that appears directly in the passage, you need to read each passage and corresponding question carefully. As you read, do the following:

- Try to understand the passage, and think about what you already know about the subject.

- If a passage has only one question, read that question extra carefully.

- If the passage or question contains words you don't understand, try to figure out what those words mean from the rest of the sentence or the entire passage.

✔ **Read each answer choice carefully.** Doing so helps you get a clearer picture of your options. If you select an answer without reading all the answers, you may end up picking the wrong one because, although that answer may seem right at first, another answer may be more correct. As you read the answer choices, do the following:

- If one answer is right from your reading and experience, mark it.

- If you aren't sure which answer is right, exclude the answers you know are wrong and then exclude answers that may be wrong.

- If you can exclude all but one answer, it's probably correct, so mark it.

Try out these tips on the sample passages and questions in the "Practicing with Sample Problems" section.

Questions about visual materials

The other type of question that appears on the Science Test is the question based on visual materials. *Visual materials* are pictures that contain information you may need to answer the corresponding questions, and they can be in the form of tables, graphs, diagrams, or maps. Understanding information in visual materials takes more practice than doing so from textual passages because many people aren't as familiar with getting information from pictures as they are with getting info from text. This section (and the practice tests in Chapters 15 and 17) can help you get the practice you need to do well on all the questions on the Science Test — including the ones based on pictures.

The following sections take a more detailed look at the different visual materials — tables, graphs, diagrams, and maps — that questions on the Science Test can refer to.

Tables

A *table* is a graphical way of organizing information (see Figure 14-1). This type of visual material allows for easy comparison between two or more sets of data. Some tables use symbols to represent information; others use words.

Science Subjects and Learning Time

Subject	Time to Prepare (Hours)	Average Grade
Earth science	10.8	A-
Biology	17.6	B+
Chemistry	17.5	B
Physics	25.2	B-

Figure 14-1: Table.

Most tables have titles that tell you what they're about. Always read the titles first so you know right away what information the tables include. If a table gives you an explanation (or *key*) of the symbols, read the explanation carefully, too; doing so helps you understand how to read the table.

Graphs

A *graph* is a picture that shows how different sets of numbers are related. On the Science Test, you can find the following three main types of graphs in Figure 14-2:

- ✔ **Bar or column graphs:** Use bars (horizontal) or columns (vertical) to present and often compare information

- ✔ **Line graphs:** Use one or more lines to connect points drawn on a grid to show the relationships between data, including changes in data over time

- ✔ **Pie graphs (also called pie charts or circle graphs):** Use arcs of circles (pieces of a pie) to show how data relates to a whole

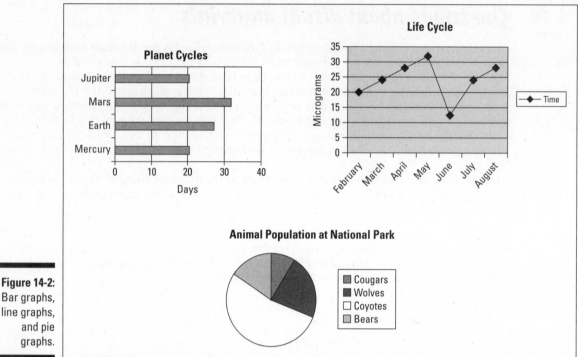

Figure 14-2:
Bar graphs,
line graphs,
and pie
graphs.

All three types of graphs usually share the following common characteristics:

- ✔ **Title:** The title tells you what the graph is about, so always read the title before reviewing the graph.

- ✔ **Horizontal axis and vertical axis:** Bar, column, and line graphs have a horizontal axis and a vertical axis. (Pie graphs don't.) Each axis is a vertical or horizontal reference line that's labeled to give you additional information.

- ✔ **Label:** The label on the axis of a graph usually contains units, such as feet or dollars. Read all axis labels carefully; they can either help you with the answer or lead you astray (depending on whether you read them correctly).

- ✔ **Legend:** Pie graphs usually have a *legend,* or printed material that tells you what each section of the graph is about. They may also contain labels on the individual pieces of the pie so that you know what each piece represents.

Graphs and tables are both often called *charts,* which can be rather confusing. To help you prepare for problems with graphs, make sure you look at and problem solve plenty of graphs before the test. Remember that many graphs show relationships. If the numbers represented on the horizontal axis are in millions of dollars and you think they're in dollars, your interpretation of the graph will be more than a little incorrect.

Diagrams

A *diagram,* such as the one in Figure 14-3, is a drawing that helps you understand how something works.

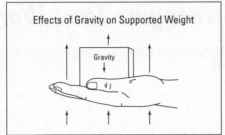

Figure 14-3:
Diagram.

Excerpted from Physical Science: What the Technology Professional Needs to Know *by C. Lon Enloe, Elizabeth Garnett, Jonathan Miles, and Stephen Swanson (Wiley).*

Diagrams on the Science Test often have the following two components:

✔ **Title:** Tells you what the diagram is trying to show you

✔ **Labels:** Indicate the names of the parts of the diagram

When you come to a question based on a diagram, read the title of the diagram first to get an idea of what the diagram is about. Then carefully read all the labels to find out the main components of the diagram. These two pieces of information can help you understand the diagram well enough to answer questions about it.

Maps

A *map* is a drawing of some section — large or small — of the earth or another planet, depending on how much space exploration has been done. Because the entire world is too large to show you on one piece of paper, a section of it is drawn to scale and presented to you on the test.

Most maps give you the following information:

✔ **Title:** Tells you what area of the world the map focuses on

✔ **Legend:** Gives you general information about the colors, symbols, compass directions, or other graphics used on the map

✔ **Labels:** Indicate what the various points on the map represent

✔ **Scale:** Tells you what the distance on the map represents in real life (For example, a map with a scale of 1 inch = 100 miles shows a distance of 500 miles on the real earth as a distance of 5 inches on the map.)

Although maps are seldom used in science passages, they are used occasionally, so you want to at least be familiar with them. The best way to get familiar with maps is to spend some time looking at road maps and world atlases, which you can find in your local library or bookstore.

Examining Preparation Strategies That Work

To get better results from the time and effort you put into preparing for the Science Test, we suggest you try the following strategies:

- ✔ **Take practice tests.** Chapters 15 and 17 give you full-length practice Science Tests. Take them. If you need more, consider purchasing additional preparation manuals that offer sample tests. Take as many of these practice tests as you can. Be cautious about time restrictions, and check your answers when you're finished. If you don't understand why some answers are correct, ask a tutor, take a preparation class, or look up the information in a book or on the Internet. Be sure you know why every one of your answers is right or wrong.

- ✔ **Create your own dictionary.** Get a notebook and keep track of all the new words (and their definitions) that you discover as you prepare for the Science Test. Make sure you understand all the science terminology you see or hear. Of course, this chore isn't one you can do in one night. Take some time and make sure this terminology becomes part of your brain.

- ✔ **Read as many passages as you can.** We may sound like a broken record, but reading is the most important way to prepare for the Science Test. After you read a paragraph from any source (textbook, newspaper article, novel, and so on), ask yourself some questions about what you read. You can also ask friends and family to ask you questions about what you read.

Check out Chapter 3 for some general test-taking strategies to help you prepare to take the GED tests.

Managing Your Time for the Science Test

As we mention earlier in this chapter, the Science Test has 50 questions that you must answer in 80 minutes, which means you have about 90 seconds to read each textual or visual passage given and answer each question. If a passage has more than one question, you have slightly more time to answer those questions because you should read the passage only once.

To help you manage your time, we recommend you check out Chapters 2 and 3 for some general time-management strategies that you can use on all the tests. For the Science Test, specifically, we suggest you focus on these two time-saving strategies:

- ✔ **For questions about passages, read the question first and then skim the material for the answer.** The passage always contains the answer, but your background knowledge in science and your familiarity with scientific terms can help you understand the material more easily and quickly. Reading the question first provides you with a guide to what is being asked and what the passage is about so that you know what to look for as you read it.

- ✔ **For questions about a visual material, such as a graph or table, read the question first and then scan the visual material.** Look at the visual material to see the big picture; questions usually don't ask about minute details.

As a general tip, answer the easiest questions first. You can then go back and spend a little more time on the more difficult questions. Remember, though, to plan ahead and leave a few minutes at the end to review your answers.

Practicing with Sample Problems

To help increase your odds of doing well on the Science Test, you want to be as familiar as you can be with what you'll encounter on the actual test. The following questions are some sample problems for the Science Test. Read each question carefully, and find the best answer based on the passages.

Questions 1 and 2 refer to the following passage.

One of the great discoveries in earth science is rocks. Rocks have many useful purposes in science. They can be used as paperweights to keep academic papers from flying away in the wind. Rocks can be used to prop laboratory doors open when the experiments go wrong and horrible smells are produced. Smooth rocks can be rubbed when pressure builds and you just need a mindless activity to get through the day.

1. According to the passage, one of the great discoveries in science is

    (1) atomic energy

    (2) static electricity

    (3) rocks

    (4) nectarines

    (5) DNA

    The correct answer is Choice (3). The important words in the question are *According to the passage*. When you see this phrase, you know to look in the passage for the answer. Because none of the answers except rocks is even remotely mentioned, rocks must be the best answer.

2. How do rocks help scientists when experiments go horribly wrong and produce terrible odors?

    (1) They can be used to smash the windows.

    (2) They can prop open the doors.

    (3) They can be thrown in anger.

    (4) They can be rubbed.

    (5) Only scientists know the answer to this.

    The correct answer is Choice (2). According to the passage, the rocks can be used to hold open the door of the lab. Rocks can also be used to smash windows and can be thrown in anger, but the passage doesn't specifically mention these uses. The passage mentions rubbing rocks as a use of rocks, but it does so in another context.

Questions 3 through 5 refer to the following passage.

Dr. Y. Kritch was a world-famous botanist. He spent his life in search of an early blooming, colorful spring flower. He first developed the onelip flower, which bloomed so early that it immediately froze in the winter weather. After many years of research, he developed a new strain of flowers called the threelip, which bloomed in the late fall, just after the first frost. Frustrated, he decided to cross-pollinate the two blooms to develop a plant that would bloom in the spring. Using a special cross-averaging-pollination process, he managed to develop a plant that would bloom in the early spring and come in many colors. In honor of the averaging process, he called it a twolip, which was later changed to tulip.

3. Why did Dr. Kritch want to develop a new flower?

    (1) He was bored.

    (2) He wanted something named after him.

    (3) He wanted to sell the flowers to stores.

    (4) He needed a gift for his wife.

    (5) Not enough information is given.

    The correct answer is Choice (5). The first four answers are all possible, but the passage doesn't mention any of them. The only correct answer is (5) because not much information is given about the doctor himself.

4. What was wrong with the onelip flower?

    (1) It bloomed so late that everyone was tired of flowers.

    (2) It never bloomed at all.

    (3) It was an ugly color.

    (4) It bloomed too early.

    (5) Not enough information is given.

    The correct answer is Choice (4). The passage states that the onelip bloomed so early that it immediately froze in the winter weather.

5. Based on the information in the passage, what can you assume a botanist does?

    (1) studies the averaging process

    (2) studies plants

    (3) freezes to death

    (4) sells flowers

    (5) not enough information given

    The correct answer is Choice (2). The passage describes how Dr. Kritch studied and developed tulip plants. Although he used the averaging process to develop the tulip, the passage doesn't mention that he studied that process. No mention is made of Dr. Kritch selling flowers or freezing to death.

Revealing Some Helpful Pointers

Here are a few pointers to remember as you take the Science Test. (See Chapter 3 for more test-taking tips that apply to all GED tests.)

✔ **Don't panic!** Your worst enemy on this or any other test is panic. Panicking takes time and energy, and you don't have a surplus of both. On the Science Test, you're expected to recognize and understand some scientific vocabulary, but, if you come across a word you don't understand, try to figure out its meaning from the rest of the sentence. If you can't do so quickly, leave it. Return to the problem at the end of the test when you know exactly how much time is left.

✔ **Remember that reading pictures is a science.** During this test, you have to answer questions based on visual materials, something you may not do every day. Remember that any visual object is like a short paragraph. It has a topic and makes comments or states facts about that topic. When you come across a question based on a visual material, the first thing to do is to figure out the content of the material. Usually, visual objects have titles that help you understand their meanings. After you figure out the main idea behind the visual object, ask yourself what information you're being given; rereading the question can be helpful. After you know these two pieces of information, you're well on your way to answering the question.

Science on the Internet

Internet sites can increase your scientific knowledge or simply introduce you to a new area of interest. If you don't have an Internet connection at home, try your local library or community center.

To save yourself time as you begin your online search for additional practice in reading science material, we suggest you check out the following sites:

✔ `www.els.net`: Contains tons of information about life sciences

✔ `www.earth.nasa.gov`: Contains lots of intriguing earth- and space-related info

✔ `www.chemistry.about.com`: Contains interesting info related to chemistry (Note that this is a commercial site, which means you'll see pesky banners and commercial links amidst the interesting and helpful information.)

✔ `www.colorado.edu/physics/2000/index.pl`: Contains some interesting physics lessons that are presented in an entertaining and informative manner

To explore on your own, go to your favorite search engine and type the science key words you're most interested in (*biology*, *earth science*, and *chemistry*, just to name a few examples).

Chapter 15

Practice Test — Science Test

● ●

*T*he Science Test consists of multiple-choice questions intended to measure general concepts in science. The questions are based on short readings that may include a graph, chart, or figure. Study the information given and then answer the question(s) following it. Refer to the information as often as necessary in answering the questions.

You have 80 minutes to answer the 50 questions in this booklet. Work carefully, but do not spend too much time on any one question. Be sure you answer every question.

Answer Sheet for Science Test

1 ① ② ③ ④ ⑤	26 ① ② ③ ④ ⑤
2 ① ② ③ ④ ⑤	27 ① ② ③ ④ ⑤
3 ① ② ③ ④ ⑤	28 ① ② ③ ④ ⑤
4 ① ② ③ ④ ⑤	29 ① ② ③ ④ ⑤
5 ① ② ③ ④ ⑤	30 ① ② ③ ④ ⑤
6 ① ② ③ ④ ⑤	31 ① ② ③ ④ ⑤
7 ① ② ③ ④ ⑤	32 ① ② ③ ④ ⑤
8 ① ② ③ ④ ⑤	33 ① ② ③ ④ ⑤
9 ① ② ③ ④ ⑤	34 ① ② ③ ④ ⑤
10 ① ② ③ ④ ⑤	35 ① ② ③ ④ ⑤
11 ① ② ③ ④ ⑤	36 ① ② ③ ④ ⑤
12 ① ② ③ ④ ⑤	37 ① ② ③ ④ ⑤
13 ① ② ③ ④ ⑤	38 ① ② ③ ④ ⑤
14 ① ② ③ ④ ⑤	39 ① ② ③ ④ ⑤
15 ① ② ③ ④ ⑤	40 ① ② ③ ④ ⑤
16 ① ② ③ ④ ⑤	41 ① ② ③ ④ ⑤
17 ① ② ③ ④ ⑤	42 ① ② ③ ④ ⑤
18 ① ② ③ ④ ⑤	43 ① ② ③ ④ ⑤
19 ① ② ③ ④ ⑤	44 ① ② ③ ④ ⑤
20 ① ② ③ ④ ⑤	45 ① ② ③ ④ ⑤
21 ① ② ③ ④ ⑤	46 ① ② ③ ④ ⑤
22 ① ② ③ ④ ⑤	47 ① ② ③ ④ ⑤
23 ① ② ③ ④ ⑤	48 ① ② ③ ④ ⑤
24 ① ② ③ ④ ⑤	49 ① ② ③ ④ ⑤
25 ① ② ③ ④ ⑤	50 ① ② ③ ④ ⑤

Science Test

Do not mark in this test booklet. Record your answers on the separate answer sheet provided. Be sure that all requested information is properly recorded on the answer sheet.

To record your answers, fill in the numbered circle on the answer sheet that corresponds to the answer you select for each question in the test booklet.

EXAMPLE:

Which of the following is the smallest unit in a living thing?

(1) tissue

(2) organ

(3) cell

(4) muscle

(5) capillary

(On Answer Sheet)

①　②　●　④　⑤

The correct answer is "cell"; therefore, answer space 3 would be marked on the answer sheet.

Do not rest the point of your pencil on the answer sheet while you are considering your answer. Make no stray or unnecessary marks. If you change an answer, erase your first mark completely. Mark only one answer space for each question; multiple answers will be scored as incorrect. Do not fold or crease your answer sheet. All test materials must be returned to the test administrator.

Note: Refer to Chapter 16 for the answers for this practice test.

DO NOT BEGIN TAKING THIS TEST UNTIL TOLD TO DO SO

Directions: Choose the <u>one best answer</u> to each question.

Questions 1 and 2 refer to the following passage.

Insulation

During the winter, you need something to keep warmth in the house and cold air out. In the summer, you need something to keep heat outside and cooler air inside. What you need is insulation.

Insulation reduces or prevents the transfer of heat (called thermal transfer) from the inside out or the outside in. Fiberglass and plastic foam provide such insulation because they contain trapped air. Normally, air is not a good insulator because the currents in air transfer the heat from one place to another. Trapping the air in small places, however, slows or prevents the transfer of heat. Think about these little packets of air the next time you sit in a warm house, safe from the frigid air of winter.

1. Why does a cinder block provide less thermal transfer than a window?

   (1) Cinder blocks are thicker.

   (2) Windows have little insulation value.

   (3) You can't see through cinder blocks.

   (4) There is no air in a cinder block.

   (5) Windows are necessary for safety.

2. Which would keep you warmest during the winter?

   (1) silk underwear

   (2) silk trousers

   (3) trousers padded with cotton

   (4) cotton underwear

   (5) fiberglass trousers

Questions 3 through 5 refer to the following passage.

Metabolism

The process of metabolism is an essential process in every living cell. Metabolism allows the cell to obtain and distribute energy, which is necessary for survival. Light from the sun is absorbed and converted into chemical energy by photosynthesis, and it is this chemical energy that is necessary for animals to survive.

One of the primary carbohydrates derived from plants is glucose. Through a process called glycolysis, energy is obtained from glucose. This reaction takes place in mitochondria and the glucose molecule is broken down into pyruvic acids, which are further broken down into molecules, such as ethanol and lactic acid. This process is cyclical as the energy produced keeps the fermentation going.

Pyruvic acids are broken down to carbon dioxide and water by respiration, which releases far more energy. What started out as sunlight has become energy that keeps animals alive.

Go on to next page

3. How do animals depend on plants to stay alive?

    (1) Plants provide animals with protective cover.

    (2) Animals need the shade provided by plants.

    (3) Cures for some diseases originate in plants.

    (4) Plants provide a comfortable environment for animals.

    (5) Plants provide animals with chemical potential energy.

4. What would happen to a plant if you covered it with a cloth that does not allow light to pass through it?

    (1) The plant would stop growing.

    (2) The leaves would shrivel.

    (3) The flower would fall off.

    (4) The plant would starve to death.

    (5) The roots would die.

5. Which chemical is key to providing animals with energy?

    (1) pyruvic acid

    (2) carbon dioxide

    (3) chlorophyll

    (4) ethanol

    (5) lactic acid

Questions 6 and 7 refer to the following passage.

Velocity and Speed

There is a difference between speed and velocity, although sometimes you see the words used interchangeably. The velocity of a body is its rate of motion in a specific direction, such as a bicycle traveling 34 miles per hour due east. Because velocity has both magnitude (34 miles per hour) and direction (due east), it can be represented by a vector.

Speed has a magnitude only. If a bicycle travels at a speed of 28 miles per hour, you know its magnitude (28 miles per hour), but not its direction. Because speed has a magnitude but not a direction, it can be represented as a scalar.

6. If force is defined as that which is required to change the state or motion of an object in magnitude and direction, how should it be represented?

    (1) wavy lines

    (2) straight line

    (3) grams

    (4) scalar

    (5) vector

7. If a person travels seven blocks at 3 miles per hour but you do not know in which direction, what would represent his or her path?

    (1) kilometers

    (2) scalar

    (3) yards

    (4) vector

    (5) linear measure

Go on to next page

Questions 8 and 9 refer to the following diagram, which is excerpted from Physical Science: What the Technology Professional Needs to Know by C. Lon Enloe, Elizabeth Garnett, Jonathan Miles, and Stephen Swanson (Wiley).

Newcomen's Steam Engine

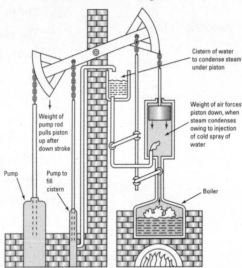

8. What properties of water and steam allow Newcomen's steam engine to operate?

    (1) Water is heavier than steam.

    (2) Steam condenses when cooled, occupying less space.

    (3) The boiler provides the energy to move the pump.

    (4) The pump rod is heavy enough to pull the arm down.

    (5) The cistern provides a positive pressure.

9. What effect does the condensation of steam in the cylinder with the piston have on the pump that fills the cistern?

    (1) controls the fire in the boiler

    (2) pumps water from the cistern to the boiler

    (3) causes the pump to fill the cistern with water

    (4) forces the piston down

    (5) sprays cold water into the main pump

Go on to next page ⟹

Question 10 refers to the following figure.

The Food Chain

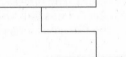

The Sun

Producers

Consumers

Decomposers

Green Plants

10. If the number of consumers in an ecosystem began to multiply without control, what would happen to the balance of the ecosystem?

   (1) The green plants would increase.

   (2) The herbivores would increase.

   (3) Consumers would starve for lack of food.

   (4) The decomposers would go out of business.

   (5) The sun would stop shining.

Go on to next page

> *Questions 11 through 14 refer to the following passage.*

The Big Bang Theory

It is hard enough to imagine the universe as it is now and even harder to create a theory about how it all began. In the 1940s, George Gamow began to develop such a theory. Georges Lemaitre, another scientist, had also been working on the problem, and Gamow used some of the ideas of Lemaitre to develop his theory.

Gamow proposed the following theory: Somewhere between 10 and 21 billion years ago, there was a giant explosion in space. Before the explosion, the universe was the size of an atomic nucleus, with a temperature of about 10 billion degrees. The explosion started the expansion of the universe. Quarks, or elemental particles, existed in huge numbers.

Within a millisecond, the universe had expanded to the size of a grapefruit. The temperature cooled to 1 billion degrees. The quarks began to clump into protons and neutrons. Minutes later, the universe was still too hot for electrons and protons to form into atoms: a super-hot, fog-like environment.

With passing time and cooling temperatures, nuclear reactions took place, and within 300,000 years, atoms of hydrogen and helium began to emerge. As the atoms formed, light began to shine. The universe was taking shape.

Gravity began to act on the atoms and transform them into galaxies. Within 1 billion years of that first great explosion, galaxies and stars began to form. Within 15 billion years, planets began to emerge from the heavy elements thrown off by the dying of stars. The universe started with a big bang and continues to grow and change according to this theory.

11. The temperature of the first tiny particles was thought to be

    (1) 1 billion degrees

    (2) 20 billion degrees

    (3) 10 billion degrees

    (4) 30 billion degrees

    (5) 15 billion degrees

12. Atoms were transformed into galaxies by

    (1) heat

    (2) pressure

    (3) centrifugal force

    (4) light

    (5) gravity

13. Quarks are

    (1) atoms

    (2) 1 billion degrees

    (3) elemental particles

    (4) hydrogen

    (5) helium

14. How is the formation of hydrogen and helium atoms related to the possible destruction from an atomic bomb?

    (1) Both use hydrogen.

    (2) No relation exists.

    (3) Both are scientific principles.

    (4) Both result from explosions.

    (5) Both are nuclear reactions.

Go on to next page

> *Questions 15 through 17 refer to the following passage.*

The Jellyfish

One of the creatures living in all the world's oceans is the jellyfish. Although it lives in the ocean, it is not a fish. The jellyfish is an invertebrate; that is, an animal lacking a backbone. Not only does it lack a backbone, but the jellyfish has no heart, blood, brain, or gills and is over 95-percent water.

The jellyfish has a body and tentacles. These tentacles are the long tendrils around the bell-like structure that contain stinging cells, which are used to capture prey. The movement of the prey triggers the sensory hair in the stinging cell, and the prey is then in trouble.

Unfortunately, people are also in trouble if they get too close to the tentacles of a jellyfish. The stings are not fatal to humans but can cause a great deal of discomfort.

15. Why is a jellyfish considered an invertebrate?

    (1) It has tentacles.

    (2) It has a small brain.

    (3) It has a primitive circulatory system.

    (4) It has no backbone.

    (5) It swims in the ocean.

16. Why do swimmers not like to be near jellyfish?

    (1) They look weird.

    (2) Swimmers can get caught in the tentacles.

    (3) Swimmers may accidentally swallow a jellyfish.

    (4) The stings are painful.

    (5) Swimmers don't like to be near ocean creatures.

17. Why do most small ocean creatures try to avoid jellyfish?

    (1) Jellyfish get in the way of the fish when they are feeding.

    (2) Jellyfish sting and eat small ocean creatures.

    (3) The fish are afraid of the strange-looking creatures.

    (4) Jellyfish and ocean creatures compete for the same food sources.

    (5) Fish cannot swim as fast as jellyfish.

Go on to next page

Questions 18 through 25 refer to the following passage.

Laws of Conservation

You are faced with laws every day. You cannot speed on the roads, and you cannot park wherever you choose.

Science has its laws, as well. One such law is that energy cannot be created or destroyed. This law, called the Law of Conservation of Energy, makes sense because you cannot create something from nothing. And if you have an electrical charge, you cannot simply make it disappear.

A further law of conservation is the Law of Conservation of Matter, which says that matter cannot be created or destroyed. This means that when a chemical change occurs, the total mass of an object remains constant. When you melt an ice cube, the water that results is neither heavier nor lighter than the original ice cube.

18. When lightning strikes a tree, much damage is done to the tree, but the lightning ceases to exist. What has happened to the lightning?

    (1) It disappears.

    (2) The energy in the lightning is transformed into something else.

    (3) The tree absorbs the lightning.

    (4) Striking the tree creates new energy to damage the tree.

    (5) It is still there, but invisible.

19. Why does science have laws?

    (1) Science is an ordered discipline.

    (2) Laws keep scientists honest.

    (3) Science needs rules to operate carefully.

    (4) Laws make it easier to study science.

    (5) Lawyers like laws.

20. When a magician makes a rabbit appear in a hat, it is an example of

    (1) physics

    (2) conservation of matter

    (3) entertainment

    (4) illusion

    (5) biology

21. When an iceberg melts, what is the result?

    (1) global warming

    (2) warmer ocean water

    (3) nothing

    (4) more food for fish

    (5) more water in the ocean

22. When you take a dead battery out of your flashlight, what has happened to its original charge?

    (1) It has been converted into light.

    (2) It has disappeared.

    (3) The battery has worn out.

    (4) The energy has been destroyed.

    (5) It went into the flashlight.

23. If you add 3 ounces of water to 1 ounce of salt, what is the effect on the final mass?

    (1) The salt will absorb the water.

    (2) You will get 1 ounce of salty water.

    (3) The salt will disappear.

    (4) The total mass will remain the same.

    (5) Some water will disappear.

Go on to next page

24. A ball rolling down a hill cannot stop by itself. What explains this?

    (1) There is a bump on the road.

    (2) The ball has no brakes.

    (3) The energy from rolling down the hill can't disappear.

    (4) The theory of the laws of conservation keep the ball from stopping.

    (5) The ball always weighs the same.

25. Conservation of energy is an example of what?

    (1) something you have to memorize

    (2) a battery commercial

    (3) a statement by a famous scientist

    (4) a law of science

    (5) the title of an article in a magazine

Questions 26 through 28 refer to the following passage.

Why Do Birds Fly South for the Winter?

Every fall, the sky is full of birds flying south for the winter. However, you can still see a few birds in the northern part of the country during the winter. Scientists have advanced theories about this phenomenon.

Some birds eat insects for food. In winter, many species of birds fly south, because that's where the food exists. In southern states, insects are available all year long, providing a banquet for the birds, whereas in the northern parts of the country, insects (as well as other food sources, such as seeds and berries) are scarce or even nonexistent during the winter. The birds fly south for winter to follow the food. In the spring, as insects once again become plentiful in the northern states, the birds still follow the food, this time to the north.

26. Why do migratory birds return to the northern states in the spring?

    (1) They miss their homes.

    (2) It gets too hot in the southern states.

    (3) They are able to find food again.

    (4) They fly north out of habit.

    (5) Birds like to fly long distances.

27. Why are insects responsible for the migration of some birds?

    (1) Insects bite the birds.

    (2) The insects lead the birds south.

    (3) Some birds eat insects.

    (4) Birds have a habit of always eating the same insects.

    (5) Insects like to chase birds.

28. Why are scientists interested in the migration of birds?

    (1) It happens regularly and apparently without explanation.

    (2) Scientists like to go south.

    (3) They like to listen to bird songs.

    (4) Scientists look for connections between travel and caterpillars.

    (5) Someone asked the scientists about it.

Go on to next page ⟶

Questions 29 and 30 refer to the following passage.

The Law of Unintended Consequences

Lake Victoria is the largest freshwater lake in Africa. It once had abundant fish, which provided protein for the local people who ate the fish. Unfortunately, a new species — the Nile Perch — was introduced into the lake by fishermen looking for a challenging fishing experience to attract their share of tourists interested in exploring the area.

The Nile Perch is an aggressive predator and had no natural enemies in Lake Victoria. It quickly ate up large numbers of the smaller fish, which affected the diets of the local population. These smaller fish ate algae and parasite-bearing snails. Without the smaller fish eating them, the live algae spread over the surface of the lake. Dead algae sank to the bottom of the lake and decayed, a process that consumed oxygen necessary for the fish living deep in the lake.

The snails, without natural predators, and the parasites they carried multiplied, creating a serious health hazard to the population. The introduction of a fish to encourage tourism had a detrimental effect on the lake and the population that depended on it.

29. What destroyed the ecological balance in Lake Victoria?

   (1) local merchants

   (2) shrinking populations of snails

   (3) freshwater lake

   (4) growing populations of smaller fish

   (5) the Nile Perch

30. Why is it never a good idea to introduce a foreign species into a stable lake?

   (1) The foreign species has plenty of predators.

   (2) The foreign species is too attractive.

   (3) The other species in the lake would not have to compete for food.

   (4) The foreign species is bad for sport fishermen.

   (5) The foreign species can upset the ecological balance.

Go on to next page

Questions 31 through 34 refer to the following table, which is adapted from Hands-On General Science Activities with Real-Life Applications *by Pam Walker and Elaine Wood (Wiley).*

Space Travel

Characteristic	Moon	Mars
Distance from Earth	239,000 miles	48,600,000 miles
Gravity	$\frac{1}{6}$ earth's gravity	$\frac{1}{3}$ earth's gravity
Atmosphere	None	Thin carbon dioxide, 1% air pressure of earth
Trip time	3 days	1.88 earth years
Communication time	2.6 seconds, round trip	10 to 41 minutes, round trip

31. If you were an aeronautical engineer planning a journey to Mars, why would you prefer to go to a space station on the moon and then launch the rocket to Mars, rather than going directly from Earth to Mars?

   (1) Lower gravity on the moon means you need less fuel for the launch.

   (2) You have more space to take off and land on the moon.

   (3) No atmosphere means an easier takeoff.

   (4) The moon is closer to Earth than Mars.

   (5) Not enough information is given.

32. If you were a communications engineer trying to establish a safety network to warn a rocket ship of dangers, where would you place the transmitter for this rocket ship's journey to Mars?

   (1) on the moon

   (2) on Earth

   (3) on Mars

   (4) at the space station

   (5) not enough information given

33. Why would a trip to the moon be a better first choice than a trip to Mars for space travelers?

   (1) You can see the moon from Earth without a telescope.

   (2) The time of the trip is much shorter.

   (3) The moon has a better atmosphere.

   (4) There are already space vehicles on the moon.

   (5) You could phone home from the moon.

34. If you held a pole-vaulting contest on the moon and Mars, on which planet could the same contestant vault higher with the same expenditure of energy?

   (1) the moon

   (2) Mars

   (3) Earth

   (4) no difference

   (5) not enough information given

Go on to next page

> *Questions 35 through 37 refer to the following passage.*

Heredity, Then and Now

How often have you seen a young child and said, "She takes after her parents." Many traits in a child do come from her parents. Physical and other characteristics, such as hair color and nose shape, are transmitted from one generation to the next. These characteristics, passed from one generation to the next, exist because of genetic code.

The first scientist to experiment with heredity was Gregor Mendel during the 19th century. Mendel experimented with pea plants and noted that characteristics appearing in "child" plants were similar to the "parent" plants. Mendel hypothesized that these characteristics were carried from generation to generation by "factors." It took many years of research to understand why children often look like their parents, but genetic code is now the basis of the study of heredity.

35. According to the passage, what is a primary determinant for characteristics of the next generation?

   (1) chance
   (2) hair color
   (3) pea plants
   (4) heredity
   (5) nature

36. What are the factors that Mendel hypothesized carried traits from one generation to the next?

   (1) plants
   (2) peas
   (3) traits
   (4) protons
   (5) genetic code

37. If you want to grow monster-sized pumpkins, from what kind of pumpkins do you want to get seeds?

   (1) orange pumpkins
   (2) doesn't matter if you have special fertilizer
   (3) monster-sized pumpkins
   (4) larger-than-average pumpkins
   (5) healthy pumpkins

Go on to next page ⟹

Questions 38 and 39 refer to the following passage.

The Space Shuttle

NASA has designed and built six space shuttles: Atlantis, Challenger, Columbia, Discovery, Endeavor, and Enterprise. The space shuttles are made up of two distinct parts: the orbiter and the booster rocket. The booster rocket provides the additional thrust to get the space shuttle away from the gravitational pull of the earth. The orbiter carries the people and payload as well as the workings of the shuttle. In a space flight, the booster is jettisoned after clearing the earth's gravitational pull, and the orbiter continues on its way.

38. Why would the booster be jettisoned?

(1) to have more fuel for later in the trip

(2) because the shuttle needs to add weight

(3) to increase the size of the shuttle

(4) to make the shuttle less maneuverable for landing

(5) because it is no longer needed

39. Which part of a shuttle carries the payload?

(1) booster

(2) cockpit

(3) orbiter

(4) rocket

(5) Challenger

Questions 40 and 41 refer to the following figure, which is excerpted from Physical Science: What the Technology Professional Needs to Know by C. Lon Enloe, Elizabeth Garnett, Jonathan Miles, and Stephen Swanson (Wiley).

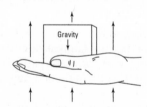

40. Work is defined as the product of force times displacement. Consider the diagram. If the force of gravity is greater than the forces being exerted by the muscles controlling the hand, what would happen?

(1) Nothing would happen.

(2) The hand would move downward.

(3) The hand would move to the right.

(4) The hand would move upward.

(5) The hand would move to the left.

41. If an athlete knows that building muscles requires doing work against a weight, what would the athlete want to change in this diagram?

(1) nothing

(2) moving the hand upward faster

(3) adding weight to the hand

(4) closing the fist as the arm is raised

(5) exhaling as the arm is raised

Go on to next page

> *Questions 42 and 43 refer to the following passage, which is adapted from* The Sciences: An Integrated Approach, *3rd Edition, by James Trefil and Robert M. Hazen (Wiley).*

Copying DNA Sequence

The polymerase chain reaction (PCR) copies a sequence of DNA. In order to do this, a strand of DNA is mixed with nucleotides (DNA precursors). Nucleotides target a specific piece of DNA, as well as polymerase, an enzyme that helps to assemble DNA. Heat is applied until the temperature reaches 200°F. The energy from the heating separates the DNA strands. The mixture is then cooled to 140°F. At this temperature, the primers attach themselves to the DNA strands. Raising the temperature to 160°F causes the nucleotides to begin to attach to the DNA strands. After all this, two copies of the DNA are created.

42. What process in the polymerase chain reaction separates the DNA strands?

    (1) heating

    (2) chemicals

    (3) pulling

    (4) gravity

    (5) chilling

43. In order to clone an organism, you require an identical DNA blueprint. Why is the PCR something a scientist who is interested in cloning would want to study?

    (1) It creates an identical copy of the DNA.

    (2) PCR clones animals.

    (3) Scientists should know everything.

    (4) A duplicate DNA structure cools clones.

    (5) The heat destroys clones.

> *Questions 44 and 45 refer to the following passage.*

Dogs and Wolves — Relatives?

Current scientific theory is that the familiar family pet, the dog, descended from the wolf, but the dog has taken a very different path. The dog was the first animal to be domesticated, right around the end of the Ice Age.

Dogs are part of an extended family called *Canidae,* which contains 38 different species. Jackals, foxes, wolves, and dogs are all part of this family. Although they are related, wolves and dogs are different. Wolves have smaller heads for the same body weight. Dogs have smaller teeth, a more curved lower jaw, and eyes that are more rounded and forward looking. At a distance, however, many of these differences are difficult to spot.

44. What feature makes the wolf better adapted to hunting in the wild?

    (1) heavier coat

    (2) larger body

    (3) larger teeth

    (4) larger paws

    (5) deeper growl

45. Of the members of the *Canidae* family that were mentioned, why is the dog the only household pet?

    (1) There are many types of dogs to choose from.

    (2) Dogs were domesticated.

    (3) Dogs are smaller than wolves.

    (4) Dogs protect people's houses.

    (5) Dogs can help the visually impaired.

Go on to next page ⟹

Questions 46 through 48 refer to the following passage.

Isotopes

Isotopes are chemical cousins. They are related to each other, but each isotope has slightly different — but related — atoms. Each of the related atoms has the same number of electrons or protons but a different number of neutrons. Because the number of electrons or protons determines the atomic number, isotopes have the same atomic number.

The number of neutrons determines the mass number. Because the number of neutrons in each isotope is different, the mass number is also different. These cousins all have different mass numbers but the same atomic number. Their chemical properties are similar but not the same. Like most cousins, they have family resemblances, but each has a unique personality.

46. What determines the atomic number?

    (1) number of isotopes

    (2) number of neutrons

    (3) number of electrons

    (4) number of atoms

    (5) number of chemicals

47. Isotopes of a chemical have the same

    (1) number of neutrons

    (2) number of atoms

    (3) mass number

    (4) size

    (5) atomic number

48. A scientist has found related atoms in two different substances. If both atoms have the same atomic number but different mass numbers, what preliminary conclusion can be reached about the atoms?

    (1) They are the same substance.

    (2) They are isotopes.

    (3) They are different substances.

    (4) One is a compound of the other.

    (5) It is too early to make any decisions.

Go on to next page

Questions 49 and 50 refer to the following passage.

How to Survive the Winter

When the temperature drops and the wind blows cold, you may think of animals that don't have homes to keep out the cold and worry about their ability to survive the winter. Not much food is available, temperatures in northern states go into the sub-zero range, and shelter is limited. How do they survive the winter?

Many animals can hibernate for the winter. Hibernation is a sleep-like condition in which the animal's heartbeat, temperature, and metabolism slow down to adapt to the colder temperatures. This dormant condition prevents their starving or freezing during the harsh winters.

49. Bears survive the winter by

    (1) going south

    (2) living in warm caves

    (3) growing a heavy winter coat

    (4) absorbing the sun's rays to keep warm

    (5) finding a safe shelter and hibernating

50. Why should you not disturb a hibernating animal?

    (1) It gets grouchy when awakened suddenly.

    (2) It needs its sleep.

    (3) It could have trouble falling asleep again.

    (4) You should never bother a wild animal.

    (5) It would not be able to find enough food to survive.

END OF TEST

Chapter 16

Answers and Explanations for the Science Test

· ·

*A*fter taking the Science Test in Chapter 15, use this chapter to check your answers. Take your time as you move through the explanations of the answers that we provide in the first section. They can help you understand why you missed the answers you did. You may also want to read the explanations for the questions you answered correctly because doing so can give you a better understanding of the thought process that helped you choose the correct answers.

If you're short on time, turn to the end of the chapter for an abbreviated answer key.

Analysis of the Answers

1. **2.** Glass contains no encapsulated air and, thus, provides neither insulation nor greater thermal flow. Choice (1), that cinder blocks are thicker, can be true, but it doesn't answer the question about heat transfer. Choice (2), that windows have little insulation value, is the best answer. Choice (3), that you can't see through cinder blocks, is true and interesting but irrelevant to the question. Choice (4), that there is no air in a cinder block, is inaccurate. Choice (5), that windows are necessary for safety, is not only irrelevant, but also incorrect. To answer this question, you need to know that good insulators contain trapped air and that glass doesn't. It's assumed that this information is general knowledge for someone at this educational level.

2. **3.** The passage says that insulation is necessary for reduced heat transfer, which keeps you warmer. All the answers except Choice (3) refer to clothing made of a single layer of material. The cotton padding acts as insulation for the trousers because the cotton contains trapped air.

3. **5.** The last paragraph of the passage states that animals must eat food with chemical potential energy, which is derived from plants. The other answers are irrelevant to the information in the passage.

This passage gives you a lot of interesting information, but because you have a time limit, you may want to read the question first and then look for the answer in the passage instead of reading the passage, reading the question, and then reading the passage again.

4. **4.** Plants produce food using energy from the sun. If you cut off the energy from the sun, you cut off the food supply. The other answers may be symptoms of a plant's starving to death, but Choice (4) sums up the information in one answer.

5. **1.** According to the passage, pyruvic acid is key to energy production. This question is a good example of why a little bit of knowledge and familiarity with the words and names used in science are helpful on these tests. All the answer choices in this question are chemical names, and some familiarity with them would make answering the question easier.

6. **5.** The passage states that velocity can be represented by a vector because it has both magnitude and direction. Force is defined as changing the state or motion of an object, either in magnitude or direction. Because a force has magnitude and direction, it's represented by a vector. The information needed to answer this question is in the last sentence of the first paragraph. You can ignore the first three answer choices completely because they have very little to do with the question. Choice (4) requires you to know the difference between a vector and a scalar. The last line of each paragraph in the passage contains the definitions you need.

7. **2.** If a person travels seven blocks from home to school, only the distance is defined. The person can go four blocks due east and three blocks due west. He or she can take a roundabout path involving all four points of the compass. You really don't know what the person is doing except somehow traveling seven blocks to school. This activity has only a magnitude and no direction, so it's represented by a scalar. After you understand the definition of a scalar, which you need to answer question 6, this question is easier to answer. You can ignore Choices (1) and (3) because they are measures of length and do not answer the question. Choice (4) is wrong because a vector has both magnitude and direction, and Choice (5) is irrelevant.

8. **2.** In the steam engine, water cools the steam, which then condenses, occupying less space. This action starts the entire cycle over again. You can eliminate the other answer choices when guessing is necessary. Choice (1) is incorrect because water and steam are both water, in different states. Their densities may be different, but their weights are the same. Only the volume differs when water turns to steam. Choice (3) is incorrect because the boiler doesn't provide the energy to move the pump, which you can see by looking at the diagram. Choice (4) isn't based on information given in the diagram. Nowhere are you told the weight of the pump rod. Choice (5) isn't based on the diagram, on fact, or on general knowledge.

9. **3.** The pump pushes water into the cistern. The other choices don't answer the question based on the information provided in the diagram. Knowing how to answer questions based on diagrams is a useful skill to have for tests like this one.

10. **3.** The producers provide food for the consumers. If the producers stay the same but the consumers increase, the consumers won't have enough food, so the consumers will starve. The other answer choices are incorrect based on the information provided.

11. **3.** The passage states that the temperature of the first tiny particles was 10 billion degrees.

 This question is excellent for practicing your skimming skills to find the answer. When you skim the passage, the words *10 billion degrees* should jump out at you. By reading the whole sentence, you confirm that your answer is correct. The other answer choices are wrong, and your skimming skills take charge. When an answer is as definite as this one, skimming the passage is usually helpful.

12. **5.** The last paragraph states that gravity transformed the atoms into galaxies. This question is another example of when a basic knowledge of science-related words can be helpful.

13. **3.** The passage states that quarks are elemental particles. This question asks for a definition. A quick skim of the passage guides you toward the last sentence in the second paragraph, which contains the definition you're looking for.

14. **5.** An atomic bomb uses a nuclear reaction to produce its massive damage. The passage states that hydrogen and helium atoms were formed by nuclear reactions. The other choices don't answer the question based on the passage. Choice (1) may be right, but it's irrelevant in this context. Choices (2) and (4) are incorrect; and Choice (3) may be interesting in another context, but it's wrong here.

15. **4.** According to the passage (third sentence in the first paragraph), invertebrates have no backbones. The other choices may be correct, but they don't answer the question. Here

and in all questions on this test, you're looking for the best answer that answers the question posed. Don't get sidetracked by other choices that are correct based on your knowledge or even based on the passage. The answer to the question posed is always the best response on a multiple-choice test.

16. **4.** Jellyfish can sting swimmers, and the stings are painful. You find this information in the last sentence of the third paragraph. The other choices don't answer the question based on the passage. For example, Choice (3) may be the stuff nightmares are based on, but the information or misinformation isn't in the passage, so you can't consider it.

17. **2.** Small ocean creatures are always on the menu for jellyfish. Creatures, in general, avoid predators — a fact that's general science knowledge.

Reading some science articles or books is good preparation for this test, but always remember not to base your answers on your prior reading. Rather, base all your answers on the material presented in the passages.

18. **2.** The passage states that energy can't be created or destroyed, so the energy from the lightning must be transformed into another type of energy. The other answer choices imply that the energy has somehow disappeared, which the passage says can't happen.

19. **1.** Science is an ordered discipline and, as such, needs laws to maintain its organization. The first sentence in the second paragraph spells out this idea. Choice (5) may be true, but it's irrelevant. Choice (2) is obviously incorrect. Choices (3) and (4) may be interesting for conversation, but they don't answer the question using the material in the passage.

20. **4.** Matter can't be created or destroyed. Thus, a rabbit can't appear except by illusion. The other answer choices seem scientific but have nothing to do with the question. Always read the question carefully to make sure you're answering it.

21. **5.** When ice melts, it turns into water. Although the amount of water in a melting iceberg is tiny compared to the amount of water in the ocean, it does add some water to the ocean. Choices (1) and (2) are incorrect because, although the melting of the iceberg and the warming of the water may be the results of global warming, these choices don't answer the question. Choices (3) and (4) are incorrect. This question is a good example of what can happen if you read a question too quickly and answer it from general knowledge. Use the information in the passage to find the best answer to the question.

22. **1.** Flashlights provide light by using the energy in the battery. The passage says that energy can't be created or destroyed, so the energy in the battery must have been converted or transformed into something else. In reality, even if you don't use a battery for an extended time, the battery grows weaker because of other reactions inside the cell. But this tidbit isn't mentioned in the passage and is just a reminder not to leave batteries in your flashlight forever.

23. **4.** If you add 3 ounces of water to 1 ounce of salt, you have 4 ounces of combined ingredients. The combined mass is the same as the sum of the individual masses. The volume may be different, but the question doesn't ask you about the volume. Choices (1) and (5) may seem to be relevant if not correct, but they don't answer the question because they have nothing to do with mass. Choice (3) is also wrong because the salt doesn't disappear; it dissolves in the water.

24. **3.** The Law of Conservation of Energy states that energy can't be created or destroyed. Thus, the energy developed by the ball rolling down the hill can't disappear. In reality, there's friction between the ball and the ground that slows it down, and the hills don't go on forever — so the ball will eventually come to rest. You may have learned this information elsewhere, but it doesn't answer the question based on the passage. No information in the passage supports Choices (1) and (5). Choice (2) may be true, but it's irrelevant, and Choice (4) is cute but incorrect.

25. **4.** Conservation of energy is a law of science. You can immediately eliminate the other answers because they are obviously irrelevant. Choice (4) is the only choice that answers the question.

26. **3.** The passage states that the lack of food in the winter months makes most birds fly south to find sources of food. When the food returns to the northern states, so do the birds. The other choices don't answer the question based on the information in the passage.

27. **3.** Some birds eat insects for their food supply. If an area has no insects, the birds move to find a new source of food. General reading in science tells you that living creatures go where the food is. Even human beings, who can choose where to live, are unlikely to move somewhere that lacks food. Other creatures have a more basic instinct to move to where there's a supply of food. Thus, the insects have a responsibility for the birds' migration — although their main contribution is being eaten.

28. **1.** Scientists are curious about anything that happens regularly that can't be easily explained. Migration is one such issue. Choice (5) may have happened, but it isn't spelled out in the passage. The key word here is *Every* at the beginning of the first sentence.

29. **5.** This question may have many answers, from sport fishermen to algae to snails. Of the potential answers given, however, Nile Perch is the best one because the introduction of this species caused all the subsequent problems.

30. **5.** This question asks you to make a general statement about foreign species of fish. Although this question doesn't ask you specifically to consider the Lake Victoria example, you're supposed to think about that example as you answer the question. Using the Lake Victoria example, you can safely say that a foreign species upsets the local ecological balance. You also know from the example that the other four choices are incorrect.

31. **1.** The less fuel you need to launch, the less you have to carry. The gravity on the moon is less than that on Earth, so you need less force and less fuel to break free of gravity. Choices (2), (3), and (4) may seem to have a ring of truth, but they don't answer the question.

32. **5.** The only locations mentioned in the table are Mars and the moon, and you're supposed to answer the question based on the material given. Thus, you don't have enough information to answer the question.

33. **2.** According to the table, it takes just 3 days to get to the moon, which is a much better first choice than the 1.88 years needed to get to Mars. The other choices are irrelevant to the question and the given table.

34. **1.** Gravity on the moon is less than that on Mars. Because gravity is the force that attracts you to the moon (or to Earth or to Mars), the less the gravity, the less the attraction between you and the surface on which you stand, and, thus, the higher and farther you can jump — which, as you may know, is the goal of a pole-vaulting contest.

35. **4.** The passage states that heredity determines the characteristics of the next generation. The only other answer choice mentioned in the passage is Choice (3), but this choice doesn't answer the question.

36. **5.** The passage states, "These characteristics, passed from one generation to the next, are called the genetic code." Thus, the best answer is Choice (5), *genetic code*.

37. **3.** If children inherit the traits of their parents, you want the desired traits of your child pumpkin to be a part of the traits of the parent pumpkins. Monster-sized pumpkin seeds have a better chance of producing extra large pumpkins than do the seeds from a regular-sized pumpkin. Although Choice (2) seems like a possibility, the passage doesn't mention the effects of fertilizer on monster-pumpkin production.

38. **5.** All the choices except Choice (5) — that the booster is no longer needed — are incorrect because they're in direct opposition to the passage. If you can quickly eliminate some or

most of the answer choices, you can save time answering the question. In this case, you can eliminate four answers, making the final choice easy and quick.

39. **3.** Because the booster is jettisoned after takeoff, the orbiter has to carry everything that continues on the trip. Choices (2), (4), and (5) are wrong and can be quickly eliminated.

40. **2.** If the force pushing down is greater than the force pushing up, the hand would move down. Although this question is based on the given diagram, which gives a general idea of what happens when a hand holds weight, the answer to the question is in the first part of the question itself. If the force of gravity (the downward force) is greater than the force of the muscles moving upward, the resultant force would be downward.

41. **3.** A larger weight in the hand would produce a greater force downward. Thus, the athlete would have to work harder against this extra weight (and, as a result, would build more muscle). Making the displacement of the hand larger would also increase the work done, but this isn't an answer choice.

42. **1.** The fourth sentence in the passage tells you that heating is the process that separates DNA strands. The other choices either don't answer the question or are wrong.

43. **1.** Cloning requires identical DNA. As you can see from the first sentence of the passage, PCR provides identical copies of DNA.

44. **3.** The larger teeth of the wolf are better for hunting. The third sentence of the third paragraph of the passage states that dogs have smaller teeth, which means wolves must have bigger teeth. Although this information isn't stated directly in the passage, it's implied. You're expected to be able to draw conclusions from the information given, so read carefully. The other answer choices are incorrect. True, some dogs have heavier coats, larger bodies, and so on, but this information isn't in the passage. You can answer the question using only information given or implied in the passage — not information from your general knowledge or prior reading.

45. **2.** The passage states that the dog was domesticated very long ago. A domesticated animal is preferable to a wild one for a household pet. The other answers may be factually correct, but they aren't part of the information included in the passage.

46. **3.** According to the first sentence of the passage, the atomic number is determined by the number of electrons or protons. Skimming the paragraph after reading the question for key words in the question makes choosing the correct answer faster and easier.

47. **5.** The last sentence of the first paragraph of the passage states that isotopes have the same atomic number.

In most cases, you don't have to memorize factual information for these tests; the passages give you the factual information you need to know. Remember that the answers are based on the factual information given.

48. **2.** The last sentence of the first paragraph of the passage states that isotopes have the same atomic number. The second sentence of the second paragraph tells you that isotopes have different mass numbers. This question requires using two bits of information from two different locations in the passage to decide on the right answer.

49. **5.** According to the first sentence of the second paragraph of the passage, bears survive the winter by finding a safe shelter and hibernating.

50. **5.** Animals hibernate in the winter when food is scarce (a fact implied from the last sentence in the second paragraph). If you wake up a hibernating animal, that animal awakes to a strange environment without its usual sources of food and probably wouldn't be able to find enough food to survive. The other answer choices may be right in some circumstances, but they don't relate to the passage. Choice (4) is good advice, but it isn't a good answer.

Answer Key

1. 2	18. 2	35. 4
2. 3	19. 1	36. 5
3. 5	20. 4	37. 3
4. 4	21. 5	38. 5
5. 1	22. 1	39. 3
6. 5	23. 4	40. 2
7. 2	24. 3	41. 3
8. 2	25. 4	42. 1
9. 3	26. 3	43. 1
10. 3	27. 3	44. 3
11. 3	28. 1	45. 2
12. 5	29. 5	46. 3
13. 3	30. 5	47. 5
14. 5	31. 1	48. 2
15. 4	32. 5	49. 5
16. 4	33. 2	50. 5
17. 2	34. 1	

Chapter 17

Another Practice Test — Science Test

• •

*T*he Science Test consists of multiple-choice questions intended to measure general concepts in science. The questions are based on short readings that may include a graph, chart, or figure. Study the information given and then answer the question(s) following it. Refer to the information as often as necessary in answering the questions.

You have 80 minutes to answer the 50 questions in this test. Work carefully, but do not spend too much time on any one question. Be sure you answer every question.

Answer Sheet for Science Test

1 ① ② ③ ④ ⑤	26 ① ② ③ ④ ⑤
2 ① ② ③ ④ ⑤	27 ① ② ③ ④ ⑤
3 ① ② ③ ④ ⑤	28 ① ② ③ ④ ⑤
4 ① ② ③ ④ ⑤	29 ① ② ③ ④ ⑤
5 ① ② ③ ④ ⑤	30 ① ② ③ ④ ⑤
6 ① ② ③ ④ ⑤	31 ① ② ③ ④ ⑤
7 ① ② ③ ④ ⑤	32 ① ② ③ ④ ⑤
8 ① ② ③ ④ ⑤	33 ① ② ③ ④ ⑤
9 ① ② ③ ④ ⑤	34 ① ② ③ ④ ⑤
10 ① ② ③ ④ ⑤	35 ① ② ③ ④ ⑤
11 ① ② ③ ④ ⑤	36 ① ② ③ ④ ⑤
12 ① ② ③ ④ ⑤	37 ① ② ③ ④ ⑤
13 ① ② ③ ④ ⑤	38 ① ② ③ ④ ⑤
14 ① ② ③ ④ ⑤	39 ① ② ③ ④ ⑤
15 ① ② ③ ④ ⑤	40 ① ② ③ ④ ⑤
16 ① ② ③ ④ ⑤	41 ① ② ③ ④ ⑤
17 ① ② ③ ④ ⑤	42 ① ② ③ ④ ⑤
18 ① ② ③ ④ ⑤	43 ① ② ③ ④ ⑤
19 ① ② ③ ④ ⑤	44 ① ② ③ ④ ⑤
20 ① ② ③ ④ ⑤	45 ① ② ③ ④ ⑤
21 ① ② ③ ④ ⑤	46 ① ② ③ ④ ⑤
22 ① ② ③ ④ ⑤	47 ① ② ③ ④ ⑤
23 ① ② ③ ④ ⑤	48 ① ② ③ ④ ⑤
24 ① ② ③ ④ ⑤	49 ① ② ③ ④ ⑤
25 ① ② ③ ④ ⑤	50 ① ② ③ ④ ⑤

Science Test

Do not mark in this test booklet. Record your answers on the separate answer sheet provided. Be sure that all requested information is properly recorded on the answer sheet.

To record your answers, fill in the numbered circle on the answer sheet that corresponds to the answer you select for each question in the test booklet.

EXAMPLE:

Which of the following is the smallest unit in a living thing?

(1) tissue

(2) organ

(3) cell

(4) muscle

(5) capillary

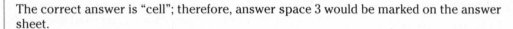

(On Answer Sheet)

① ② ● ④ ⑤

The correct answer is "cell"; therefore, answer space 3 would be marked on the answer sheet.

Do not rest the point of your pencil on the answer sheet while you are considering your answer. Make no stray or unnecessary marks. If you change an answer, erase your first mark completely. Mark only one answer space for each question; multiple answers will be scored as incorrect. Do not fold or crease your answer sheet. All test materials must be returned to the test administrator.

Note: Refer to Chapter 18 for the answers for this practice test.

DO NOT BEGIN TAKING THIS TEST UNTIL TOLD TO DO SO

Directions: Choose the <u>one best answer</u> to each question.

Questions 1 through 3 refer to the following passage.

Hibernating Plants

Tulips are beautiful flowers that come up early every spring. They are fragile in appearance but manage to survive the uncertain weather of spring, blooming for a while, and then sleeping for the rest of the year. The next year, they are ready to peek out of the earth and brighten your spring again.

Tulips survive because they grow from bulbs. Each bulb stores moisture and food during good weather. When the weather turns, the plant hibernates: The roots and leaves dry out and fall off, but the bulb develops a tough outer skin to protect itself. The bulb becomes dormant until the following spring, when the whole cycle begins again.

1. Which part of the tulip allows it to survive a rough winter?

    (1) the leaves

    (2) the buds

    (3) the bulb

    (4) the roots

    (5) the stem

2. If you wanted an early blooming plant to give your garden color in spring, which of the following would you plant?

    (1) rose

    (2) petunia

    (3) tulip

    (4) begonia

    (5) impatiens

3. When you are enjoying your garden in spring or summer, the flowers that look so pretty are composed of cells. These cells are the basic unit of all living things in the universe. In addition to flowers, weeds, trees, and even you are composed of cells. Although garden plants are composed of cells, the cells are different from plant to plant. That is why some plants produce roses and others produce dandelions.

    Which of the following is not composed of cells?

    (1) dogs

    (2) flowers

    (3) gravity

    (4) Sir Isaac Newton

    (5) the forest

Go on to next page

> Questions 4 and 5 refer to the following passage.

Gunpowder

As you watch a Western on television, have you ever wondered how the bullet is propelled out of the gun when the trigger is pulled?

Bullets are made of two parts, the jacket and the projectile. The jacket is filled with gunpowder and an ignition device, and when the ignition device is hit, the gunpowder explodes, hurling the projectile out of the barrel of the gun.

4. In the movies, guns with blank cartridges are used for effect. What part of the cartridge would be different from a cartridge used for target practice?

(1) bullet

(2) casing

(3) barrel

(4) gunpowder

(5) projectile

5. If you wanted to reduce the force with which a projectile was hurled out of the barrel, what would you change?

(1) Use a smaller jacket.

(2) Use a smaller projectile.

(3) Use a smaller gun.

(4) Use less gunpowder in the jacket.

(5) Use more gunpowder.

> Questions 6 and 7 refer to the following passage.

Rocket Propulsion

Have you ever wondered how a rocket ship moves? Perhaps you have seen science-fiction movies in which a captain uses a blast of the rocket engines to save the ship and its crew from crashing into the surface of a distant planet.

Usually, a fuel, such as the gas in a car, needs an oxidizer, like air, to create combustion, which powers the engine. In space, there is no air and, thus, no oxidizer. The rocket ship, being a clever design, carries its own oxidizer. The fuel used may be a liquid or a solid, but the rocket ship always has fuel and an oxidizer to mix together. When the two are mixed and combustion takes place, a rapid expansion is directed out the back of the engine. The force pushing backward moves the rocket ship forward. In space, with no air, the rocket ship experiences no resistance to the movement. The rocket ship moves forward, avoids the crash, or does whatever the crew wants it to do.

6. Why is the rocket engine the perfect propulsion method for space travel?

(1) It's very powerful.

(2) It can operate without an external oxidizer.

(3) It carries a lot of fuel.

(4) You can't hear the noise it makes.

(5) It accelerates quickly.

7. Fuel on a rocket ship may be

(1) an oxidizer

(2) a gas

(3) an air

(4) an expansion

(5) a liquid

Go on to next page

Questions 8 through 16 refer to the following passage.

Where Does All the Garbage Go?

When we finish using something, we throw it away, but where is away? In our modern cities, away is usually a landfill site, piled high with all those things that we no longer want. A modern American city generates solid waste or garbage at an alarming rate. Every day, New York City produces 17,000 tons of garbage and ships it to Staten Island, where it is added to yesterday's 17,000 tons in a landfill site. We each produce enough garbage every five years to equal the volume of the Statue of Liberty. In spite of all the efforts to increase recycling, we go on our merry way producing garbage without thinking about where it goes.

In any landfill, gone is not forgotten by nature. By compacting the garbage to reduce its volume, we slow the rate of decomposition, which makes our garbage last longer. In a modern landfill, the process produces a garbage lasagna. There's a layer of compacted garbage covered by a layer of dirt, covered by a layer of compacted garbage and so on. By saving space for more garbage, we cut off the air and water needed to decompose the garbage and, thus, preserve it for future generations. If you could dig far enough, you might still be able to read forty-year-old newspapers. The paper may be preserved, but the news is history.

One of the answers to this problem is recycling. Any object that can be reused in one form or another is an object that shouldn't be found in a landfill. Most of us gladly recycle our paper, which saves energy and resources. Recycled paper can be used again and even turned into other products. Recycling old newspapers is not as valuable as hidden treasure, but when the cost of landfills and the environmental impact of producing more and more newsprint is considered, it can be a bargain. If plastic shopping bags can be recycled into a cloth-like substance which can be used to make reusable shopping bags, maybe American ingenuity can find ways to reduce all that garbage being stored in landfills before the landfills overtake the space for cities.

8. Why are modern landfills as much a part of the problem as a part of the solution?

    (1) They look very ugly.

    (2) They take up a lot of valuable land.

    (3) The bacteria that aid decomposition do not thrive.

    (4) Newspapers are readable after 50 years.

    (5) Archeologists have no place to dig.

9. Why is recycling paper important?

    (1) It looks neater.

    (2) It reduces the need for new landfill sites.

    (3) Newspaper is not biodegradable.

    (4) It saves money.

    (5) Newspapers do not fit into compost heaps.

10. Why is solid waste compacted in a modern landfill?

    (1) to reduce the odor

    (2) to help the bacteria decompose the waste

    (3) to make the landfill look better

    (4) to reduce the amount of space it occupies

    (5) to speed up the nitrogen cycle

11. What is the modern landfill compared to?

    (1) an efficient way of ridding cities of solid waste

    (2) a garbage lasagna

    (3) a place for bacteria to decompose solid waste

    (4) a site for archeologists to explore

    (5) a huge compost bin

Go on to next page

12. Why is it important for cities to establish recycling programs?

    (1) It makes people feel good about their garbage.

    (2) It is cheaper to recycle.

    (3) Recycling lets someone else look after your problem.

    (4) You are running out of bacteria to decompose waste.

    (5) It is cheaper than the cost of new land-fill sites.

13. What can individual Americans do to reduce the amount of waste that is going into the landfills?

    (1) Eat less.

    (2) Reuse and recycle as much as possible.

    (3) Stop using paper.

    (4) Import more nitrogen.

    (5) Grow more bacteria.

14. Bacteria provide what helpful purpose in composting?

    (1) They help get rid of illness.

    (2) They make rodents sick.

    (3) They are part of the inorganic cycle.

    (4) They help decompose composting waste.

    (5) They make yogurt taste distinctive.

15. If municipalities lose money recycling paper, why do they continue?

    (1) The politicians don't know they are losing money.

    (2) Municipalities don't have to make money.

    (3) The public likes to recycle paper.

    (4) The cost is less than acquiring more landfill sites.

    (5) Recycling paper has become part of urban life.

16. How does recycling paper save money for the city?

    (1) Recycling trucks run on diesel fuel.

    (2) New landfill sites cost money to buy.

    (3) Municipalities don't have to burn the paper.

    (4) In a landfill site, the heavy machinery uses a lot of fuel.

    (5) Newspapers have to be delivered.

Go on to next page

> *Questions 17 and 18 refer to the following passage.*

Air Bags

Most new cars are equipped with air bags. In a crash, the air bags quickly deploy, protecting the driver and front-seat passenger by inflating to absorb the initial force of the crash. Air bags deploy so quickly and with such force that they can injure a short adult sitting too close to the dashboard or a child in a car seat. This safety device has to be treated with respect. With the proper precautions, air bags save lives. In fact, a person in the front seat of a modern car equipped with air bags who also wears a seat belt stands a much better chance of surviving a crash than an unbelted person. The two safety devices work together to save lives but must be used properly.

17. In a front-end collision, what absorbs the force of the crash?

    (1) air bags

    (2) the car's frame

    (3) the seats

    (4) padded dashboards

    (5) the windshield

18. Where is the safest place for an infant in a car seat in a car equipped with air bags?

    (1) in the rear seat

    (2) in the front seat

    (3) on the right side of the car

    (4) on the left side of the car

    (5) where the infant can be tended by an adult

Go on to next page

Questions 19 through 22 refer to the following diagram, which is excerpted from The Sciences: An Integrated Approach, 3rd Edition, by James Trefil and Robert M. Hazen (Wiley).

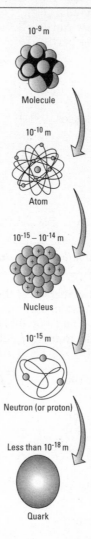

10^{-9} m

Molecule

10^{-10} m

Atom

$10^{-15} - 10^{-14}$ m

Nucleus

10^{-15} m

Neutron (or proton)

Less than 10^{-18} m

Quark

19. According to this diagram, what is the building block upon which the other particles are made?

(1) atom

(2) molecule

(3) neutron

(4) quark

(5) proton

20. According to this diagram, how many times larger is a molecule than a quark?

(1) 100

(2) 1,000

(3) 1,000,000

(4) 1,000,000,000

(5) 10,000,000,000

Go on to next page

21. Scientists thought that the atom was the smallest particle that existed, but they were wrong. There are smaller particles than the atom, and the atom is not itself a solid. If people cannot see atoms, how can scientists know that there are smaller particles than atoms?

    (1) They guess.

    (2) They experiment.

    (3) They use powerful magnifying glasses.

    (4) They use logic.

    (5) Another scientist told them.

22. The seat you are sitting on seems solid, but in reality, it is composed of atoms. Each of the atoms is composed of a nucleus, which is composed of neutrons and protons, but much of the space occupied by an atom is just empty space. This means that the chair you are sitting on is mostly empty space. It follows that when you stand on the floor of a building, you are ultimately being supported by

    (1) wood

    (2) concrete

    (3) girders

    (4) atoms

    (5) chemical reactions

Questions 23 and 24 refer to the following passage.

The Surface of the Moon

The surface of the moon is a hostile, barren landscape. Astronauts have found boulders as large as houses in huge fields of dust and rock. They've had no maps to guide them but have survived, thanks to their training for the mission.

23. What is it about the lunar landscape that may make landing there dangerous?

    (1) Astronauts have to consider the possibility of hostile aliens.

    (2) The moon is full of large, uncharted spaces with very large boulders.

    (3) The moon has unlit landing fields with uncertain footings.

    (4) Not all maps of the moon are accurate.

    (5) Spacecraft has poor brakes for this type of terrain.

24. What aspect of the moon makes the height of a boulder unimportant for the astronauts moving about?

    (1) Astronauts have training in flying.

    (2) There are special tools for flying over boulders.

    (3) Astronauts can drive around an obstruction.

    (4) Low gravity makes climbing easier, if it's necessary.

    (5) The boulder is not that big.

Go on to next page

Questions 25 and 26 refer to the following passage.

Pushing Aside the Water

If you fill a glass right to the brim with water, you have to drink it at its present temperature. If you decide that you want to add ice, the water spills over the brim. The ice has displaced an amount of water equal to the volume of the ice.

When you lower yourself into a luxurious bubble bath in your tub, the water rises. If you could measure the volume of that rise, you could figure out the volume of your body. Because you would displace a volume of water in the tub equal to the volume of your body, the new combined volume of you plus the water, minus the original volume of the water, equals the volume of your body. Next time you sink slowly into that hot bathwater, make sure that you leave room for the water to rise or make sure that you are prepared to mop the floor.

25. When you sink into a tub of water, you displace

   (1) your weight in water

   (2) a lot of water

   (3) bubbles

   (4) a volume equal to the volume of your body

   (5) the soap

26. If you wanted to find the volume of an irregularly shaped object, how could you do it?

   (1) Put the object in a pre-measured volume of water and measure the increase.

   (2) Measure the object and calculate the volume.

   (3) Weigh the object and calculate the volume.

   (4) Put the object in an oven and heat it.

   (5) Look it up.

Go on to next page ⟹

> *Questions 27 through 29 refer to the following passage.*

Newton's First Law of Motion

In 1687, Isaac Newton proposed three laws of motion. These laws are not the types of laws that we are familiar with; they are statements of a truth in the field of physics. Newton's First Law of Motion states that a body at rest prefers to remain at rest and a body in motion prefers to stay in motion unless acted upon by an external force. One example you may be familiar with is the game of billiards. Each of the balls will remain in its position unless hit by the cue ball. Once hit, the ball will continue to roll until the friction of the table's surface or an external force stops it.

Inertia is the tendency of any object to maintain a uniform motion or remain at rest. This law has been adopted in current language. When we say that businesses or people are being held back because of their inertia, we mean that they will either languish in their immobility or refuse to change direction in spite of all the input from employees and advisors. In 1687 when Newton was formulating his First Law of Motion, he was not aware of the profound effect it would have on the world of science and common language.

27. If your car becomes stuck in a snow bank, what must you do to free it?

    (1) Apply a force downward to increase the traction of the wheels.

    (2) Leave it at rest until it wants to move.

    (3) Apply a force in the direction you want it to move.

    (4) Sit on the hood to increase the weight on the front tires.

    (5) Blame Newton.

28. A company that refuses to change its ideas is said to suffer from

    (1) downturns

    (2) stability

    (3) manipulation

    (4) inertia

    (5) poor management

29. When you are driving at a steady speed on the highway, why does it take great effort to stop suddenly?

    (1) Cars should have the right of way.

    (2) It takes too much power to start driving again.

    (3) Pedestrians should stay in parks.

    (4) Your car tends to continue at the same rate.

    (5) Driving is difficult enough without distractions.

Go on to next page

> Question 30 refers to the following passage.

Newton's Second Law of Motion

Newton's Second Law of Motion states that when a body changes its velocity because an external force is applied to it, that change in velocity is directly proportional to the force and inversely proportional to the mass of the body. That is, the faster you want to stop your car, the harder you must brake. The brakes apply an external force that reduces the velocity of the car. The faster you want to accelerate the car, the more force you must apply. Increasing the horsepower of an engine allows it to apply greater force in accelerating. That is why drag racer cars seem to be all engine.

30. If you want a car that accelerates quickly, which attributes give you the best acceleration?

    (1) lightweight and two doors

    (2) high horsepower and automatic transmission

    (3) automatic transmission

    (4) automatic transmission and two doors

    (5) lightweight and high horsepower

> Question 31 refers to the following passage.

Newton's Third Law of Motion

Newton's Third Law of Motion states that for every action there is an equal and opposite reaction. If you stand on the floor, gravity pulls your body down with a certain force. The floor must exert an equal and opposite force upward on your feet, or you would fall through the floor.

31. A boxer is punching a punching bag. What is the punching bag doing to the boxer?

    (1) bouncing away from the boxer

    (2) reacting with a force equal and opposite to the force of his punch

    (3) swinging with a velocity equal to that of the punch

    (4) swinging back with a force greater than that of the punch

    (5) remaining still

Go on to next page

Questions 32 through 34 refer to the following passage.

Why Don't Polar Bears Freeze?

Watching a polar bear lumber through the frigid Arctic wilderness, you may wonder why it doesn't freeze. If you were there, you would likely freeze. In fact, you may feel cold just looking at photographs of polar bears.

Professor Stephan Steinlechner of Hanover Veterinary University in Germany set out to answer the question of why polar bears don't freeze. Polar bears have black skin. This means that, in effect, polar bears have a huge solar heat collector covering their body. Covering this black skin are white hollow hairs. These hairs act as insulation, keeping the heat inside the fur covering. This is like an insulated house. The heat stays in for a long period of time.

This is an interesting theory and does answer the question, except you may still wonder how they keep warm at night, when the sun isn't out!

32. The most important element in retaining the polar bear's body heat is its

    (1) paws

    (2) scalp

    (3) skin

    (4) blood

    (5) hair

33. What is the polar bear's solar heat collector?

    (1) caves

    (2) ice

    (3) its furry coat

    (4) the snow

    (5) its skin

34. If you had to live in the arctic, what sort of clothing would be most appropriate?

    (1) insulated coats

    (2) silk underwear

    (3) black clothing with fur covering

    (4) white clothing with fur covering

    (5) heavy wool

Go on to next page

Questions 35 and 36 refer to the following diagram, which is excerpted from The Sciences: An Integrated Approach, *3rd Edition, by James Trefil and Robert M. Hazen (Wiley).*

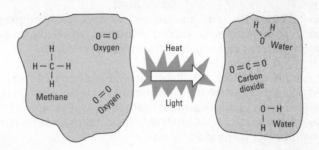

35. When methane burns, it produces light, heat, carbon dioxide, and water. Why would natural gas be a good choice for keeping your house warm in winter?

    (1) The chemical reaction produces carbon dioxide.

    (2) The chemical reaction produces light.

    (3) The chemical reaction produces water.

    (4) The chemical reaction uses oxygen.

    (5) The chemical reaction produces heat.

36. If firefighters were faced with a methane fire, what would they want to eliminate to put out the fire?

    (1) heat

    (2) light

    (3) water

    (4) carbon dioxide

    (5) oxygen

Questions 37 and 38 refer to the following passage.

Paternity Testing

DNA has become part of everyone's vocabulary, and several crime shows on television use it as a key plot element. DNA has put criminals in jail and freed others. It is used as proof in trials and is an important dramatic tool on many television dramas and talk shows.

Another use for DNA is not as dramatic. Because a child inherits the DNA of his or her parents, DNA testing can prove paternity. This is an example of a practical use for a scientific discovery.

37. Paternity testing compares the DNA of the child with the DNA of the

    (1) mother

    (2) father

    (3) father's aunt

    (4) father and grandfather

    (5) both sides of the family

38. Why is there no need for maternity testing when a child is born?

    (1) A mother's DNA is always the same as her children's.

    (2) Fathers are liable for support.

    (3) Mothers give birth to their children.

    (4) It makes a better drama.

    (5) Fathers may have more than one child.

Go on to next page

Questions 39 through 44 refer to the following passage.

Space Stuff

Each space flight carries items authorized by NASA, but the quirky little items carried in astronauts' pockets are what catch the interest of collectors. Auction sales have been brisk for material carried aboard various space flights.

On the second manned Mercury flight, Gus Grissom carried two rolls of dimes. He was planning to give these to the children of his friends after he returned to Earth. If you carried two rolls of dimes around Earth, they would be worth ten dollars. When Gus Grissom returned to Earth, however, these dimes became space mementos, each worth many times its face value.

Although NASA does not permit the sale of items carried aboard space missions, many items have found their way to market. Eleven Apollo 16 stamps, autographed by the astronauts, sold for $27,000 at auction, but the corned beef sandwich that John Young offered to Gus Grissom never returned to Earth.

39. What did Gus Grissom plan to do with his rolls of dimes?

    (1) Sell them at auction.

    (2) Use them in vending machines.

    (3) Give them to children.

    (4) Donate them to charity.

    (5) Keep them as souvenirs.

40. What happened to John Young's corned beef sandwich?

    (1) It is in storage.

    (2) It was sold.

    (3) It was left on the moon.

    (4) It was eaten.

    (5) Not enough information is given.

41. What is so special about items carried in an astronaut's pocket?

    (1) Weightlessness changes their composition.

    (2) They have been in space.

    (3) Lunar radiation affects them.

    (4) The pockets are made of a special material.

    (5) They are autographed.

42. What would NASA authorize astronauts to carry into space?

    (1) toys to bring home to their kids

    (2) a bulletproof vest

    (3) an extra cup of coffee for the flight

    (4) government documents

    (5) tools for experiments

43. Why would autographed stamps be worth so much money?

    (1) They are rare when personally autographed.

    (2) Stamps always become valuable.

    (3) People collect autographs.

    (4) Astronauts don't give autographs.

    (5) Auctions always get high prices.

44. Why would the contents of an astronaut's pocket become so valuable after a space flight?

    (1) NASA told them not to carry things in their pockets.

    (2) Auctions increase the value of articles.

    (3) Collectors value anything that exists in limited quantities.

    (4) Space travel makes articles magical.

    (5) The astronauts held out for the highest price.

Go on to next page ⟹

Questions 45 and 46 refer to the following passage.

Work

When we think of work, we think of people sitting at desks operating computers or building homes or making some other effort to earn money. When a physicist thinks of work, she probably thinks of a formula — force exerted over a distance. If you don't expend any energy — resulting in a force of zero — or if your force produces no movement, no work has been done. If you pick up your gigantic super-ordinary two-pound hamburger and lift it to your mouth to take a bite, you do work. If you want to resist temptation and just stare at your hamburger, you do no work. If your friend gets tired of you playing around and lifts your hamburger to feed you, you still do no work, but your friend does. In scientific terms, two elements are necessary for work to be done: a force must be exerted and the object to which the force has been exerted must move.

45. If the formula for work is Work = Force × Distance, how much more work would you do in lifting a 10-pound barbell 3 feet instead of 2 feet?

    (1) half as much
    (2) 3 times as much
    (3) ⅓ as much
    (4) 1½ times as much
    (5) 2⅓ times as much

46. While you may see that you do work in climbing a flight of stairs, why do you also do work when you descend a flight of stairs?

    (1) It is hard to climb down stairs.
    (2) You have traveled a distance down the stairs.
    (3) You feel tired after descending stairs.
    (4) You have exerted a force over a distance.
    (5) If you do it at work, it's work.

Go on to next page

Questions 47 and 48 refer to the following figure and passages, which are excerpted from Physical Science: What the Technology Professional Needs to Know, *by C. Lon Enloe, Elizabeth Garnett, Jonathan Miles, and Stephen Swanson (Wiley).*

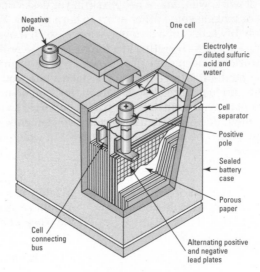

Lead-Acid Storage Battery

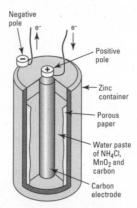

Dry-Cell Battery

The Lead-Acid Storage Battery

One battery you rely on is the 12-volt lead-acid storage battery used in cars and trucks. This battery is composed of six separate cells, each developing about 2 volts. By connecting the six cells in series, the overall voltage becomes the sum, or 12 volts.

The Dry-Cell Battery

The traditional dry-cell or flashlight battery is a zinc-carbon battery. It derives its name from the fact that the liquid portion has been replaced by a moist paste of ammonium chloride, manganese dioxide, and carbon. These components are the anode portion of the cell, and the zinc container serves as the cathode.

Go on to next page

47. If you wanted a 48-volt lead-acid battery, how many cells would it need?

    (1) 24

    (2) 26

    (3) 28

    (4) 36

    (5) 48

48. What replaces the liquid-acid portion of the lead-acid battery in a dry-cell battery?

    (1) a moist paste

    (2) a powder

    (3) dry acid

    (4) carbon and zinc

    (5) a stick of acid

Go on to next page

> *Questions 49 and 50 refer to the following passage.*

The Cell and Heredity

Each cell in a living organism consists of a membrane surrounding a cytoplasm. The cytoplasm is like jelly and has a nucleus in its center. Chromosomes are part of the nucleus. They are important because they store DNA. DNA stores the genetic code that is the basis of heredity.

49. What determines what traits you inherit from your parents?

    (1) the cell

    (2) the atom

    (3) the nucleus

    (4) the neutron

    (5) DNA

50. What part of the chromosome carries the genetic code?

    (1) membrane

    (2) cytoplasm

    (3) nucleus

    (4) atom

    (5) DNA

END OF TEST

Chapter 18

Answers and Explanations for the Science Test

∙ ∙

After taking the Science Test in Chapter 17, use this chapter to check your answers. Take your time as you move through the explanations of the answers that we provide in the first section. They can help you understand why you missed the answers you did. You may also want to read the explanations for the questions you answered correctly because doing so can give you a better understanding of the thought process that helped you choose the correct answers.

If you're short on time, turn to the end of the chapter for an abbreviated answer key.

 If you have trouble finishing the entire Science Test in Chapter 17 in the allotted time, turn to Chapter 16 and read over the answers to the first Science Test (which you can take in Chapter 15). Underline the sentence or sentences that tell you the correct answer to each question. Mark each passage in the test in Chapter 15 to indicate whether you can skim it or you need to read the entire passage to find the answer.

Analysis of the Answers

1. **3.** The passage describes how the bulb changes to allow the tulip to survive the winter. The complete explanation of how the bulb enables the tulip to survive is in the second paragraph.

2. **3.** The passage states that tulips bloom early and grow each year from the bulb.

3. **3.** All the answer choices except gravity are living substances that are made up of cells. Gravity is a force, not a living substance.

4. **5.** Because the projectile is the only part that leaves the gun, and because movie producers and directors don't want to hurt anyone, the guns are altered so that the projectile does no harm. In most cases, there's no projectile and the gun just makes a noise and a flash — nothing comes out of the barrel. The bullet still operates in a similar way with flash and noise, but the nonexistent projectile is harmless.

5. **4.** The force that propels the projectile out of the barrel is the explosion of the gunpowder in the jacket. The force of the explosion is determined by the amount of powder in the jacket. If there's less powder in the jacket, there's less force propelling the projectile out of the barrel.

6. **2.** In space, there's no oxidizer to take part in the chemical reaction needed for combustion. A rocket ship carries its own oxidizer and, thus, can travel through airless space.

7. **5.** The passage states that "the fuel used may be a liquid or a solid." This question asks for only part of the information given in the passage.

8. **3.** The passage states that with the methodology used for burying solid waste in a modern landfill, the bacteria needed for decomposition can't survive. The reason for using landfills is that they require less space — not that they promote decomposition. Thus, the landfill and the processes used within it are as much a part of the problem as part of the solution.

9. **2.** Recycling reduces the need for new landfill sites. In large cities, land is expensive and few people want to live next to a landfill site. Even if you remove the garbage by shipping it elsewhere, as New York City does, it still has to be dumped somewhere. This information, which the passage states, agrees with what you may have read in newspapers and seen on television. This passage is an example of a passage where previous knowledge blends in with the stated material.

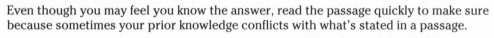

   Even though you may feel you know the answer, read the passage quickly to make sure because sometimes your prior knowledge conflicts with what's stated in a passage.

10. **4.** Solid waste is compacted to reduce the amount of space it occupies, which also happens to make the landfill last longer. The waste is compacted in spite of the fact that doing so slows down decomposition and lengthens the life of the garbage.

11. **2.** A modern landfill is compared to garbage lasagna because it's made up of alternating layers of compacted garbage and dirt. This method prevents timely decomposition.

12. **5.** The passage states that recycling is cheaper than continuing to acquire new landfill sites. Choice (2) looks like a possible answer, but it isn't complete because it doesn't explain why recycling is cheaper. Be sure to read the answers carefully — you don't want to choose an incomplete answer. The other answer choices don't address the question in light of the material presented in the passage.

13. **2.** As long as you dispose of waste by taking it to the curb or the dump, there will be an excess amount of waste being disposed of. Every piece of waste that you can reuse or recycle lives on to be useful again and, thus, eliminates some of the waste in America.

14. **4.** The passage states that bacteria decompose waste. Unfortunately, modern methods of waste disposal in landfills reduce the effectiveness of the bacteria.

15. **4.** Landfill sites are more expensive to acquire than the cost of recycling. In most cities, people hope to find new uses for recycled materials, which could increase the value of garbage.

16. **2.** Recycling reduces the amount of space required in landfill sites. These sites are large and expensive for any city to buy. Needing fewer landfill sites (or smaller landfill sites) would save money.

   You may notice a theme developing in these questions — something you may see as a pattern of answers. Be wary of looking for themes or patterns when answering questions on this test. If you think you've found one, be cautious because the theme or pattern may exist only in your head.

17. **1.** The purpose of the airbag, according to the passage, is to absorb some of the forces in a front-end crash. Choice (2) is incorrect because the passage doesn't mention anything about the car's frame as part of the energy-absorbing mechanism. Choices (3) and (5) would do little in the way of absorbing force in a crash. Padded dashboards provide minimal protection, but they're not as good as airbags.

   One or more answer choices to a question may be correct according to your memory, but if the passage doesn't mention them, don't choose them. A correct answer in a multiple-choice question is either mentioned or suggested in the passage.

18. **1.** An infant is safest in the rear seat because, when deployed, the air bag is powerful enough to injure a small person (according to the third sentence of the first paragraph). The other four answer choices seem reasonable, but they're incorrect because the passage doesn't mention them.

19. **4.** The diagram (going from bottom to top) indicates the process of building up a molecule. The quark is the smallest particle, and the molecule is the largest. Sometimes you have to read a diagram in an unfamiliar way to answer the question.

20. **4.** According to the diagram, a quark is 10^{-18} m across and a molecule is 10^{-9} across. The molecule would be $10^{-9} \div 10^{-18} = 1 \div 10^{-9}$ or 1,000,000,000 times the size of a quark.

    A number with a negative exponent, like 10^{-9}, equals 1 ÷ 10 to the positive power of the negative exponent (for example, $10^{-9} = 1 \div 10^{9}$).

21. **2.** Scientists often develop experiments to test theories about items that are invisible to the naked eye. Curiosity drives scientists to try to find answers; experimentation proves that smaller particles than atoms exist. The other answers don't directly answer the question.

22. **4.** The passage states that everything is composed of atoms. As a result, the floor must be composed of atoms. Choices (1) and (2) are building materials and are themselves made of atoms. Choice (3) is a fabricated part of a building and is made of atoms, and Choice (5) doesn't even come close to answering the question.

23. **2.** Landing a spaceship on large boulders is impossible, and the lack of charts makes accidentally meeting a boulder a possibility. A boulder as big as a house could do major damage to a spaceship. The passage states that there are such large boulders on the surface of the moon and that there are few accurate charts of the surface.

24. **4.** The moon has less gravity than Earth. Climbing requires lifting your weight against the force of gravity. It's easier to climb on the moon. With greatly reduced gravity, astronauts can jump fairly high. Whether or not they could jump over a house-sized boulder remains to be seen.

25. **4.** The passage tells you that you would displace a volume equal to your own volume. Choice (1) looks like it may be correct, but the passage is about volume, not weight.

26. **1.** The object would displace a volume of water equal to its volume. Thus, putting an object in a pre-measured volume of water is one way to measure the volume of an irregularly shaped object.

27. **3.** According to Newton, a force must be applied to move an object at rest. Newton, who never drove a car, said that you have to apply an external force on the object at rest (the car in this question) in the direction you want it to move. If you want your car to move deeper into the snow, you push it down. If you have a crane or a helicopter, which the passage doesn't mention, you apply a force upward to lift it out of the snow. Choice (3) is the best answer.

28. **4.** You find the answer to this question in the second paragraph of the passage.

29. **4.** When driving at a uniform rate of speed, the car resists changes in speed. The car wants to continue to travel at the same speed. To change that speed suddenly, you must apply great effort to your brakes.

30. **5.** Newton's Second Law of Motion states that when a body changes its velocity because an external force is applied to it, that change in velocity is directly proportional to the force and inversely proportional to the mass of the body. If you decrease the weight of the body and increase the size of the external force, the acceleration increases.

31. **2.** Newton's Third Law of Motion states that for every action there's an equal and opposite reaction. If the boxer is exerting a force on the punching bag, the bag is exerting an equal and opposite force on the boxer.

32. **5.** The passage states that the hair acts as insulation, retaining the polar bear's body heat.

33. **5.** The passage states that the polar bear's dark skin collects heat from the sun.

34. **3.** If you were in the Arctic, you'd want to duplicate the experience of the polar bear. Black clothing with a fur covering is the best answer.

35. **5.** In cold weather, you need a source of heat to warm your house, and methane produces heat in the chemical reaction. The other answers are incorrect.

36. **5.** Methane requires oxygen to produce light and heat. If there's no oxygen, the methane can't burn.

37. **2.** Paternity refers to the male half of a couple. If mothers were tested, it would be called maternity testing.

38. **3.** No one ever has any doubt on the day of the birth about who gave birth to a child. The mother is always obvious on that day. If the child were separated from the mother after birth, maternity testing could be an issue. But the question specifically asks about the day the baby is born.

39. **3.** According to the passage, Gus Grissom planned to give the dimes to the children of his friends.

40. **5.** The passage tells you that the sandwich wasn't returned to Earth, but nothing more. The passage doesn't tell you what happened to it. Any of the other answer choices besides Choice (5) are speculation. On these tests, you need to stick to the information you're given.

41. **2.** Because being in space is a rare occurrence, anything that has been there takes on a certain importance. Collectors want objects that are rare and about to get rarer.

42. **5.** The purpose of space flights is scientific research, so you're looking for an item associated with carrying out experiments or performing the daily routines of space travel. None of the other choices fills the bill.

43. **1.** Anything autographed by a famous person is valuable. When the object autographed is also available in limited quantities, it becomes more valuable still.

44. **3.** Collectors like to collect unique things. Few items are as unique as something that has flown in space.

45. **4.** Because the force remains constant, the work done is proportional to the distance traveled, which means you would do 3 ÷ 2 or 1½ times as much work.

46. **4.** Walking down the stairs, you have to exert a force against the force of gravity for a distance (the definition of work in physics). In real life, it seems easier to walk down a flight of stairs than walk up it, but, in both cases, work is being done.

47. **1.** If you want a 48-volt lead-acid battery, and each cell produces 2 volts, you need 24 cells (48 ÷ 2 = 24).

48. **1.** The moist paste replaces the acid in the battery.

49. **5.** DNA stores the genetic code, which determines heredity, and you get your DNA from your parents.

50. **5.** DNA in the chromosome stores the genetic code, which determines heredity. Yes, this answer is the same answer as Question 49, but the question is different. Read the questions carefully, and don't spend your time looking for patterns or tricks.

Answer Key

1. **3**	18. **1**	35. **5**
2. **3**	19. **4**	36. **5**
3. **3**	20. **4**	37. **2**
4. **5**	21. **2**	38. **3**
5. **4**	22. **4**	39. **3**
6. **2**	23. **2**	40. **5**
7. **5**	24. **4**	41. **2**
8. **3**	25. **4**	42. **5**
9. **2**	26. **1**	43. **1**
10. **4**	27. **3**	44. **3**
11. **2**	28. **4**	45. **4**
12. **5**	29. **4**	46. **4**
13. **2**	30. **5**	47. **1**
14. **4**	31. **2**	48. **1**
15. **4**	32. **5**	49. **5**
16. **2**	33. **5**	50. **5**
17. **1**	34. **3**	

Part V
Checking Your Comprehension: The Language Arts, Reading Test

The 5th Wave   By Rich Tennant

"C'mon Fogelman-talk! And I don't want to hear any of your non-parallel sentence structures, incomplete sentences, or dangling participles!"

In this part . . .

Here you get to find out everything you ever wanted to know about the Language Arts, Reading Test. You discover what types of materials you're expected to read and answer questions about and how the test is formatted. You also find out some strategies that can help you do your best on this test, as well as a summary of what to read before the tests to increase your chances for success. Finally, you get a chance to take two full-length practice tests.

The practice tests are serious business — as long as you choose to treat them that way. They give you a chance to see how you'd do on a real test and to check your answers. As a bonus, this part offers you detailed answer explanations you can read if you don't understand why answers are what they are.

Chapter 19

Reading between the Lines: Encountering the Language Arts, Reading Test

---

In This Chapter

▶ Identifying the skills the Language Arts, Reading Test covers

▶ Figuring out how the test is formatted

▶ Preparing for the different types of questions on this test

▶ Checking out a few helpful strategies and managing your time for this test

▶ Trying out some sample problems

---

*I*n a nutshell, the Language Arts, Reading Test determines how well you read and understand what you've read. Sounds simple enough, right? If you're looking for a few more details about the types of passages and questions that appear on this test, you've come to the right place. This chapter covers those topics and many more.

 To do well on this test, you have to be in the practice of reading different types of material and comprehending what you read. If you're not a big fan of reading, start with something simple, like a daily newspaper or a weekly news magazine. Every day, switch off the TV for an hour and read something instead. Gradually advance to how-to books (like this one) and short stories from an *anthology* (a fancy name for a collection of short stories or poems). Eventually, begin reading novels, longer poems, and plays.

Looking at the Skills the Language Arts, Reading Test Covers

You may not understand why the GED wants to test your knowledge of literature comprehension. However, in today's society, being able to comprehend, analyze, and apply something you've read is an important skill set to have. The questions on the Language Arts, Reading Test focus on the following skills (which you're expected to be able to use as you read passages of prose, poetry, and plays):

✔ **Comprehension (20 percent):** Questions that test your *comprehension* skills assess your ability to read a source of information, understand what you've read, and restate the information in your own words. If you understand the passage, you can rephrase what you read without losing the meaning of the passage. You can also create a summary of the main ideas presented in the passage and explain the ideas and implications of the passage.

✔ **Application (15 percent):** Questions that test your *application* skills assess your ability to use the information you read in the passage in a new situation, such as when you're answering questions. Application-focused questions are most like real life because they often ask you to apply what you read in the passage to a real-life situation. Being able to read a users' manual and then use the product it came with is a perfect example of using your application skills in real life.

✔ **Analysis (30 to 35 percent):** Questions that test your *analysis* skills assess your ability to draw conclusions, understand consequences, and make inferences after reading the passage. To answer these questions successfully, you have to make sure your conclusions are based on the written text in the passage and not on your background knowledge or the book you read last week. Questions that focus on your ability to analyze what you read try to find out whether you appreciate the way the passage was written and see the cause-and-effect relationships within it. They also expect you to know when a conclusion is being stated and analyze what it means in the context of the passage.

✔ **Synthesis (30 to 35 percent):** Questions that test your *synthesis* skills assess your ability to take information in one form and in one location and put it together in another context. Here you get a chance to make connections between different parts of the passage and compare and contrast them. You may be asked to talk about the tone, point of view, style, or purpose of a passage — and saying the purpose of a passage is to confuse and confound test takers isn't the answer.

Some questions on this test may ask you to use information in the passages combined with information from the text of the questions to answer them. So make sure you read everything written in the test booklet — you never know where an answer may come from.

Understanding the Test Format

The Language Arts, Reading Test measures your ability to understand and interpret prose and poetry passages. It's plain and simple — no tricks involved. You don't have to do any math to figure out the answers to the questions. You just have to read, understand, and use the material presented to you to answer the corresponding questions. The passages in this test are similar to the works a high school student would come across in English class, and they're taken from two specific sources: literary text and nonfiction text (we discuss both areas in further detail in the next section).

To help you feel more comfortable with taking the Language Arts, Reading Test, we're here to give you a better idea of what this test looks like on paper. It consists of 40 multiple-choice questions and a number of textual passages to go with them. You have 65 minutes to complete the test, which means you have a little over 1½ minutes to complete each question (and read the passage that goes with it).

Before each passage in the test is a question in bold — called a *purpose question*. Keep in mind that you don't have to answer the purpose question; its sole job is to help you focus on what's important in the passage that follows it. The purpose question suggests the purpose for reading the passage and can give you hints about what the questions that follow will ask.

A passage of 200 to 400 words or a poem of 8 to 25 lines follows each purpose question. The passages in this test may come from workplace (on-the-job) materials or from academic reading materials. Thirty of the questions (or 75 percent of them) are based on literary texts (including plays, poetry, short stories, novels, and so on), and the other ten questions (or 25 percent) are based on nonfiction texts (including biographies, reviews, memos, directions, and so on). After each passage, you have to answer four to eight multiple-choice questions.

Passages are passages. Although the next section describes what types of passages appear on the Language Arts, Reading Test to help you prepare, don't worry so much about what type of passage you're reading. Instead, spend your time understanding what information the passage presents to you.

Identifying the Types of Questions and Knowing How to Prepare for Them

To help you get comfortable with answering the questions on the Language Arts, Reading Test, you probably want to have a good idea of what these types of questions look like. The good news is that we focus on the two main types of questions in this section. We also give you some practical advice you can use as you prepare to take this test.

The simplest advice we can give to someone about to take this test is to read. In the previous sections of this chapter, we outline what's being tested and give you an idea of how much of the test focuses on each type of passage. Now comes the part you have to do yourself — the reading. Read everything you can and decide what kind of reading you're doing. Ask yourself questions about everything you read — even if that means asking yourself questions about the sides of cereal boxes. Read instruction manuals for products you own — you may surprise yourself by learning something new about some of your more complicated electronic possessions.

Literary passages

The Language Arts, Reading Test includes at least one passage from each of the following literary texts (and plenty of questions to go with them):

- **Drama:** *Drama* (that is, a play) tells a story using the words and actions of the characters. The description of the place and costumes are in the stage directions or in the head of the director. As you read passages from drama, try to imagine the dramatic scene and see the characters and their actions in your head. Doing so makes drama easier to understand.

  Stage directions are usually printed in italics, *like this*. Even though you're not an actor in the play, pay attention to the stage directions. They may provide you with valuable information you need to answer the questions that follow the passage.

- **Poetry:** *Poetry* is the concentrated juice of literature, meaning that the ideas and emotions are closely packed and aren't always visible during your first reading. Read poetry slowly and carefully. If you take your time, poetry can make sense and be quite beautiful. As a matter of fact, popular music is often written as poetry. (Leonard Cohen is a wonderful example of a poet who can and does sing his poems.) We know you aren't taking this test as entertainment, but try to enjoy the poetry as much as you can.

  As you prepare for this test, read a lot of poetry — even if you hate it. Some poetry is beautiful and moving, and, if you read enough, you're sure to find at least one piece that you come to enjoy. After you read a poem, decide what the poet is saying and how he or she is saying it. Why does the poet use certain words? What images are in the poem? Taking the time to practice asking these types of questions after reading poetry can really prepare you for the poetry portion of this test.

- **Prose fiction:** *Prose fiction* refers to novels and short stories. As you may already know, *fiction* is writing that comes straight from the mind of the author (in other words, it's made up; it's not about something that really happened). The only way to become familiar with prose fiction is to read as much fiction as you can. After you read a book, try to talk about it with other people who have read the book.

  This test includes prose fiction written during the following three time periods (look in the library for books written during these periods to get some ideas of what to read):

- Before 1920
- Between 1920 and 1960
- After 1960

The difference between the time periods is usually evident in the words used and the situations described, but when the prose was written isn't the most important part of the passages. Spend your time reading and understanding the main ideas in the passages, and don't worry too much about when they were written. Just try to recognize that some passages are newer and some are older.

Nonfiction passages

As far as the nonfiction text on this test is concerned, you may have to read passages from any of the following sources (and answer questions about them, too, of course):

- **Critical reviews of visual and performing arts:** These prose passages are reviews written by people who have enough knowledge of the visual or performing arts to be critical of them. You can find examples of good critical reviews in the library, in some daily papers, and on the Internet. Enter *critical review* into your favorite search engine, and you'll get more critical reviews than you have time to read.

  To prepare for this part of the test, try to read critical reviews of books, movies, restaurants, and the like as often as you can. The next time you go to a movie, watch television, or go to a play, write your own critical review (what you thought of the piece of work). Put some factual material into your review, and make suggestions for improvement. Compare what the real critics have to say with your own feelings about the movie, television show, or play. Do you agree with their opinions?

- **Nonfiction prose:** *Nonfiction prose* is prose that covers a lot of ground — and all the ground is real. Nonfiction prose is material that the author doesn't create in his or her own mind — it's based on fact or reality. In fact, this book is classified as nonfiction prose, and so are the newspaper articles you read every day. The next time you read the newspaper or a magazine, tell yourself, "I'm reading nonfiction prose." Just don't say it out loud in a coffee shop or in your break room at work — or people may start to look at you in strange ways.

- **Workplace and community documents:** You run across these types of passages in the job- and community-related areas of life. The following are some examples:

  - **Mission statements:** Organizations and companies often write mission statements to tell the world what the company's role is in the community. You may have your own mission statement: "I live to party" or "I hate reading," for example. Of course, you may have to change it if you want to pass this test.

  - **Goal (or vision) statements:** Companies and organizations may also have goal statements, which tell the world what they intend to accomplish. The goal statement for your study group may be as follows: "We're all going to pass the GED tests on our first attempt."

  - **Rules for employee behavior:** Every company, school, or organized group has rules for behavior. Some are written down, while others are unspoken but understood. Some of the passages on this test come from real or imaginary rules of behavior. You probably already know how to read them.

  - **Legal documents:** Legal documents are drafted by lawyers and may include leases, purchase contracts, and bank statements. If you aren't familiar with legal documents, collect some examples from banks or libraries and review them. If you can explain these types of documents to a friend, you understand them.

- **Letters:** You certainly know what a *letter* is: a written communication between two people. It's not very often that you get to read other people's letters without getting into trouble — here's your chance.

✔ **Manuals:** Every time you invest in a major purchase, you get a users' manual that tells you how to use the item. Some manuals are short and straightforward; others are long and complicated. It took me so long to read the manual that came with my new camera that I thought my hobby was reading manuals, not taking pictures.

Examining Preparation Strategies That Work

Now that you know what to read to prepare for this test, you need to focus on how to read. You can't easily skim the type of poetry and prose that appears on the test. You need to read each question and passage carefully to find the right answer.

Keep the following reading tactics in mind as you prepare for the test:

✔ **Read.** Read whatever you have available, but also look for the specific types of texts that we discuss in the preceding sections. Become a reading addict. Read labels, cereal boxes, novels, magazines, poems, plays, short stories, and newspapers. Read everything and anything. And don't stop with just reading — also digest and think about everything you read, just as you're asked to do on this test. When you read, read carefully. If reading poetry and drama is unfamiliar to you, read them even more carefully. The more carefully you read any material, the easier it'll be for you to get the right answers on the test.

✔ **Ask questions.** Ask yourself questions about what you've read. Do you understand the main ideas well enough to explain them to a stranger? (Note that we don't advise going up to strangers to explain things to them in person. Pretend you're going to explain it to a stranger and do all the talking in your head. If you want to explain what you read to someone in person, ask your friends and family to lend you an ear — or two.)

Ask for help if you don't understand something you read. You may want to form a study group and work with other people. If you're taking a test-preparation course, ask the instructor for help when you need it. If you have family, friends, or co-workers who can help, ask them.

✔ **Use a dictionary.** Not many people understand every word they read, so use a dictionary. Looking up unfamiliar words increases your vocabulary, which, in turn, makes passages on the Language Arts, Reading Test easier to understand. If you have a Thesaurus, use it, too. Often knowing a synonym for the word you don't know is helpful. Plus, it improves your Scrabble game.

✔ **Use new words.** A new word doesn't usually become part of your vocabulary until you put it to use in your everyday language. When you come across a new word, make sure you know its meaning and try to use it in a sentence. Then try to work it into conversation for a day or two. After a while, this challenge can make each day more exciting.

✔ **Practice.** Practice taking the Language Arts, Reading Tests in Chapters 20 and 22. Do the questions, and check your answers. Look at the explanations of the answers that we provide in Chapters 21 and 23. Don't move on to the next answer until you understand the preceding one. If you want more sample tests, look for additional test-prep books at your bookstore or local library. You can also find some abbreviated tests on the Internet. Enter *GED test questions* or *GED test questions + free* into your favorite search engine, and check out some of the results.

Take as many practice tests as you can. Stick to the time limits, and keep the testing situation as realistic as possible. When you go to the test center for the official test, you will feel more at ease because you practiced.

This test doesn't test you on anything but reading. All the information you need to answer the questions is given in the passages or in the text of the questions that accompany the passages. You're not expected to recognize the passage and answer questions about what comes before it or what comes after it in context of the entire work. The passages are complete in themselves, so just focus on what you read.

Many people get hung up on the poetry and drama passages. Don't stress. Keep in mind that these literary genres are just different ways of telling a story and conveying feelings. If you're not familiar with them, read poems and plays before taking this test. Discuss what you have read with others; you may even want to consider joining (or starting) a book club that discusses poems and/or plays.

Managing Your Time for the Language Arts, Reading Test

As we mention earlier in this chapter, the Language Arts, Reading Test consists of 40 questions that you have to answer in 65 minutes, which averages out to just over 1½ minutes per question. When you begin the test, the best way to manage your time is to answer the easiest questions first. Then move to the more difficult questions and spend a little more time on those questions.

Throughout the test, keep track of the time. You don't want to run out of time before you finish answering all the questions. Arrange your time to leave a little extra time for the sections you have the most difficulty with. If you have difficulty with poetry, leave a bit of extra time for poetry-based questions, and use less time for the prose sections. Keep in mind, however, that this test is a timed test, so you can't spend limitless time on any one question. If you do, you won't have time to finish — and finishing is definitely important. Check out Chapters 2 and 3 for some general time-management tips.

Practicing with Sample Problems

The following passage and sample problems give you some idea of what the Language Arts, Reading Test questions look like.

Choose the one best answer to each question. Questions 1 through 5 refer to the following passage.

DOES EMPLOYMENT NEED A NEW FACE?
Facilities for Access to Creative Enterprise (FACE)
Originally founded in 1982 to train unemployed youth in small "hand skill" craft workshops, this project provides occupational and entrepreneurial skills as an alternative to traditional manufacturing jobs. Beginning with glass engraving and sign writing, FACE now offers training in more than 200 hand skill occupations, including antique restoration, clothing manufacturing, graphic design, masonry, sail making, specialist joinery, weaving, and wood turning. Funded through the Youth Training Scheme, FACE provides 800 training places in the west and northeast of England under the premise that even if the young people can't secure employment, they at least will have the skills to create their own businesses.

Based on its experience, FACE has developed, with the Royal Society of Arts, a Certificate in Small Business and Enterprise Skills. The aim of the certificate is "to develop the basic skills of enterprise across a range of occupational sectors, within small business and in general employment and which are applicable in a wide range of personal and social contexts outside work." Competencies include self-evaluation, decision making, initiative taking, resource and time management, opportunism and self-motivation, problem solving, and learning-to-learn skills, as well as communication and number skills vital to personal effectiveness.

1. What is the overall purpose of the FACE project?

    (1) to provide manufacturing jobs

    (2) to engrave glass

    (3) to train unemployed youth

    (4) to write signs

    (5) to restore antiques

The correct answer is Choice (3). The overall purpose of the FACE project is to train unemployed youth. Glass engraving, sign writing, and antique restoring are just some of the skills the youth may develop through FACE. Manufacturing jobs are in short supply, resulting in the need for entrepreneurial skills.

2. Which of the following is not an example of a hand skill craft occupation?

    (1) weaving

    (2) wood turning

    (3) sail making

    (4) specialist joinery

    (5) robotic assembly

The correct answer is Choice (5). Robotic assembly is a high-tech computer-assisted approach to manufacturing that seeks to replace workers with robots. The other answers — weaving, wood turning, sail making, and joinery (carpentry) — are all examples of hand skill craft occupations according to the passage.

3. How can young people best secure employment northeast of England?

    (1) by engaging in traditional manufacturing

    (2) by creating new enterprises

    (3) by joining the Royal Society of Arts

    (4) by obtaining a Certificate in Small Business

    (5) by going to one of 800 training places

The correct answer is Choice (2). The best way for youth to secure employment is to "create new enterprises," as the passage states. Jobs are being lost in traditional manufacturing. The Royal Society, business certificate, and training places don't refer directly to securing employment.

4. Who helped FACE develop the Certificate in Small Business and Enterprise Skills?

   (1) Youth Training Scheme

   (2) west and northeast England

   (3) hand skill workshops

   (4) Royal Society of Arts

   (5) occupational sectors

   The correct answer is Choice (4). The Royal Society of Arts assisted FACE in developing the Certificate in Small Business and Enterprise Skills. The Youth Training Scheme, while providing funding for FACE, wasn't directly involved with the Certificate. Hand skill workshops and occupational sectors have no direct relation to the Certificate. Choice (2) — west and northeast England — refers only to locations.

5. Which competency is not included in training for the Certificate?

   (1) self-evaluation

   (2) anger management

   (3) decision making

   (4) problem solving

   (5) number skills

   The correct answer is Choice (2). Anger management isn't mentioned in the passage as one of the competencies; all the other skills are.

Revealing Some Helpful Pointers

This chapter includes several tips to help you achieve greatness on this test. This section hits on a few other general pointers that can help give you the edge you're looking for. As you work your way through the Language Arts, Reading Test, keep the following pointers in mind:

- ✔ **Look at the purpose question.** Before every passage is a purpose question (see the "Understanding the Test Format" section for details). Be sure to read it. You don't have to answer it, but it gives you a direction for reading the passage. Take any clues that you can get.

- ✔ **Ferret out the meaning of new words from the surrounding text.** Even the best readers sometimes come to a word they don't recognize or understand. Luckily, the sentences around a new word can give you clues to the meaning of the word. Ask yourself, "What word would make sense in place of the one I don't know?"

- ✔ **Recognize that everything's important.** In this test, information may be hiding in many places. It may be in explanatory notes set off in square brackets [like this]. It may be hiding in stage directions, usually printed in italics, *like this*. It may be hidden in the speaker's name before the dialogue. Read everything and skip nothing.

- ✔ **Develop your reading speed.** Reading is wonderful, but reading quickly is even better — it gets you through the test with time to spare. Check out *Speed Reading For Dummies* by Richard Sutz with Peter Weverka (Wiley), or do a quick Internet search to find plenty of material that can help you read faster. Whatever method you use, try to improve your reading rate without hurting your overall reading comprehension.

Chapter 20

Practice Test — Language Arts, Reading Test

• •

The Language Arts, Reading Test consists of excerpts from fiction and nonfiction. Each excerpt is followed by multiple-choice questions about the reading material.

Read each excerpt first and then answer the questions following it. Refer back to the reading material as often as necessary in answering the questions.

Each excerpt is preceded by a purpose question. The purpose question gives a reason for reading the material. Use the purpose questions to help focus your reading. You are not required to answer these purpose questions. They are given only to help you concentrate on the ideas presented in the reading material.

You have 65 minutes to answer the 40 questions in this booklet. Work carefully, but do not spend too much time on any one question. Be sure you answer every question.

Answer Sheet for Language Arts, Reading Test

1 ① ② ③ ④ ⑤   21 ① ② ③ ④ ⑤

2 ① ② ③ ④ ⑤   22 ① ② ③ ④ ⑤

3 ① ② ③ ④ ⑤   23 ① ② ③ ④ ⑤

4 ① ② ③ ④ ⑤   24 ① ② ③ ④ ⑤

5 ① ② ③ ④ ⑤   25 ① ② ③ ④ ⑤

6 ① ② ③ ④ ⑤   26 ① ② ③ ④ ⑤

7 ① ② ③ ④ ⑤   27 ① ② ③ ④ ⑤

8 ① ② ③ ④ ⑤   28 ① ② ③ ④ ⑤

9 ① ② ③ ④ ⑤   29 ① ② ③ ④ ⑤

10 ① ② ③ ④ ⑤   30 ① ② ③ ④ ⑤

11 ① ② ③ ④ ⑤   31 ① ② ③ ④ ⑤

12 ① ② ③ ④ ⑤   32 ① ② ③ ④ ⑤

13 ① ② ③ ④ ⑤   33 ① ② ③ ④ ⑤

14 ① ② ③ ④ ⑤   34 ① ② ③ ④ ⑤

15 ① ② ③ ④ ⑤   35 ① ② ③ ④ ⑤

16 ① ② ③ ④ ⑤   36 ① ② ③ ④ ⑤

17 ① ② ③ ④ ⑤   37 ① ② ③ ④ ⑤

18 ① ② ③ ④ ⑤   38 ① ② ③ ④ ⑤

19 ① ② ③ ④ ⑤   39 ① ② ③ ④ ⑤

20 ① ② ③ ④ ⑤   40 ① ② ③ ④ ⑤

Language Arts, Reading Test

Do not mark in this test booklet. Record your answers on the separate answer sheet provided. Be sure that all requested information is properly recorded on the answer sheet.

To record your answers, fill in the numbered circle on the answer sheet that corresponds to the answer you select for each question in the test booklet.

EXAMPLE:

It was Susan's dream machine. The metallic blue paint gleamed, and the sporty wheels were highly polished. Under the hood, the engine was no less carefully cleaned. Inside, flashy lights illuminated the instruments on the dashboard, and the seats were covered by rich leather upholstery.

The subject ("it") of this excerpt is most likely

(1) an airplane

(2) a stereo system

(3) an automobile

(4) a boat

(5) a motorcycle

(On Answer Sheet)
① ② ● ④ ⑤

The correct answer is "an automobile"; therefore, answer space 3 would be marked on the answer sheet.

Do not rest the point of your pencil on the answer sheet while you are considering your answer. Make no stray or unnecessary marks. If you change an answer, erase your first mark completely. Mark only one answer space for each question; multiple answers will be scored as incorrect. Do not fold or crease your answer sheet. All test materials must be returned to the test administrator.

Note: Refer to Chapter 21 for the answers for this practice test.

Directions: Choose the <u>one best answer</u> to each question.

Questions 1 through 6 refer to the following poem, "Concord Hymn," by Ralph Waldo Emerson (1886).

WHAT WAS "THE SHOT HEARD 'ROUND THE WORLD"?

Line   By the rude bridge that arched the flood,
     Their flag to April's breeze unfurled,
     Here once the embattled farmers stood,
     And fired the shot heard round the world.

(05)   The foe long since in silence slept;
     Alike the conqueror silent sleeps;
     And Time the ruined bridge has swept
     Down the dark stream which seaward creeps.

     On this green bank, by this soft stream,
(10)   We set today a votive stone;
     That memory may their deed redeem,
     When, like our sires, our sons are gone.

     Spirit, that made those heroes dare
     To die, and leave their children free,
(15)   Bid Time and Nature gently spare
     The shaft we raise to them and thee.

1. What is the best phrase to describe where the farmers made their stand?

    (1) by the rough-structured span

    (2) beside the flood

    (3) under the flag

    (4) in April's breeze

    (5) over the arch

2. What were the farmers ready for?

    (1) negotiations

    (2) vacation

    (3) retreat

    (4) war

    (5) celebrations

3. Why are foes and conquerors silent?

    (1) They've gone away.

    (2) They've all since died.

    (3) They lost the battle.

    (4) They won the war.

    (5) They live together peacefully.

4. What has happened to the bridge?

    (1) It was rebuilt after the battle.

    (2) It's not a memory now.

    (3) It hasn't been swept away.

    (4) It never existed.

    (5) Only the ruins now remain.

5. What does a "votive stone" in line 10 refer to?

    (1) a monument to the fallen

    (2) a new bridge to cross the stream

    (3) a memorial celebration

    (4) a flag-raising ceremony

    (5) a family reunion

6. What does "the shot heard round the world" (line 4) refer to?

    (1) only time will tell

    (2) the unfurling of a flag

    (3) an event about to begin

    (4) the sleeping foes

    (5) the setting of a votive stone

Go on to next page ⟹

> *Questions 7 through 12 refer to the following excerpt from Garrison Keillor's* Prodigal Son *(1989).*

WHERE DOES EVIL COME FROM?

Line **DWIGHT:** *(sitting at table, reading newspaper)* Morning.

DAD: You see your brother this morning?

DWIGHT: In bed.

DAD: I promised Harry Shepherd I'd be over to his place by seven-thirty. He's got a
(05) lost sheep out on the mountain wild and steep.

DWIGHT: Says here that fatted calves are down one and three-quarter shekels on the
Damascus market, Dad. Makes me wonder if maybe lean calves wouldn't have a
higher profit margin, and then we could spend more time in the vineyard — Dad, are
you listening to me?

(10) **DAD:** I'm worried about your brother.

DWIGHT: We can't afford to stand still, Dad. Look at the Stewarts — they're buying
up land left and right! You've got to move ahead or you lose ground . . . .

WALLY: *(thickly)* Morning, Dad. Morning, Dwight. *(He sits down, groans, puts his head
in his hands.)*

(15) **DAD:** You look a little peaked, son.

WALLY: I donno — it's some kind of morning sickness, Dad. I feel real good at night
and then I wake up and hurt all over.

DWIGHT: I noticed a couple empty wineskins behind the fig tree this morning.

WALLY: I dropped them, and they spilled! Honest!

(20) **DAD:** Where were you taking them?

WALLY: I was putting them outside! Wine's got to breathe, you know. And so do I,
Dad. I've got a real breathing problem here. I'm worried about my health, Dad. I read
an article the other day in Assyrian Digest that says bad feelings may be environmental. I donno. Maybe I need to get away for a while, Dad. Get my head straight. Work
(25) out some things.

7. Why does Wally's father think Wally
    doesn't feel well this morning?

    (1) Wally feels badly that he spilled some
        wine.

    (2) Wally works on a tree farm in Judea.

    (3) Wally drank too much wine.

    (4) Wally needs a vacation.

    (5) Wally wants to run the business.

8. What is the setting for the play?

    (1) breakfast table

    (2) fig tree

    (3) market

    (4) bed

    (5) vineyard

Go on to next page

9. Why did Dwight feel it would be better to raise lean calves?

   (1) less profit

   (2) fat is bad for you

   (3) more profit

   (4) more expensive to produce

   (5) better than goats

10. Why isn't Dad paying attention to Dwight?

    (1) He wants to help find a lost sheep.

    (2) He wants to spend time in the vineyard.

    (3) He wants to buy more land.

    (4) He is reading the paper.

    (5) He is worried about Wally.

11. Why do you think Wally is late for breakfast?

    (1) He is sick.

    (2) He has a hangover.

    (3) He is doing the chores.

    (4) He is reading an article.

    (5) He is working in the fields.

12. What comparison does Wally make between himself and wine?

    (1) They both are sweet.

    (2) They both like to travel.

    (3) They both need to breathe.

    (4) They are both precious.

    (5) They both cause problems.

Go on to next page

> *Questions 13 through 18 refer to the following excerpt from Jack London's "In a Far Country" (1899).*

HOW CAN I MAKE MY FORTUNE?

Line   When the world rang with the tale of Arctic gold, and the lure of the North gripped the heartstrings of men, Carter Weatherbee threw up his snug clerkship, turned the half of his savings over to his wife, and with the remainder bought an outfit. There was no romance in his nature — the bondage of commerce had crushed all that; he was simply tired of the
(05)   ceaseless grind, and wished to risk great hazards in view of corresponding returns . . . and there, unluckily for his soul's welfare, he allied himself with a party of men.

There was nothing unusual about this party, except its plans. Even its goal, like that of all the other parties, was the Klondike. But the route it had mapped out to attain that goal took away the breath of the hardiest native, born and bred to the vicissi-
(10)   tudes of the Northwest. Even Jacques Baptiste, born of a Chippewa woman and a renegade voyageur (having raised his first whimpers in a deerskin lodge north of the sixty-fifth parallel, and had the same hushed by blissful sucks of raw tallow), was surprised. Though he sold his services to them and agreed to travel even to the never-opening ice, he shook his head ominously whenever his advice was asked.

(15)   Percy Cuthfert's evil star must have been in the ascendant, for he, too, joined this company of Argonauts. He was an ordinary man, with a bank account as deep as his culture, which is saying a good deal. He had no reason to embark on such a venture — no reason in the world, save that he suffered from an abnormal development of sentimentality. He mistook this for the true spirit of romance and adventure.

13. What caused Carter Weatherbee to leave his job?

   (1) Arctic gold
   (2) a woman
   (3) his snug clerkship
   (4) half of his savings
   (5) the heartstrings of men

14. What is meant by "bondage of commerce" in line 4?

   (1) the corresponding returns
   (2) the romance in his nature
   (3) the drudgery of life as a clerk
   (4) the risk of great hazards
   (5) half of his savings

15. What was the goal of the party?

   (1) to find the old trails
   (2) to reach the Klondike
   (3) to map out a route
   (4) to tell the tale of the Arctic
   (5) to buy outfits

16. How would you best describe the chosen route to the Klondike?

   (1) blissful
   (2) hardy
   (3) hushed
   (4) ominous
   (5) surprising

17. Why was Jacques Baptiste important to the party?

   (1) He was a native of the Northwest.
   (2) He was born of a Chippewa woman.
   (3) He was a renegade voyageur.
   (4) He was born in a deerskin lodge.
   (5) He sucked raw tallow.

18. Why do you think Percy Cuthfert joined the party?

   (1) to show that he is an ordinary man
   (2) to fill his bank account
   (3) to seek romance and adventure
   (4) to be able to say a good deal
   (5) because of his abnormal development

Go on to next page

> *Questions 19 through 24 refer to the following excerpt from James Baldwin's "Sonny's Blues"*
> *(1957).*

WHY DOES SONNY FEEL SORRY?

Line   DEAR BROTHER,

You don't know how much I needed to hear from you. I wanted to write you many a
time but I dug how much I must have hurt you and so I didn't write. But now I feel like
a man who's been trying to climb up out of some deep, real deep and funky hole and
(05)   just saw the sun up there, outside. I got to get outside.

I can't tell you much about how I got here. I mean I don't know how to tell you. I guess
I was afraid of something or I was trying to escape from something and you know I
have never been very strong in the head (smile). I'm glad Mama and Daddy are dead
and can't see what's happened to their son and I swear if I'd known what I was doing I
(10)   would never have hurt you so, you and a lot of other fine people who were nice to me
and who believed in me.

I don't want you to think it had anything to do with me being a musician. It's more
than that. Or maybe less than that. I can't get anything straight in my head down here
and I try not to think about what's going to happen to me when I get outside again.
(15)   Sometime I think I'm going to flip and *never* get outside and sometime I think I'll come
straight back. I tell you one thing, though, I'd rather blow my brains out than go
through this again. But that's what they all say, so they tell me.

Your brother,
SONNY

19. Why didn't Sonny write to his brother
    (lines 1 and 2)?

    (1) He was lazy.

    (2) He felt guilty.

    (3) He was too busy.

    (4) He was afraid.

    (5) He was in a hole.

20. Where do you think Sonny is writing from?

    (1) a funky hole

    (2) inside the place

    (3) a prison cell

    (4) another space

    (5) a deep place

21. What is the meaning of "strong in the head"
    (line 8)?

    (1) physically fit

    (2) humorous

    (3) happy

    (4) intelligent

    (5) angry

22. Why is Sonny glad his parents are dead
    (lines 8 and 9)?

    (1) They escaped from something that no
        one knows about.

    (2) They never have to hurt him.

    (3) They were afraid of something.

    (4) They knew a lot of other fine people
        from the neighborhood.

    (5) They cannot see what has happened to
        their son.

Go on to next page ⟶

23. What is Sonny most afraid of while inside?
    (1) flipping before he gets out
    (2) getting anything straight
    (3) being a musician
    (4) coming straight back
    (5) blowing his brains out

24. How does Sonny feel about his brother?
    (1) He blames him.
    (2) He hates him.
    (3) He likes him.
    (4) He likes his music.
    (5) He rejects him.

Go on to next page

> Questions 25 through 30 refer to the following excerpt from Tim O'Brien's The Things They Carried *(1990)*.

WHAT WERE THE THINGS THEY CARRIED?

Line First Lieutenant Jimmy Cross carried letters from a girl named Martha, a junior at
Mount Sebastian College in New Jersey. They were not love letters, but Lieutenant
Cross was hoping, so he kept them folded in plastic at the bottom of his rucksack. In
the late afternoon, after a day's march, he would dig his foxhole, wash his hands
(05) under a canteen, unwrap the letters, hold them with the tips of his fingers, and spend
the last hour of light pretending. He would imagine romantic camping trips into the
White Mountains in New Hampshire. He would sometimes taste the envelope flaps,
knowing her tongue had been there. More than anything, he wanted Martha to love
him as he loved her, but the letters were mostly chatty, elusive on the matter of love.
(10) She was a virgin, he was almost sure. She was an English major at Mount Sebastian,
and she wrote beautifully about her professors and roommates and midterm exams,
about her respect for Chaucer and her great affection for Virginia Woolf. She often
quoted lines of poetry; she never mentioned the war, except to say, Jimmy, take care
of yourself. The letters weighed 10 ounces. They were signed Love, Martha, but
Lieutenant Cross understood that Love was only a way of signing and did not mean
(15) what he sometimes pretended it meant. At dusk, he would carefully return the letters
to his rucksack. Slowly, a bit distracted, he would get up and move among his men,
checking the perimeter, then at full dark he would return to his hole and watch the
night and wonder if Martha was a virgin.

25. When did Jimmy read Martha's letters?

    (1) after a day's march

    (2) in his foxhole

    (3) under a canteen

    (4) at the bottom of his rucksack

    (5) in the first light of day

26. How would you best describe their relationship?

    (1) lovers

    (2) strangers

    (3) acquaintances

    (4) siblings

    (5) no relationship

27. How did Jimmy demonstrate his affection?

    (1) He washed his hands.

    (2) He wrapped the letters.

    (3) He held the letters by the tips of his fingers.

    (4) He read the letters at the last hour of light.

    (5) He tasted the envelope flaps.

28. What does the phrase "mostly chatty" (line 9) tell you about Martha's feelings toward Jimmy?

    (1) She cares deeply.

    (2) She is just being friendly.

    (3) She is infatuated.

    (4) She has a casual interest.

    (5) She has no feelings for Jimmy at all.

29. How do you know Martha enjoyed writing letters?

    (1) Her letters were thick and chatty.

    (2) She showed much respect for Chaucer.

    (3) She was an English major.

    (4) She wrote beautifully.

    (5) She wrote about her professors and roommates.

30. What do you think the letters really meant to Jimmy?

    (1) an interesting hobby

    (2) a pleasing pastime

    (3) a way to escape boredom

    (4) a sense of hope for the future

    (5) profound disappointment

Go on to next page

> *Questions 31 through 35 refer to the following excerpt, written by Dale Shuttleworth (originally printed in the* Toronto Star, *January 2008).*

WHAT IS THE HISTORY OF THE SOCIAL ENTERPRISE MOVEMENT?

Line The Center for Social Innovation, a renovated warehouse in the Spadina Ave. area of Toronto houses 85 "social enterprises," including organizations concerned with the environment, the arts, social justice, education, health, technology and design. Tribute has been paid to the "social enterprise movement" in Quebec and Vancouver
(05) for providing the impetus for this very successful venture.

Toronto, Ontario also has provided leadership in the areas of community education and community economic development — essential components in the creation of social enterprises. In 1974, the Toronto Board of Education assisted in the establishment of the Learnxs Foundation Inc. as part of its Learning Exchange System.

(10) The foundation represented an additional source of support for the burgeoning "alternatives in education" movement. In 1973, the Ontario government had imposed ceilings on educational spending and together with reduced revenue due to declining enrolment the Toronto board had limited means to fund innovative and experimental programs. The Learnxs Foundation was an independent "arms-length" non-profit
(15) charitable enterprise, which could solicit funds from public and private sources and generate revenue through the sale of goods and services to support innovative programs within the Toronto system.

What followed during the 1970s was a series of Learnxs-sponsored demonstration projects as a source of research and development in such areas as: school and com-
(20) munity programs to improve inner-city education; a series of small enterprises to employ 14- to 15-year-old school leavers; Youth Ventures — a paper recycling enterprise employing at-risk youth; Artsjunction — discarded material from business and industry were recycled for use as craft materials for visual arts classes; Toronto Urban Studies Centre — a facility to encourage the use of the city as a learning envi-
(25) ronment; and Learnxs Press — a publishing house for the production and sale of innovative learning materials.

The York Board of Education and its school and community organizations jointly incorporated the Learning Enrichment Foundation (LEF), modeled on Learnxs. Originally devoted to multicultural arts enrichment, LEF during the 1980s joined with
(30) parental groups and the school board to establish 13 school-based childcare centers for infants, pre-school and school-age children.

In 1984, LEF was asked by Employment and Immigrant Canada to convene a local committee of adjustment in response to York's high rate of unemployment and plant closures. Outcomes of the work of the Committee included:

(35) York Business Opportunities Centre: In 1985, with support from the Ontario Ministry of Industry, Trade & Technology, LEF opened the first small business incubator operated by a non-profit charitable organization.

Microtron Centre: This training facility was devoted to micro-computer skills, word and numerical processing, computer-assisted design, graphics and styling, and elec-
(40) tronic assembly and repair.

Go on to next page ⟶

Microtron Bus: This refurbished school bus incorporated eight workstations from the Microtron Centre. It visited small business, industry and service organizations on a scheduled basis to provide training in word and numerical processing for their employees and clients.

(45) In 1996, the Training Renewal Foundation was incorporated as a non-profit charity to serve disadvantaged youth and other displaced workers seeking skills, qualifications and employment opportunities. Over the years TRF has partnered with governments, employers and community organizations to provide a variety of services including job-creation programs for: immigrants and refugees, GED high school equivalency,
(50) café equipment technicians, coffee and vending service workers, industrial warehousing and lift truck operators, fully expelled students, youth parenting, construction craft workers and garment manufacturing.

31. The Center for Social Innovation is

    (1) a new restaurant

    (2) a center housing social enterprises

    (3) the head office of a charity

    (4) part of LEF

    (5) a small enterprise to employ school leavers

32. The Learnxs Foundation supported

    (1) homeless people

    (2) scholarships for students specializing in computer studies

    (3) innovative programs

    (4) art programming

    (5) recycling projects

33. Artsjunction specialized in

    (1) making maps

    (2) assisting new artists in finding studios

    (3) helping artists learn about the city

    (4) publishing art booklets

    (5) distributing discarded materials to visual arts classes

34. The Microtron bus helped

    (1) provide transportation for computer science students to their labs

    (2) provide training in word and numerical processing to employees and clients

    (3) train auto mechanics in the digital controls in the new cars

    (4) the center establish social enterprises

    (5) train young people as bus drivers

35. The Training Renewal Foundation serves

    (1) as a social innovator for youth

    (2) as a patron of the center

    (3) dinner to the homeless

    (4) disadvantaged youth and displaced workers

    (5) as a business incubator

Go on to next page

Questions 36 through 40 refer to the following excerpt.

HOW MUST EMPLOYEES BEHAVE?

Line It is expected that employees behave in a respectful, responsible, professional manner. Therefore, each employee must do the following:

• Wear appropriate clothing and use safety equipment where needed.

(05) • Refrain from the use and possession of alcohol and/or illicit drugs and associated paraphernalia throughout the duration of the work day.

• Refrain from associating with those who pass, use, and are under the influence of illicit drugs and/or alcohol.

• Address all other employees and supervisors with courtesy and respect, using non-offensive language.

(10) • Accept the authority of supervisors without argument. If you consider an action unfair, inform the Human Resources department.

• Respect the work environment of this company and conduct oneself in a manner conducive to the growth and the enhancement of our business.

(15) • Refrain from inviting visitors to our place of work in order to keep the premises secure.

• Promote the dignity of all persons, regardless of gender, creed, or culture and conduct oneself with dignity.

If the employee chooses *not* to comply:

(20) • On the first offense, the employee meets with his or her supervisor. A representative from Human Resources may choose to attend.

• On the second offense, the employee meets with the Vice President of Human Resources before returning to work.

• On the third offense, the employee is dismissed.

36. Which requirement relates to employee appearance?

  (1) The employee must refrain from using alcohol.

  (2) The employee must not use associated paraphernalia.

  (3) The employee must wear appropriate clothing.

  (4) The employee must use courtesy and respect.

  (5) The employee must use non-offensive language.

37. Which requirement addresses relations with supervisors?

  (1) Accept authority.

  (2) Contribute to business growth and enhancement.

  (3) Use non-offensive language.

  (4) Do not use drugs and alcohol.

  (5) Refrain from associating.

Go on to next page

38. Which requirement is concerned with the growth and enhancement of the business?

    (1) conducive to growth

    (2) enhancement of self

    (3) dressing unprofessionally

    (4) personal conduct

    (5) inviting visitors

39. How are safety and security protected?

    (1) by promoting dignity

    (2) by not inviting others in

    (3) by the types of interaction

    (4) through meetings with supervisors

    (5) by being respectful and responsible

40. What are the penalties for continued non-compliance?

    (1) You meet with the president of the company.

    (2) Your salary goes up.

    (3) You must avoid your supervisor.

    (4) You have to take behavior classes.

    (5) You are fired.

END OF TEST

Chapter 21

Answers and Explanations for the Language Arts, Reading Test

· ·

After taking the Language Arts, Reading Test in Chapter 20, use this chapter to check your answers. Take your time as you move through the explanations of the answers that we provide in the first section. They can help you understand why you missed the answers you did. You may also want to read the explanations for the questions you answered correctly because doing so can give you a better understanding of the thought process that helped you choose the correct answers.

If you're short on time, turn to the end of the chapter for an abbreviated answer key.

Analysis of the Answers

1. **1.** They stood by the "rude bridge" (or *rough-structured span*) to make their stand. Although a flag and an arch are mentioned in the poem, they aren't the best answers. Neither the flood (meaning the river) nor the April breeze is a plausible answer.

2. **4.** The farmers were ready for war. The fact that they were "embattled" (another word for fighting) and firing shots shows this. They definitely weren't having negotiations (instead, they seem resolute) or taking a vacation, nor were they retreating or celebrating.

3. **2.** They've all since died *(sleeping silently)*. They haven't just gone away because they won or lost the war, nor are they living together peacefully.

4. **5.** The bridge has fallen into ruins. The other answers are incorrect: The bridge did exist (obviously), and it wasn't rebuilt after the battle (as indicated by the fact that it's no longer there), and it was swept away.

5. **1.** The "votive stone" represents a memorial to the fallen. A new bridge, celebration, ceremony, and reunion aren't appropriate answers — they just don't make sense in the context of the poem.

6. **3.** The shot heard round the world refers to the beginning of an event, specifically, the American Revolution. The tone of the poem tells you this answer, in descriptions of the flag as "unfurling" and the farmers as "embattled." You don't, of course, have to know which war it was.

7. **3.** Wally isn't feeling well because he drank too much wine. You have to draw this conclusion from Dwight's saying that he "noticed a couple empty wineskins behind the fig tree this morning."

8. **1.** Breakfast table is correct because the characters had just sat down for breakfast. The other locations — fig tree, market, bedroom, and vineyard — although mentioned in the excerpt, aren't the setting of the play.

9. **3.** Dwight felt it would be better to raise lean calves because they would represent more profit. Two of the answers — less profit and more expensive — are the opposite of what's stated in the passage. High fat content may be true, but it isn't mentioned in the passage. Goats aren't mentioned in the passage, either.

10. **5.** Dad isn't paying attention to Dwight because he is worried about Wally. Lost sheep, time in the vineyard, buying more land, and reading the paper aren't the best reasons for Dad's distraction.

11. **2.** Wally had been drinking wine the night before and is suffering from a hangover. The other reasons given — sickness, chores, reading, and working — aren't appropriate answers, based on the passage.

12. **3.** Both Wally and the wine need to breathe. Wally says, "Wine's got to breathe, you know. And so do I, Dad."

13. **1.** Carter left his job because he was lured by the promise of Arctic gold. Leaving his snug clerkship may be partially correct, but it isn't the best answer. The passage doesn't mention "a woman," except his wife, who stays behind. "Half of his savings" and "the heartstrings of men" don't answer the question.

14. **3.** He wanted to escape his everyday drudgery in life as a clerk. "Bondage of commerce" refers to his dislike of his day routine in the business world. His need for wealth (returns), romance, risk taking, and savings are different factors that don't apply to the question.

15. **2.** The text says that "Even its [the party's] goal . . . was the Klondike."

16. **4.** It was "ominous" because there was a foreboding of ill-fortune. Throughout the passage, words such as "unluckily," "ominously," and "evil star . . . in the ascendant" give the passage an ominous feeling. The route certainly was not blissful or hushed. "Surprising" doesn't make sense, and "hardiest" refers to a native of the region.

17. **1.** The fact that Jacques was native-born and raised in the Northwest made him important to the party. The fact that he was a renegade voyageur, born of a Chippewa woman in a deerskin lodge where he sucked tallow, isn't as relevant as his knowledge of the area is to his importance to the party.

18. **3.** Percy was seeking some romance and adventure in his otherwise mundane life. The fact that he was an ordinary man with a bank account, who spoke a good deal and was abnormally sentimental, aren't the best answers.

19. **2.** Sonny felt guilty at not having written sooner. The other answers — that he was lazy, busy, afraid, and in a hole — may relate to Sonny's behavior, feelings, or location, but they aren't the best answers.

20. **3.** The passage points out that Sonny has been sent to prison. The other choices, while mentioned in the excerpt, don't adequately describe his location.

21. **4.** "Strong in the head" refers to being smart or intelligent. Humorous, happy, and angry aren't characteristics related to strength or ability. Physically fit relates to the whole body, not the brain.

22. **5.** Sonny would be embarrassed if his parents knew he had been sent to prison.

23. **1.** Sonny is afraid he'll flip (or lose his mind) before being released from prison. Being a musician doesn't refer to his life in prison. "Getting anything straight" doesn't mean anything and is a trick question. The other two choices — coming straight back and blowing his brains out — refer to things that may happen after he leaves prison, not while inside it.

24. **3.** You know from the first sentence and from lines 10 and 11 that Sonny likes his brother and appreciates what his brother has done for him.

25. **1.** Jimmy finally got a chance to read Martha's letters after a day's march. The question asks *when* he read the letters. In the first light of day is incorrect (the passage refers to the "last hour of light.") The other choices refer to *where,* so they can't possibly be correct.

26. **3.** Martha saw Jimmy as just an acquaintance, while he wished they could be lovers. Strangers, siblings, and no relationship are incorrect answers.

27. **5.** He tasted the flaps of envelopes that he knew her tongue had sealed. This shows how much he cared for her. The other actions — washing his hands and wrapping the letters — are other ways to describe his feelings for her, but they aren't as strong as his tasting the envelope flaps. Holding the letters with the tips of his fingers and reading them at the last hour of light don't describe his feelings.

28. **2.** Martha enjoyed writing to Jimmy on a purely friendly basis. To say she cared deeply (she didn't), was infatuated (she wasn't), had a casual interest (it was more than casual), or had no feelings at all (she does have some feelings) don't correctly describe her interest.

29. **1.** The fact that her letters were thick and chatty indicates that she enjoyed writing letters. Her respect for Chaucer, her status as an English major, and her beautiful writing aren't the best answers. Professors and roommates don't relate to her enjoyment.

30. **4.** The letters served as a source of hope for the future. Other answers — an interesting hobby, a pleasing pastime, an escape from boredom, and profound disappointment — may all be true, but they don't indicate the real reason for Jimmy's deep interest in the letters.

31. **2.** The column specifically states that the center houses 85 social enterprises. Choice (1) is totally wrong and can be instantly eliminated on first reading. The other answers have a ring of correctness because the column is about social enterprises, charities, LEF, and school leavers, but they have nothing to do with the center and, thus, are wrong.

32. **3.** The column states that the Learnxs Foundation supports innovative programs. All the other answers except for Choice (1) are mentioned or implied in the column; however, they aren't correct answers to the question. You have to read carefully and double-check the facts. Just because something is mentioned or is familiar doesn't mean it's the right answer to the question.

33. **5.** The passage clearly spells out that Artsjunction's function is to distribute discarded materials to visual arts classes. The other answers may be worthy of effort on behalf of some charity or agency, but they aren't the mandate of Artsjunction.

34. **2.** The column is very specific about the purpose of the Microtron bus. It provided services to employees and clients of small businesses in word and numerical processing. The other answers sound like they could be right, but, after rereading the column, you can see that they aren't.

When you're trying to answer these questions under time constraints, try to remember exactly what the passage said. If you only think you remember, go back as quickly as you can and skim the piece for key words. In this case the key word is *Microtron.*

35. **4.** The passage very precisely spells out the mandate of the Training Renewal Foundation as being to serve disadvantaged youth and displaced workers. The other answers may be worthy activities for any charity, but they aren't stated as part of the mandate and, thus, are wrong as answers. Choice (3) is just wrong and is a play on another meaning of *serves.* You can immediately exclude this answer and have only four others to consider.

36. **3.** Employees should wear appropriate clothing to project a professional appearance and maintain safety standards. The other requirements — such as refraining from alcohol use, not associating with paraphernalia, being respectful, and using non-offensive language — don't relate to appearance.

37. **1.** Employees must accept the authority of supervisors, as is stated clearly in the passage.

38. **4.** Employees must conduct themselves professionally so that the business grows and improves.

39. **2.** To ensure safety and security, employees shouldn't invite other people in. The promotion of dignity, interaction, supervisors, and respect don't directly relate to ensuring safety and security.

40. **5.** Repeated instances of non-compliance lead to dismissal. The other answers aren't backed up by the passage.

Answer Key

1. **1**	15. **2**	28. **2**
2. **4**	16. **4**	29. **1**
3. **2**	17. **1**	30. **4**
4. **5**	18. **3**	31. **2**
5. **1**	19. **2**	32. **3**
6. **3**	20. **3**	33. **5**
7. **3**	21. **4**	34. **2**
8. **1**	22. **5**	35. **4**
9. **3**	23. **1**	36. **3**
10. **5**	24. **3**	37. **1**
11. **2**	25. **1**	38. **4**
12. **3**	26. **3**	39. **2**
13. **1**	27. **5**	40. **5**
14. **3**		

Chapter 22

Another Practice Test — Language Arts, Reading Test

••

*T*he Language Arts, Reading Test consists of excerpts from fiction and nonfiction. Each excerpt is followed by multiple-choice questions about the reading material.

Read each excerpt first and then answer the questions following it. Refer back to the reading material as often as necessary in answering the questions.

Each excerpt is preceded by a purpose question. The purpose question gives a reason for reading the material. Use the purpose questions to help focus your reading. You are not required to answer these purpose questions. They are given only to help you concentrate on the ideas presented in the reading material.

You have 65 minutes to answer the 40 questions in this test. Work carefully, but do not spend too much time on any one question. Be sure you answer every question.

Answer Sheet for Language Arts, Reading Test

1 ① ② ③ ④ ⑤   21 ① ② ③ ④ ⑤

2 ① ② ③ ④ ⑤   22 ① ② ③ ④ ⑤

3 ① ② ③ ④ ⑤   23 ① ② ③ ④ ⑤

4 ① ② ③ ④ ⑤   24 ① ② ③ ④ ⑤

5 ① ② ③ ④ ⑤   25 ① ② ③ ④ ⑤

6 ① ② ③ ④ ⑤   26 ① ② ③ ④ ⑤

7 ① ② ③ ④ ⑤   27 ① ② ③ ④ ⑤

8 ① ② ③ ④ ⑤   28 ① ② ③ ④ ⑤

9 ① ② ③ ④ ⑤   29 ① ② ③ ④ ⑤

10 ① ② ③ ④ ⑤   30 ① ② ③ ④ ⑤

11 ① ② ③ ④ ⑤   31 ① ② ③ ④ ⑤

12 ① ② ③ ④ ⑤   32 ① ② ③ ④ ⑤

13 ① ② ③ ④ ⑤   33 ① ② ③ ④ ⑤

14 ① ② ③ ④ ⑤   34 ① ② ③ ④ ⑤

15 ① ② ③ ④ ⑤   35 ① ② ③ ④ ⑤

16 ① ② ③ ④ ⑤   36 ① ② ③ ④ ⑤

17 ① ② ③ ④ ⑤   37 ① ② ③ ④ ⑤

18 ① ② ③ ④ ⑤   38 ① ② ③ ④ ⑤

19 ① ② ③ ④ ⑤   39 ① ② ③ ④ ⑤

20 ① ② ③ ④ ⑤   40 ① ② ③ ④ ⑤

Language Arts, Reading Test

Do not mark in this test booklet. Record your answers on the separate answer sheet provided. Be sure that all requested information is properly recorded on the answer sheet.

To record your answers, fill in the numbered circle on the answer sheet that corresponds to the answer you select for each question in the test booklet.

EXAMPLE:

It was Susan's dream machine. The metallic blue paint gleamed, and the sporty wheels were highly polished. Under the hood, the engine was no less carefully cleaned. Inside, flashy lights illuminated the instruments on the dashboard, and the seats were covered by rich leather upholstery.

The subject ("it") of this excerpt is most likely

(1) an airplane

(2) a stereo system

(3) an automobile

(4) a boat

(5) a motorcycle

(On Answer Sheet)
① ② ● ④ ⑤

The correct answer is "an automobile"; therefore, answer space 3 would be marked on the answer sheet.

Do not rest the point of your pencil on the answer sheet while you are considering your answer. Make no stray or unnecessary marks. If you change an answer, erase your first mark completely. Mark only one answer space for each question; multiple answers will be scored as incorrect. Do not fold or crease your answer sheet. All test materials must be returned to the test administrator.

Note: Refer to Chapter 23 for the answers for this practice test.

Directions: Choose the <u>one best answer</u> to each question.

Questions 1 through 6 refer to the following poem by Sheila Sarah Franschman (2010).

WHAT IS SPECIAL ABOUT MUIR WOODS?

Line Under the worn wooden sign ushering one and all
To wander along the broad plank path
And feast your eyes on the majestic redwoods
Some on earth longer than 1,000 years
(05) Their outer layers bathed in shades of brown and black
Towering above but below the clouds
Gazing now at the branches entwined in lovers knots
Nature providing the streams meandering through
Feeding the nourishments required to sustain
(10) Through the times
Fog settles on the highest branches
Elevating trees into the heavens above
Small animals dart about the ground cover
And birds choose between plant and branch
(15) The four seasons offer different hues
While spring follows a babbling stream,
Ending in catch basins
And summer opens to sunlight exposing their vulnerability
And their strength
(20) Fall foliage turns to red and yellow,
With a hint of orange
While winter envelopes the landscape
Wearing a coat of white
Vulnerable now
(25) Waiting again for seasons to renew themselves
For people and animals
To wander again along the broad plank path.

1. What is the overall setting for the poem?

   (1) a backyard

   (2) a barn

   (3) a city street

   (4) a forest

   (5) a playground

2. Some redwood trees live as long as

   (1) 400 years

   (2) 1,000 years

   (3) 200 years

   (4) 1,500 years

   (5) 80 years

Go on to next page

3. When the author writes, "The four seasons offer different hues," she means that

    (1) Different birds and animals populate the setting each season.

    (2) Leaves change color every season.

    (3) Falling leaves make the streams change color.

    (4) Fog filters the light differently during the winter.

    (5) The colors of the setting change with the seasons.

4. In which season does the author describe the setting as "vulnerable?"

    (1) spring

    (2) summer

    (3) fall

    (4) winter

    (5) not enough information given

5. When someone looks at a redwood tree, what color(s) do they see?

    (1) green and red

    (2) red

    (3) brown and black

    (4) red and yellow

    (5) orange

6. What provides the nourishment for the giant trees to grow?

    (1) nature

    (2) gardeners

    (3) park workers

    (4) animals

    (5) birds

Go on to next page

> *Questions 7 through 12 refer to the following excerpt from George Bernard Shaw's* Major Barbara *(1905).*

WHY IS UNDERSHAFT INTERESTED IN THE SALVATION ARMY?

Line **UNDERSHAFT:** One moment, Mr. Lomax. I am rather interested in the Salvation Army. Its motto might be my own: Blood and Fire.

LOMAX: *(shocked)* But not your sort of blood and fire, you know.

UNDERSHAFT: My sort of blood cleanses: my sort of fire purifies.

(05) **BARBARA:** So does ours. Come down tomorrow to my shelter — the West Ham Shelter — and see what we are doing. We're going to march to a great meeting in the Assembly at Mile End. Come and see the shelter and then march with us: It will do you a lot of good. Can you play anything?

UNDERSHAFT: In my youth I earned pennies, and even shillings occasionally, in the
(10) streets and in public house parlors by my natural talent for stepdancing. Later on, I became a member of the Undershaft Orchestra Society, and performed passably on the tenor trombone.

LOMAX: *(scandalized, putting down the concertina)* Oh I say!

BARBARA: Many a sinner has played himself into heaven on the trombone, thanks to
(15) the Army.

LOMAX: *(to BARBARA, still rather shocked)* Yes; but what about the cannon business, don't you know? *(to UNDERSHAFT)* Getting into heaven is not exactly in your line, is it?

LADY BRITOMART: Charles!!!

LOMAX: Well; but it stands to reason, don't it? The cannon business may be neces-
(20) sary and all that; we can't get along without cannons; but it isn't right, you know. On the other hand, there may be a certain amount of tosh about the Salvation Army — I belong to the Established Church myself — but still you can't deny that it's religion; and you can't go against religion, can you? At least unless you're downright immoral, don't you know.

7. Why did Barbara invite Undershaft to the shelter?

   (1) to march in the band

   (2) to attend a great meeting

   (3) to earn pennies

   (4) to stepdance

   (5) to be with them in the Assembly

8. What does stepdancing for pennies tell you about Undershaft?

   (1) He has natural talent.

   (2) He frequented public houses.

   (3) He had an impoverished youth.

   (4) He performed passably.

   (5) He was a skilled musician.

Go on to next page

9. What can Undershaft contribute to the march?

    (1) stepdancing

    (2) pennies

    (3) shillings

    (4) trombone playing

    (5) natural talent

10. How would you describe Lomax's treatment of Undershaft?

    (1) friendly

    (2) bitter

    (3) encouraging

    (4) philosophical

    (5) critical

11. Why might Undershaft's motto be "Blood and Fire"?

    (1) He makes cannons.

    (2) He plays the trombone.

    (3) He is a sinner.

    (4) He doesn't belong to the Established Church.

    (5) He marches for the Salvation Army.

12. How do you know Barbara is committed to doing good?

    (1) She is in the Salvation Army.

    (2) She operates a shelter.

    (3) She joins in marches.

    (4) She plays the concertina.

    (5) She recruits others to join.

Go on to next page ⟹

> Questions 13 through 18 refer to the following excerpt from Washington Irving's "Rip Van Winkle," (1819).

WHAT CAN YOU LEARN FROM THE MOUNTAINS?

Line
Whoever has made a voyage up the Hudson must remember the Kaatskill Mountains. They are a dismembered branch of the great Appalachian family, and are seen away to the west of the river, swelling up to a noble height, and lording it over the surrounding country. Every change of season, every change of weather, indeed, every hour of
(05) the day, produces some change in the magical hues and shapes of these mountains, and they are regarded by all the good wives, far and near, as perfect barometers. When the weather is fair and settled, they are clothed in blue and purple, and print their bold outlines on the clear evening sky; but, sometimes, when the rest of the landscape is cloudless, they will gather a hood of gray vapors about their summits, which,
(10) in the last rays of the setting sun, will glow and light up like a crown of glory.

At the foot of these fairy mountains, the voyager may have descried the light smoke curling up from a village, whose shingle-roofs gleam among the trees, just where the blue tints of the upland melt away into the fresh green of the nearer landscape. It is a little village of great antiquity, having been founded by some of the Dutch colonists, in
(15) the early times of the province, just about the beginning of the government of the good Peter Stuyvesant, (may he rest in peace!) and there were some of the houses of the original settlers standing within a few years, built of small yellow bricks brought from Holland, having latticed windows and gablefronts, surmounted with weather-cocks.

13. How would you locate the Kaatskill Mountains?

   (1) Ask directions.

   (2) Journey up the Hudson.

   (3) Look for a dismembered branch.

   (4) Notice fresh green.

   (5) Enjoy the surrounding country.

14. According to lines 5 and 6, how do the wives tell the weather?

   (1) with perfect barometers

   (2) by the clear evening sky

   (3) with the crown of glory

   (4) through gray vapors

   (5) with magical hues and shapes

15. What might you look for to find the village?

   (1) fairy mountains

   (2) shingle-roofs

   (3) light smoke curling

   (4) blue tints

   (5) great antiquity

16. Who originally founded the village?

   (1) Peter Stuyvesant

   (2) the great Appalachian family

   (3) the voyager

   (4) Dutch colonists

   (5) the government

17. Why is the phrase "may he rest in peace!" (line 16) used after Peter Stuyvesant?

   (1) He has since died.

   (2) He was an original settler.

   (3) He was a voyager.

   (4) He was a soldier.

   (5) He was the governor.

18. What materials came from Holland?

   (1) weather-cocks

   (2) yellow bricks

   (3) latticed windows

   (4) gablefronts

   (5) shingle-roofs

Go on to next page

> Questions 19 through 24 refer to the following excerpt from Richard Wright's "The Man Who Was Almost a Man," from Eight Men (1961).

WHAT DO YOU NEED TO BE A MAN?

Line   Dave struck out across the fields, looking homeward through paling light . . . One of these days he was going to get a gun and practice shooting, then they couldn't talk to him as though he were a little boy. He slowed, looking at the ground. Shucks, Ah ain scareda them . . . even ef they are biggern me! Aw, Ah know whut Ahma do. Ahm

(05)   going by ol Joe's sto n git that Sears Roebuck catlog n look at them guns. Mebbe Ma will lemme buy one when she gits mah pay from ol man Hawkins. Ahma beg her t gimme some money. Ahm ol ernough to hava gun. Ahm seventeen. Almost a man. He strode, feeling his long loose-jointed limbs. Shucks, a man oughta hava little gun aftah he done worked hard all day.

(10)   He came in sight of Joe's store. A yellow lantern glowed on the front porch. He mounted steps and went through the screen door, hearing it bang behind him. There was a strong smell of coal oil and mackerel fish. He felt very confident until he saw fat Joe walk in through the rear door, then his courage began to ooze.

"Howdy, Dave! Whutcha want?"

(15)   "How yuh, Mistah Joe? Aw, Ah don wanna buy nothing. Ah jus wanted t see ef yuhd lemme look at tha catlog erwhile."

"Sure! You wanna see it here?"

"Nawsuh. Ah wants t take it home wid me. Ah'll bring it back termorrow when Ah come in from the fiels."

(20)   "You plannin on buying something?"

"Yessuh."

"Your ma lettin you have your own money now?"

"Shucks. Mistah Joe, Ahm gittin t be a man like anybody else!"

19. What was Dave's place of employment?
    (1) Joe's store
    (2) Sears Roebuck
    (3) Hawkins's fields
    (4) with his Ma
    (5) unemployed

20. Why did he want "to get a gun" in line 2?
    (1) to show he wasn't "scareda" the others
    (2) to prove he wasn't unemployed
    (3) to make his Ma proud
    (4) to impress Joe
    (5) to get a better job

21. From where did Dave hope to get a gun?
    (1) from "Joe's sto"
    (2) from "ol man Hawkins"
    (3) from Ma
    (4) from the Sears Roebuck "catlog"
    (5) from field hands in the field

22. How would you find Joe's store at night?
    (1) by the smell of mackerel
    (2) by the banging screen door
    (3) by the smell of coal oil
    (4) by a yellow lantern glow
    (5) through the rear door

Go on to next page

23. Why do you think Dave asked to take the catalog home?

    (1) He lost his nerve.

    (2) It was too dark to read.

    (3) He had to be home for supper.

    (4) He makes his own money.

    (5) He had to ask his mother's permission.

24. What must Dave do to get the gun?

    (1) Find it in the catalog.

    (2) Convince Ma to give him the money.

    (3) Persuade Joe to place the order.

    (4) Return the catalog to Joe.

    (5) Get ol man Hawkins's permission.

Go on to next page

> Questions 25 through 30 refer to the following excerpt from Saul Bellow's "Something to Remember Me By" (1990).

HOW DID IT ALL BEGIN?

Line It began like any other winter school day in Chicago — grimly ordinary. The temperature a few degrees above zero, botanical frost shapes on the windowpane, the snow swept up in heaps, the ice gritty and the streets, block after block, bound together by the iron of the sky. A breakfast of porridge, toast, and tea. Late as usual, I stopped for
(05) a moment to look into my mother's sickroom. I bent near and said, "It's Louie, going to school." She seemed to nod. Her eyelids were brown, her face was much lighter. I hurried off with my books on a strap over my shoulder.

When I came to the boulevard on the edge of the park, two small men rushed out of a doorway with rifles, wheeled around aiming upward, and fired at pigeons near the
(10) rooftop. Several birds fell straight down, and the men scooped up the soft bodies and ran indoors, dark little guys in fluttering white shirts. Depression hunters and their city game. Moments before, the police car had loafed by at ten miles an hour. The men had waited it out.

This had nothing to do with me. I mention it merely because it happened. I stepped
(15) around the blood spots and crossed into the park.

25. What words best describe the appearance of a winter school day in Chicago?

   (1) botanical frost
   (2) swept in heaps
   (3) grim and gritty
   (4) iron sky
   (5) block after block

26. What do you find out about the state of Louie's home life in lines 4 and 5?

   (1) He ate porridge, toast, and tea.
   (2) He was late, as usual.
   (3) He carried books on a strap.
   (4) His face was much lighter.
   (5) His mother was sick.

27. What were the men doing in the doorway?

   (1) hunting for game
   (2) having target practice
   (3) staying out of the weather
   (4) hiding from police
   (5) making their way to the park

28. How do you know the men were good shots?

   (1) They ran indoors.
   (2) They were small men.
   (3) They had rifles.
   (4) Several birds fell.
   (5) Pigeons were near the rooftop.

29. What adjective best describes the hunters?

   (1) angry
   (2) hungry
   (3) happy
   (4) brave
   (5) careless

30. Why didn't Louie tell the police about what he saw?

   (1) He was in a hurry to get to school.
   (2) His mother was sick.
   (3) It had nothing to do with him.
   (4) The guys were his friends.
   (5) They were depression hunters.

Go on to next page

Questions 31 through 35 refer to the following excerpt from Russell Hart's Photography For
Dummies, 2nd Edition (Wiley).

WHAT'S THE SECRET TO LOADING BATTERIES?

Line   If you've ever had to figure out where to stick batteries in your child's latest electronic acquisition, then loading batteries in your point-and-shoot shouldn't be a challenge. Turn off your camera when you install them; the camera may go crazy opening
and closing its lens. (Some cameras turn themselves off after you install new batter-
(05)   ies, so you have to turn them back on to shoot.)

With big point-and-shoot models, you typically open a latched cover on the bottom to
install batteries. More compact models have a battery compartment under a door or
flap that is incorporated into the side or grip of the camera. You may have to pry
open such doors with a coin.

(10)   More annoying are covers on the bottom that you open by loosening a screw. (You
need a coin for this type, too.) And most annoying are battery covers that aren't hinged
and come off completely when you unscrew them. If you have one of these, don't
change batteries while standing over a sewer grate, in a field of tall grass, or on a pier.

Whether loading four AAs or a single lithium, make sure that the batteries are cor-
(15)   rectly oriented as you insert them. You'll find a diagram and/or plus and minus markings, usually within the compartment or on the inside of the door.

If your camera doesn't turn on and the batteries are correctly installed, the batteries
may have lost their punch from sitting on a shelf too long. Which is where the battery
icon comes in.

(20)   If your camera has an LCD panel, an icon tells you when battery power is low.

31. Where will you be installing the batteries?

(1) an electronic acquisition

(2) a children's toy

(3) a big point-and-shoot

(4) a camera

(5) a flashlight

32. What is the easiest model in which to
replace the batteries?

(1) compact models

(2) big point-and-shoots

(3) screw bottoms

(4) covers not hinged

(5) covers that come off completely

33. Why should locations such as sewer grates
and tall grass be avoided when changing
batteries?

(1) Water can get in the camera.

(2) Your lens may get dirty.

(3) The glare would ruin the picture.

(4) Your film would get exposed.

(5) The battery cover may be lost.

Go on to next page ⟹

34. How do you ensure that the batteries are correctly oriented?

    (1) Use four AAs.

    (2) Use a single lithium.

    (3) Empty the compartment.

    (4) Find a diagram.

    (5) Check the inside of the film box.

35. What tells you whether the batteries are low?

    (1) the LCD panel

    (2) the battery icon

    (3) the battery compartment

    (4) a single lithium battery

    (5) markings on the diagram

Go on to next page

Questions 36 through 40 refer to the following excerpt, written by Sheila Sarah Franschman (2010).

WHAT'S THE MOST COMFORTABLE WAY TO SEE THE SIGHTS?

Line   San Francisco is a walking town and I trudged up and down the hills until my legs were
ready for a vacation. I walked through Chinatown; explored Union Square; looked up at
Coit Tower; down at the Golden Gate from the bridge; meandered in Fisherman's Wharf
and, of course, shopped Macy's and Barney's. While looking at a pair of comfortable shoes
(05)   in a store window, I noticed, tucked away among the souvenir shops, an innocuous store
front selling tours. What an original idea — seeing San Francisco seated instead of walking.

The next day a small white tour bus picked me up from my hotel at 8.15 a.m., a little
earlier than I would have preferred, but the anticipation of seeing beautiful California
while seated got me going. The bus was comfortable and not very crowded, and I
(10)   found a window seat with its view of the world or at least Mason Street.

Traveling the spectacular windswept coastline of northern California I anticipated the highlight of the trip, called the seventeen-mile drive. I watched as the suburbs of San Francisco
faded into the distance and each mile took us closer to our destination. I looked at the pictures in the brochure and wondered if the reality was as glorious as the photographs.

(15)   The driver explained that this was a century-old route that was originally used by tourists
in covered wagons. Now, it was a gated community with luxury hotels and golf courses,
which are still the main attraction after all these years, but I was not there to see people
swinging clubs. I was there to see the power of the waves and the stillness of the deserted
beaches. I could tolerate golfers, oblivious to anything except their game, playing on the
(20)   world famous Pebble Beach Golf Links as long as I could commune with my beloved ocean.

Soon enough I saw it. The ocean pounded the beach, lapping up sand only to spit it out
again in a swirl of water. I was one with the ocean, and the rhythm of the waves washed
away all present-day concerns. This is what I had come to California to experience.

There are about twenty stops along the route and I watched in wonderment as we slowed
(25)   to enjoy each one. Stopping first at Point Joe, I disembarked with camera in tow, awe-struck
by the power of the waves and the beauty of the scenery. From this vista point, the terrain
is studded by rocks jutting above the turbulent waters that stream around them. Standing
against the backdrop of sky meeting water, people recorded memories to take back home.

People dressed in early winter attire stepped gingerly down steep terrain weathered
(30)   by the elements to get a closer look at the magnificent beach spread before them. All
of us on the bus had entered the seventeen-mile drive experience.

As the bus passed countless coves and scenic views, we encounter pure white sand
while curious people move in a dream sequence aimlessly wandering about. I had
entered the reality of Pebble Beach, the sand danced in the waves resembling an
(35)   unfinished canvas which engulfed me and swirled my imagination.

At the next stop, the Lone Cypress stands majestically perched on the rocky cliff watching over the Pacific Ocean, a symbol and landmark inspiring amateur photographers
trying to capture the grandeur on a silicon chip. This tree, growing from a rock, is used
as a trademark for the resort and typifies the pioneer spirit that must have been part of
(40)   each early Californian as they struggled with nature for their existence. Now, sitting on
a comfortable bus, I experienced the beauty of the area surrounded by native pine and
cypress trees, twisted by nature becoming a foil for the Lone Cypress. I admire the
independence and strength of this tree and the early pioneers as I continue my journey.

Go on to next page ⟩

(45) The Ghost tree, a Monterey Cypress, bleached white from ocean spray, stands as a monument to nature's fury and beauty. Along the cliffs are other blanched Cypress trees, standing like a phalanx of apparitions haunting me. I have seen the raw beauty of California.

36. What means of getting around San Francisco did the author use at first?

    (1) public transit

    (2) bus

    (3) walking

    (4) automobile

    (5) limousine

37. What was the highlight of the author's trip?

    (1) the Golden Gate Bridge

    (2) Chinatown

    (3) Carmel

    (4) the seventeen-mile drive

    (5) Union Square

38. In reality, the seventeen-mile drive is

    (1) a gated community

    (2) a deserted highway

    (3) a golf course

    (4) a luxury hotel

    (5) a beach resort

39. What impressed the author at Point Joe?

    (1) the power of the waves and the beauty of the scenery

    (2) the rhythm of the waves

    (3) the manicured lawns

    (4) the sea lions

    (5) the covered wagons

40. The Lone Cypress has become famous because it is

    (1) very old

    (2) used as a trademark for the resort

    (3) growing out of a rock

    (4) much taller than the other trees

    (5) very well kept

END OF TEST

Chapter 23

Answers and Explanations for the Language Arts, Reading Test

. . . .

After taking the Language Arts, Reading Test in Chapter 22, use this chapter to check your answers. Take your time as you move through the explanations of the answers that we provide in the first section. They can help you understand why you missed the answers you did. You may also want to read the explanations for the questions you answered correctly because doing so can give you a better understanding of the thought process that helped you choose the correct answers.

If you're short on time, turn to the end of the chapter for an abbreviated answer key.

Analysis of the Answers

1. **4.** From the description in the first part of the poem (trees, stream, birds, small animals, and so on), you can tell that the setting is a forest. None of the other answers fit the setting described in the poem.

2. **2.** The poem states that the redwood trees can live longer than 1,000 years (line 4). The other answers are factually incorrect. This question is a good example of when skimming can help you find an answer quickly because it's asking for a factual and numeric answer.

3. **5.** The author describes in detail the changes in color of the settings for each season. The other answers may look like they may be right, but there's no evidence in the poem to support them.

4. **4.** The author writes, "While winter envelopes the landscape / Wearing a coat of white / Vulnerable now." The other seasons aren't described in this manner, so you know winter is the answer. Choice (5) is incorrect as more than enough information is given to answer the question. If you read the question and then skim the poem, you stand a very good chance of efficiently getting the right answer.

5. **3.** The author describes the trees as "bathed in shades of brown and black." If you have some knowledge of redwood trees, you know that the wood is red — not the bark. The other colors may be mentioned in the poem but they aren't referring to the redwood trees.

6. **1.** The author says that nature provides the needed nourishment and that the streams carry it to the trees. Although the other answers are feasible, they're incorrect based on the poem. You must answer the questions based on only the information given in the passage. Don't let any prior knowledge sway you from this task. The correct answer is always in the passage.

7. **1.** Barbara was recruiting players for her marching band and saw Undershaft as a candidate. The other answer choices (attending a meeting, earning pennies, stepdancing, and being in the Assembly) don't express her interest in Undershaft.

8. **3.** You know Undershaft had an impoverished youth because he had to stepdance for pennies to survive. During this time, poor children danced as entertainment for people who might throw them pennies. This way of living was a bit above begging in that the children provided some entertainment for the money donated.

9. **4.** Undershaft was a trombone player who could contribute his musical talents to the marching band. Stepdancing, pennies, or shillings aren't contributions to the band. Natural musical talent could be a correct answer, but because a more specific answer exists, you need to rule out this one.

10. **5.** Lomax criticizes Undershaft's work as a cannon manufacturer, implying that Undershaft won't get to heaven because of his work with cannons. Lomax may be bitter and he may be philosophical, but those words don't describe his treatment of Undershaft. "Friendly" and "encouraging" certainly don't describe Lomax's demeanor, either.

11. **1.** Undershaft's motto could be "Blood and Fire" because he manufactures cannons used to kill people in war. Playing the trombone, being a sinner, belonging to the Church, and marching aren't related to blood and fire.

12. **2.** Barbara doesn't just preach about good works; she operates a shelter to help poor people. This reason is stronger than the other choices given, such as being in the Salvation Army, joining in marches, playing the concertina, or recruiting others.

13. **2.** To locate the Kaatskill Mountains, you need to journey up the Hudson. A dismembered branch, fresh green, and surrounding the country aren't locations that can better help you locate the mountains. Although asking directions may work, this approach isn't mentioned in the passage.

14. **5.** The wives use the magical hues and shapes of the mountains to forecast the weather. Other factors, such as the evening sky, gray vapors, or the crown of glory, aren't as good of indicators. A barometer is an instrument to measure air pressure.

15. **3.** To help you locate the village, you first need to look for light smoke curling from chimneys. You can't see the other sign, shingle-roofs, as soon as you can see the smoke. Mountains, tents, and great antiquity aren't signs for locating villages.

16. **4.** The Dutch colonists were the newcomers who founded the village. Peter Stuyvesant established the government. The great Appalachian family refers to the mountains. The voyager discovered the village in his travels.

17. **1.** Peter Stuyvesant, who had headed the government, had since died. The other answer choices describe Stuyvesant as an original settler, a voyager, a soldier, and a governor, but they don't refer to his death.

18. **2.** Settlers brought yellow bricks from Holland to build the houses. Other materials, such as weather-cocks, windows, gablefronts, and shingle-roofs, were locally acquired.

19. **3.** Dave worked as a field hand on the Hawkins's farm. He hopes his mother will let him buy a gun with his wages from Hawkins. He wasn't unemployed, and he didn't work at Joe's store, Sears Roebuck, or with his Ma.

20. **1.** He wants to show the other field hands that he isn't scared of them. Dave mentions that he isn't afraid of them just before he first discusses buying the gun.

21. **4.** Dave had to purchase the gun through the Sears Roebuck catalog. Joe didn't keep guns in his store. Mr. Hawkins, Ma, and the field hands aren't sources of guns.

22. **4.** Joe kept a yellow lantern glowing on the porch. Other answer choices, such as the smell of mackerel, the banging screen door, the coal oil smell, and the rear door, may also help you find the store, but they aren't the best indicators.

23. **1.** Dave lost his nerve and was afraid to ask Joe to see guns in the catalog. The other possibilities — it was too dark, he needed to get home for supper, he made his own money, and he had to ask for his mother's permission — aren't the best answers.

24. **2.** Dave would have to convince Ma to give him the money to buy the gun. The other reasons, including finding it in the catalog, persuading Joe, returning the catalog, or getting ol man Hawkins's permission, either aren't relevant or aren't as important as convincing Ma to give him the money.

25. **3.** The winter sky was grim and the streets were gritty in Chicago. Botanical frost refers to the windowpane. Snow was swept in heaps for block after block. The iron sky is only one characteristic, and it isn't the most important.

26. **5.** Louie was living with his mother, who was very ill and confined to bed. Other answers describing Louie's breakfast, his punctuality, his books, and his complexion aren't good descriptions of the focus of his home life.

27. **1.** The men were hunting pigeons (game) for food. You can see that having target practice, staying out of the weather, hiding from the police, and going to the park are inappropriate answers if you've read the passage thoroughly.

28. **4.** They were able to knock several birds from the sky. The other answer choices — that the men were running indoors, were small in size, and had rifles or that the pigeons were near the rooftop — don't answer the question.

29. **2.** The hunters and their families must have been hungry for food to hunt pigeons in the street. The other adjectives — angry, happy, brave, and careless — don't adequately describe why they were hunting.

30. **3.** What Louie saw had nothing to do with him, and he didn't want to get involved. Other possible answers — that he was hurrying to school, his mother was sick, or he was friends with the guys or that the guys were depression hunters — don't relate to why Louie wouldn't tell the police.

31. **4.** The batteries are installed in a camera. Other answer choices, such as electronics, a children's toy, or a flashlight, have no meaning in this excerpt. Point-and-shoot, while another term for a camera, isn't the best answer.

32. **2.** The easiest model in which to replace batteries is in the point-and-shoot camera. The other answer choices — compact models, screw bottoms, and different types of covers — don't relate directly to the question.

33. **5.** Avoid all the locations mentioned so that you don't lose your battery cover if you drop it. Sewer grates and tall grass are places where the cover could easily be lost. The rest of the answer choices refer to issues other than losing battery covers.

34. **4.** To ensure that the batteries are correctly oriented, you must find the diagram and use it. Other choices, such as using four AAs or a single lithium, emptying the compartment, or checking inside the film box, don't answer the question.

35. **2.** You must check the battery icon to see whether the batteries are low. According to the passage, the LCD panel, compartment, lithium battery, and diagram markings aren't correct answers.

36. **3.** At first, the author walked around San Francisco. The author used the bus for a trip outside the city after she walked around the city itself, and the passage doesn't mention public transit, automobiles, or limousines. You can pick this answer easily by reading the questions first and then skimming the passage.

37. **4.** The author states quite emphatically that the seventeen-mile drive was the highlight of the trip. The author saw all the other places, but none elicited the response of the seventeen-mile drive.

38. **1.** In the passage, the bus driver explained to the passengers that the seventeen-mile drive is really a gated community. It also contains a golf course and a luxury hotel, but it is a gated community itself. You have to read the questions and passage carefully to make sure of the answer. Skimming may have provided you with three possible answers (3, 4, and 5) and one unlikely but still possible answer (2). More careful reading provides only one correct answer (1).

39. **1.** The first answer is a direct quote from the passage, so you know right away that it's right. The other answers are possible but not specifically mentioned as impressing the author. Two of the answers (3 and 4) aren't located at Point Joe, one answer (5) is from another century, and the last answer (2) isn't specifically associated with Point Joe. When you find a direct quote that answers the question, choosing the right answer is easy to do.

40. **2.** The Lone Cypress is used as a trademark for the resort and, for this reason, has become famous. The other answers may or may not be right, but they aren't specifically mentioned by the author. You can use only items that are specifically mentioned or directly implied as your answer. Other answers may be possible, but the answer you want is the one that's there in the passage.

Answer Key

1. **4**	15. **3**	28. **4**
2. **2**	16. **4**	29. **2**
3. **5**	17. **1**	30. **3**
4. **4**	18. **2**	31. **4**
5. **3**	19. **3**	32. **2**
6. **1**	20. **1**	33. **5**
7. **1**	21. **4**	34. **4**
8. **3**	22. **4**	35. **2**
9. **4**	23. **1**	36. **3**
10. **5**	24. **2**	37. **4**
11. **1**	25. **3**	38. **1**
12. **2**	26. **5**	39. **1**
13. **2**	27. **1**	40. **2**
14. **5**		

Part VI

Counting All the Possible Solutions: The Mathematics Test

The 5th Wave   By Rich Tennant

"I hear you think you got all the angles figured. Well, maybe you do and maybe you don't. Maybe the ratios of the lengths of corresponding sides of an equiangular right-angled triangle are equal, then again, maybe they're not – let's see your equations."

In this part . . .

*T*his part includes ways to use the mathematics you've learned over the years to pass the Mathematics Test. Here you discover why this test has different answer forms and how to use them. To help you build confidence for this part of the GED, we show you that you really do know a lot about math — and that you may have been too frightened of the subject before to think about everything you know. We do our best to show you that math can be fun — or at least not horrible — and we offer you strategies that can help you do your best on this test.

Like the other test parts, this part includes two complete practice tests. Take the allotted time to answer these problems, and then be sure to check your answers to see if you were right. If you don't answer a question or two (or more) correctly, use the explanations we provide to help you understand how to work out the problems.

Before you start preparing for the Mathematics Test, remember this: You can conquer math — and this part will help you do just that.

Chapter 24

Safety in Numbers: Facing the Mathematics Test, Parts I and II

. . . .

In This Chapter

▶ Getting a handle on the skills being tested and the test format

▶ Preparing for the test using a few tried-and-true strategies

▶ Knowing how to tackle the different question types

▶ Practicing some time-management skills for the Math Test

▶ Doing a few practice problems

. . . .

Welcome to the dreaded Mathematics Test. Although you may have done everything to avoid math in high school, you can't escape this test if you want to pass the GED. To tell you the truth, test takers really do have nightmares about this test, but don't worry! This chapter helps you prepare not for having nightmares but for taking the test successfully.

Most of the questions in the other GED tests are about reading comprehension: You're given a passage and are expected to understand it well enough to correctly answer the questions that follow. Although you can prepare for the other tests by doing a lot of reading and taking sample tests, you don't have to come in with a lot of knowledge or great skills in the test areas themselves.

The Mathematics Test, however, tests your understanding of mathematical concepts and your ability to apply them to situations you may find in the real world, which means you have to spend time solving as many problems as you can and improving your math skills as much as possible before you take this test. This chapter gives you some tips and tricks for studying for the GED Mathematics Test.

Looking at the Skills the Math Test Covers

Math isn't scary, and it has yet to appear as the villain in any major Hollywood horror films (at least that we know about). In fact, math can even be fun when you put your mind to it. In any case, the Mathematics Test assesses your abilities in math, so you have to be ready for it. This is the one GED subject that requires a special way of thinking and understanding — improving your ability to think mathematically will make your job of passing this test easier.

To do well on the Mathematics Test, you need to have a general understanding of numbers, their relationships to one another, measurements, geometry, data analysis and statistics, probability, patterns, functions, and algebra. (If you don't know what we mean by these terms, check out the next section "Understanding the Test Format.") In essence, to be successful on this test, you need to have the mathematical knowledge base that most high school graduates have and you need to know how to apply it to solve real-life problems. If, after reading this chapter, you're still worried about solving different math problems, take some time to go through a few high school math books at your local library or sign up for a math prep class or a math study group.

Understanding the Test Format

The Mathematics Test consists of two parts, each with 25 questions. You have 90 minutes to complete both parts. Part I allows you to use a calculator; Part II bans the calculator in favor of your brain. (You're given scratch paper to use for rough calculations.) You have to pass both parts to pass this test.

A formula sheet is provided for you to use during the test. Keep in mind that you may not need all the formulas provided, and you may not need a formula for every question. Part of the fun of math is knowing which formula to use for which problems and figuring out when you don't need one at all.

The Mathematics Test is different from all the other tests in the GED because you have different ways to answer the questions on this test. This test assesses the following four areas. Each of the four areas gets approximately equal billing on the test. You can expect to find between 5 and 7 questions (or 20 to 30 percent of the total number of questions) on each area.

- **Number operations and number sense:** Surprise, surprise — these problems deal with numbers. Here's a breakdown of the two topics in this category:

    - *Number operations* are the familiar actions you take in math problems and equations, such as addition, subtraction, multiplication, and division. You probably mastered these operations in grade school; now all you have to do is practice them.

    - *Number sense* is the ability to understand numbers. You're expected to be able to recognize numbers (not a difficult task), know their relative values (that 5 is larger than 3, for example), and know how to use them (which takes us back to number operations). In addition, number sense includes the ability to *estimate* (or approximate) the result of number operations — which is always a handy skill on a timed test.

- **Measurement and geometry:** Here, you get a chance to play with mathematical shapes and manipulate them in your head. You get to use the Pythagorean relationship (or theorem) to do all sorts of interesting calculations, and you get to use measurements to do things like find the volume of ice cream in a cone or the amount of paint you need to cover a wall. If you relax, you can have fun with these questions and then maybe even use a lot of the knowledge in real life. This category breaks down into two topics:

    - *Measurement* involves area, volume, time, and the distance from here to there. Measurement of time is a good thing to know when taking any test because you want to make sure you run out of questions before you run out of time!

    - *Geometry* is the part of mathematics that deals with measurement. It also deals with relationships and properties of points, lines, angles, and planes. This branch of math requires you to draw and use diagrams.

- **Data analysis, statistics, and probability:** If you pay attention and practice the concepts in this category, you'll be able to think more clearly about the next political poll that shows that every representative of the party sponsoring the poll is good and all others are evil. This category breaks down into the following types:

    - *Data analysis* allows you to analyze data. You probably already practice this skill without realizing it. When you read about stock performance or lack of performance, calculate or read about baseball statistics, or figure out how many miles per gallon your car gets, you're doing data analysis.

    - Statistics and probability are part of data analysis. *Statistics* is the interpretation of collections of random numbers and can be used to prove one thing or another; *probability* tells you how often an event happens.

- **Algebra, functions, and patterns:** You most likely use these concepts in everyday life, although you may not know that you do. Here's a breakdown of the three types in this category:

- *Algebra* is a form of mathematics used to solve problems by using letters to represent unknown numbers, creating equations from the information given, and solving for the unknown numbers — thus, turning them into known numbers. If you ever said something like, "How much more does the $10 scarf cost than the $7.50 one?" you were really solving this equation: $7.50 + x = 10.00$.

- *Functions* are part of mathematics. They involve the concept that one number can be determined by its relationship with another. A dozen always consists of 12 units, for example. If you were buying two dozen eggs, you'd be buying $12 \times 2 = 24$ eggs.

- *Patterns* are the predictable repeat of a situation. For example, if someone told you the first four numbers in a pattern were 1, 2, 3, 4 and asked you what the next number was, you'd say "5" pretty fast. This simple pattern involves adding one to each number to get the next one. Most patterns get more complicated than this one, but, if you keep your wits about you, you can figure out how to solve them.

Make sure you understand how to solve problems involving these four math concepts. (The "Practicing with Sample Problems" section later in this chapter gives you examples on how to do so.) If you already have a firm grasp on these topics, go ahead and take the practice tests in Chapters 25 and 27. However, if you need to review most of this material, read the following sections for more info, and take the mini–practice test in this chapter. You can check your answers and read the explanations when you're done. If you need to review certain concepts even more, be sure to do so. Then you can take the full practice tests.

Identifying the Types of Questions and Knowing How to Tackle Them

The Mathematics Test breaks down into four main types of questions. If you have a basic understanding of these question types, you can avoid any surprises when you sit down to the take the test. The following sections explain the four types of questions you encounter on this test and offer advice on how to prepare for them so you can solve them with ease when you see them on the test.

Multiple-choice questions

Most of the questions on the GED tests are *multiple choice.* In these questions, you're given five possible answers, and you have to choose the one best answer. Most of the multiple-choice questions on the Mathematics Test give you some information or show you figures and ask you to solve the problem based on that info or those figures. But you may also see the following special types of questions:

✔ **Set-up questions:** These questions don't expect you to calculate specific answers but ask you what steps you'd take to solve them. Before you declare this type of question to be your favorite, keep in mind that you still have to choose the correct way to solve the problem. You just get to skip the final step of calculating the answer.

✔ **Not-enough-information questions:** These questions don't give you enough information to calculate specific answers. The only right answer is "not enough information given." Only 4 percent of the questions on the test are of this type, so if you answer more than two questions this way, you may not be looking at the questions carefully enough.

Some of the questions on this test may have extra information — just ignore it. Of course, you have to make sure the information you decide is extra really is extra. You don't want to disregard anything essential to solving the problem.

Because you're assessed no penalty for guessing, if you don't know the answer to a question, guess. Although you can't get a point for a blank answer, you can get a point for eliminating all but the most possible answer and marking it (if you're correct, of course).

Alternate-format questions

Alternate-format questions ask you to calculate the answers without choosing from five possible answers. For these questions, you write down real numbers or fill in actual graphs. Because the Mathematics Test is machine graded, you can't just write down numbers on paper. Instead, you use an alternate-format grid, which comes in one of two formats (see the following two sections).

The test has about ten questions that require you to record your answers on an alternate-format grid. Don't panic: Just concentrate on reading the instructions and calculating your answers.

Standard grid

Questions that require you to use a standard grid (see Figure 24-1) to record your answers are very similar to multiple-choice questions except that they don't give you five choices. When you come up with your answer on a standard-grid question, record it on the standard grid by writing the numbers in the open spaces and filling in the corresponding circles below the numbers. (If you don't fill in the circles, you can't get a point for your answer.)

Before

After

Figure 24-1:
A standard
grid.

Here are a few tips to keep in mind as you work your way through the standard-grid questions:

✔ **No answer entered on a standard grid can be a mixed number.** If your answer is a *mixed number* (a whole number and a fraction), convert your answer to a decimal before entering it on the grid. You convert to a decimal by dividing the top number of the fraction by the bottom number and adding that decimal to the whole number; for example, 1¾ becomes 1.75. If, on the other hand, your answer is an *improper fraction* (one in which the top number is larger than the bottom number), you have the choice of entering the number this way on the grid or converting it to a decimal and entering that number.

  ✔ **No answer entered on a standard grid can be negative.** If you come up with an
    answer that's a negative number, check your calculations because it's wrong.

Coordinate-plane grid

Questions that require you to use a coordinate-plane grid to record your answers are
mostly geometry problems. The *coordinate-plane grid* is a two-dimensional graph with
circles placed at regular points. You indicate your answer by filling in a circle to indicate a
point on the graph (as with all other questions on this test, make sure you fill in the circles
completely). Take a look at the coordinate-plane grid in Figure 24-2 for the point (3, 2).

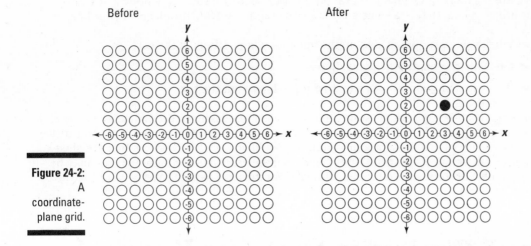

Figure 24-2:
A
coordinate-
plane grid.

The best way to prepare for questions with coordinate-plane grids is to practice geometry
questions. Borrow a high school geometry textbook to find your fill of sample questions.
Just be sure you understand the answers to those questions, too. If you feel the need for
even more geometry problems, check out *Math Word Problems For Dummies* by Mary Jane
Sterling (Wiley). With all the problems in this book and that book, you should have all the
practice you need.

If you spend all your time doing problems to be 100 percent sure that you know everything
there is to know, you may never get the chance to take the tests to prove what you know. So
just do the best you can in the time you have before you take the GED tests.

Questions with a calculator

Part I of the Mathematics Test lets you use a calculator — not just any calculator, however.
On test day, you'll receive a special calculator — the Casio FX-260 solar calculator — to use
on this part of the Mathematics Test. This calculator may seem like a real bonus, but don't
forget that you have to return it along with your test booklet. If you're calculator-phobic or
worried about using a scientific calculator, try to get your hands on one to practice with
before the test. You can check out an interesting video on how to use the calculator at
www.acenet.edu/programs/gedts/media/calc.wmv.

You're probably familiar with calculators that add, subtract, multiply, and divide. The Casio
FX-260, however, is a scientific calculator, which means it does all those operations and a
whole lot more. The Casio FX-260 calculates fractions, percents, exponents, problems
involving parentheses, and so on. Note that you won't necessarily use all the keys on the
calculator to take the test. Many test centers require you to preview a short film on how to
use the calculator before the Mathematics Test. Call your local administrator to find out
whether the film is available at your site.

Being given a calculator to use in Part I of the Mathematics Test has a downside, too. Because test takers can use a calculator, the questions in this part tend to be a bit harder with more steps than in the noncalculator part. However, in general, if you know how to set up the problems, the calculator makes them easier for you to solve.

Questions without a calculator

Part II of the Mathematics Test doesn't let you use a calculator — unless you count the calculator you were born with (that's right, your brain). You're given scratch paper on the test, but the more questions you practice in your head, the easier the noncalculator test questions will be. Here are some easy ways to practice solving problems in your head:

- ✔ When you go shopping, add up the items as you put them in the cart.

- ✔ Calculate discounts when you shop.

- ✔ Be the first at your table in a restaurant to figure out the tip.

For multiple-choice questions, sometimes it's easier and faster to estimate the answer to a question. For example, 4.2×8.9 is almost 4×9, which equals 36. If you see only one answer that's close to 36, that answer is probably correct. If you see five answers that are close to 36, however, you need to spend time calculating the exact answer. Although you may be able to solve problems in your head, always work them on paper to verify you have the correct answer.

Examining Preparation Strategies That Work

To get ready for the Mathematics Test, you first have to relax and realize that math is your friend — perhaps not a lifetime friend but a friend at least until you finish this test. You also need to consider that you've been using math all your life (and probably didn't even know it). When you tell a friend that you'll be over in 20 minutes, for example, you use math. When you see a sale sign in the store and mentally figure out whether or not you can afford the sale-priced item, you use math. When you complain about the poor mileage your car gets (and can prove it), you use math. Lucky for you, we're here to help you get more familiar with math (and how to use it) so that you're ready for everything the Mathematics Test throws at you. The following are some strategies you can implement to help you get better results:

- ✔ **Read and make sure you understand what you read.** What all the GED tests have in common is that they all assess, in one way or another, reading comprehension; if you can't read and understand the questions, you can't answer them. As we mention time and time again in this book, just reading isn't always enough — you have to stop and ask yourself questions about what you read. A good way to practice this skill is to find an old math textbook. Don't worry about the grade level or even the content. If it's full of problems to solve, it'll work. Read through each problem and ask yourself these questions: What does this problem want me to find? What is the answer in general terms?

  If you need more practice reading and understanding math problems, go to the "Practicing with Sample Problems" section later in this chapter or check out one of the following (all published by Wiley):

  - *Basic Math and Pre-Algebra For Dummies* by Mark Zegarelli

  - *Basic Math and Pre-Algebra Workbook For Dummies* by Mark Zegarelli

  - *Math Word Problems For Dummies* by Mary Jane Sterling

✓ **Solve the problem with the information on the page — not with the information you may have in your head.** Some questions may not give you enough information to solve the problem. For example, a question may ask for a conclusion that you can't make from the information given on the page. Even if you know some information that would help you solve the problem, don't use it. The people who write the test questions include and exclude information for a purpose — extra information can make guessing more difficult and separate the test takers who are paying attention from those who aren't, and, sometimes, extra information is put in to make the question a bit more realistic. They don't depend on you to add information.

You bring with you to the test the knowledge of what the basic operations are and how to use them. You aren't expected to know the dimensions of some fictional character's room or how well Alice does on her reading scores. You're expected to know how to solve problems and to leave the specifics of the problems to the tester.

✓ **Realize that not every question is solvable.** Some questions don't include enough information to solve the problem, or they ask a question that can't be answered with the information given in the question. If you come across a question you can't answer, don't panic! Reread the question to make sure it can't be answered.

One clue that a question may not be able to be answered is an answer choice that says, "Not enough information given." Don't assume this clue means you don't have enough information, though, because some questions that can be solved include this answer choice to make you think. Use this clue only when you've already determined that the question can't be solved.

✓ **Take the practice tests in this book, and check your answers.** Turn to Chapters 25 and 27 to take the full-length practice tests. Hold yourself to the test's time constraints, and make sure you answer all the questions. Then be sure to check your answers and read through all the answer explanations in Chapters 26 and 28. Going through the answers shows you on which areas of the test you need extra help.

Try not to be intimidated by the word *math* or the subject as a whole. A math teacher once said that mathematicians are lazy people — they always use the easiest way to find the right answer. We don't want to insult or irritate any mathematicians by calling them lazy, but finding the easiest way to solve a problem is usually the right way. If your way is too long and complicated, it's probably not right.

Managing Your Time for the Math Test

The Mathematics Test allows you 90 minutes to complete 50 questions (you get 45 minutes to answer the first 25 questions, followed by a short break, and then you get another 45 minutes for the last 25 questions). For the mathematically inclined, that equals 1 minute and 48 seconds for each question. If you want some time to review your answers, you have less than 1½ minutes for each question. To help you manage your time for the Mathematics Test, check out the following suggestions (refer to Chapters 2 and 3 for some general time-management tips):

✓ **Experiment.** You need a second person to complete this exercise. After finding a friend to help you, close your eyes and try to estimate the length of 1½ minutes. Indicate the beginning and end of the time by tapping the table with a finger or a pencil, and have your friend measure and report on your accuracy. Repeat this exercise many times until you can estimate 1½ minutes repeatedly and accurately. Next, pick a question from the "Practicing with Sample Problems" section later in this chapter, and try to do it in 1½ minutes. Being able to manage your time is the most important indicator of success on any test like the GED.

If you can keep to your schedule of less than 1½ minutes per question, you'll have enough time to go over your answers and make any changes necessary after you finish solving all the questions.

With such a tight schedule for taking the Mathematics Test, there's clearly no time to panic. Aside from the fact that panicking distracts you from your overall goal, it also takes time — and you have very little time to spare. So relax and just do your best — save the panicking for another day.

✔ **Time yourself.** If you don't see what's being asked by a question within a few seconds, reread the question and try again. If it still isn't clear, go on to the next question. Spending all your time trying to solve one problem at the expense of the others isn't a good idea. Watch your watch. Put it on the table in front of you. If it doesn't have a second hand or a second indicator, consider borrowing one that does.

Practice timing yourself as you work your way through the practice tests in Chapters 25 and 27. Getting familiar with how to keep track of your time before you get to the real test can help you make sure you run out of questions before you run out of time.

✔ **Speed-read.** The key to developing your speed-reading skills is making sure you don't sacrifice your understanding of the material you're reading along the way. Follow these steps to improve your speed-reading skills:

1. Find any book with short paragraphs and calculate the number of words in two typical paragraphs. The easiest way to do so is to count the number of words in three consecutive lines and divide by three. (Isn't it interesting how math creeps into everything?) Write down the average number of words per line so you don't forget it, and multiply it by the number of lines in a paragraph to figure out the number of words in the paragraph.

2. Now recruit your friend for help again. At a signal from your friend, start to read the paragraph and signal when you're finished. You can then calculate how long it took you to read a word by dividing the time you spent reading by the number of words.

3. Read other paragraphs in the same way, but try to read them faster. You may try leading your eyes with your fingers by moving your finger across the line of text and slowly speeding up the rate you read. Check out *Speed Reading For Dummies* by Richard Sutz (Wiley) for more tips and practice ideas. If you think increasing your reading speed would increase your test scores or reduce your anxiety about finishing all the questions in the allotted time, this book is a good one to look at for help.

Practicing with Sample Problems

The best way to get ready for the Mathematics Test is to practice problems. You encounter problems on this test that evaluate your skills in a wide variety of areas, so check out the sample problems in this section to help you prepare for all of them. We provide several examples for each skill on the test. At the end of this section, we give you another minitest to help you practice even more. You can then check out Chapters 25 and 27 for additional practice.

Number operations and number sense

To do well on the questions that address number operations and number sense, you need to be able to use numbers in equivalent forms, such as integers, fractions, decimals, percents, exponents, and scientific notation, and recognize equivalences ($\frac{5}{50} = \frac{1}{10} = 0.1 = 10\%$). You need to know how to use whole numbers, decimals, fractions, percents, ratios, proportions, exponents, roots, and scientific notation when appropriate and how to decide which operation to use to solve problems. For these types of problems, you also want to be able to relate basic arithmetic operations to one another (for example, knowing that addition and subtraction are opposite operations: $5 + 2 = 7$ and $7 - 2 = 5$). Finally, you must know how to perform calculations with pencil and paper, with a calculator, and in your head, as well as how to estimate the solution to a problem to ensure that your answer is reasonable.

Try out the following example problems for practice with number operations and number sense:

1. Vlad is shopping for a new shirt because all the stores are having end-of-season sales. Sam's Special Shirts offers Vlad 20% off all his purchases while Hardworking Harry's Haberdashery has a special sale offering five shirts for the price of four. Which is the better deal?

   (1) neither

   (2) Sam's Special Shirts

   (3) both are the same

   (4) Hardworking Harry's Haberdashery

   (5) not enough information given

In this case, the correct answer is Choice (3) because five shirts for the price of four represents a 20% discount. Consider buying four shirts for $10 each and getting one more free. Then your five shirts would cost you $40 or an average price of $8 each, which is 20% off the regular price ($10). Keep in mind that the same prices are often stated in different ways.

2. Lillian is drawing a scale diagram of her apartment to take with her while shopping for rugs. If she has taken all the measurements in the apartment, what operation would she use to draw the scale drawing?

   (1) decimals

   (2) exponents

   (3) ratios

   (4) scientific notation

   (5) addition

The correct answer is Choice (3). A scale drawing involves representing one dimension with a smaller one while keeping the shape of the room the same. Lillian may have decided to represent 1 foot in real life by 1 inch on her drawing (a ratio of 1 foot to 1 inch), resulting in a 12-foot wall being represented by a 12-inch line. Not all the answers are operations and would have to be excluded immediately.

3. Sylvia couldn't fall asleep one night and got to wondering how much water her bedroom would hold if she filled it to the ceiling. She measured all the walls and knew all the measurements, including length, width, and height. What operation should she use to calculate how many cubic feet of water would be needed to fill the room?

   (1) addition

   (2) subtraction

   (3) multiplication

   (4) division

   (5) roots

The correct answer is Choice (3) because the formula to calculate the volume of a room is to multiply the length by the width by the height. (The formula for calculating volume is listed on the formula sheet provided with the Mathematics Test — see Chapters 25 and 27.)

4. Hassan has developed a new trick to play on his classmates. He asks them to write down their ages and multiply by 4, divide by 2, then subtract 6, and, finally, add 8. When they tell him the resulting number, Hassan can always tell them their age. If one of his friends tells Hassan the resultant number is 52, how old is he?

   (1) 33

   (2) 25

   (3) 52

   (4) 24

   (5) 26

   The correct answer is Choice (2). Hassan knows that multiplication and division are opposite operations, which means that multiplying by 4 and dividing by 2 produces a number twice the original. Addition and subtraction are opposites, too, so subtracting 6 and adding 8 results in a number 2 larger than the original. If the number Hassan's friend tells him is 52, Hassan simply has to subtract 2 from the resultant number (52) and divide by 2, giving him an answer of 25.

5. Susie is shopping for a few groceries. She buys a loaf of bread for $1.29 and a half-gallon of milk for $1.47. She sees her favorite cheese on sale for $2.07. If she has $5.00 in her purse, can she buy the cheese?

   (1) unsure

   (2) yes

   (3) not enough money

   (4) too much information

   (5) not enough information

   The correct answer is Choice (2). The simplest way to solve this problem is to add the cost of the bread and milk to get $2.76. The cheese is $2.07, which added to the $2.76 gives you a total of $4.83, which is less than $5.00. You can also estimate the result by adding $1.30 (approximation of $1.29) and $1.50 (approximation of $1.47) to get $2.80. If you then add $2.10 (approximation of $2.07) for the cheese, the result is $4.90, which is less than $5.00. Using approximations can help you answer some questions quickly and give you an idea of whether or not an answer you achieved using a calculator makes sense.

Measurement and geometry

To do well on the questions that address measurements and geometry, you need to be able to solve problems involving geometric figures using the ideas of perpendicularity, parallelism, congruence, and similarity. You need to know how to "see" geometric figures and their translations and rotations, as well as how to understand and use the Pythagorean relationship (or theorem) to solve problems. You also must be able to calculate and use the *slope* of a line (which is rise over run), the *y-intercept* of a line (the point at which the line crosses the *y*-axis), and the *intersection* of two lines (where two lines meet). And you need to know how to use coordinates to describe and draw geometrical figures on a graph.

You must be able to identify, estimate, and convert units of metric and customary measurement and solve problems involving uniform rates (miles per hour, for example). You need to be able to read and interpret scales, meters, and gauges. In addition, you need to know how to solve questions involving length, perimeter, area, volume, angle measurements, capacity weight, and mass. Finally, you need to be able to predict how a change in length and width affects the perimeter, area, and volume of an object.

Try out the following example problems for practice with measurement and geometry:

1. Alvin is drawing a diagram of his room. He has drawn the line representing the floor and is ready to draw the line representing the wall. How would that line be related to the line representing the floor?

   (1) congruent

   (2) parallel

   (3) similar

   (4) perpendicular

   (5) equal

   The correct answer is Choice (4) because walls are perpendicular to floors (if they weren't, the room would probably collapse).

2. Olga designed a logo consisting of an equilateral triangle in a circle for a new company. She designed it with one vertex of the triangle pointing north-northeast. The client said she liked the design but preferred that the vertex of the triangle point due south. What rotation would Olga have to perform to satisfy her client?

   (1) 90 degrees to the right

   (2) 45 degrees to the left

   (3) 110 degrees to the right

   (4) 135 degrees to the left

   (5) 135 degrees to the right

   The correct answer is Choice (5). If you visualize the equilateral triangle drawn within the circle with one vertex pointing north-northeast, you can see that the vertex is 45 degrees above the horizontal, which is due east. To go from due east to due south requires a rotation of 90 degrees to the right. The entire rotation would consist of 45 degrees + 90 degrees = 135 degrees to the right. If reading about this problem is confusing, draw it. Diagrams often make problems easier to visualize.

3. Georgio wants to climb a ladder perched beside his house to check the condition of the eaves, which are 22 feet above the ground. For safety, the ladder should be placed 10 feet from the house. What would be the minimum length of ladder he would need to reach the eaves, rounded to the nearest foot?

   (1) 24

   (2) 25

   (3) 26

   (4) 27

   (5) 28

   The correct answer is Choice (2). You represent a ladder perched against a house by a right-angled triangle with the vertical height of 22 feet and a base of 10 feet. The ladder represents the hypotenuse of the triangle. To calculate the length of the ladder, you have to use the Pythagorean relationship. If you represent the length of the ladder as x,

   $x = \sqrt{10^2 + 22^2} = \sqrt{100 + 484} = 24.166091$. Because you want the ladder to be long enough to reach the wall, it has to be 25 feet long.

Pythagoras, a Greek mathematician, proved that the square of the hypotenuse of a right-angled triangle is equal to the sum of the squares of the other two sides. The *hypotenuse* is the side opposite the right angle. You find the Pythagorean relationship on the formula sheet you get with your test, so don't forget to check it for important information you may need as you work through the test.

4. Calvin and Kelvin, carpenters extraordinaire, are building a staircase for their clients, the Coalmans. The stairway is to bridge a space 10 feet high, and the distance from the front of the bottom step to the back of the top step is 14 feet. What is the slope of the stairway to 2 decimal places?

(1) 0.68

(2) 0.69

(3) 0.70

(4) 0.71

(5) 0.72

The correct answer is Choice (4). To calculate the slope, you have to divide the rise by the run. That is $\frac{10}{14} = 0.7142857$, or 0.71 to 2 decimal places.

The *slope* of a line is rise over run (see the following figure). Thus, the slope of a stairway is equal to the distances above the floor of the last step over the distance from the front of the first step to the back of the top step.

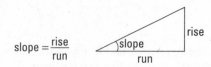

5. Describe where the point (–4, –4) would be on a graph by drawing it on the coordinate-plane grid.

The point (–4, –4) would be 4 units to the left of the *y*-axis and 4 units below the *x*-axis (see the following grid).

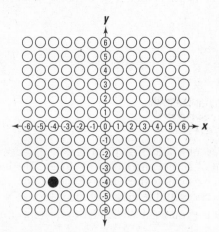

6. Felix and Francis have just bought new cars. Felix, being American, has a car with a speedometer graduated in customary units. Francis, being Canadian, has a speedometer graduated in metric units. When they're driving in Felix's car at a speed of 55 miles per hour, what would Francis's speedometer read in kilometers per hour?

    (1) 160

    (2) 88

    (3) 55

    (4) 77

    (5) 100

    The correct answer is Choice (2). Because 1 mile = 1.6 kilometers, 55 miles = 88 kilometers (55 × 1.6). The speeds are both in units per hour, so 55 mph = 88 kph.

7. Aaron wants to paint the floor of his apartment. His living room/dining room is 19 feet by 16 feet, his bedroom is 12 feet by 14 feet, and his hallways are 6 feet by 8 feet. Bowing to pressure from his friends, he has decided not to paint the floor of the kitchen or the bathroom. How many square feet of floor must he paint?

    (1) 304

    (2) 520

    (3) 250

    (4) 216

    (5) 560

    The correct answer is Choice (2). To find the area, you multiply the length by the width. The area of the living room/dining room is 19 × 16 = 304 square feet, the area of the bedroom is 12 × 14 = 168 square feet, and the area of the hallway is 6 × 8 = 48 square feet. The total area is the sum of the room areas or 304 + 168 + 48 = 520 square feet.

8. Read the following meter and enter the reading on the standard grid.

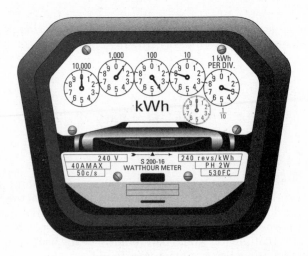

    The correct answer is 1,483. To show the answer of 1483 on a standard grid, you simply darken the circles for the numbers 1, 4, 8, and 3, in that order (as shown in the following grid).

Questions 9 and 10 are based on the following information:

April is considering two apartments. They are of equal size except for the bedrooms. Bedroom A is 19 feet by 14 feet and bedroom B is 17 feet by 16 feet.

9. How many square feet larger is the larger bedroom?

   (1) 9

   (2) 8

   (3) 7

   (4) 6

   (5) 5

The correct answer is Choice (4). The area of bedroom A is $19 \times 14 = 266$ square feet. The area of bedroom B is $17 \times 16 = 272$ square feet. Bedroom B is larger by $272 - 266 = 6$ square feet.

10. April wants an area rug for the larger bedroom that would cover the floor leaving a space 1 foot from each wall. If the rug had a fringe all the way around it, how many feet long would the fringe be?

    (1) 58

    (2) 29

    (3) 85

    (4) 55

    (5) 88

The correct answer is Choice (1). The measure of the fringe is the perimeter of the rug. Because the rug would cover the floor 1 foot in from each wall, the length of the rug would be $17 - 2 = 15$ feet, and the width would be $16 - 2 = 14$ feet. The reason why you have to subtract 2 from each measurement is that the rug would be 1 foot from each wall, resulting in a rug that was 2 feet shorter than the room in each dimension. Perimeter $= 2(l + w)$, where l is the length and w is the width, so the perimeter of the rug $= 2(15 + 14) = 2(29) = 58$ feet.

Data analysis, statistics, and probabilities

To do well on the types of questions that address analyzing data, stats, and probabilities, you need to be able to construct, understand, and draw inferences from tables, charts, and graphs. You need to understand the difference between correlation and causation, and you need to be able to draw graphs based on the data presented and ensure that the graphs make sense. You also must know how to predict from data using an informal line of best fit.

For this portion of the GED, you must know how to calculate the mean, median, and mode of a group of data and evaluate what happens to these numbers when the data is changed. You also need to be able to recognize bias in statistical conclusions and make predictions from data produced by experiments or theoretical probabilities.

Try out the following example problems for practice with data analysis, stats, and probabilities:

Questions 1 and 2 refer to the following table.

Car Manufacturer	Sales — July 2009 (In Thousands)	Sales — July 2008 (In Thousands)	% Change
Commonwealth	90	105	−14
Frisky	175	147	+19
Goodenough	236	304	−22
Horsesgalore	99	64	+55
Silkyride	24	16	+50

1. From the table, which car manufacturer showed the greatest percentage increase in sales?

    (1) Commonwealth

    (2) Frisky

    (3) Goodenough

    (4) Horsesgalore

    (5) Silkyride

    The correct answer is Choice (4). The greatest percentage increase was Horsesgalore with a 55% increase in sales.

2. From the table, which of the following conclusions could be drawn from the data?

    (1) Car sales are increasing across the board.

    (2) Car sales are decreasing across the board.

    (3) Small manufacturers are selling more cars.

    (4) Large manufacturers are selling more cars.

    (5) No generalization is possible from this data.

    The correct answer is Choice (5). From the data given, no generalization is possible; some big manufacturers have rising sales, some have falling sales. This fact eliminates the first four statements.

Question 3 refers to the following table.

Week	Calories Consumed	Weight (Pounds)	Height (Feet/Inches)
1	12,250	125	5 ft. 1.5 in.
2	15,375	128	5 ft. 1.5 in.
3	13,485	128	5 ft. 1.5 in.
4	16,580	130	5 ft. 1.5 in.
5	15,285	129	5 ft. 1.5 in.

3. Alan kept track of his caloric intake, his weight, and his height for a period of five weeks. What conclusion can you draw from his observations?

(1) Eating a lot makes you taller.

(2) Some weeks Alan was hungrier than others.

(3) Eating more calories will make you gain weight.

(4) Eating more calories will make you taller.

(5) There's no correlation between the data presented.

The correct answer is Choice (3). The more Alan ate, the heavier he became (which represents a possible causal relationship). The table provides no basis for the other answers.

If two values change in tune with each other, they have a *correlating* relationship. For example, there's a positive correlation between height and age during the teenage years. In other words, you get taller as you get older. If one event leads to another or causes another, the events form a *causal* relationship. For example, eating all the red jellybeans alters the percentage of orange jellybeans in a mixture of equal numbers of each color because eating a red jellybean removes it from the pool of jellybeans, which originally had the same number of each color. As a result, the percentage of orange jellybeans increases.

4. Connect the following points to draw a geometric figure on the coordinate-plane grid: (3,1), (–4, –3), (–5,5).

The correct answer should look like this:

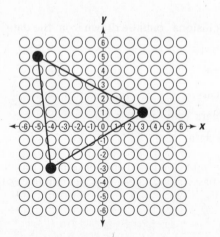

Be prepared to draw graphs from data presented, but always remember that the only way to draw a graph for a question on this test is to use a coordinate-plane grid, which has size limitations. Always be sure that your graph makes sense. If the trend is declining, the graph should be headed downward toward the *x*-axis (horizontal axis). Negative values always appear on the left side of the *y*-axis (vertical axis) or below the *x*-axis.

Question 5 refers to the following table, which shows Sheila's marks in her final year of high school.

Subject	Grade (%)
Literature	94
Mathematics	88
Physical Education	86
Science	92
Spanish	90

5. On a standard grid, mark the mean grade that would result from a 6-point drop in Sheila's Spanish grade.

The mean mark with her grade in Spanish falling 6 points would be
$(94 + 88 + 86 + 92 + 84) \div 5 = 88.8$. Here's what it would like on the standard grid:

8	8	.	8
/	/	/	
.	.	.	●	.
0	0	0	0	0
1	1	1	1	1
2	2	2	2	2
3	3	3	3	3
4	4	4	4	4
5	5	5	5	5
6	6	6	6	6
7	7	7	7	7
8	●	●	8	●
9	9	9	9	9

Questions 6 and 7 refer to the following table, which shows the results Julio got from measuring and interviewing several of his classmates about their heights and birth months.

Month of Birth	Height
March	5 ft. 4 in.
June	5 ft. 6 in.
March	5 ft. 1 in.
January	5 ft. 8 in.
August	5 ft. 5 in.
January	5 ft. 4 in.

6. What month would produce the shortest people according to this theory? Using the months as the *x*-axis and the inches in height as the *y*-axis, record the point that would represent the inches in the height on the coordinate-plane grid.

The graph should look like this:

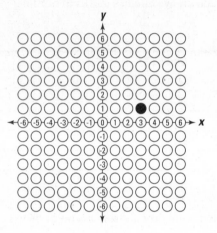

7. From the graph of Julio's results, what conclusion, if any, can be reached?

(1) No conclusions can be reached.

(2) People born in the colder months are taller.

(3) People born in March are shorter.

(4) People born in the warm months are similar in height.

(5) Two of Julio's classmates were born in each of January and March.

The correct answer is Choice (5). The only conclusion that can be reached from such a small, biased sample is about the number of his classmates who were born in each month.

Question 8 refers to the following table.

Person Interviewed	*Flavor Preference*			
	Chocolate	*Vanilla*	*Strawberry*	*Peanut*
Donalda's mother	No	No	Yes	No
Donalda's father	No	No	Yes	No
Donalda's brother	No	No	No	Yes
Donalda's sister	No	No	Yes	No

8. Donalda collected the information in the table as part of her research on the most popular flavor of ice cream. After interviewing several subjects and entering her data into the table, she came up with the following conclusions. Which is the most believable?

   (1) Nobody likes chocolate ice cream.

   (2) Nobody likes vanilla ice cream.

   (3) Strawberry ice cream is the most popular flavor in the world.

   (4) No conclusion is possible from this data.

   (5) Peanut ice cream is the second most popular flavor in America.

   The correct answer is Choice (4). The sample Donalda used is biased because the subjects are all related. A proper sample in an experiment is selected randomly. Because the data is from a biased sample, no conclusions can be drawn from the results.

   Question 9 refers to the following table.

Age at Marriage for Those Who Divorce in America

Age	Women	Men
Under 20 years old	27.6%	11.7%
20 to 24 years old	36.6%	38.8%
25 to 29 years old	16.4%	22.3%
30 to 34 years old	8.5%	11.6%
35 to 39 years old	5.1%	6.5%

9. The information in this table indicates that to reduce the chance of divorce:

   (1) Younger women should marry older men.

   (2) Older men should marry younger women.

   (3) Nobody should get married.

   (4) Fewer men get divorced than women.

   (5) You can't draw conclusions from this table.

   The correct answer is Choice (5). This table is a compilation of statistics and reflects the situation as of the date the statistics were gathered. You can't realistically draw conclusions from this type of data, except to state things such as, "5.1% of women aged 35 to 39 got divorced." Just because someone presents you with a table of data doesn't mean you can draw general conclusions from it.

Question 10 refers to the following table.

Make and Model	Price
Hopper Model A1	$249.99
Vacuous Vacuum Company Model ZZ3	$679.99
Clean-R-Up Special Series	$179.00
Electrified Home Upright	$749.99
Super Suction 101	$568.99

10. Pierre is looking for a vacuum cleaner for his apartment. He is on a limited budget and wants to spend the least he can for his purchase. He has been told by his best friend that spending around the mean amount for a vacuum cleaner will get him an average unit. His father claims that spending about the median amount is the smartest way to get a good deal. Which vacuum cleaner comes the closest to satisfying both criteria?

   (1) Hopper Model A1

   (2) Vacuous Vacuum Company Model ZZ3

   (3) Clean-R-Up Special Series

   (4) Electrified Home Upright

   (5) Super Suction 101

The correct answer is Choice (5). You can calculate the mean price by adding all the prices and dividing the sum by the number of prices: (249.99 + 679.99 + 179.99 + 749.99 + 568.99) ÷ 5 = $485.79. To determine the median price, you put all the prices in order; the middle one is the median. In this case the median is $568.99 because it's in the middle of the prices: 749.99, 679.99, 568.99, 249.99, 179.99. The machine that comes closest to satisfying both criteria is the Super Suction 101 because its price is the same as the median. The difference between the price of the Super Suction 101 and the mean price is $194.20. The difference between the price of the Hopper Model A1 and the mean price is $235.80, leaving the Super Suction 101 the clear mathematical winner.

One thing to keep in mind is that the mathematical problems on this test aren't always reflections of reality. The technique used for buying vacuum cleaners in question 10 isn't a reasonable way of buying anything, but it's a good question because it tests your knowledge of the mean, median, and subtraction.

Algebra, functions, and patterns

To do well in the types of questions that address algebra, functions, and patterns, you need to be able to draw graphs or tables, create verbal descriptions and equations to represent presented data, and use the same data with different forms of representation. You need to understand that the same function may be used in different problems. You have to know how to solve problems using algebraic expressions and equations and how to evaluate formulas. You need to understand direct and indirect variation, use them to solve problems, and see patterns in tables and graphs. You also need to be able to explain how a change in one quantity in an equation results in changes in the other quantities in the equation. Finally, you must be able to understand, use, and solve problems involving linear, quadratic, and exponential functions.

Try out the following example problems for practice with algebra, functions, and patterns:

Question 1 refers to the following table.

Annual Production of the Wonderful World of Widgets	
Year	*Annual Production (In Million Units)*
2009	43
2008	29
2007	72
2006	70
2005	71

1. The general manager of the Wonderful World of Widgets wants to present these figures in a visual, easily understood way to the board of directors to help them understand the effect that the downturn in the economy is having on the production of widgets. What would be the best way to present the figures?

(1) a graph

(2) a series of tables

(3) verbal descriptions

(4) pictures of the plant exterior

(5) a movie of how widgets are used in America

The best answer is Choice (1). A graph is a visual representation of data; it's easily understood and can be used to compare data visually. You could use some of the other choices to represent the data, but they would all be more complex than a graph.

2. Rachel and Ronda were planning for their first apartment, and they decided to split the required shopping tasks. Rachel was responsible for finding out how much it would cost to carpet their living room, and Ronda was responsible for finding out how much it would cost to paint the walls in the bedroom. What formula would they need to use to get an answer that would let them figure out the price for each job?

(1) $P = 2(l + w)$

(2) $A = l \times w$

(3) $V = l \times w \times d$

(4) $A = \pi r^2$

(5) $C = \pi d$

The correct answer is Choice (2). In each case, Rachel and Ronda have to calculate the area of the space they're dealing with to get a price for the carpet and the paint. The formula for area is $A = l \times w$.

3. Roger and Ekua went shopping together. Ekua spent twice as much for clothing as Roger did. If their total expenditure for clothing was $90.00, how much did Roger spend for clothing?

   (1) $60.00

   (2) $90.00

   (3) $40.00

   (4) $30.00

   (5) $20.00

   The correct answer is Choice (4). If you represent the amount of money Roger spent by x, the amount of money that Ekua spent is $2x$. You can represent their spending by the equation $90 = x + 2x$ or $3x = 90$, in which case $x = 30$. So Roger spent $30.00 for clothing.

4. Evaluate the following formula to 2 decimal places:

   $$N = \sqrt{a + c - 2ac}, \text{ if } a = 25 \text{ and } c = 9$$

   (1) 34.67

   (2) 20.40

   (3) 22.47

   (4) no answer

   (5) 27.99

   The correct answer is Choice (4). You can't find the square root of a negative number, and $2ac$ will always be larger than $a + c$, which makes the difference of the two negative.

5. Solve the following equation for x:

   $$x = 2y + 6z - y^2, \text{ if } y = 6 \text{ and } z = 2$$

   (1) 12

   (2) 11

   (3) −12

   (4) −11

   (5) none of the above

   The correct answer is Choice (3). You can solve this equation by substituting 6 for y and 2 for z, which produces this equation: $2(6) + 6(2) - 6^2 = -12$

   Question 6 refers to the following table.

Subject	Height	Shoe Size
1	5 in. 3 ft.	5
2	5 in. 9 ft.	8
3	5 in. 6 ft.	5½
4	6 in. 1 ft.	10
5	5 in. 7 ft.	6

6. Althea has a theory about the men in her class. She has decided that the taller men have larger shoe sizes than the shorter men. To prove her theory, she asked several of the men to measure themselves and tell her their shoe sizes. From her observations, she created the preceding table.

Using her observations, Althea decided to graph the results to see if there's any credibility to her theory. Draw the point that would represent the shoe size of the median height on the coordinate-plane grid if the *y*-axis represents shoe sizes.

The grid should look like this:

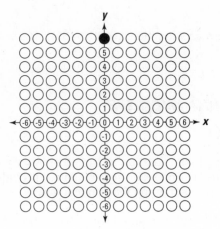

As you can see from the grid, the shoe size of the median height is 6 and that is marked on the grid. Althea doesn't have a proper theory (but she does have an interesting observation). You can see this by looking at the table but her table is of a very limited sample and thus proves nothing.

7. The students in a math class are looking at the equation $A = l \times w$. The teacher asks what result doubling the length *(l)* would have on the area *(A)*. What answer is correct?

(1) none

(2) makes it two times larger

(3) makes it four times larger

(4) makes it three times larger

(5) can't determine the result without the value of *w*

The correct answer is Choice (2). In this linear equation, any multiple of one term results in the same multiple of the answer. Multiplying *l* by 2 results in multiplying *A* by 2.

As you prepare for the Mathematics Test, you definitely want to remember this rule about equations: Whatever you do to one side, you must do to the other side.

Question 8 refers to the following table.

a	b	F
1	2	−16
2	1	−3
3	2	−18
2	3	−35
3	4	x

8. Herman developed the following function to amuse himself: $F = 2a + 3b^2 - 2ab$. He kept track of his results in this table.

Using Herman's function, what is the value of x?

(1) 53

(2) 82

(3) 88

(4) 66

(5) 42

The correct answer is Choice (4). Using Herman's function, $x = 2(3) - 3(4)(4) - 2(3)(4) = 6 - 48 - 24 = 66$.

A little pretest to help you prepare for the Mathematics Test

For some extra practice for the Mathematics Test, take this short pretest. After you finish each question in this pretest, check your answer and read the explanation provided. The more you know and the more you practice, the better you'll do on test day.

1. A wall is 20 feet long and 8 feet high. If all of it is to be painted with two coats of blue paint, how many square feet of wall have to be covered?

(1) 56

(2) 160

(3) 230

(4) 320

(5) 40

The correct answer is Choice (4). The area of the wall is $20 \times 8 = 160$ square feet. Each coat requires that you paint 160 square feet, but because you have to paint two coats, the answer is $2 \times 160 = 320$. If your first choice for the answer was Choice (2), you forgot about the second coat of paint. If you picked Choice (1), you confused perimeter with area. Remember that *perimeter* is the distance all the way around an object — in this case $2(20 + 8) = 56$. Choice (4) is the correct answer with the first two digits reversed (in other words, it's a reminder to check your answers carefully!). Reversing digits under the stress of time limits isn't impossible or unusual. Choice (5) is just plain wrong. You can eliminate this answer immediately, leaving you with four answers to consider.

2. Barry earns $1,730 per month after taxes. Each month, he spends $900 for rent and $600 for living expenses like food and utilities. How much does he have left over to buy luxuries and spend on entertainment?

(1) $170

(2) $230

(3) $390

(4) $320

(5) $180

The correct answer is Choice (2). Barry spends $900 + $600 = $1,500 for rent and living expenses. He has $1,730 - $1,500 = $230 left over. The other answer choices are simply wrong. Some of them may look correct if you don't know how to do the question.

3. On Monday, Mary walked 12 blocks. On Tuesday, she walked 10 blocks, and, on Wednesday, she walked 14 blocks. If she wants to beat her average trip for those three days on Thursday, at least how many blocks must she walk?

    (1) 10

    (2) 11

    (3) 9

    (4) 13

    (5) 12

    The correct answer is Choice (4). Her average trip for those three days was $(12 + 10 + 14) \div 3 = 36 \div 3 = 12$ blocks. To beat her average, she has to walk 13 blocks on Thursday. If she walks 12 blocks, she will equal (not beat) her average trip. All the other answers are less than her average.

4. Solve the following equation for x: $3x + 12 = 24$

    (1) 12

    (2) 24

    (3) 3

    (4) 4

    (5) 36

    The correct answer is Choice (4). If $3x + 12 = 24$, you can subtract 12 from both sides so that $3x = 24 - 12$, or $3x = 12$, or $x = 4$. Again, remember the cardinal rule of equations: Whatever you do to one side, you must do to the other.

5. Where are all the points with an x-coordinate of -4 located on a graph?

    (1) 4 units above the x-axis

    (2) 4 units to the left of the x-axis

    (3) 4 units from the y-axis

    (4) 4 units above the y-axis

    (5) 4 units to the left of the y-axis

    The correct answer is Choice (5). All points with x-coordinates that are negative are located to the left of the y-axis (the vertical axis). Therefore, if a point has an x-coordinate of -4, it's located on a line 4 units to the left of the y-axis.

Revealing Some Helpful Pointers

As you prepare for the Mathematics Test, do the following:

✔ **Master arithmetic fundamentals.** About half the test depends on basic arithmetic (addition, subtraction, multiplication, division, decimals, and fractions). The better you know the fundamentals, the better you can do on this test.

✔ **Understand how to solve problems.** To get a handle on how to solve basic mathematical problems, do a lot of practice problems before the test. The more problems you solve, the more natural solving problems will become. Borrow or buy as many math books as you can, and use the sample questions in them to develop your problem-solving skills.

(Be sure to get one that has answers in the back so you can check your work.) Check every answer immediately after you work the question. If you answered it incorrectly, figure out why. If you can't answer it, ask someone to explain the solution to you.

✔ **Understand the rules of math.** Textbooks are full of rules, theorems, hypotheses, and so on. Read over as many of these rules as you can, and try to explain the main ones to a friend. If you can explain a particular rule (the Pythagorean theorem, for example) to a friend and he or she understands it, you've mastered the rule. If you can't explain it, ask someone to help you better understand the rule.

✔ **Take practice tests.** See Chapters 25 and 27 for two full-length practice tests. If two aren't enough, buy or borrow additional test-prep books that include sample Mathematics Tests. Be strict about time constraints. After checking your answers, figure out why you missed the problems and correct your mistakes.

The only part of the test you can't duplicate is the feeling of sitting in the examination room just before you start the test. But the more practice tests you take, the more comfortable you'll be when test day finally arrives.

Chapter 25

Practice Test — Mathematics Test: Parts I and II

● ●

*T*he Mathematics Test consists of multiple-choice and alternate-format questions intended to measure general mathematics skills and problem-solving ability. The questions are based on short readings that often include a graph, chart, or figure.

Like the Language Arts, Writing Test, the Mathematics Test is made up of two parts. Part I allows you to use a calculator to help you answer the questions; Part II doesn't. Each part consists of 25 questions.

You have 45 minutes to complete each part. Work carefully, but do not spend too much time on any one question. Be sure to answer every question.

Formulas you may need are given on the page before the first test question in each part. Only some of the questions will require you to use a formula. Not all the formulas given will be needed.

Some questions contain more information than you will need to solve the problem; other questions do not give enough information. If the question does not give enough information to solve the problem, the correct answer choice is "not enough information given."

Note: The GED test administrator will collect your calculator when you finish Part I of the Mathematics Test. After you turn in your calculator and the administrator tells you to begin Part II, you can move on to that part.

Answer Sheet for Mathematics Test: Part 1

1 ① ② ③ ④ ⑤

2 ① ② ③ ④ ⑤

3

4 ① ② ③ ④ ⑤

5 ① ② ③ ④ ⑤

6 ① ② ③ ④ ⑤

7 ① ② ③ ④ ⑤

8

9 ① ② ③ ④ ⑤

10 ① ② ③ ④ ⑤

11 ① ② ③ ④ ⑤

12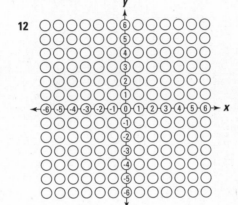

13 ① ② ③ ④ ⑤

14 ① ② ③ ④ ⑤

15 ① ② ③ ④ ⑤

16 ① ② ③ ④ ⑤

17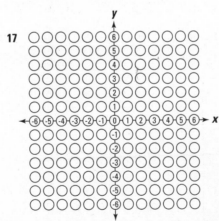

18 ① ② ③ ④ ⑤

19 ① ② ③ ④ ⑤

20 ① ② ③ ④ ⑤

21 ① ② ③ ④ ⑤

22 ① ② ③ ④ ⑤

23 ① ② ③ ④ ⑤

24 ① ② ③ ④ ⑤

25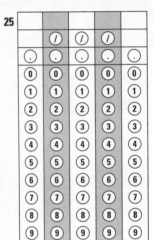

Answer Sheet for Mathematics Test: Part II

1 ① ② ③ ④ ⑤   12 ① ② ③ ④ ⑤   20

2 ① ② ③ ④ ⑤   13

3 ① ② ③ ④ ⑤

4 ① ② ③ ④ ⑤

5 ① ② ③ ④ ⑤

6 ① ② ③ ④ ⑤

7

14 ① ② ③ ④ ⑤   21 ① ② ③ ④ ⑤

15 ① ② ③ ④ ⑤   22 ① ② ③ ④ ⑤

23 ① ② ③ ④ ⑤

24 ① ② ③ ④ ⑤

16   25 ① ② ③ ④ ⑤

8 ① ② ③ ④ ⑤

9 ① ② ③ ④ ⑤

10 ① ② ③ ④ ⑤

11

17 ① ② ③ ④ ⑤

18 ① ② ③ ④ ⑤

19 ① ② ③ ④ ⑤

Mathematics Test: Part 1

The use of calculators is allowed in Part I only.

Do not write in this test booklet. The test administrator will give you a blank paper for your calculations. Record your answers on the separate answer sheet provided. Be sure all information is properly recorded on the answer sheet.

To record your answers, fill in the numbered circle on the answer sheet that corresponds to the answer you select for each question in the test booklet.

EXAMPLE:

If a grocery bill totaling $15.75 is paid with a $20.00 bill, how much change should be returned?

(1) $5.25

(2) $4.75

(3) $4.25

(4) $3.75

(5) $3.25

(On Answer Sheet)

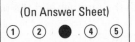

The correct answer is "$4.25"; therefore, answer space 3 would be marked on the answer sheet.

Do not rest the point of your pencil on the answer sheet while you are considering your answer. Make no stray or unnecessary marks. If you change an answer, erase your first mark completely. Mark only one answer space for each question; multiple answers will be scored as incorrect. Do not fold or crease your answer sheet. All test materials must be returned to the test administrator.

Note: Refer to Chapter 26 for the answers for Parts I and II of this practice test.

Calculator Directions

To prepare the calculator for use the ***first*** time, press the ⎡ON⎤ (upper-rightmost) key. "DEG" will appear at the top-center of the screen and "0" at the right. This indicates the calculator is in the proper format for all your calculations.

To prepare the calculator for ***another*** question, press the ⎡ON⎤ or the red ⎡AC⎤ key. This clears any entries made previously.

To do any arithmetic, enter the expression as it is written. Press ⎡=⎤ (equals sign) when finished.

EXAMPLE A: 8 – 3 + 9

First press ⎡ON⎤ or ⎡AC⎤

Enter the following: ⎡8⎤ , ⎡–⎤ , ⎡3⎤ , ⎡+⎤ , ⎡9⎤ , ⎡=⎤

The correct answer is 14.

If the expression in parentheses is to be multiplied by a number, press ⎡×⎤ (multiplication sign) between the number and the parenthesis sign.

EXAMPLE B: 6(8 + 5)

First press ⎡ON⎤ or ⎡AC⎤

Enter the following: ⎡6⎤ , ⎡×⎤ , ⎡(⎤ , ⎡8⎤ , ⎡+⎤ , ⎡5⎤ , ⎡)⎤ , ⎡=⎤

The correct answer is 78.

To find the square root of a number

  ✔ Enter the number.
  ✔ Press the ⎡SHIFT⎤ (upper-leftmost) key ("SHIFT" appears at the top-left of the screen).
  ✔ Press ⎡x^2⎤ (third from the left on top row) to access its second function: square root.

DO NOT press ⎡SHIFT⎤ and ⎡x^2⎤ at the same time.

EXAMPLE C: $\sqrt{64}$

First press ⎡ON⎤ or ⎡AC⎤

Enter the following: ⎡6⎤ , ⎡4⎤ , ⎡SHIFT⎤ , ⎡x^2⎤ , ⎡=⎤

The correct answer is 8.

To enter a negative number, such as –8

  ✔ Enter the number without the negative sign (enter 8).
  ✔ Press the "change sign" (⎡+/–⎤) key, which is directly above the ⎡7⎤ key.

All arithmetic can be done with positive and/or negative numbers.

EXAMPLE D: –8 – (–5)

First press ⎡ON⎤ or ⎡AC⎤

Enter the following: ⎡8⎤ , ⎡+/–⎤ , ⎡–⎤ , ⎡5⎤ , ⎡+/–⎤ , ⎡=⎤

The correct answer is –3.

The Standard Grid

Mixed numbers, such as 3½, cannot be entered in the standard grid. Instead, represent them as decimal numbers (in this case, 3.5) or fractions (in this case, ⅞). In addition, no answer on a standard grid can be a negative number, such as –8.

To record your answer for a standard-grid question

✔ Begin in any column that will allow your answer to be entered.

✔ Write your answer in the boxes on the top row.

✔ In the column beneath a fraction bar or decimal point (if any) and each number in your answer, fill in the circle representing that character.

✔ Leave blank any unused column.

EXAMPLE:

The scale on a map indicates that ½ inch represents an actual distance of 120 miles. In inches, how far apart on the map will the two towns be if the actual distance between them is 180 miles?

The answer to the above example is ¾, or 0.75 inch. A few examples of how the answer could be gridded are shown below.

Points to remember:

✔ The answer sheet will be machine scored. **The circles must be filled in correctly.**

✔ Mark no more than one circle in any column.

✔ Grid only one answer even if there is more than one correct answer.

✔ Mixed numbers, such as 3½, must be gridded as 3.5 or ½.

✔ No answer on a standard grid can be a negative number.

The Coordinate-Plane Grid

To record an answer on the coordinate-plane grid, you must have an *x*-value and a *y*-value. No answer for a coordinate-plane question will have a value that is a fraction or decimal.

Mark only the <u>one</u> circle that represents your answer.

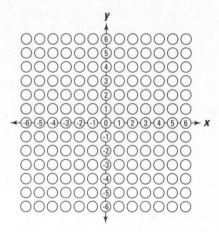

EXAMPLE:

The coordinates of point A, shown on the graph below, are (2,–4).

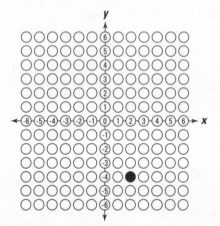

The coordinates of point B, not shown on the graph, are (–3,1). What is the location of point B?

DO NOT MARK YOUR ANSWER ON THE GRAPH ABOVE.

Mark your answer on the coordinate-plane grid on the answer sheet (at right).

CORRECT RESPONSE:

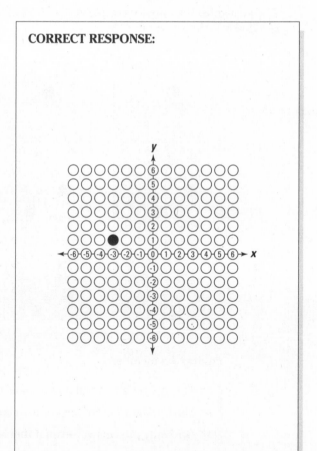

Formulas

AREA of a:

square	Area = side^2
rectangle	Area = length × width
parallelogram	Area = base × height
triangle	Area = ½ × base × height
trapezoid	Area = ½ × (base$_1$ + base$_2$) × height
circle	Area = π × radius^2; π is approximately equal to 3.14

PERIMETER of a:

square	Perimeter = 4 × side
rectangle	Perimeter = (2 × length) + (2 × width)
triangle	Perimeter = side$_1$ + side$_2$ + side$_3$

CIRCUMFERENCE of a circle — Circumference = π × diameter; π is approximately equal to 3.14

VOLUME of a:

cube	Volume = side^3
rectangular solid	Volume = length × width × height
square pyramid	Volume = ⅓ × (base edge)^2 × height
cylinder	Volume = π × radius^2 × height; π is approximately equal to 3.14
cone	Volume = ⅓ × π × radius^2 × height; π is approximately equal to 3.14

COORDINATE GEOMETRY

distance between points = $\sqrt{\left(x_2 - x_1\right)^2 + \left(y_2 - y_1\right)^2}$; (x_1, y_1) and (x_2, y_2) are two points in a plane

slope of a line = $\dfrac{y_2 - y_1}{x_2 - x_1}$; (x_1, y_1) and (x_2, y_2) are two points on the line

PYTHAGOREAN RELATIONSHIP

$a^2 + b^2 = c^2$; a and b are sides, and c is the hypotenuse of a right triangle

MEASURES OF CENTRAL TENDENCY

mean = $\dfrac{x_1 + x_2 + \cdots + x_n}{n}$; where the xs are the values for which a mean is desired, and n is the total number of values for x

median = the middle value of an odd number of *ordered* scores, and halfway between the two middle values of an even number of *ordered* scores

SIMPLE INTEREST — interest = principal × rate × time

DISTANCE — distance = rate × time

TOTAL COST — total cost = (number of units) × (price per unit)

DO NOT BEGIN TAKING THIS TEST UNTIL TOLD TO DO SO

Directions: Choose the <u>one best answer</u> to each question.

1. Dharma is making sale signs for the Super Summer Sale at the Super Saver Swim Shop. Sales tax in Dharma's state is 5%. She makes a series of signs:

   Sign A: ½ off all merchandise

   Sign B: Buy one item, get the second item of equal value free

   Sign C: 50% off all merchandise

   Sign D: Nine times your sales tax back

   What would a shrewd consumer notice about the signs?

   (1) Sign A offers a better buy.

   (2) Sign C offers the worst deal.

   (3) Sign D offers the worst deal.

   (4) Sign B offers a better deal.

   (5) All signs offer the same deal.

2. Daryl is framing a picture. He draws the following diagram to help him make it:

   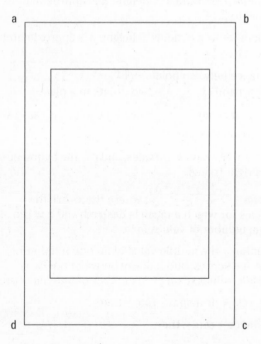

   Which of the following is true about the above diagram?

   (1) *ab* must be perpendicular to *ad*

   (2) *ab* must be parallel to *bc*

   (3) *ad* must be parallel to *ab*

   (4) *ab* and *dc* must be perpendicular

   (5) *ab* and *ad* must be parallel

3. The Hammerhill family is building a deck behind their house. The deck is to be 16 feet long and 21 feet wide, and the decking material was priced at $45.00 a square yard. What would be the cost, in dollars, of the decking material? Mark the answer on the standard grid on the answer sheet.

4. Margaret Millsford, the Chief Financial Officer of Aggravated Manufacturing Corporation, has to report to the Board of Directors. She has been instructed to analyze the sales of each of the company's product lines and recommend dropping the least profitable line. She found that although the per-unit profit of each of their lines was the same, the volume produced differed. She prepared the following graph to back up her recommendation:

   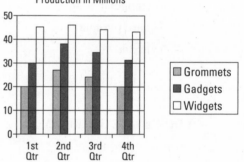

   What should be her recommendation of the least profitable line to drop?

   (1) widgets

   (2) grommets

   (3) gadgets

   (4) grommets and widgets

   (5) gadgets and widgets

Go on to next page

5. Quan wants to build steps down from the 6-foot-high porch behind his house. The bottom step should be 7 feet away from the house to allow for a gentle slope. How long, in feet, will the steps be (answer to two decimal places)?

   (1) 8.22

   (2) 13.00

   (3) 2.92

   (4) 13.22

   (5) 9.22

6. Alice was trying to explain how the length of time she could run each morning had improved each month since she started, except for the month she twisted her ankle. She drew the following graph to show her friends Mary and Kevin the average length of time (in minutes) she ran each day each month:

   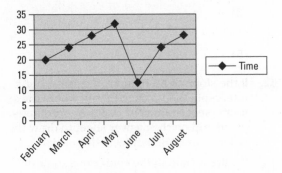

   In which month did Alice twist her ankle?

   (1) June

   (2) February

   (3) August

   (4) September

   (5) May

7. Dominic and Paula were comparing their report cards, as follows:

   Dominic's Report Card

Subject	Grade (%)
Mathematics	63
Social Studies	76
Science	65
Language Arts	84
Physical Education	72

   Paula's Report Card

Subject	Grade (%)
Mathematics	80
Social Studies	64
Science	76
Language Arts	72
Physical Education	88

   The teacher told them that the ratio of their total marks was very close. What is the ratio of Paula's marks to Dominic's marks on these report cards?

   (1) 9:10

   (2) 18:19

   (3) 10:9

   (4) 19:18

   (5) 2:1

8. In the series, 4, 6, 10, 18, . . . , which is the first term that is a multiple of 11? Mark the answer on the standard grid on the answer sheet.

Go on to next page

9. Simone follows the stock market very carefully. She has been carefully following Cowardly Corporation the last few months, keeping track of her research in the following table:

Date	Closing Price (In U.S. Dollars)
August 7	15.03
August 17	16.12
September 1	14.83
September 9	15.01
September 16	14.94
September 20	15.06
September 23	15.17
September 24	15.19

Simone bought shares of the stock on September 24 and wants to make money before selling it. She paid 3% commission to her broker for buying and will pay the same again for selling. What is the lowest price (in U.S. dollars) for which Simone can sell each of her shares in order to break even?

(1) 16.48

(2) 16.13

(3) 15.66

(4) 20.00

(5) 15.99

10. If $22.4 = \dfrac{56a}{5a + 10}$, what is the value of a?

(1) 0

(2) –56

(3) 4

(4) –4

(5) 56

Questions 11 and 12 refer to the following graph.

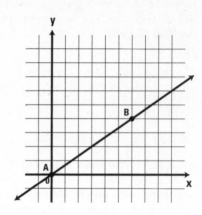

11. Calculate the slope of the line AB.

(1) ⅔

(2) ½

(3) ⅐

(4) ¼

(5) –½

12. If the slope of AB remains the same, but it intercepts the y-axis at C(0,4), where does it intersect the x-axis? Use the coordinate-plane grid on the answer sheet to draw the point where AB intersects the x-axis.

13. If a fire is built in the center of a square barbeque pit, where is the safest place to stand to avoid the intense heat of the fire?

(1) at a corner

(2) along the left side

(3) along the right side

(4) 6 feet from the middle

(5) not enough information given

Go on to next page

14. Lydia and Wayne are shopping for carpets for their home and are looking for the best carpet at the best price. Carnie's Carpets offers them a wool carpet for $21.50 per square yard. Flora's Flooring says they will match that same carpet for only $2.45 per square foot, while Dora's Deep Discount offers them an 8-by-12 foot rug of the same carpet material for $210.24. What is the lowest price per square foot offered to Lydia and Wayne?

    (1) $24.50

    (2) $2.45

    (3) $21.90

    (4) $2.19

    (5) $2.39

15. Miscellaneous Appliances Limited is concerned about its output at Plant A. For its annual report, company officials prepared the following graphs to show the output for each quarter of the last two years:

Output at Plant A – 2007

Output at Plant A – 2008

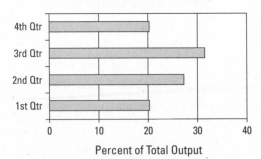

Which quarter showed a dramatic decrease in production in 2008?

    (1) 3rd quarter

    (2) 1st quarter

    (3) 4th quarter

    (4) 2nd quarter

    (5) no significant change

16. The Ngs are looking to expand their two-story house and have calculated that they need at least another 630 square feet to live comfortably. They want to use the basement level for storage and the rest for living. A contractor quotes them $15.80 per square foot for the renovation without redecoration. A real estate agent tells them that they can increase the value of their home by about $18,000 by building the addition. If they want to add as much additional space as possible for the $18,000 they will recover, how much additional space, in square feet, should they add on?

    (1) 630

    (2) 1,260

    (3) 1,620

    (4) 1,140

    (5) 1,329

17. In an experiment involving throws of a 20-sided die, the following results were obtained:

Throw	Left-Handed	Right-Handed
1	2	4
2	4	12
3	5	2
4	9	6
5	11	13
6	10	15
7	4	17
8	6	3
9	7	5

Using the coordinate-plane grid on the answer sheet, plot the point representing the combined medians of the throws using the median of the left-handed results as the *x*-value and the median of the right-handed results as the *y*-value.

Go on to next page

18. LeeAnne is shopping for a new vehicle. She drives about 18,000 miles per year. She is most concerned about the cost of gasoline and other operating costs, like insurance and maintenance. She expects gasoline to average $3.50 a gallon during the five years she will own the car and is basing her decision on that price. As she shops, she makes the following chart:

Type of Vehicle	Miles per Gallon	Operating Costs per Mile
SUV	12.8	$0.78
Sedan	19.6	$0.48
2-door	19.5	$0.54
All-wheel drive	17.2	$0.62
Sports car	18.6	$0.66

Based on her criteria, which car should LeeAnne buy?

(1) SUV

(2) sedan

(3) 2-door

(4) all-wheel drive

(5) sports car

19. Tom is worried about getting to the GED testing center on time. He knows that he averages 40 miles per hour on the route to the tests. If the test site is 47 miles from Tom's house, and he wants to arrive 20 minutes early, how much time does he have to leave for travel and waiting?

Choose the answer that indicates which operations need to be performed and the order in which they need to be performed to answer this question.

(1) add then divide

(2) multiply then add

(3) divide then add

(4) add then multiply

(5) divide then multiply

20. Leonora has just received her mid-term report card. Her grades are as follows:

Leonora's Report Card

Subject	Grade (%)
English	84
Geography	78
Mathematics	68
Physical Education	77
Physics	82

Her average grade is 77.8%. In order to get into the college of her choice, she needs an average of 80%. English is her best subject. By how many percentage points will her English score have to go up, assuming all her other subjects stay the same, to get into college?

(1) 7

(2) 8

(3) 9

(4) 10

(5) 11

21. Sonia has an amazing recipe for rice. For each 1 cup of rice, she adds 2 cups of vegetable soup and a quarter cup of lentils. This weekend, she is having a large dinner party and figures she needs to cook 3½ cups of rice for her guests. How much of the other two ingredients should she use?

(1) 7 cups of soup and ⅞ cup of lentils

(2) 3½ cups of soup and ½ cup of lentils

(3) 7 cups of soup and 1 cup of lentils

(4) 1 cup of soup and 7 cups of lentils

(5) 6 cups of soup and ⅞ cup of lentils

Go on to next page

22. In drawing cards from a deck, any single card has an equal chance of being drawn. After six cards have been drawn and removed, what is the probability of drawing an ace of hearts if it has not yet been drawn?

    (1) 1:52

    (2) 1:50

    (3) 1:48

    (4) 1:46

    (5) 1:44

23. The Symons are redecorating a room in their house. They have some interesting ideas. They want to put a rug on the floor surrounded by a border of tiles. They are considering teak paneling halfway up each wall. In addition, they may cut away part of the ceiling to put in a skylight. This is a diagram of their room:

    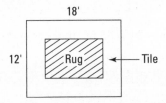

    The rug costs $7.50 a square foot, and tile costs $9.00 a square foot. One rug they like is 16 feet by 10 feet, leaving just a little area around the rug for tiles. At the store, however, they see another rug that is only 12 feet by 8 feet, but it's just the right pattern and colors for their room. Which floor treatment is less expensive?

    (1) both are the same cost

    (2) the larger rug

    (3) the smaller rug without the paneling

    (4) the smaller rug

    (5) not enough information given

24. Brad is a secret shopper for the Friendly Furniture store. His job is to go to competitive stores and price a series of items to make sure his employer can advertise that he has the best prices. His boss wants to start a new advertising campaign: "Friendly Furniture — always lower than the average price of our competitors." Brad's job is to shop several stores to make sure the claim is accurate. Brad's results are recorded in the following table:

Item	Store A	Store B	Store C	Store D	Friendly Furniture
Couch	$1,729	$1,749	$1,729	$1,699	$1,719
Dining room set	$4,999	$4,899	$5,019	$4,829	$4,899
Loveseat	$1,259	$1,199	$1,279	$1,149	$1,229
Coffee table	$459	$449	$479	$429	$449
Reclining chair	$759	$799	$739	$699	$739

Which item cannot be advertised as "lower than the average price?"

(1) couch

(2) dining room set

(3) loveseat

(4) coffee table

(5) reclining chair

25. In a pistachio-eating contest, Sarah eats 48 pistachios in 18 minutes. If she could maintain her rate of eating pistachios, how many could she eat in 2 hours? Record your answer on the standard grid on the answer sheet.

END OF PART I

Mathematics Test: Part II

The use of calculators is <u>not</u> allowed in Part II.

Do not write in this test booklet. The test administrator will give you a blank paper for your calculations. Record your answers on the separate answer sheet provided. Be sure all information is properly recorded on the answer sheet.

To record your answers, fill in the numbered circle on the answer sheet that corresponds to the answer you select for each question in the test booklet.

EXAMPLE:

If a grocery bill totaling $15.75 is paid with a $20.00 bill, how much change should be returned?

(1) $5.25

(2) $4.75

(3) $4.25

(4) $3.75

(5) $3.25

(On Answer Sheet)

① ② ● ④ ⑤

The correct answer is "$4.25"; therefore, answer space 3 would be marked on the answer sheet.

Do not rest the point of your pencil on the answer sheet while you are considering your answer. Make no stray or unnecessary marks. If you change an answer, erase your first mark completely. Mark only one answer space for each question; multiple answers will be scored as incorrect. Do not fold or crease your answer sheet. All test materials must be returned to the test administrator.

If you finish Part II early, you may return to Part I, but without the calculator.

Note: Refer to Chapter 26 for the answers for Parts I and II of this practice test.

The Standard Grid

Mixed numbers, such as 3½, cannot be entered in the standard grid. Instead, represent them as decimal numbers (in this case, 3.5) or fractions (in this case, ½). No answer on a standard grid can be a negative number, such as –8.

To record your answer for a standard-grid question

✔ Begin in any column that will allow your answer to be entered.

✔ Write your answer in the boxes on the top row.

✔ In the column beneath a fraction bar or decimal point (if any) and each number in your answer, fill in the circle representing that character.

✔ Leave blank any unused column.

EXAMPLE:

The scale on a map indicates that ½ inch represents an actual distance of 120 miles. In inches, how far apart on the map will the two towns be if the actual distance between them is 180 miles?

The answer to the above example is ¾, or 0.75 inch. A few examples of how the answer could be gridded are shown below.

Points to remember:

✔ The answer sheet will be machine scored. **The circles must be filled in correctly.**

✔ Mark no more than one circle in any column.

✔ Grid only one answer even if there is more than one correct answer.

✔ Mixed numbers, such as 3½, must be gridded as 3.5 or ½.

✔ No answer on a standard grid can be a negative number.

The Coordinate-Plane Grid

To record an answer on the coordinate-plane grid, you must have an *x*-value and a *y*-value. No answer for a coordinate-plane question will have a value that is a fraction or decimal.

Mark only the <u>one</u> circle that represents your answer.

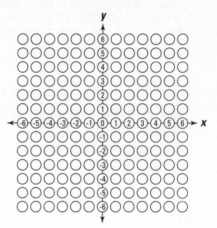

EXAMPLE:

The coordinates of point A, shown on the graph below, are (2,–4).

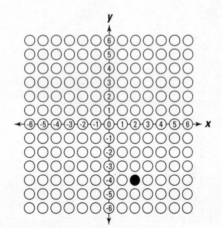

The coordinates of point B, not shown on the graph, are (–3,1). What is the location of point B?

DO NOT MARK YOUR ANSWER ON THE GRAPH ABOVE.

Mark your answer on the coordinate-plane grid on the answer sheet (at right).

CORRECT RESPONSE:

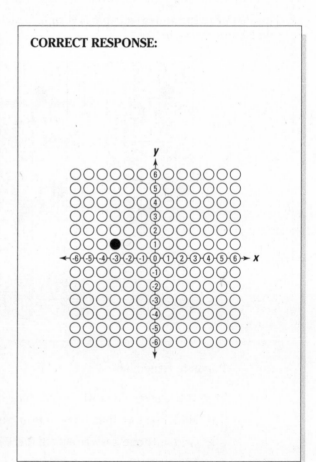

Formulas

AREA of a:

square	Area = side^2
rectangle	Area = length × width
parallelogram	Area = base × height
triangle	Area = ½ × base × height
trapezoid	Area = ½ × (base$_1$ + base$_2$) × height
circle	Area = π × radius^2; π is approximately equal to 3.14

PERIMETER of a:

square	Perimeter = 4 × side
rectangle	Perimeter = (2 × length) + (2 × width)
triangle	Perimeter = side$_1$ + side$_2$ + side$_3$

CIRCUMFERENCE of a circle   Circumference = π × diameter; π is approximately equal to 3.14

VOLUME of a:

cube	Volume = side^3
rectangular solid	Volume = length × width × height
square pyramid	Volume = ⅓ × (base edge)^2 × height
cylinder	Volume = π × radius^2 × height; π is approximately equal to 3.14
cone	Volume = ⅓ × π × radius^2 × height; π is approximately equal to 3.14

COORDINATE GEOMETRY   distance between points = $\sqrt{\left(x_2 - x_1\right)^2 + \left(y_2 - y_1\right)^2}$; (x_1, y_1) and (x_2, y_2) are two points in a plane

slope of a line = $\frac{y_2 - y_1}{x_2 - x_1}$; (x_1, y_1) and (x_2, y_2) are two points on the line

PYTHAGOREAN RELATIONSHIP $a^2 + b^2 = c^2$; a and b are sides, and c is the hypotenuse of a right triangle

MEASURES OF CENTRAL TENDENCY   **mean** = $\frac{x_1 + x_2 + \cdots + x_n}{n}$; where the xs are the values for which a mean is desired, and n is the total number of values for x

median = the middle value of an odd number of *ordered* scores, and halfway between the two middle values of an even number of *ordered* scores

SIMPLE INTEREST   interest = principal × rate × time

DISTANCE   distance = rate × time

TOTAL COST   total cost = (number of units) × (price per unit)

DO NOT BEGIN TAKING THIS TEST UNTIL TOLD TO DO SO

Directions: Choose the <u>one best answer</u> to each question.

1. Kevin wants to paint his room, which is 9 feet 5 inches long, 8 feet 3 inches wide, and 8 feet 2 inches high. The label on the paint can cautions that air must be exchanged in the room every 12 minutes. When Kevin looks for exhaust fans to keep the air moving, he finds that they are calibrated in cubic feet per minutes. What operation does Kevin have to perform first to figure out which size fan he needs?

   (1) multiplication

   (2) division

   (3) addition

   (4) subtraction

   (5) square root

2. Which of these shapes has the same relationship to the horizontal after a 90-degree rotation about a point on the perimeter?

   (1) square

   (2) isosceles triangle

   (3) circle

   (4) pentagon

   (5) not enough information given

3. In a large company, the top four positions are organized as follows:

   Each department has the following budget:

Department	Budget ($ Millions)
Operations	14.7
Human Resources	2.1
Marketing	5.6

   What is the ratio of the largest budget to the smallest budget?

   (1) 7:1

   (2) 14:1

   (3) 5:2

   (4) 7:5

   (5) 14:5

Go on to next page

4. A company has doubled its sales from the 1st to the 3rd quarters. Which graph indicates this pattern?

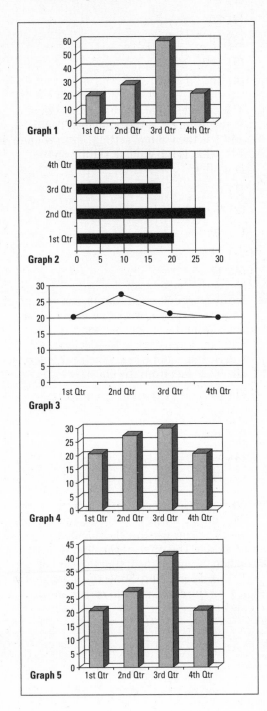

Graph 1

Graph 2

Graph 3

Graph 4

Graph 5

(1) Graph 1

(2) Graph 2

(3) Graph 3

(4) Graph 4

(5) Graph 5

5. A 6-foot tall forester standing some 16 feet from a tree uses his digital rangefinder to calculate the distance between his eye and the top of the tree to be 25 feet. How tall is the tree?

(1) $\sqrt{41}$

(2) $\sqrt{881}$

(3) $\sqrt{256}$

(4) $\sqrt{97}$

(5) not enough information given

6. Lawrie is trying to save money and keeps her money in both checking and savings accounts. Each week, she puts $24.00 from her paycheck into her savings account. However, the fourth week she overdraws her checking account by $7.50, and the bank transfers the money from her savings account. For providing this service, the bank charges Lawrie $10.00. What is her savings account balance after the fourth week?

(1) $88.50

(2) $96.00

(3) $86.00

(4) $78.50

(5) $24.00

7. Sarah is negotiating the price of a chair for her room. The original price was $96.00. Store A offers her ⅓ off. Store B offers her a discount of 30%. How much will she save by taking the lower price? Use the standard grid on the answer sheet to record your answer in dollars.

Go on to next page

Questions 8 through 10 are based on the following information and figure.

While a rock band is setting up for a concert, the audio engineer is calibrating the amplifiers used for the concert. He has an instrument that develops and displays a graph for each setting on the amplifier controls. The graph appears like this:

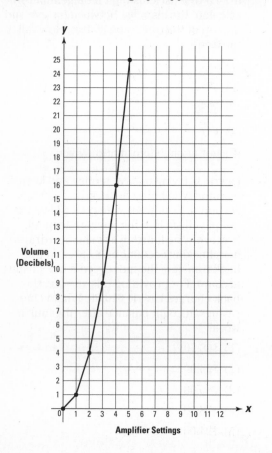

Amplifier Settings

8. From the graph, calculate the volume in decibels for a setting of 10 on the amplifier.

   (1) 20

   (2) 30

   (3) 50

   (4) 100

   (5) 10

9. The equation that produced this graph is $V = S^2$, where V is the volume in decibels and S is the volume setting. If the volume is 144, what is the volume setting on the amplifier?

   (1) 8

   (2) 9

   (3) 10

   (4) 11

   (5) 12

10. In this particular auditorium, the volume of sound decreases by half for every 10 feet away from the stage a person sits. If the volume at the stage is 144 decibels, what will be the volume in decibels for a person sitting 20 feet from the stage?

    (1) 24

    (2) 36

    (3) 48

    (4) 60

    (5) 72

11. Gary and Georgina George bought a new car and are trying to estimate the gas mileage. The new car travels 240 miles at a cost of $54.00. The price of gasoline is $2.70 per gallon. They estimate that the car will get 18 miles per gallon. Show the actual mileage on the standard grid on the answer sheet.

Go on to next page

Question 12 is based on the following figures, which are reprinted from Physical Science: What the Technology Professional Needs to Know by C. Lon Enloe, Elizabeth Garnett, Jonathan Miles, and Stephen Swanson (Wiley).

Questions 14 through 16 refer to the following table.

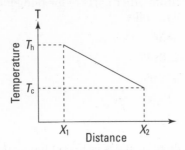

Average Mileage and Annual Fuel Cost of Selected Vehicles

Vehicle	Mileage (Miles per Gallon)		Annual Cost ($)*
	City	Highway	
A	23	28	840
B	21	29	875
C	19	25	1,000
D	18	24	1,050
E	17	22	1,105
F	16	22	1,167
G	15	21	1,235
H	14	19	1,314
I	13	18	1,400
J	12	16	1,823

*Annual cost includes 15,000 miles driven annually; 55% of the miles in the city and 45% on the highway; standard price of fuel

12. If the person pictured wants to remain at a constant temperature, what geometrical shape should he follow as a path?

    (1) hexagon

    (2) ellipse

    (3) line

    (4) square

    (5) circle

13. Igor is in charge of the swimming pool at the local recreation center. The pool is 120 feet long and 24 feet wide and holds 12,902 cubic feet of water. What is the average depth of the pool in feet? Record your answer on the standard grid on the answer sheet.

14. If you were in the market for a car, how much could you save, in dollars, over a three-year period, by buying the most economical car over the least economical car?

    (1) 840

    (2) 983

    (3) 2,520

    (4) 5,469

    (5) 2,949

15. What is the difference in miles per gallon between the mean city mileage and the median of the city mileages for these vehicles?

    (1) 1⅔

    (2) ⅓

    (3) 17

    (4) 2½

    (5) 2

Go on to next page

16. Graph the results for Vehicle A on the coordinate-plane grid, with the difference between city and highway mileage as the appropriate point on the *y*-axis.

17. In order to solve a problem in her mathematics class, Jan had to solve the following set of equations:

    $2x + 3y = 10$

    $5x + 6y = 13$

    What is the correct value of *y*?

    (1) +4

    (2) –8

    (3) –6

    (4) +6

    (5) +8

18. An international survey found the following information about participation in adult education:

    ### Percent of Population over Age 21 Participating in Adult Education in the Year 2003

Country	Total Participation Rate (%)
Denmark	62.3
Hungary	17.9
Norway	43.1
Portugal	15.5
United States	66.4

    Compare the participation rates of the countries with the highest and lowest participation rates by calculating approximately how many more adults participate in adult education in the country with the highest participation rate than in the country with the lowest participation rate.

    (1) 2 times as many

    (2) 4 times as many

    (3) 6 times as many

    (4) 8 times as many

    (5) not enough information given

19. Gordon has the following six bills to pay this month:

Bill Payable To	Amount
Bedding by Vidalia	$23.00
Chargealot Credit Corp.	$31.00
Dink's Department Store	$48.00
Furniture Fit for a Princess Shoppe	$13.00
Highest Fidelity Sound Shop	$114.00
Overpriced Gas Corporation	$39.00

    Each month, he allocates $250.00 to pay his bills. This month, his bills are over this budget. How much extra money must he find from other parts of his budget to pay all of his bills?

    (1) $8.00

    (2) $268.00

    (3) $28.00

    (4) $18.00

    (5) $38.00

20. If a flight of stairs is 15 feet long, and the second floor is 9 feet above the floor below, how much floor space in length will the staircase occupy? Use the standard grid on the answer sheet to record your answer.

21. Andrew just bought a small circular swimming pool for his children to play in. The diameter of the pool is 12 feet, and Andrew can fill it safely to a depth of 9 inches. If a cubic foot of water weighs 62.42 pounds, how many pounds does the water in Andrew's pool weigh?

    (1) approximately 27,000

    (2) approximately 2,700

    (3) approximately 53,000

    (4) approximately 1,300

    (5) approximately 5,300

Go on to next page

22. If Giorgio borrows $100 for one year and three months and repays $108 dollars including simple interest, what rate of interest was he charged?

    (1) 6.4%

    (2) 8.0%

    (3) 4.0%

    (4) 4.6%

    (5) 8.4%

23. Chico went shopping for some groceries for his family. His shopping list was as follows:

    - 2 pounds of apples
    - 5 bananas
    - 1 container of milk
    - 1 loaf of bread

    If apples were $.79 a pound, bananas $.23 each, milk $1.27 a carton, and bread $.98 a loaf, what is the approximate total cost of the groceries?

    (1) $3.90

    (2) $4.10

    (3) $4.90

    (4) $5.50

    (5) $6.00

24. What is the next number in the series: 4, 7, 12, 19, . . . ?

    (1) 28

    (2) 26

    (3) 24

    (4) 32

    (5) 30

25. A rectangle 5 units long and 4 units high is represented on a graph. If three of the corners are placed at (3,2), (3,−2), and (−2,2), where should the fourth corner be placed?

    (1) (−2,2)

    (2) (2,−2)

    (3) (−2,−2)

    (4) (2,2)

    (5) (5,4)

END OF TEST

Chapter 26

Answers and Explanations for the Mathematics Test

A fter taking the Mathematics Test in Chapter 25, use this chapter to check your answers. Take your time as you move through the explanations of the answers for Parts I and II that we provide in the first two sections. They can help you understand why you missed the answers you did. You may also want to read the explanations for the questions you answered correctly because doing so can give you a better understanding of the thought process that helped you choose the correct answers.

If you're short on time, turn to the end of the chapter for abbreviated answer keys for Parts I and II of the Mathematics Test.

Analysis of the Answers for Part 1

Note: In all the following explanations, the answers given are the ones that would be read from the display on the calculator if the correct numbers were entered. Calculators always calculate to the maximum number of digits possible on their display. It is up to the person operating the calculator to either set the number of decimal places, if possible, or to make sense of the answer.

1. **3.** This problem tests your understanding of numbers and their equivalents (integers, fractions, decimals, and percents) in a real-world situation. Signs A, B, and C give customers 50% off. Sign D gives them 45% (9 × 5% sales tax). Sign D offers the least discount.

2. **1.** This problem involves measurement and geometry and tests your understanding of perpendicular and parallel lines in a geometrical figure. Frames are rectangles. Each pair of opposite sides must be parallel for this to be a rectangle.

3. **1680 on standard grid.** This problem tests your knowledge and mastery of number operations and number sense. Use the calculator because numerous conversions are involved, including the following:

    Area of the deck is 16 × 21 = 336 square feet

    9 square feet = 1 square yard

    $^{336}/_9$ = 37⅓ square yards

    1 square yard of decking costs $45.00

    37⅓ square yards of decking costs $1,680.00

4. **2.** This problem tests your data-analysis skills. You're asked to interpret and draw inferences from the bar graph. Because the profit per unit is the same for all products, the product selling the least units provides the lowest profit. In each quarter, according to the bar graph, grommets sold the fewest numbers. Grommets were the least profitable product and, therefore, are recommended as the one to drop.

5. **5.** This problem tests your skills in measurement and geometry. You're asked to use the Pythagorean relationship to calculate a distance. This is a good question on which to use the calculator because it involves squaring, adding, and calculating the square root.

The *Pythagorean relationship* says that the square of the hypotenuse of a right-angled triangle is equal to the sum of the squares of the other two sides. (You may remember this term being called the *Pythagorean theorem.*) The hypotenuse is the side opposite the right angle.

To help you figure out this problem, draw a sketch that looks something like this:

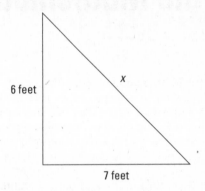

In the sketch, x represents the length of the hypotenuse. Thanks to the Pythagorean relationship, which you're given on the formula sheet of the Mathematics Test, you know that the square of x is equal to the square of 6 plus the square of 7, or

$6^2 + 7^2 = x^2$

$36 + 49 = 85$

Then $x^2 = 85$

$x = 9.22$

The length of the stairs is 9.22 feet, rounded to two decimal places.

6. **1.** Alice has converted her story into a graph, and you're being asked to interpret the line graph in conjunction with her story. Because her average daily time had been increasing until May, dropped in June, and recovered in July and August, you can assume that the twisted ankle slowed her down. It likely happened in June.

7. **4.** Number operations are involved in solving this problem. You're asked to average a set of grades for each person and compare them using a ratio. You can simplify this question using the calculator.

The total of Paula's marks is 80 + 64 + 76 + 72 + 88 = 380.

The total of Dominic's marks is 63 + 76 + 65 + 84 + 72 = 360.

Because you divide each total by 5 to get the averages for Paula and Dominic, you can simply use the ratio of the totals to get the answer because it will equal the ratio of the averages. (Note that if one of the students had six grades and the other had five, for example, you'd have to use the ratio of the averages, not of the totals.)

The ratio of Paula's marks to Dominic's marks is 380:360, which you can simplify by dividing top and bottom by 20 to get 19:18. Note that Choice (2) is the ratio of Dominic's marks to Paula's marks, but that's not what the question asked for.

8. **66 on standard grid.** This problem involves algebra, functions, and patterns. The numbers 4, 6, 10, 18, . . . form a pattern (also called a *series*). After looking carefully at the series, you see that the second term is formed by subtracting 1 from the first term and multiplying by 2. Try this on the third number: $(6 - 1) \times 2 = 10$. You've found your pattern. Continuing the series: 4, 6, 10, 18, 34, 66, . . . , the first term you come to that is a multiple of 11 is 66.

9. **3.** This problem involves data analysis and manipulation of numbers and is best done using the calculator. Most of the information given is irrelevant, except to decide that Simone may have bought at a high point. The important price to consider is $15.19. In addition to this price per share, Simone has to pay her broker 3% commission.

Therefore, her final price per share on September 24 is $15.19 + $.03(15.19) = $15.6457. Because you're dealing with money, you have to round the number to two decimal places, making her final price per share $15.65. This amount of money came out of her bank account for each share she bought.

If she decides to sell the shares at this price, $15.65, she has to pay her broker another 3% commission, or $.03(15.65) = $0.4695. Rounded to two decimals, she has to pay a commission of $0.47 per share. She then receives the value of the shares, $15.65, minus the commission of $0.47, for a total of $15.18 per share. That is, for each share she sells, the broker deposits $15.18 into her account. Notice that this amount is less than the amount she paid for each share.

In order to break even, Simone has to receive $15.65 per share — after the commission. Set the equation up this way:

$1x - x(0.03) = 15.65$, where x is the selling price

$1x - 0.03x = 15.65$, where x is the selling price

$0.97x = 15.65$

Now divide both sides by 0.97 and $x = 16.13$.

10. **4.** This question involves algebra. You have to solve a linear equation, as follows:

$$22.4 = \frac{56a}{5a + 10}$$

Cross-multiply and write this equation as $22.4(5a + 10) = 56a$

Getting rid of the parentheses, the equation looks like this: $112a + 224 = 56a$

Bringing all the as to the left and the numbers to the right, you have: $112a - 56a = -224$

Combining the as, you have: $56a = -224$

Divide both sides by 56 to get one a on the left: $a = -4$

11. **1.** This question tests your skills in measurement and geometry. You're asked to find the slope of a line drawn for you.

The *x-axis* runs horizontally across the paper. The *y-axis* runs vertically, up and down the paper. The *origin* is where the two axes (that's the plural of axis) intersect. Points to the left of the *y*-axis have negative *x*-values. Points below the *x*-axis have negative *y*-values. The *x-intercept* of a line is the point where the line cuts the *x*-axis. The *y-intercept* of a line is the point where the line cuts the *y*-axis. All lines parallel to the *x*-axis have slopes of 0.

The slope of a line is the rise over the run. The rise is 4 and the run is 6. This means that the slope is ⁴⁄₆ or ⅔ (divide top and bottom by 2 to simplify).

12. **(–6,0) on coordinate-plane grid.** This question tests your skills in measurement and geometry. You're asked to identify the *x*-intercept and the *y*-intercept and to draw a line with a slope of ⅔ on the coordinate-plane grid.

If you draw a line through the point on the *y*-axis having the same slope, it crosses the *x*-axis at (–6,0). Simply count over 3 points to the left (the run), down 2 (the rise), and you're at (–3,2). But you're asked for the *x*-intercept, so repeat this process. Go over 3 more points to the left and down 2 more, and you're at (–6,0).

13. **5.** This question doesn't provide enough information for you to give an accurate answer. If the fire were rectangular in shape, the answer would be different from a circular fire, or an irregularly shaped fire. The question provides information only about the shape of the barbeque.

14. **4.** Consider the price per square foot at each store:

    Carnie's Carpets: $21.50 per square yard = $21.50 ÷ 9 = $2.39 per square foot

    Flora's Flooring: $2.45 per square foot

    Dora's Deep Discount: The area of an 8-by-12 foot rug is $8 \times 12 = 96$ square feet. The cost for 96 square feet is $210.24 or $210.24 ÷ 96 = $2.19 per square foot.

15. **1.** In this question, you're asked to analyze graphs to identify patterns in a workplace situation.

    In the first graph for 2007, the third quarter produces about half the output for the year. In the second graph, the third quarter of 2008 produces only a little over 30% of the output. The best answer for this question is the third quarter.

16. **4.** This problem involves measurement, specifically, area and money. Assuming that the estimate for renovation is accurate, the number of square feet of renovation that the Ngs can afford for $18,000 is $18,000 ÷ 15.80 square feet = 1,139.24 square feet. Round this number to 1,140 because you usually don't add part of a square foot.

17. **(6,6) on coordinate-plane grid.** This problem involves data analysis, statistics, and probability. You're being asked to graph a point representing the medians of two sets of data. First, find the median (the middle number, when put in order) of the first set of numbers. The median is 6. Then find the median of the second set of numbers. Again, it is 6.

    Neatness doesn't count in your rough work. Don't spend time making beautiful tables on your scratch paper. Just sketch out the answer.

18. **2.** This problem is based on measurement using uniform rates, and it asks you to make a decision based on factual information. To figure the cost of gasoline over the five years, set up the problem this way:

    $$18,000 \text{ miles} \times \frac{1 \text{ gallon}}{12.8 \text{ miles}} \times \frac{\$3.50}{\text{gallon}} \times 5 \text{ years}$$

    To figure the operating costs over five years, set up the problem this way:

    $$18,000 \text{ miles} \times \frac{\$0.78}{\text{mile}} \times 5 \text{ years}$$

    To help you decide which car LeeAnne should buy, create a chart like the following:

Vehicle Type	Miles/ Gallon	Total Gas Costs	Operating Costs/Mile	Total Operating Cost	Total Cost
SUV	12.8	$24,609.38	$0.78	$70,200.00	$94,809.38
Sedan	19.6	$16,071.43	$0.48	$43,200.00	$59,271.43
2-door	19.5	$16,153.83	$0.54	$48,600.00	$64,753.83
All-wheel drive	17.2	$18,313.94	$0.62	$55,800.00	$74,113.94
Sports car	18.6	$16,935.47	$0.66	$59,400.00	$76,335.47

    From these figures, you can see that the sedan is the best buy.

19. **3.** This problem involves number operations. Instead of asking you for the answer, which is pretty simple, you're asked to provide the operations that are required to solve the problem. First, you divide (miles to site ÷ miles per hour), and then you add (the amount of time Tom wants to arrive early).

20. **5.** This question involves data analysis. You're asked to apply measures of central tendency (the mean) and analyze the effect of changes in data on this measure. If Leonora's present average is 77.8% and she wants to get an average of 80%, she needs enough marks to get an additional 2.2% (80 – 77.8).

Because she is taking five subjects, she requires 5 extra points for each percent increase. Thus, she requires $2.2 \times 5 = 11$ additional points. The problem says that English is her best subject, so she would need the 11 extra points in English.

21. **1.** This question tests your ability to figure out how a change in the amount of rice used results in changes to the amount of soup and lentils needed.

    Because each cup of rice requires 2 cups of soup, 3½ cups of rice require $2 \times 3\frac{1}{2} = 7$ cups of soup.

    Because each cup of rice requires ¼ cup of lentils, 3½ cups of rice require $3\frac{1}{2} \times \frac{1}{4} = \frac{7}{2} \times \frac{1}{4} = \frac{7}{8}$ cup of lentils.

22. **4.** This question is a test in probability. You're asked to figure out the probability of an event occurring. If you had an entire deck of 52 cards, the probability of drawing an ace of hearts would be 1:52. If you remove 6 cards and none of them is the ace of hearts, you may as well have a 46-card deck (52 – 6). The probability of drawing an ace of hearts from a 46-card deck is 1:46.

23. **2.** This problem tests your measurement skills. You're asked to predict the impact of changes in the linear dimensions of the rug on its area and cost. Choice (3) seems logical, but the question never mentions the cost of the paneling, so you can't consider it as an answer.

    Draw a sketch of the room with the larger rug. It will have a tiled area around it. You have to figure out how many square feet of tile and carpet you need for this floor treatment, as follows:

    The area of the room is $18 \times 12 = 216$ square feet.

    The larger rug will cover $16 \times 10 = 160$ square feet of the floor. This leaves 56 square feet (216 – 160) to be covered with tile. The cost of the rug is $\$7.50 \times 160 = \$1,200$. The cost of the tile is $\$9.00 \times 56 = \$504.00$. The total cost is $\$1,200.00 + \$504.00 = \$1,704.00$.

    The smaller rug will cover $12 \times 8 = 96$ square feet of the floor. This leaves $216 - 96 = 120$ square feet to be covered with tile. The cost of the rug is $\$7.50 \times 96 = \$720.00$. The cost of the tile is $\$9.00 \times 120 = \$1,080.00$. The total cost is $\$720.00 + \$1,080.00 = \$1,800.00$. The smaller rug will cost more for the entire floor treatment.

    Tile costs more per square foot than carpeting, so you know without doing any figuring that having more tile will result in higher costs.

24. **3.** This question is an exercise in data analysis. You're asked to compare sets of data based on the mean (average) prices of four other stores. You can summarize the average prices on a sketch table like this one:

Item	Store A	Store B	Store C	Store D	Average Price	Friendly Furniture
Couch	$1,729.00	$1,749.00	$1,729.00	$1,699.00	$1,726.50	$1,719.00
Dining room set	$4,999.00	$4,899.00	$5,019.00	$4,829.00	$4,936.50	$4,899.00
Loveseat	$1,259.00	$1,199.00	$1,279.00	$1,149.00	$1,221.50	$1,229.00
Coffee table	$459.00	$449.00	$479.00	$429.00	$454.00	$449.00
Reclining chair	$759.00	$799.00	$739.00	$699.00	$749.00	$739.00

    You can see that the only item Friendly Furniture sells for over the average price is the loveseat, which is the answer to the question.

25. **320 on standard grid.** This question tests your knowledge of number operations by asking you to solve a problem involving calculations. Sarah ate $48 \div 18$ pistachios per minute. In 2 hours or 120 minutes, she could eat $120 \times \frac{48}{18} = 320$.

Analysis of the Answers for Part II

1. **1.** This question is about number operations; it asks you to select the appropriate operation to solve a problem. Because the first operation performed is to find the volume of the room, and the formula for volume is length × width × height, the first operation you use to solve the problem is multiplication.

2. **5.** This question tests your knowledge of measurement and geometry. You're asked to visualize and describe geometrical figures under a 90-degree rotation. Each of the figures is changed by the rotation. Try drawing each of these shapes, picking a point on the perimeter and rotating it 90 degrees. Because this is a timed test, try drawing one or two, noticing that they change quite a bit. Use your imagination to check the rest. After discovering that none of the four shapes has the same relationship to the horizontal after a 90-degree rotation about a point on its perimeter, you have your answer — not enough information given.

3. **1.** This question tests your data-analysis skills by asking you to interpret a chart and answer a question involving calculation.

   The largest budget is the Operations budget, while the smallest budget is Human Resources. The ratio between these two budgets is 14.7 to 2.1 or 7:1 (dividing both sides by 2.1).

   If you wanted to do this in your head, notice that 14:2 (the approximate ratio between the Operations budget and the Human Resources budget) is double 7:1.

4. **5.** This question tests your knowledge of patterns by asking you to compare different graphs to extract information. Graph 5 has the first and third quarters in the required ratio.

5. **5.** This problem involves measurement and geometry, and it asks you to use the Pythagorean relationship to solve a problem.

   You can't actually solve this problem, however. Because the rangefinder is measuring the distance from the forester's eye and you don't know how high his eye is above the ground, you can't calculate the height of the tree. You can calculate the distance from the forester's eye to the top of the tree by using the Pythagorean relationship, but the question asks for the height of the tree (which is the distance from the ground — not the forester's eye — to the top of the tree). Thus, you don't have enough information.

6. **4.** This question tests your knowledge of number operations by asking you to perform several operations to calculate an answer. After the fourth week, Lawrie would've deposited 4 × $24.00 = $96.00. There would've been two withdrawals totaling $7.50 + $10.00 = $17.50. Her balance after the fourth week would be $96.00 − $17.50 = $78.50.

7. **3.20 on standard grid.** This question tests your skills in using percentages and discounts. Store A offers Sarah ⅓ off or 96 ÷ 3 = $32.00 off the original price. Store B offers her 30% off. 30% is 0.30, so she'll get 96 × 0.30 = $28.80 off the original price. By buying at store A, she'd get the chair for $32.00 − $28.80 = $3.20 less. Thus, she'd save $3.20.

8. **4.** This question tests your skills by asking you to use information from a graph to solve a problem. From the graph, you can figure out that the volume in decibels is the square of the volume setting. For a volume setting of 4, the volume is 16 decibels. Therefore, for a setting of 10, the volume is 100 decibels (10^2).

9. **5.** This question tests your skills in algebra by asking you to solve equations. The equation given is $V = S^2$. If $S^2 = 144$, the square root of 144 is 12. Thus, the answer is 12.

10. **2.** If the volume decreases by half for every 10 feet away from the stage you get and the volume at the stage is 144 decibels, a person sitting 10 feet from the stage would hear at a volume of 72 decibels (144 ÷ 2), and a person sitting 20 feet from the stage would hear at a volume of 36 decibels (72 ÷ 2).

11. **12 on standard grid.** This question involves number operations. You're asked to calculate the average miles per gallon for a vehicle. Rather than provide you with the number of gallons used, you're given the cost of gasoline and the cost of the 240-mile trip. To calculate

the amount of fuel used, you divide $54.00 by $2.70 to get 20 gallons. You can do this operation mentally to speed things up. Next, you divide the miles, 240, by the fuel used, 20 gallons, to get the mileage, 12 miles per gallon ($240 \div 20 = 12$).

12. **5.** This question tests your skills in measurement and geometry. To remain at a constant temperature, you have to remain at a constant distance from the fire.

The path of a point that travels a constant distance from a point is a circle.

13. **4.48 on standard grid.** This problem tests your ability to do calculations and use a formula: Volume = length × width × depth. Thus, 12,902 cubic feet = 120 feet × 24 feet × average depth. The average depth $= \dfrac{12,902}{(120 \times 24)} = 4.48$ (the answer is rounded).

14. **5.** This question tests your ability to make a decision based on data presented in a table and then to use that information to answer a question. The least economical car costs $1,823 to drive for a year, while the most economical car costs $840 for the same time under the same conditions. The difference in cost for one year is $1,823 – $840 = $983. The cost for three years is $983 × 3 = $2,949.

15. **1.** This question tests your ability to analyze data using the mean and median to answer a question about the data given. The mean of the city mileages is the sum of the mileages divided by 10 (the number of entries), which equals 16.8. The median of the mileages is the one midway between the two in the middle, or 16.5. The difference between the two numbers (16.8 – 16.5) is ⅓ (or 0.3).

16. **(0,5) on coordinate-plane grid.** This question tests your ability to analyze data by representing data graphically.

For Vehicle A, the difference between the city and highway mileage is 5 mpg (28 – 23). The point you want on the *y*-axis is (0,5), which you need to mark on the coordinate-plane grid.

17. **5.** This question tests your skill in algebra by asking you to solve a system of linear equations:

$2x + 3y = 10$

$5x + 6y = 13$

Remember that a *linear equation* is one in which the powers of the variables are all equal to 1. To solve this system, you have to eliminate *x* by multiplying each equation by a number that allows you to subtract one from the other and end up with just *y*s. Multiply the first equation by 5 and the second equation by 2:

$5(2x + 3y = 10) = 10x + 15y = 50$

$2(5x + 6y = 13) = 10x + 12y = 26$

Subtract the second equation from the first, and you get $3y = 24$; $y = 8$. (Note that you can also multiply the second equation by –2 and add the two equations together. Either way gets you the same answer.)

18. **2.** This question asks you to analyze a situation presented in a table. The table tells you that the country with the highest participation rate is the United States, with a participation rate of 66.4. The country with the lowest participation rate is Portugal, with a participation rate of 15.5. Because you're asked for an approximation, you can say that the participation rate in the United States is 60 and in Portugal is 15, which means that 4 times as many adults participate in adult education in the United States than in Portugal.

19. **4.** This problem involves number operations. The total amount of Gordon's bills is $23.00 + $31.00 + $48.00 + $13.00 + $114.00 + $39.00 = $268.00. If Gordon allocates only $250.00 to pay these bills, he ends up $268.00 – $250.00 = $18.00 short. Be wary of Choice (2), which is a special trap for people who don't read the question carefully.

20. **12 on standard grid.** This question tests your ability to use the Pythagorean relationship to solve a problem.

If the hypotenuse is 15 feet and the vertical height is 9 feet, the square of the third side is equal to $15^2 - 9^2$, which equals $225 - 81$, which equals 144. The square root of 144 is 12, so 12 is your answer.

21. **5.** This problem tests your knowledge of measurement and geometry by asking you to solve a problem involving volume and weight. You can do this problem in your head, but we take you through the steps using calculations first.

The formula for volume of a cylinder (the cylinder is the circular inside of the pool to a height of 9 inches) is $\pi \times r^2 \times h$, where π = approximately 3.14, r = radius, and h = height. If the diameter is 12 feet, the radius is 6 feet. If the height is 9 inches, it's $\frac{9}{12}$ feet, which can be simplified to $\frac{3}{4}$ feet.

In a formula, don't forget that all units must be the same; that is, feet and feet or inches and inches.

The volume is $(3.14)(6 \times 6)(\frac{3}{4})$ = 85.59 cubic feet.

Because 1 cubic foot weighs 62.42 pounds, the weight of 85.59 cubic feet is 85.59×62.42 = 5,343 or 5,300 rounded to the nearest hundred.

To do this problem in your head, multiply 6×6 to get 36. Multiply 36 by $\frac{3}{4}$ to get 27, and multiply 27 by 3 to get 81. The approximate volume of the pool is 81 cubic feet, which isn't bad for an approximation. For your purposes, say the volume is 80 cubic feet, which is still close. The weight of a cubic foot of water is 62.42 pounds, so round it to 60 pounds. Now, multiply 80 by 60 to get 4,800, which is closest to Choice (5). You can go with that approximation because it's very close to one of the answers.

22. **1.** This question tests your ability to evaluate an answer using a formula. This formula, $I = p \times r \times t$ isn't in the format you want because you want to calculate the rate, which means solving for r. You can change the equation to $r = \frac{I}{p \times t}$, which allows you to calculate the rate from the information given. Substituting into this equation, you get $r = \frac{8}{100 \times 1.25}$. (Remember that 1 year and 3 months is $1\frac{1}{4}$ or 1.25 of a year.)
Then $r = \frac{8}{125}$ = 0.064 = 6.4%.

23. **3.** This question involves number operations. You're asked to calculate — in your head — the answer to a problem.

To use mental math to solve this problem, round everything. Consider the apples at $.80 a pound, bananas at $.20 each, milk at $1.30, and a loaf of bread at $1.00. The total for this approximation is $(2 \times \$.80) + (5 \times \$.20) + \$1.30 + \$1.00 = \$4.90$. Looking at the answer choices, Choice (3) is the only one close to this approximation.

24. **1.** This question tests your knowledge of patterns by asking you to figure out the next number in a series. By looking at the series, it looks like each number is the square of the placement of the number in the list, plus 3. That is, the first number is 1^2 plus 3, or 4. The second number is 2^2 plus 3, or 7. The third term is 3^2 (or 9) plus 3, or 12. The fifth term would be 5^2 (or 25) plus 3, which is 28.

25. **3.** This question tests your skills in geometry by asking you to visualize a graph of an object. Because the object is a rectangle, the opposite sides are equal in length and are parallel, the fourth corner will be 2 units to the left of the y-axis, giving it an x-coordinate of –2, and 2 units below the x-axis, giving it a y-coordinate of –2. Therefore, the point would be (–2,–2).

The *x-coordinate* is the distance from the *y*-axis, and the *y-coordinate* is the distance from the *x*-axis.

Answer Key for Part 1

1. **3**

2. **1**

3. **1680** (on standard grid)

4. **2**

5. **5**

6. **1**

7. **4**

8. **66** (on standard grid)

9. **3**

10. **4**

11. **1**

12.

13. **5**

14. **4**

15. **1**

16. **4**

17.

18. **2**

19. **3**

20. **5**

21. **1**

22. **4**

23. **2**

24. **3**

25. **320** (on standard grid)

Answer Key for Part II

1. **1**

2. **5**

3. **1**

4. **5**

5. **5**

6. **4**

7. **3.20** (on standard grid)

8. **4**

9. **5**

10. **2**

11. **12** (on standard grid)

12. **5**

13. **4.48** (on standard grid)

14. **5**

15. **1**

16.

17. **5**

18. **2**

19. **4**

20. **12** (on standard grid)

21. **5**

22. **1**

23. **3**

24. **1**

25. **3**

Chapter 27

Another Practice Test — Mathematics Test: Parts I and II

● ●

*T*he Mathematics Test consists of multiple-choice and alternate-format questions intended to measure general mathematics skills and problem-solving ability. The questions are based on short readings that often include a graph, chart, or figure.

Like the Language Arts, Writing Test, the Mathematics Test is made up of two parts. Part I allows you to use a calculator to help you answer the questions; Part II doesn't. Each part consists of 25 questions.

You have 45 minutes to complete each part. Work carefully, but do not spend too much time on any one question. Be sure to answer every question.

Formulas you may need are given on the page before the first test question in each part. Only some of the questions will require you to use a formula. Not all the formulas given will be needed.

Some questions contain more information than you will need to solve the problem; other questions do not give enough information. If the question does not give enough information to solve the problem, the correct answer choice is "not enough information given."

Note: The GED test administrator will collect your calculator when you finish Part I of the Mathematics Test. After you turn in your calculator and the administrator tells you to begin Part II, you can move on to that part.

Answer Sheet for Mathematics Test: Part 1

1 ① ② ③ ④ ⑤

2
	/	/	/	
.	.	.	.	.
0	0	0	0	0
1	1	1	1	1
2	2	2	2	2
3	3	3	3	3
4	4	4	4	4
5	5	5	5	5
6	6	6	6	6
7	7	7	7	7
8	8	8	8	8
9	9	9	9	9

3 ① ② ③ ④ ⑤

4 ① ② ③ ④ ⑤

5 ① ② ③ ④ ⑤

6
	/	/	/	
.	.	.	.	.
0	0	0	0	0
1	1	1	1	1
2	2	2	2	2
3	3	3	3	3
4	4	4	4	4
5	5	5	5	5
6	6	6	6	6
7	7	7	7	7
8	8	8	8	8
9	9	9	9	9

7 ① ② ③ ④ ⑤

8 ① ② ③ ④ ⑤

9 ① ② ③ ④ ⑤

10
	/	/	/	
.	.	.	.	.
0	0	0	0	0
1	1	1	1	1
2	2	2	2	2
3	3	3	3	3
4	4	4	4	4
5	5	5	5	5
6	6	6	6	6
7	7	7	7	7
8	8	8	8	8
9	9	9	9	9

11 ① ② ③ ④ ⑤

12 ① ② ③ ④ ⑤

13
	/	/	/	
.	.	.	.	.
0	0	0	0	0
1	1	1	1	1
2	2	2	2	2
3	3	3	3	3
4	4	4	4	4
5	5	5	5	5
6	6	6	6	6
7	7	7	7	7
8	8	8	8	8
9	9	9	9	9

14 ① ② ③ ④ ⑤

15 ① ② ③ ④ ⑤

16 ① ② ③ ④ ⑤

17 ① ② ③ ④ ⑤

18
	/	/	/	
.	.	.	.	.
0	0	0	0	0
1	1	1	1	1
2	2	2	2	2
3	3	3	3	3
4	4	4	4	4
5	5	5	5	5
6	6	6	6	6
7	7	7	7	7
8	8	8	8	8
9	9	9	9	9

19 ① ② ③ ④ ⑤

20 ① ② ③ ④ ⑤

21 ① ② ③ ④ ⑤

22 ① ② ③ ④ ⑤

23 ① ② ③ ④ ⑤

24 ① ② ③ ④ ⑤

25 ① ② ③ ④ ⑤

Answer Sheet for Mathematics Test: Part II

1 ① ② ③ ④ ⑤

2 ① ② ③ ④ ⑤

3 ① ② ③ ④ ⑤

4 ① ② ③ ④ ⑤

5 ① ② ③ ④ ⑤

6 ① ② ③ ④ ⑤

7 ① ② ③ ④ ⑤

8 ① ② ③ ④ ⑤

9 ① ② ③ ④ ⑤

10 ① ② ③ ④ ⑤

11 ① ② ③ ④ ⑤

12 ① ② ③ ④ ⑤

13 ① ② ③ ④ ⑤

14 ① ② ③ ④ ⑤

16 ① ② ③ ④ ⑤

17 ① ② ③ ④ ⑤

18 ① ② ③ ④ ⑤

19 ① ② ③ ④ ⑤

21 ① ② ③ ④ ⑤

22 ① ② ③ ④ ⑤

24 ① ② ③ ④ ⑤

25 ① ② ③ ④ ⑤

Mathematics Test: Part 1

The use of calculators is allowed in Part I only.

Do not write in this test booklet. The test administrator will give you a blank paper for your calculations. Record your answers on the separate answer sheet provided. Be sure all information is properly recorded on the answer sheet.

To record your answers, fill in the numbered circle on the answer sheet that corresponds to the answer you select for each question in the test booklet.

EXAMPLE:

If a grocery bill totaling $15.75 is paid with a $20.00 bill, how much change should be returned?

(1) $5.25

(2) $4.75

(3) $4.25

(4) $3.75

(5) $3.25

(On Answer Sheet)

① ② ● ④ ⑤

The correct answer is "$4.25"; therefore, answer space 3 would be marked on the answer sheet.

Do not rest the point of your pencil on the answer sheet while you are considering your answer. Make no stray or unnecessary marks. If you change an answer, erase your first mark completely. Mark only one answer space for each question; multiple answers will be scored as incorrect. Do not fold or crease your answer sheet. All test materials must be returned to the test administrator.

Note: Refer to Chapter 28 for the answers for Parts I and II of this practice test.

Calculator Directions

To prepare the calculator for use the ***first*** time, press the | ON | (upper-rightmost) key. "DEG" will appear at the top-center of the screen and "0" at the right. This indicates the calculator is in the proper format for all your calculations.

To prepare the calculator for ***another*** question, press the | ON | or the red | AC | key. This clears any entries made previously.

To do any arithmetic, enter the expression as it is written. Press | = | (equals sign) when finished.

EXAMPLE A: $8 - 3 + 9$

First press | ON | or | AC |

Enter the following: | 8 |, | – |, | 3 |, | + |, | 9 |, | = |

The correct answer is 14.

If the expression in parentheses is to be multiplied by a number, press | × | (multiplication sign) between the number and the parenthesis sign.

EXAMPLE B: $6(8 + 5)$

First press | ON | or | AC |

Enter the following: | 6 |, | × |, | (|, | 8 |, | + |, | 5 |, |) |, | = |

The correct answer is 78.

To find the square root of a number

✔ Enter the number.

✔ Press the | SHIFT | (upper-leftmost) key ("SHIFT" appears at the top-left of the screen).

✔ Press | x² | (third from the left on top row) to access its second function: square root.

DO NOT press | SHIFT | and | x² | at the same time.

EXAMPLE C: $\sqrt{64}$

First press | ON | or | AC |

Enter the following: | 6 |, | 4 |, | SHIFT |, | x² |, | = |

The correct answer is 8.

To enter a negative number, such as –8

✔ Enter the number without the negative sign (enter 8).

✔ Press the "change sign" (| +/– |) key, which is directly above the | 7 | key.

All arithmetic can be done with positive and/or negative numbers.

EXAMPLE D: $-8 - (-5)$

First press | ON | or | AC |

Enter the following: | 8 |, | +/– |, | – |, | 5 |, | +/– |, | = |

The correct answer is –3.

The Standard Grid

Mixed numbers, such as 3½, cannot be entered in the standard grid. Instead, represent them as decimal numbers (in this case, 3.5) or fractions (in this case, ½). In addition, no answer on a standard grid can be a negative number, such as –8.

To record your answer for a standard-grid question

- Begin in any column that will allow your answer to be entered.

- Write your answer in the boxes on the top row.

- In the column beneath a fraction bar or decimal point (if any) and each number in your answer, fill in the circle representing that character.

- Leave blank any unused column.

EXAMPLE:

The scale on a map indicates that ½ inch represents an actual distance of 120 miles. In inches, how far apart on the map will the two towns be if the actual distance between them is 180 miles?

The answer to the above example is ¾, or 0.75 inch. A few examples of how the answer could be gridded are shown below.

Points to remember:

- The answer sheet will be machine scored. **The circles must be filled in correctly.**

- Mark no more than one circle in any column.

- Grid only one answer even if there is more than one correct answer.

- Mixed numbers, such as 3½, must be gridded as 3.5 or ½.

- No answer on a standard grid can be a negative number.

The Coordinate-Plane Grid

To record an answer on the coordinate-plane grid, you must have an *x*-value and a *y*-value. No answer for a coordinate-plane question will have a value that is a fraction or decimal.

Mark only the <u>one</u> circle that represents your answer.

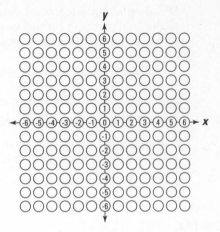

EXAMPLE:

The coordinates of point A, shown on the graph below, are (2,–4).

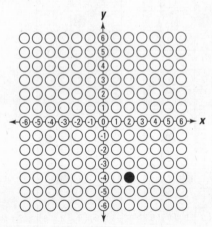

The coordinates of point B, not shown on the graph, are (–3,1). What is the location of point B?

DO NOT MARK YOUR ANSWER ON THE GRAPH ABOVE.

Mark your answer on the coordinate-plane grid on the answer sheet (at right).

CORRECT RESPONSE:

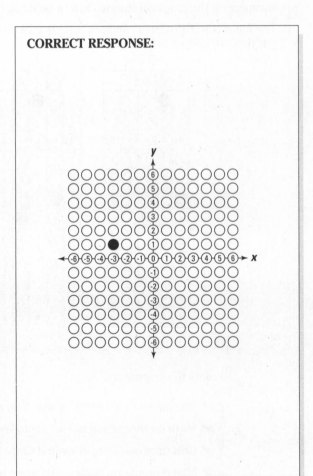

Formulas

AREA of a:

square	Area = side^2
rectangle	Area = length × width
parallelogram	Area = base × height
triangle	Area = ½ × base × height
trapezoid	Area = ½ × (base$_1$ + base$_2$) × height
circle	Area = π × radius^2; π is approximately equal to 3.14

PERIMETER of a:

square	Perimeter = 4 × side
rectangle	Perimeter = (2 × length) + (2 × width)
triangle	Perimeter = side$_1$ + side$_2$ + side$_3$

CIRCUMFERENCE of a circle — Circumference = π × diameter; π is approximately equal to 3.14

VOLUME of a:

cube	Volume = side^3
rectangular solid	Volume = length × width × height
square pyramid	Volume = ⅓ × (base edge)^2 × height
cylinder	Volume = π × radius^2 × height; π is approximately equal to 3.14
cone	Volume = ⅓ × π × radius^2 × height; π is approximately equal to 3.14

COORDINATE GEOMETRY

distance between points = $\sqrt{\left(x_2 - x_1\right)^2 + \left(y_2 - y_1\right)^2}$; (x_1, y_1) and (x_2, y_2) are two points in a plane

slope of a line = $\dfrac{y_2 - y_1}{x_2 - x_1}$; (x_1, y_1) and (x_2, y_2) are two points on the line

PYTHAGOREAN RELATIONSHIP

$a^2 + b^2 = c^2$; a and b are sides, and c is the hypotenuse of a right triangle

MEASURES OF CENTRAL TENDENCY

mean = $\dfrac{x_1 + x_2 + \cdots + x_n}{n}$; where the xs are the values for which a mean is desired, and n is the total number of values for x

median = the middle value of an odd number of *ordered* scores, and halfway between the two middle values of an even number of *ordered* scores

SIMPLE INTEREST — interest = principal × rate × time

DISTANCE — distance = rate × time

TOTAL COST — total cost = (number of units) × (price per unit)

DO NOT BEGIN TAKING THIS TEST UNTIL TOLD TO DO SO

Directions: Choose the <u>one best answer</u> to each question.

Question 1 refers to the following table.

Room Level Dimensions (In Feet)

Dining Room	9.71 x 8.01
Living Room	19.49 x 10.00
Kitchen	13.78 x 7.09
Solarium	19.00 x 8.01
Master Bedroom	13.78 x 12.40
Second Bedroom	11.42 x 8.60

1. Singh has bought a new apartment and wants to carpet the living room, dining room, and master bedroom. If he budgets $35.00 per square yard for carpeting and installation, how much should he budget for these rooms?

    (1) $1,674.08

    (2) $1,457.08

    (3) $1,724.91

    (4) $1,500.08

    (5) $1,745.08

2. After asking for directions to a restaurant, Sarah was told it was 1,000 yards ahead, but her car's odometer reads distances in miles and tenths of miles. How many miles should she drive to find the restaurant to the nearest tenth? Write your answer on the standard grid on the answer sheet.

3. Arthur is making a circular carpet made up of small pieces of cloth glued to a backing. If he wants a carpet that is 7 feet 8 inches across, including a 2-inch fringe all around the carpet, how many square feet of backing does he need to cover, rounded to one decimal place?

    (1) 168.9

    (2) 45.72

    (3) 54.7

    (4) 42.2

    (5) 45.7

4. The vertices of a triangle are A(–6,4), B(–8,–6), and C(8,7). Which side is the longest?

    (1) AB

    (2) BC

    (3) CA

    (4) AC

    (5) not enough information given

Question 5 refers to the following graph.

Results of Flipping Unbalanced Coins

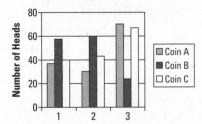

5. As an experiment, a class flips three coins 100 times each and charts the results. The coins are not accurately balanced. From the chart, which coin during which series of tosses is closest to being balanced?

    (1) coin B, third set

    (2) coin C, third set

    (3) coin A, second set

    (4) coin B, first set

    (5) coin C, first set

6. Sam and Arnold were eating ice cream cones. Arnold wondered what volume of ice cream his cone would hold. Sam measured the cone and found it to be 2½ inches across the top and 5½ inches high. How many cubic inches of ice cream would the cone hold, rounded to one decimal place, if it were filled to the top of the cone? Record your answer on the standard grid on the answer sheet.

Go on to next page

7. Donna is very involved with speed walking. In order to keep from getting too bored, she has started counting how many breaths she takes for each of her steps. She figured that she takes 3 breaths for every 27-inch step. How many breaths does she take in a 1,000-yard walk?

   (1) 5,332

   (2) 1,280

   (3) 2,126

   (4) 4,767

   (5) 4,000

8. Yvonne is studying a map. She is 47 miles due south of where she wants to go, but the road goes 17 miles due west to an intersection that then goes northeast to her destination. Approximately how much farther must she travel because of the way the road goes?

   (1) 3 miles

   (2) 20 miles

   (3) 16 miles

   (4) 50 miles

   (5) 45 miles

Questions 9 and 10 are based on the following information.

Carlos wants to buy a used car. He has been told that a car loses 4.3 cents from its book value for every mile over 100,000 that it has traveled. He sees just the car he wants, but it has 137,046 miles on the odometer. If the book value of the car is $13,500, what is the car actually worth?

9. Estimate the realistic value of the car to the nearest $10.

   (1) $10,907

   (2) $13,750

   (3) $87,046

   (4) $12,020

   (5) $11,000

10. Calculate the realistic value of the car to the nearest dollar. Record your answer on the standard grid on the answer sheet.

11. Elena wants to draw a mural on the wall of her house. The wall is 9 feet high and 17 feet long. In order to plan the mural, she draws a scale drawing of the area for the mural on a piece of paper 11 inches long. How high, in inches, should the drawing be to maintain scale?

    (1) 6.2

    (2) 5.8

    (3) 8.5

    (4) 9.0

    (5) 5.0

12. If the slope of a line is 0.75, and $y_2 = 36$, $y_1 = 24$, and $x_1 = 12$, what is the value of x_2?

    (1) 14

    (2) −28

    (3) 28

    (4) −14

    (5) 22

Questions 13 and 14 are based on the following table.

Literacy Rates in Selected Countries

Country	Population	Literacy Rate (%)
China	1,315,844,000	90.9
Cuba	11,269,000	99.8
Ethiopia	77,431,000	35.9
Haiti	8,895,000	54.8
India	1,103,371,000	61.0
Israel	6,725,000	97.1
Russia	143,202,000	99.4
South Africa	47,432,000	82.4
United States	298,213,000	99.0

13. If the literacy rates of China, the United States, and Russia were compared, how many times larger would the greatest literacy rate be than the least? Record your answer, rounded to one decimal point, on the standard grid on the answer sheet.

Go on to next page

14. How many more people (in millions) are literate in India than Israel?

   (1) 109

   (2) 666

   (3) 90

   (4) 100

   (5) 103

15. The probability of an event taking place, P, is equal to the number of ways a particular event can occur, divided by the total number of ways, M, or $P = N \div M$. To test this theory, a student removes all the picture cards from a deck. What is the probability that a card less than the number 6 will be drawn? (Aces are low in this case.)

   (1) 1 in 3

   (2) 1 in 5

   (3) 1 in 2

   (4) 1 in 4

   (5) 1 in 6

Questions 16 and 17 are based on the following information.

   Peter's grades in his final year of high school classes are 81, 76, 92, 87, 79, and 83.

16. In order to get a scholarship, Peter's median grade must be above the median grade for the school, which is 82. By how many points is he above or below that standard?

   (1) 4

   (2) 2

   (3) 1

   (4) 0

   (5) 3

17. If Peter's goal is to graduate with a mean grade of 90%, by how many total points is he failing to achieve his goal?

   (1) 42

   (2) 43

   (3) 44

   (4) 45

   (5) 46

18. Olga has a propane-powered car. She was told it was safe to fill her cylindrical propane tank at a rate of 1¾ cubic feet per minute. If the propane tank measures 4.8 feet long and 2.1 feet in diameter and is empty, how long, in minutes, will it take to fill it? Record your answer, rounded to one decimal, on the standard grid on the answer sheet.

19. The formula for compound interest on a loan is $M = P(1 + i)^n$, where M is the final amount including the principal, P is the principal amount, i is the rate of interest per year, and n is the number of years invested.

   If Amy invested the $1,574 she got as gifts for graduating from elementary school in a Guaranteed Investment Certificate paying 3.75% compound interest calculated annually for the seven years until she graduates from college, how much money would she have?

   (1) $341.18

   (2) $1,978.18

   (3) $462.67

   (4) $2,036.67

   (5) $1,878.18

20. Consider the equation $E = mc^2$. If the value of m triples and the value of c remains constant, what is the effect on E?

   (1) 36 times larger

   (2) 9 times larger

   (3) 27 times larger

   (4) 3 times larger

   (5) no effect

21. An accident investigator calculates a car's speed during a skid by multiplying the following: the square root of the radius of the curve that the center of mass, r, follows × a constant, k, × the drag factor of the road, m. If the speed calculated was 47 miles per hour and the drag factor was 0.65, what was the radius of the curve that the car's center of mass followed?

   (1) 11.6

   (2) 8.5

   (3) 5.8

   (4) 4.9

   (5) not enough information given

Go on to next page

22. Vladimir is designing gas tanks for trucks. The length of the tanks is fixed, but the diameter can vary from 3 to 4 feet. How many more cubic feet of gas does the largest tank hold?

    (1) 8.50

    (2) 3.00

    (3) 2.75

    (4) 4.75

    (5) not enough information given

Questions 23 through 25 are based on the following table.

Summary of Winning Numbers in Seven Consecutive Lottery Draws

Draw Number	Winning Numbers
1	8, 10, 12, 23, 25, 39
2	1, 29, 31, 34, 40, 44
3	1, 14, 26, 38, 40, 45
4	1, 6, 14, 39, 45, 46
5	10, 12, 22, 25, 37, 44
6	13, 16, 20, 35, 39, 45
7	10, 16, 17, 19, 37, 42

23. Based only on the results in the table and assuming that there are 49 possible numbers in the set to be drawn, what are your chances of drawing a 1 in your first draw?

    (1) 1 in 343

    (2) 3 in 343

    (3) 3 in 7

    (4) 1 in 49

    (5) not enough information given

24. If you had to pick one number in this lottery, what would be the odds based on these results that a number greater than 25 would appear in the winning numbers?

    (1) 26 in 49

    (2) almost certain

    (3) 20 in 49

    (4) 17 in 49

    (5) 21 in 26

25. Louise had a theory that the median of the winning numbers in each draw in this lottery would be very close. Considering the winning numbers presented, is Louise's hypothesis accurate?

    (1) not at all

    (2) almost always

    (3) about half the time

    (4) occasionally

    (5) about a quarter of the time

END OF PART I

Mathematics Test: Part II

The use of calculators is <u>not</u> allowed in Part II.

Do not write in this test booklet. The test administrator will give you a blank paper for your calculations. Record your answers on the separate answer sheet provided. Be sure all information is properly recorded on the answer sheet.

To record your answers, fill in the numbered circle on the answer sheet that corresponds to the answer you select for each question in the test booklet.

EXAMPLE:

If a grocery bill totaling $15.75 is paid with a $20.00 bill, how much change should be returned?

(1) $5.25

(2) $4.75

(3) $4.25

(4) $3.75

(5) $3.25

(On Answer Sheet)

① ② ● ④ ⑤

The correct answer is "$4.25"; therefore, answer space 3 would be marked on the answer sheet.

Do not rest the point of your pencil on the answer sheet while you are considering your answer. Make no stray or unnecessary marks. If you change an answer, erase your first mark completely. Mark only one answer space for each question; multiple answers will be scored as incorrect. Do not fold or crease your answer sheet. All test materials must be returned to the test administrator.

If you finish Part II early, you may return to Part I, but without the calculator.

Note: Refer to Chapter 28 for the answers for Parts I and II of this practice test.

The Standard Grid

Mixed numbers, such as 3½, cannot be entered in the standard grid. Instead, represent them as decimal numbers (in this case, 3.5) or fractions (in this case, ½). No answer on a standard grid can be a negative number, such as –8.

To record your answer for a standard-grid question

- Begin in any column that will allow your answer to be entered.

- Write your answer in the boxes on the top row.

- In the column beneath a fraction bar or decimal point (if any) and each number in your answer, fill in the circle representing that character.

- Leave blank any unused column.

EXAMPLE:

The scale on a map indicates that ½ inch represents an actual distance of 120 miles. In inches, how far apart on the map will the two towns be if the actual distance between them is 180 miles?

The answer to the above example is ¾, or 0.75 inch. A few examples of how the answer could be gridded are shown below.

Points to remember:

- The answer sheet will be machine scored. **The circles must be filled in correctly.**

- Mark no more than one circle in any column.

- Grid only one answer even if there is more than one correct answer.

- Mixed numbers, such as 3½, must be gridded as 3.5 or ½.

- No answer on a standard grid can be a negative number.

The Coordinate-Plane Grid

To record an answer on the coordinate-plane grid, you must have an *x*-value and a *y*-value. No answer for a coordinate-plane question will have a value that is a fraction or decimal.

Mark only the <u>one</u> circle that represents your answer.

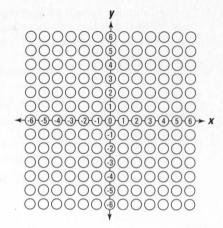

EXAMPLE:

The coordinates of point A, shown on the graph below, are (2,–4).

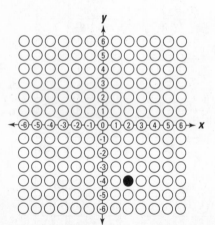

The coordinates of point B, not shown on the graph, are (–3,1). What is the location of point B?

DO NOT MARK YOUR ANSWER ON THE GRAPH ABOVE.

Mark your answer on the coordinate-plane grid on the answer sheet (at right).

CORRECT RESPONSE:

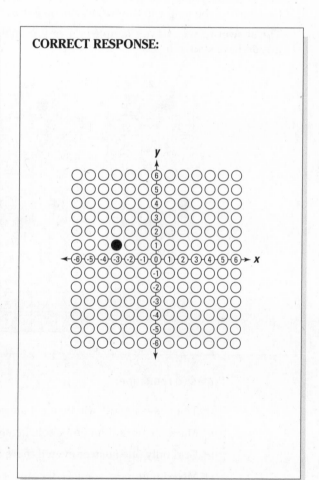

Formulas

AREA of a:

square	Area = side^2
rectangle	Area = length × width
parallelogram	Area = base × height
triangle	Area = ½ × base × height
trapezoid	Area = ½ × (base$_1$ + base$_2$) × height
circle	Area = π × radius^2; π is approximately equal to 3.14

PERIMETER of a:

square	Perimeter = 4 × side
rectangle	Perimeter = (2 × length) + (2 × width)
triangle	Perimeter = side$_1$ + side$_2$ + side$_3$

CIRCUMFERENCE of a circle — Circumference = π × diameter; π is approximately equal to 3.14

VOLUME of a:

cube	Volume = side^3
rectangular solid	Volume = length × width × height
square pyramid	Volume = ⅓ × (base edge)^2 × height
cylinder	Volume = π × radius^2 × height; π is approximately equal to 3.14
cone	Volume = ⅓ × π × radius^2 × height; π is approximately equal to 3.14

COORDINATE GEOMETRY

distance between points = $\sqrt{\left(x_2 - x_1\right)^2 + \left(y_2 - y_1\right)^2}$; (x_1, y_1) and (x_2, y_2) are two points in a plane

slope of a line = $\dfrac{y_2 - y_1}{x_2 - x_1}$; (x_1, y_1) and (x_2, y_2) are two points on the line

PYTHAGOREAN RELATIONSHIP $a^2 + b^2 = c^2$; a and b are sides, and c is the hypotenuse of a right triangle

MEASURES OF CENTRAL TENDENCY

mean = $\dfrac{x_1 + x_2 + \cdots + x_n}{n}$; where the xs are the values for which a mean is desired, and n is the total number of values for x

median = the middle value of an odd number of *ordered* scores, and halfway between the two middle values of an even number of *ordered* scores

SIMPLE INTEREST interest = principal × rate × time

DISTANCE distance = rate × time

TOTAL COST total cost = (number of units) × (price per unit)

DO NOT BEGIN TAKING THIS TEST UNTIL TOLD TO DO SO

Directions: Choose the <u>one best answer</u> to each question.

1. Jerry has started a business selling computers. He can buy a good used computer for $299 and sell it for $449. The only question he has is will he make money. If his overhead (rent, light, heating, and cooling) amounts to $48 per unit and his taxes amount to $3 per unit, how many computers will he have to sell to make $700 per week profit?

    (1) 6

    (2) 9

    (3) 7

    (4) 8

    (5) 10

2. To be awarded a scholarship at Constant College, a student must score above the median of all the students in his or her year and have a mean of at least 90%. Georgio was hoping for a scholarship. Here are his marks:

    Mathematics: 94

    Applied Science: 92

    English: 87

    Spanish: 96

    Physics: 90

    The median mark for the graduating students was 86.5. How many percentage points above the required minimum mean score did Georgio score?

    (1) 3.2

    (2) 1.8

    (3) 86.5

    (4) 91.8

    (5) 93.2

Question 3 refers to the following table.

Geothermal-Electric Capacity in Selected Countries in 2004

Country	Installed Capacity (Megawatts)
China	6
Italy	502
New Zealand	248
Russia	26
United States	1,850

3. What is the approximate ratio of Installed Capacity of the largest to the smallest?

    (1) 1850:26

    (2) 274:2

    (3) 308:1

    (4) 5:4

    (5) 803:1

4. Elayne wants to buy a new fuel-efficient car. She notices that a new car is advertised as getting 100 mpg in city driving and 70 mpg on the highway. After a week of record keeping, she produces the following table for her old car.

Day	City Driving (Miles)	Highway Driving (Miles)
Monday	30	5
Tuesday	35	25
Wednesday	25	10
Thursday	30	20
Friday	20	5
Saturday	5	70
Sunday	5	75

If her old car gets 18 mpg in the city and 12 mpg on the highway and gas costs $2.70 a gallon, how much would she save in a week by buying this new fuel-efficient hybrid car?

    (1) $12.15

    (2) $22.50

    (3) $57.60

    (4) $47.25

    (5) $69.75

Go on to next page

Question 5 refers to the following table.

Interest Rates Offered by Different Car Dealerships

Dealer	Interest Rate Offered
A	Prime + 2%
B	7.5%
C	½ of prime + 5%
D	Prime + 20% of prime for administrative costs

5. Donald is confused. He is looking for a new car, but each dealership offers him a different interest rate. If the prime lending rate is 6%, which dealer is offering Donald the best terms to finance his car?

   (1) Dealer D

   (2) Dealer C

   (3) Dealer B

   (4) Dealer A

   (5) not enough information given

6. The formula for average deviation in statistics is as follows:

   Average deviation $= \dfrac{|x|}{n}$, where x is the deviation, $|x|$ is the absolute value of x, and n is the number of values.

   If the values for the deviation are -7, $+6$, $+2$, -13, -9, and $+17$, what is the average deviation?

   (1) 5

   (2) 6

   (3) 7

   (4) 8

   (5) 9

7. Henry wanted to find out how many people watched *Four's a Mob,* the newest sitcom. He did a survey of 12 of his favorite friends and found that 10 of them had seen the last episode. Knowing that the population of the United States is more than 288,000,000, Henry calculated that 240,000,000 people watched his new favorite sitcom. What is wrong with Henry's conclusion?

   (1) There are more people than that in the United States.

   (2) His sample is too small.

   (3) Some people may have gone out that evening.

   (4) His calculation is wrong.

   (5) Nothing is wrong.

Questions 8 and 9 are based on the following information.

   In September, Ken and Ben wanted to lose some weight by the following July. They figured that by supporting each other, eating a balanced diet with reduced calories, and exercising, they could lose 0.5 pound per week.

8. What mathematical operation(s) would you use to calculate the amount of weight they could lose between the beginning of September and the end of June?

   (1) division

   (2) counting and adding

   (3) division and counting

   (4) counting and multiplication

   (5) subtraction

9. If they stuck to their plans, approximately how much could they each lose between the beginning of September and the end of June?

   (1) 20 pounds

   (2) 50 pounds

   (3) 30 pounds

   (4) 36 pounds

   (5) 48 pounds

Go on to next page ⇨

10. Mary and Samantha are planning a 900-mile trip. Mary says that she can drive at an average speed of 45 miles per hour. Samantha says that she will fly, but it takes her 45 minutes to get to the airport and 1 hour and 15 minutes to get from the airport to her destination after she lands. If she has to be at the airport 3 hours before take-off and the airplane travels an average of 300 mph, how many hours will Samantha have to wait for Mary?

    (1) 2

    (2) 8

    (3) 9

    (4) 12

    (5) 16

Question 11 refers to the following information and graph.

The Queenly Hat Company of Lansing, Michigan, produces designer hats for women who feel that a hat completes an outfit. Their sales vary from quarter to quarter and factory to factory. The chart below reflects their sales for one year.

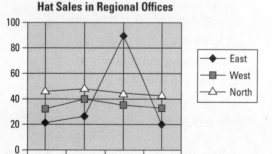

11. Of the three factories, which factories and in which quarters are sales figures approximately in the ratio of 2:1?

    (1) east and west in 2nd quarter

    (2) west and north in 3rd quarter

    (3) east and north in 3rd quarter

    (4) west and east in 1st quarter

    (5) east and west in 1st quarter

Questions 12 and 13 are based on the following table.

Life Expectancy for Urban Dwellers

Age (In Years)	Males	Females
10	61.4	67.3
20	50.3	55.1
30	40.4	45.1
40	32.8	36.5
50	22.1	26.4
60	15.2	17.8
70	9.9	10.7

12. From the data presented in the table, what interpretation could be reached?

    (1) Women age better than men.

    (2) Men live longer than women in all age categories.

    (3) The number of years yet to live decreases with increasing age.

    (4) Urban dwellers live longer than rural dwellers in all age categories.

    (5) Not enough information is given.

13. From the data presented, hypothesize why women live longer than men in an urban environment.

    (1) Women take better care of their health.

    (2) A greater percentage of men work in an urban setting.

    (3) Men are involved in more auto accidents in an urban setting.

    (4) Rural populations live longer.

    (5) Not enough information is given.

Go on to next page

14. The cost of a finished item is equal to 2 times the production cost, plus 120% of the overhead costs at the retail level, plus profit. If three stores, A, B, and C, each sell the product, and store B has a 50% raise in rent, how will this affect the selling price for the item?

    (1) The selling price would go down.

    (2) The selling price would remain the same.

    (3) The selling price would go up.

    (4) Everybody would raise their prices.

    (5) Everybody would lower their prices.

15. Sol wanted to write the population of the United States in scientific notation for a project he was working on. If the population of the United States is 288,257,352, what is the value for *x*, if he wrote the population out as 28.8×10^x? Mark your answer on the standard grid on the answer sheet.

16. Harry and Karry are preparing for the big race. They have been keeping track of their times in the following table:

Comparative Times

Harry's Times (In Seconds)	Karry's Times (In Seconds)
15.6	15.9
14.9	16.1
16.0	15.8
15.8	16.2
16.1	14.8

    What conclusion can you reach from comparing their mean times?

    (1) Karry is slightly faster.

    (2) Harry is slightly slower.

    (3) They are about even.

    (4) Karry has a higher mean time.

    (5) Harry has a higher mean time.

17. Maria bought an apartment. The total floor area is 1,400 square feet. If the ceilings are 9 feet high, and her air system withdraws and replaces 63 cubic feet of air each minute, how long, in minutes, does it take to withdraw and replace all the air in her apartment?

    (1) 180

    (2) 200

    (3) 220

    (4) 240

    (5) 260

18. Peter is emptying his swimming pool. He can pump 9 cubic feet of water per minute. If his pool measures 45 feet by 12 feet with an average depth of 4 feet, when will his pool be empty if he starts pumping at noon on Tuesday?

    (1) 9:00 a.m. on Wednesday

    (2) 4:00 a.m. on Wednesday

    (3) 6:00 p.m. on Tuesday

    (4) 2:00 p.m. on Tuesday

    (5) 4:00 p.m. on Tuesday

19. Mohammed works in sales. He compares his average paychecks for the last four weeks and finds that he has earned an average of $420.00 per week for the four-week month. If he earned $480.00 the first week, $400.00 the third week, and $550.00 the final week, how much did he earn the second week of the month?

    (1) $250.00

    (2) $280.00

    (3) $340.00

    (4) $190.00

    (5) $300.00

20. Georgia started shopping with $500.00 in her purse. When she returned home after shopping, she had $126.00 in her purse and $83 in credit card receipts. How much did she spend shopping? Record your answer in dollars on the standard grid on the answer sheet.

Go on to next page

21. If you open a can flat along the seam and cut almost all the way around each end, what shape would you end up with?

    (1) a circle

    (2) a rectangle with a circle on each end

    (3) a rectangle

    (4) a circle with two rectangles on each end

    (5) a cone

22. Sonya's car uses gasoline in direct proportion to her speed. If she increases her average speed by 10 miles per hour to save time, what is the economic consequence?

    (1) She would save time.

    (2) She would save money.

    (3) She would arrive at about the same time.

    (4) She would spend more money on fuel.

    (5) She would spend the same amount as before.

23. A circle is drawn with its center at the origin and a diameter of 8 units. Where will the circumference intersect the negative y-axis? Mark this point on the coordinate-plane grid on the answer sheet.

24. An accurate fuel gauge reads ⅛ full. If the fuel tank holds 24 gallons, how many gallons of fuel will fill it?

    (1) 18

    (2) 19

    (3) 20

    (4) 21

    (5) 22

25. As part of a mathematics test, Ying was given the following equations to solve:

    $4x + 2y = 20$

    $2x + 6y = 35$

    What is the value of y?

    (1) 4

    (2) 5

    (3) 6

    (4) 7

    (5) 8

END OF TEST

Chapter 28

Answers and Explanations for the Mathematics Test

After taking the Mathematics Test in Chapter 27, use this chapter to check your answers. Take your time as you move through the explanations of the answers for Parts I and II that we provide in the first two sections. They can help you understand why you missed the answers you did. You may also want to read the explanations for the questions you answered correctly because doing so can give you a better understanding of the thought process that helped you choose the correct answers.

If you're short on time, turn to the end of the chapter for abbreviated answer keys for Parts I and II of the Mathematics Test.

Analysis of the Answers for Part I

Note: In all the following explanations, the answers given are the ones that would be read from the display on the calculator if the correct numbers were entered. Calculators always calculate to the maximum number of digits possible on their display. It is up to the person operating the calculator to either set the number of decimal places, if possible, or to make sense of the answer.

1. **3.** In this question, you're given more information than you need. You're given the dimensions of every room in the apartment, but Singh doesn't want to carpet all of them. Because you can use the calculator in this part of the test, you can calculate an accurate answer. The first thing to do is calculate the area of each of the rooms Singh wants to carpet.

Area = length × width, and the length and width must be in the same units.

Here are the areas you come up with:

Living room: $19.49 \times 10.00 = 194.90$

Dining room: $9.71 \times 8.01 = 77.7771$

Master bedroom: $13.78 \times 12.40 = 170.872$

The calculator doesn't put a zero at the end of a number, so the area of the master bedroom has one fewer decimal point than the others, but that's okay.

Next, you have to total the areas: $194.9 + 77.7771 + 170.872 = 443.5491$.

Because the lengths and widths are in feet, the answer is in square feet, BUT the cost of the carpet is in square yards. To convert square feet into square yards, you divide by 9: $443.5491 \div 9 = 49.283233$, which is the area in square yards.

You don't need all these decimal places, but because they're already entered into the calculator, you can keep them.

The carpet budget was for $35.00 a square yard, so you have to multiply the total area Singh wants to carpet by the cost per square yard: $49.283233 \times 35.00 = 1724.9131$.

You need an answer in dollars and cents, so you have to round to two decimal points. (The third decimal integer is 2, so you need to round down.) Therefore, the budget for the carpet is $1,724.91 — Choice (3).

This isn't a good question for guessing because you can't logically eliminate any of the answers without doing the calculations.

2. **0.6 (on standard grid).** To convert yards into miles, you have to divide the number of yards you want to convert into miles by 1,760 (because one mile equals 1,760 yards). 1,000 yards is about 0.57 miles ($1,000 \div 1,760 = 0.568181818$). Odometers usually read to one decimal point, so Sarah should drive about 0.6 miles, rounded up because the second decimal place is larger than 5, which would be just past the restaurant.

3. **5.** The circular carpet has a diameter of 7 feet 8 inches, and it has a 2-inch fringe all the way around it. To calculate the diameter that will be covered by the backing, you have to subtract the width of the fringe (which you get by multiplying 2 inches by 2 because the fringe adds 2 inches to both sides of the circle):

7 feet 8 inches – 4 inches = 7 feet 4 inches

Because the units must be the same to calculate the area, you need to convert the diameter into inches: 7 feet 4 inches = $7 \times 12 + 4 = 88$ inches.

The diameter is twice the radius, thus the radius of the covered area = $^{88}/_2 = 44$ inches.

Now you can use the formula for the area of a circle given on the formula page, $A = \pi \times r^2$, where π is approximately 3.14. Thus, the area is $3.14 \times 44 \times 44 = 6,079.04$ square inches.

Because the question asks for an answer in square feet, you have to convert square inches to square feet by dividing by 144 (12 inches = 1 foot; $12^2 = 144$):

$6,079.04 \div 144 = 42.215555$ or 42.2, rounded to one decimal place.

Choice (4) is what you would've calculated if you forgot to subtract the fringe, and Choice (1) is the result of using the diameter in the formula rather than the radius. Choice (2) is the result of not reading the question carefully; it's close, but it has two decimal places.

4. **2.** This question tests your skills in geometry by asking you to calculate the lengths of sides of a triangle when given the *vertices* (corners of a triangle).

The length of the line joining the points (x_1, y_1) and (x_2, y_2) is $\sqrt{(x_2 - x_1)^2 + (y_2 - y_1)^2}$. Thus, when you substitute the three points of the triangle into this equation, you get the following lengths of *AB, BC,* and *CA* (or *AC*):

$$AB = \sqrt{(-8 - [-6])^2 + (-6 - 4)^2} = 10.198039 = 10.20$$

$$BC = \sqrt{(-8 - [-8])^2 + (7 - [-6])^2} = 20.615528 = 20.62$$

$$CA = \sqrt{(-8 - [-6])^2 + (-7 - 4)^2} = 11.180339 = 11.18$$

From these lengths, you can see that the longest side of the triangle is *BC.*

If you sketch out a graph and locate the points of this triangle, *BC* is obviously the longest side. Sketching could save you a lot of time calculating when the answer is this obvious, so try sketching first.

5. **4.** This question asks you to draw an inference from a graph. Looking carefully at the graph, Coin B in the first set comes closest to 50%, which is the theoretical chance of a head or tail landing when the coin is balanced.

6. **9.0 (on standard grid).** The shape of an ice cream cone is a cone, and the volume of a cone = ⅓ × π × radius² × height, where π is approximately equal to 3.14 (this equation appears on the formula sheet given to you on the test).

   To make the calculations simpler using the calculator, change the fractions to decimals:

   2½ = 2.5, 5½ = 5.5, and ⅓ = 0.3333333

   Now you have to insert the values from the question into the equation (remember that you find the radius by dividing the diameter by 2):

   Volume = 0.3333333 × 3.14 × (2.5 ÷ 2)² × 5.5 = 8.9947896, or 9.0 cubic inches, rounded to one decimal place

   Record your answer on the standard grid.

7. **5.** This problem asks you to solve a problem using basic operations. If Donna takes 3 breaths for every 27-inch step and she walks 1,000 yards (which equal 36,000 inches because there are 36 inches in a yard), she takes 36,000 ÷ 27 = 1,333.3 steps. If she takes 3 breaths per step, she takes 3 × 1,333.3 = 3,999.9 or 4,000 breaths during her 1,000-yard walk.

8. **2.** This problem is a test of your knowledge of how to use the Pythagorean relationship. Sketch out a map for this problem: Due south and due west are at right angles. So Yvonne's journey is a triangle, with the last part of Yvonne's journey as the hypotenuse. Pythagoras (the guy who, as you may expect, came up with the Pythagorean relationship) said that the square of the hypotenuse of a right triangle is equal to the sum of the squares of the other two sides. Thus, the square of the last leg of Yvonne's journey equals $47^2 + 17^2 = 2,498$. The square root of 2,498 is 49.98. Because none of the numbers in this problem has any numbers beyond the decimal point, you can round the answer to 50. However, the question asks how much farther she traveled: She ended up traveling 17 + 50 = 67 miles and would have traveled 47 miles. Therefore, she traveled 67 − 47 = 20 miles farther.

9. **4.** If you want to use approximate values in this problem, you could say that the car depreciates about 4 cents a mile over 100,000 miles. This car is about 37,000 miles over that milestone, which means it has depreciated about 4 × 37,000 cents. You want to solve this in terms of dollars, though. To change cents into dollars, you divide by 100 (because each dollar has 100 cents): 4 × 370 = 1,480.

   You can then subtract this approximate value from the original price: $13,500 − $1,480 = $12,020.

10. **11,907 (on standard grid).** Using the same calculation that you use in problem 9, but using exact values, you get 13,500 − (4.3 × 37,046) ÷ 100 = 11,907.02 or $11,907, when rounded to the nearest dollar.

11. **2.** This problem tests your skills in geometry by asking you to solve a problem involving similarity of geometrical figures. In order to draw a scale drawing, the lengths and widths must be reduced in the same ratio. If the wall is 17 feet or (17 × 12 = 204 inches), and the paper is 11 inches long, the ratio of paper length to real length is 11:204. The width of the drawing must stay in the same ratio. If the height of the drawing is *H*, then

    11:204 = H(9 × 12) or 11:204 = H(108). In other words, $\dfrac{11}{204} = \dfrac{H}{108}$. By cross-multiplying, you get

    H = (11 × 108) ÷ 204 = 5.8. Note that the answer is rounded.

12. **3.** This question tests your skills in algebra by asking you to evaluate a term in an equation. The equation for the slope of a line is $\dfrac{y_2 - y_1}{x_2 - x_1}$.

    Substituting into the equation, you get $0.75 = \dfrac{36 - 24}{x_2 - 12}$

    Then, because 0.75 is the same thing as ¾, you can say the following: $\dfrac{3}{4} = \dfrac{12}{x_2 - 12}$

Cross-multiplying, you get the following:

$$3(x_2 - 12) = 4 \times 12$$
$$3x_2 - 36 = 48$$
$$3x_2 = 48 + 36$$
$$3x_2 = 84$$
$$x_2 = \frac{84}{3} = 28$$

13. **1.1 (on standard grid).** From the table, you can see that the highest literacy rate is Russia at 99.4% and the lowest is China at 90.9%. Looking at Russia and the United States, you can see that their literacy rates are so close that, for all intents and purposes, they're equal, and, thus, there's no need to calculate the comparison.

    If we consider the literacy rate for Russia divided by that for China, we get 99.4 ÷ 90.9 = 1.093509351 or 1.1, rounded to one decimal place.

    The literacy rate of Russia is 1.1 times the literacy rate of China.

14. **2.** The population of India is 1,103,371,000 of which 61.0% are literate. To calculate the number of literate people in India, calculate 61.0% of 1,103,371,000: 1,103,371,000 × 0.61 = 673,056,310.

    Note that you have to change 61.0% to a decimal, 0.61, before you can do the calculation.

    The population of Israel is 6,725,000 of which 97.1% are literate. To calculate the number of literate people in Israel, calculate 97.1% of 6,725,000: 6,725,000 × 0.971 = 6,529,975.

    To calculate how many more illiterate people there are in India, you have to subtract the number of illiterate people in Israel from the number in India: 673,056,310 – 6,529,975 = 666,526,335. Thus, there are 666,526,335 more illiterate people in India than in Israel, which really doesn't tell you anything except that the population of India is substantially larger than that of Israel. The answer is 2,666 million.

    Choice (1) is the number of illiterate people in India, which the question didn't ask for directly. The other answers are just wrong.

    In problems involving calculating big numbers, be careful reading the digits from the calculator and copying them to the page, and recheck the numbers.

15. **3.** This question tests your ability to calculate a probability. Use the formula given ($P = N \div M$) to calculate the results. To draw a card less than 6, the possible cards to be drawn are 5 (less than 6) × 4 (the number of suits) = 20. The total possible number of cards is 52 (total cards in a deck) – the picture cards (4 jacks, 4 queens, and 4 kings), which is 52 – 12 = 40. Now, using the equation, the probability is 20 ÷ 40 = ½. This is another way of writing 1 in 2.

16. **4.** This question tests your skills in statistics by asking you to solve a problem involving the median of a group of numbers. Peter's median grade was 82, which you find by putting his marks in ascending order — 76, 79, 81, 83, 87, 92 — and taking the grade that's right in the middle. If you had an odd number of grades, choosing the grade that's in the middle would be easy. Because you have an even number of grades, the median is the mean (or average) of the two middle numbers, or $\frac{81+83}{2} = 82$.

17. **1.** This question is a test of your skills in data analysis. Peter's average grade was (81 + 76 + 92 + 87 + 79 + 83) ÷ 6 = 83. He failed to meet his goal by 7%. Each percent is equivalent to one point per subject, or 7 × 6 = 42 points.

18. **9.5 (on standard grid).** This question tests you on your skills in measurement involving uniform rates, such as miles per hour, gallons per minute, or, in this case, cubic feet per minute. The tank fills at a uniform rate, which means you can do the question without

getting involved in a series of calculations. The volume of a cylinder = π × radius² × height. Substitute the numbers from the question into this equation:

Volume of cylinder = $3.14 \times (2.1 \div 2)^2 \times 4.8 = 16.61688$ or 16.6

The safe fill rate is 1¾ or 1.75 cubic feet per minute. It would take $16.6 \div 1.75 = 9.4857142$ or 9.5 minutes (rounded to the nearest tenth) to fill the tank.

19. **4.** Using the formula given, you can calculate the total amount she would have at the end of seven years:

$M = P (1 + i)^n$

$M = \$1,574 (1 + .0375)^7$

$M = \$1,574 (1.0375)^7$

$M = \$2,036.67$

20. **4.** This question tests your knowledge of equations by asking you to analyze how a change in one quantity in an exponential equation, $E = mc^2$, results in a change in another quantity. The variation between E and m in this function is linear and direct, which means that whatever happens to m also happens to E. If m is 3 times larger, so is E.

21. **5.** This question tests your ability to figure out when you don't have enough information to complete a problem. Without the value of the constant, the answer can be anything.

22. **5.** Without the length of the tank, you don't have enough information to answer the question.

23. **4.** This question tests your skills in probability. If there are 49 possible numbers in a set, the probability of drawing any one number is 1 in 49.

24. **3.** This problem tests your skills in data analysis by asking you to make inferences from data. If there are 49 numbers drawn in each draw, the odds of drawing a number greater than 25 is 20 in 49. If you count the numbers greater than 25 in the table, you find 20 of them.

Although there's a lot of data in the table, lottery draws are discrete events (they aren't dependent on one another), and the results of one don't affect the results of another. Thus, you can consider only one draw for this question.

25. **4.** This question tests your knowledge of statistics and measures of central tendency (in this case, the median). Consider the following adaptation of the given table. (The median is always the middle number when numbers are lined up from smallest to largest; when you have an even number of numbers, as you do here, take the two middle numbers, add them, and divide by 2 to get the median.)

Summary of Winning Numbers in Seven Consecutive Lottery Draws

Draw Number	*Winning Numbers*	*Median*
1	8, 10, 12, 23, 25, 39	17.5
2	1, 29, 31, 34, 40, 44	32.5
3	1, 14, 26, 38, 40, 45	32.0
4	1, 6, 14, 39, 45, 46	26.5
5	10, 12, 22, 25, 37, 44	23.5
6	13, 16, 20, 35, 39, 45	27.5
7	10, 16, 17, 19, 37, 42	18.0

Louise's theory is a curious one in that she seems to have no basis for it. When considering the numbers presented, two of the medians are close, so the best answer is *occasionally*.

Analysis of the Answers for Part II

1. **4.** To calculate the basic cost of the computer, you have to add the net cost plus the overhead (299 + 48 + 3 = 350). Because each computer costs Jerry $350 and he sells it for $449, he has a net profit of $99 (449 – 350 = 99).

   To calculate the number of computers he'd have to sell to make $700 a week, divide the amount of profit he wants to make by the gross cost of each computer:

   700 ÷ 99 = 7.070707071

   Because you can't sell less than one of a computer, the correct answer is 8.

2. **2.** Georgio's mean mark was (94 + 92 + 87 + 96 + 90) ÷ 5, or 459 ÷ 5, or 91.8. Because the minimum requirement was 90%, Georgio was 91.8 – 90 = 1.8% above the minimum, which is Choice (2). If you answered Choice (4), you forgot to subtract the minimum mark.

3. **3.** The largest installed capacity is the United States with 1,850 megawatts, and the smallest is China with 6 megawatts. To calculate the ratio, you have to divide the largest by the smallest or divide 1,850 by 6, which gives you 308.3333333, which is approximately 308. The ratio is 308:1

4. **3.** The simplest way to figure out this problem is to create a chart by figuring out the costs of the old car per day and the costs of the new car per day by dividing the miles driven by the mileage and multiplying by the cost per gallon. For example, on Monday, Elayne spends this much for her old car in the city: 30 miles ÷ 18 mpg × $2.70 = $4.50.

   After you find out how much Elayne spends on her old car and would spend on her new car per day, you have to add the costs for the seven days of the week together to get the costs per week for each car.

Day	City Driving	Cost in Old Car	Cost in New Car	Highway Driving	Cost in Old Car	Cost in New Car
Mon	30	$4.50	$0.81	5	$1.13	$0.19
Tues	35	$5.25	$0.95	25	$5.63	$0.96
Wed	25	$3.75	$0.68	10	$2.25	$0.39
Thurs	30	$4.50	$0.81	20	$4.50	$0.77
Fri	20	$3.00	$0.54	5	$1.13	$0.19
Sat	5	$0.75	$0.14	70	$15.75	$2.70
Sun	5	$0.75	$0.14	75	$16.88	$2.89
TOTAL	**150**	**$22.50**	**$4.05**	**210**	**$47.25**	**$8.10**

The savings are the difference between the old car's costs and the new car's costs:

($22.50 + $47.25) – ($4.05 + $8.10) = $57.60.

5. **1.** This question tests your ability to use number operations. If you adapt the table, it looks like this:

Interest Rates Offered by Different Car Dealerships

Dealer	Interest Rate Offered	Equivalent Rate
A	Prime + 2%	8% (6% + 2%)
B	7.5%	7.5%
C	½ of prime + 5%	8% (½ of 6% + 5% = 3% + 5%)
D	Prime + 20% of prime for administration	7.2% (6% + [20% of 6%] = 6% + 1.2%)

Dealer D is offering the best terms for financing the car.

6. **5.** This question tests your skills in algebra because it asks you to use an equation to solve a problem.

   Using the formula given in the question, you can figure out that the average deviation is (7+6+2+13+9+17) ÷ 6 = 54 ÷ 6 = 9. Because the absolute values are used, the numbers without the signs are used. You divide by 6 because there are six values to consider.

   The *absolute value* (what's inside the two vertical lines) of a number is its value without regard to its sign. So, the absolute value of a negative number is always a positive number.

7. **2.** In statistics, for results to be valid, samples must be large and random. In this question, the sample is too small to tell anyone anything of statistical significance, and the entire sample consists of friends, not randomly selected people. The best answer is that the sample was too small.

8. **4.** This question tests your skills in number operations by asking you to select the appropriate operations to solve this problem. To solve it, you count the number of weeks between September and the end of June and multiply by 0.5 (that is, 0.5 pound) to get the answer, so you use counting and multiplication.

9. **1.** This question tests your skills in using estimation to solve a problem involving number operations. There are ten months between the beginning of September and the end of June. If you estimate that there are 4 weeks in each month (there are actually about 4.3 weeks per month), there are 40 weeks in this period of time. Each of them could lose about 20 pounds (40 × 0.5).

10. **4.** This question tests your skills in measurement to solve a problem involving uniform rates. If Mary can drive at an average speed of 45 miles per hour, it will take her 900 ÷ 45 = 20 hours to drive the 900 miles. Samantha, on the other hand, will travel at 300 miles per hour on a plane for a time of 900 ÷ 300 = 3 hours, but she will add 45 + 75 (1 hour and 15 minutes is 75 minutes) + 180 (that's 3 hours in minutes) = 300 minutes. 300 minutes is 5 hours (300 ÷ 60). Her total trip would be 3 hours + 5 hours = 8 hours in duration, or 12 hours shorter than Mary's trip.

11. **3.** Looking at the graph, in the third quarter, the east plant seems to have produced twice (ratio of 2:1) as many hats as the north plant.

   This answer is considered an approximation because the graphs aren't perfectly accurate.

12. **3.** This question tests your ability to interpret data presented in a table. The data presented is the number of years left to live at different age levels. The only valid interpretation you can reach from this data is that the number of years yet to live decreases with increasing age, which is Choice (3).

   Read the answers as carefully as you read the questions. Women may have a greater life expectancy, but that doesn't necessarily mean they age better or worse than men. That's a topic for another question.

13. **5.** This question tests your skills in data analysis by asking you to evaluate arguments. You also have to discover whether you have enough information to decide on a reason for why women live longer than men. In this case, you don't have enough information in the table to develop any hypothesis, which means Choice (5) is correct. In question 12, you have enough information to make a broad, sweeping generalization, but that isn't the case in this question. Always read questions carefully to make sure the question is answerable before choosing an answer.

14. **3.** This question tests your skills in analysis by asking you to explain how a change in one quantity affects another quantity. The price of the article is set by a linear function involving the overhead (the costs of doing business that don't change with how many products you sell — things like rent, utility bills, salaries, and so on), the cost of acquiring the item, and the profit. If any of these numbers go up, the selling price goes up, too, which is why the correct answer is Choice (3). In this equation, each of the terms affects the answer in a linear manner. If the rent goes up, either the selling price goes up or the profit goes down, but, in either situation, the raise in rent will have an effect on the basic cost of an item and, thus, the selling price, as well.

15. **7 (on standard grid).** This question tests your skills in number operations by asking you to write a large number in scientific notation. To write 288,257,352 in scientific notation, you start with an approximation — 288,000,000 is close enough. The number of zeros defines the power of x. The population could be written as 288×10^6. Because Sol wants to write it more properly as $28.8 \times$ a power of ten, the power would have to be one higher than 6, or 7.

16. **4.** This question tests your skills in statistics by asking you to compare measurements of central tendency (the means or averages). Harry's mean time is (15.6 + 14.9 + 16.0 + 15.8 + 16.1) ÷ 5 = 15.68. Karry's mean time is (15.9 + 16.1 + 15.8 + 16.2 + 14.8) ÷ 5 = 15.76. Karry has a higher mean time (which means that Harry is slightly faster).

17. **2.** This question tests your skills in measurement by asking you to solve a problem involving volume. If the total floor area is 1,400 square feet and the ceilings are 9 feet high, the volume of the apartment is $1,400 \times 9 = 12,600$ cubic feet. If the air system can replace 63 cubic feet per minute, it requires $12,600 \div 63 = 200$ minutes to withdraw and replace all the air, which is Choice (2). The other answer choices are wrong, but Choices (1) and (3) are close enough that if you tried to do the question using approximations you might become confused.

REMEMBER

When some of the answers are close in value, it's worth the extra effort to do the calculations instead of estimating.

18. **5.** This question tests your skills in measurement and geometry. You have to solve a problem involving uniform rates. Peter's swimming pool holds $45 \times 12 \times 4 = 2,160$ cubic feet of water. He can pump 9 cubic feet per minute. It would take him $2,160 \div 9 = 240$ minutes. To get from hours to minutes, divide by 60 (because every hour has 60 minutes). So it would take Peter $240 \div 60 = 4$ hours to empty his pool. If he started pumping at noon on Tuesday, Peter would finish four hours later, which is at 4:00 p.m. on Tuesday.

TIP

An easy way to simplify this problem is to divide one number by 9 first: $45 \div 9 = 5$. Then you can multiply: $5 \times 12 \times 4 = 240$. This calculation is easier to do in your head than the other way.

19. **1.** This question tests your skills in algebra by asking you to analyze data used to calculate the mean of a set of numbers. If Mohammed earned an average of $420.00 for four weeks, he earned a total of $420 \times 4 = \$1,680.00$. The other three weeks he earned $480.00 + $400.00 + $550.00 = \$1,430.00$. The remaining week he earned $1,680.00 - $1,430.00 = \$250.00$.

20. **457 (on standard grid).** This question tests your skills in number operations. Georgia spent $500.00 - $126.00 = \$374.00$ plus $83.00 in credit card purchases. $374.00 + $83.00 = \$457.00$, or 457 in dollars on the standard grid.

21. **2.** This question tests your skills in geometry and spatial visualization. If you opened a can flat along the seam, you'd have a rectangle and two circles, one on each end. Questions of this type require the use of imagination. Imagine a can and cut it along the seam in your head, and then cut around the bottom and top to make it lay flat. The result would be a rectangle from the can itself and a circle on each end from the top and bottom.

22. **4.** This question tests your skills by asking you to read carefully to answer a question. If Sonya's car uses gasoline in direct proportion to her speed, the faster she goes, the more gas she uses. The more gas she uses, the more it costs her to drive, which is an economic consequence — so Choice (4) is correct. Choice (1) isn't an economic consequence, although it is true in fact.

Read the answers carefully. A right answer that doesn't answer the question is wrong.

23. **(0,–4) on coordinate-plane grid.** If the center is at the origin and the diameter (which is twice the radius) is 8 units, the circle will intersect each of the axes (that's the plural of axis) at a distance of 4 units from it. Therefore, it intersects the negative y-axis at (0,–4).

24. **4.** If the gauge reads ⅛ full, it has 24 ÷ 8 = 3 gallons of fuel left in it. Because it holds 24 gallons, it needs 24 – 3 = 21 gallons to fill it.

25. **2.** To solve these equations, you need to subtract one from the other and end up with just ys. To get rid of one of the variables using this method, you need to have the same coefficient in front of the variable you're planning to eliminate. You can multiply each term of an equation by a number and still maintain the equation. Here's how:

Multiply the second equation by 2 and leave the first equation as it is (or multiply by 1, which is the same thing):

$1(4x + 2y = 20) = 4x + 2y = 20$

$2(2x + 6y = 35) = 4x + 12y = 70$

Subtract, and you get $10y = 50$; $y = 5$.

Note that you can also multiply the second equation by –2 and add the two equations together. Either way gets you the same answer.

Answer Key for Part 1

1. **3**
2. **0.6** (on standard grid)
3. **5**
4. **2**
5. **4**
6. **9.0** (on standard grid)
7. **5**
8. **2**
9. **4**
10. **11,907** (on standard grid)
11. **2**
12. **3**
13. **1.1** (on standard grid)

14. **2**
15. **3**
16. **4**
17. **1**
18. **9.5** (on standard grid)
19. **4**
20. **4**
21. **5**
22. **5**
23. **4**
24. **3**
25. **4**

Answer Key for Part II

1. **4**

2. **2**

3. **3**

4. **3**

5. **1**

6. **5**

7. **2**

8. **4**

9. **1**

10. **4**

11. **3**

12. **3**

13. **5**

14. **3**

15. **7** (on standard grid)

16. **4**

17. **2**

18. **5**

19. **1**

20. **457** (on standard grid)

21. **2**

22. **4**

23.

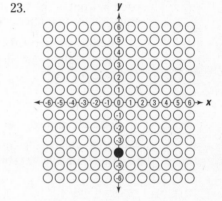

24. **4**

25. **2**

Part VII
The Part of Tens

The 5th Wave

By Rich Tennant

In this part . . .

This part — which appears in all *For Dummies* books — includes lists of tens that amaze, astonish, astound, amuse, clarify, edify, educate, elucidate, expound, and explain. (Note that we use ten verbs here.)

This part gives you tips for succeeding on the GED tests, maximizing your test scores, and using that wonderful diploma after you pass all the tests.

If you use the material in this book seriously and have some fun with what we provide you, you'll be prepared for the tests. Only you can make a difference in your life. Start with this part and make up your own list of how a GED diploma will change your life for the better.

Chapter 29

Ten (Plus One) Surefire Ways to Maximize Your GED Test Scores

. . . .

In This Chapter
▶ Finding ways to improve your skills for each test
▶ Giving yourself time to study and sleep
▶ Preparing yourself for the big day

. . . .

*O*f course you want to do well on the GED — otherwise, you wouldn't be reading this book. But we also know that your time is limited, so this chapter gives you ten (er, eleven — we got a little carried away!) ideas and tips for doing well on your tests.

Studying Subject-Matter Books

If you've taken all the practice tests in this book (see Chapters 5, 7, 10, 12, 15, 17, 20, 22, 25, and 27), you may have identified key areas in which you're lacking skills. Although those practice tests can't predict your score, they do give you practice and a general idea of your strengths and weaknesses. If you didn't get 80 percent correct on any of the sample tests, you need to improve your skills in that area.

We recommend that you visit your local bookstore or library for the many *For Dummies,* *CliffsNotes,* and *CliffsQuickReview* books (Wiley) that are meant just for students. For example, consider the following fun, interesting, and easy-to-read *For Dummies* books that can either improve your skills or simply make you more familiar with (and, therefore, more comfortable with) certain subjects:

✔ *Algebra For Dummies* by Mary Jane Sterling (mathematics)

✔ *Algebra II For Dummies* by Mary Jane Sterling (mathematics)

✔ *Algebra Workbook For Dummies* by Mary Jane Sterling (mathematics)

✔ *Anatomy and Physiology For Dummies* by Donna Rae Siegfried (science)

✔ *Astronomy For Dummies,* 2nd Edition, by Stephen P. Maran (science)

✔ *Biology For Dummies* by Donna Rae Siegfried (science)

✔ *The Civil War For Dummies* by Keith D. Dickson (social studies)

✔ *Congress For Dummies* by David Silverberg (social studies)

✔ *English Grammar For Dummies,* 2nd Edition, by Geraldine Woods (language arts)

✔ *Everyday Math For Dummies* by Charles Seiter (mathematics)

✔ *Geography For Dummies* by Charles Heatwole (social studies, science)

✔ *Geometry For Dummies,* 2nd Edition, by Mark Ryan (mathematics)

- *Poetry For Dummies* by The Poetry Center, John Timpane, and Maureen Watts (language arts)

- *Politics For Dummies,* 2nd Edition, by Ann DeLaney (social studies)

- *Shakespeare For Dummies* by John Doyle and Ray Lischner (language arts)

- *Supreme Court For Dummies* by Lisa Paddock (social studies)

- *U.S. History For Dummies,* 2nd Edition, by Steve Wiegand (social studies)

- *Vocabulary For Dummies* by Laurie E. Rozakis (language arts)

- *World History For Dummies,* 2nd Edition, by Peter Haugen (social studies)

- *World War II For Dummies,* by Keith D. Dickson (social studies)

To find out what other helpful *For Dummies* books have been published since this book was written, check out www.dummies.com.

Consider browsing through the *For Dummies* travel books to help with social studies. You may also want to review some of the *For Dummies* workplace books on managing people and running a business to get acquainted with workplace reading material, which often appears on the Language Arts, Reading Test.

The *CliffsNotes Literature* series helps you study specific books, plays, poems, and short stories. Although the Language Arts, Reading Test doesn't test your knowledge of literature, reading literature is always a good way to help you prepare for that test. Consider reading one or two of Shakespeare's plays and other drama, poetry from 1600 to the present, novels from 1920 to the present, and recent short stories. If you're unsure about anything you read, pick up the *CliffsNotes* book on that piece of literature, and discover what you may have missed on your first reading. To find a *CliffsNotes* title for the literature you're reading, go to www.cliffsnotes.com.

Books in the *CliffsQuickReview* and *CliffsAP* series may also be helpful. Note that the *CliffsAP* series is geared toward Advance Placement students who are in high school but are trying to take tests that allow them to earn college credits. *Cliffs* and *CliffsQuickReview* books are geared specifically to high school and college students who are struggling to understand a particular subject matter. Before buying any books, browse through each title you're considering to make sure it meets your needs.

Make full use of your library (including interlibrary loans) so that you don't end up spending all your hard-earned money on books. Here are just a few of the most helpful *CliffsNotes* books related to GED test areas:

- *Cliffs Math Review for Standardized Tests* by Jerry Bobrow (mathematics)

- *Cliffs Memory Power for Exams* by William Browning (general)

- *Cliffs Verbal Review for Standardized Tests* by William Covino and Peter Orton (language arts)

- *CliffsAP Biology,* 3rd Edition, by Phillip Pack (science)

- *CliffsAP Chemistry,* 4th Edition, by Bobrow Test Preparation Services (science)

- *CliffsAP English Language and Composition,* 3rd Edition, by Barbara Swovelin (language arts)

- *CliffsAP English Literature and Composition,* 2nd Edition, by Allan Casson (language arts)

- *CliffsAP United States History,* 3rd Edition, by Paul Soifer and Abraham Hoffman (social studies)

- *CliffsQuickReview Algebra I* by Jerry Bobrow (mathematics)

- *CliffsQuickReview Algebra II* by Edward Kohn and David Alan Herzog (mathematics)
- *CliffsQuickReview American Government* by Paul Soifer, Abraham Hoffman, and D. Stephen Voss (social studies)
- *CliffsQuickReview Anatomy and Physiology* by Phillip Pack (science)
- *CliffsQuickReview Astronomy* by Charles Peterson (science)
- *CliffsQuickReview Basic Math and Pre-Algebra* by Jerry Bobrow (mathematics)
- *CliffsQuickReview Biology* by I. Edward Alcamo and Kelly Schweitzer (science)
- *CliffsQuickReview Chemistry* by Harold D. Nathan and Charles Henrickson (science)
- *CliffsQuickReview Economics* by John Duffy (social studies)
- *CliffsQuickReview Geometry* by Edward Kohn (mathematics)
- *CliffsQuickReview Linear Algebra* by Steven A. Leduc (mathematics)
- *CliffsQuickReview Physical Geology* by Mark J. Crawford (social studies)
- *CliffsQuickReview Physics* by Linda Huetinck and Scott Adams (science)
- *CliffsQuickReview Psychology* by Theo Sonderegger (social studies)
- *CliffsQuickReview U.S. History I* by Paul Soifer and Abraham Hoffman (social studies)
- *CliffsQuickReview U.S. History II* by Paul Soifer and Abraham Hoffman (social studies)
- *CliffsQuickReview Writing, Grammar, Usage, and Style* by Jean Eggenschwiler and Emily Dotson Biggs (language arts)

Some preparation books (books like this one that prepare you to take the GED tests) also include tutoring in test-content areas. (Those books are usually from 800 to 1,000 pages long, which is far more pages than this book had room for.) Visit your bookstore or local library and look for an up-to-date test-preparation book that gives you at least two additional sets of practice tests, is easy to understand, and includes some skill-building material in the areas in which you need help. You may also want to try taking an Official GED Practice Test. This test is available at testing centers and preparation classes. The official practice test can help you predict your score. This score allows you to see how close you are to passing the real GED.

You may also want to check out *The SAT I For Dummies,* 6th Edition, by Geraldine Woods and *The ACT For Dummies,* 4th Edition, by Michelle Rose Gilman, Veronica Saydak, and Suzee Vlk (Wiley). Although they're aimed at juniors and seniors who are taking college-entrance exams, if you can master the review material and sample questions, you prepare yourself not only for the GED but also for college-entrance exams after you receive your diploma.

Enrolling in a GED Preparation Class

If you like to interact with other people and prefer a teacher to guide you through your preparation, consider taking a *GED preparation class:* a class designed to prepare you to take and pass the GED tests. These classes are generally offered free of charge.

To find a class in your location, ask around: Question people you know who have taken the GED, administrators and teachers at your local high school or college, or workers at your local GED testing center. You may also be able to take distance-learning courses (which means you do your assignments on your own and contact your instructor via the Internet), which may be a good choice for you.

After deciding on a few potential classes, visit the class or instructor, if possible. Make sure that his or her teaching style matches your learning style. The preparation class will be a big investment of your time, so shop around wisely.

After choosing a preparation class, form a study group — a small group of other GED test takers who help each other with study questions. Then you can help each other study and ask each other questions about different aspects of the test. Not to mention, you can still go out with your friends and have a good time without boring everyone by talking only about the GED tests.

Be wary before committing to a group, though: If the other group members' idea of studying is to party for three hours to get ready for five minutes of study, and you want to study for three hours to get ready for five minutes of social activity, you won't be happy. Talk to the other members of the study group and listen to what the goals are for the group. If you can find a suitable group, make a commitment and enjoy your new friends.

Scheduling Time to Study

Whether you study on your own or with an instructor, set aside time each day to study. Stick to your schedule as if your grade depends on it (and, by the way, it does!). Study regularly by doing the following:

1. **Take practice tests to find out with which subject area(s) you struggle.**

   Check each answer on the practice tests, and read all the answer explanations. Make sure you understand your mistakes.

2. **Focus your studies on the subject area(s) in which you're weak.**

3. **Take more practice tests.**

Preparing for the Test in Your Mind

To make yourself less anxious about the GED tests, visualize yourself at the tests. In your mind, see yourself enter the room, sit down at the desk, hear the instructions, and pick up your pen or pencil. Go through this routine in your mind until it begins to feel familiar. Then see yourself opening the question booklet and skimming the questions (questions that are likely familiar to you because you've taken many practice tests). See yourself noting the easy questions and beginning to answer them. By repeating this visual sequence over and over again in your mind, it becomes familiar — and what's familiar isn't nearly as stressful as what's unfamiliar.

Getting Good Rest the Week before the Test

As part of your plan for preparation, include some social time, some down time, and plenty of time for rest because everyone performs better when well rested. In fact, your memory and ability to solve problems improve remarkably when you're properly rested.

Whatever you do, don't panic about your upcoming tests and stay up all night (or every night for a week) right before your tests. Instead, plan your last week before the test so that you get plenty of sleep and are mentally and physically prepared for the test.

Wearing Comfortable Clothes

Consider the following situation. You're about to sit for approximately seven and a half hours on what is probably an uncomfortable chair. The room may be too warm or too cold.

So, choosing from the following answers, what's the appropriate dress for the GED tests?

(1) formal dress because this is an important occasion

(2) a parka over a bathing suit because one can never predict the weather

(3) something very comfortable so that you can concentrate on the tests

(4) your best clothes because you need to impress others

(5) whatever is handiest in your closet

If you answered Choice (3), you have the idea. Dress comfortably and in layers. All of your concentration should be on the tests, not your clothes, not on the people around you, and not on the conditions in the room.

Making Sure You Have Proper Identification

To take the GED tests, you need acceptable picture identification. Because what's *acceptable* may vary from state to state, check with your state GED office or your local testing center (or check the information they send to you after you sign up) before the test.

The picture I.D. required is usually a driver's license or passport; at any rate, it's usually something common and easy to obtain. Just check in advance for what's required, and make sure you have it ready for the tests.

Practicing Your Route to the Test Site

On certain days, you just don't want to get lost. These days include your wedding day, an important interview, and the day you're taking the GED tests. Make sure you plan a route from your home to the testing site. Map it out and practice getting to the test center.

Leave extra time for surprises. You never know when your street could be declared an elephant crossing and a pack of elephants decides to meander across your road. The crowd and elephants could make you late for the tests unless you allow yourself some extra time.

Arriving Early

Consider the following two scenarios:

✔ Test Taker One arrives 15 seconds before the beginning of the tests and feels nothing but panic. Test Taker One barely arrives at the desk in time to lift a pencil and begin the test. Test Taker One is so distracted that he or she takes 15 minutes to calm down, and by then, the first test is well underway.

✔ Test Taker Two arrives 40 minutes early. Test Taker Two has time to drink some coffee and relax before the test. Sitting calmly at the desk, Test Taker Two relaxes, listens to the instructions, and begins to take the first test in a relaxed manner.

Which test taker would you rather be? Leave early for the test! Let other people stress and panic. Be the relaxed, prepared test taker.

A couple of weeks before the tests, confirm the time your test is supposed to begin. You may receive a letter of confirmation before your testing date. If not, follow up with the testing center with a phone call.

Starting with Easy Questions

As you open each test, start with the easy questions — the ones you know you can do. As soon as you get the test, skim the questions, identify the easy ones, and do those problems first. Only after doing so are you ready to tackle the other questions in a relaxed, confident mood.

Whatever you do, don't mark in the test book as you move through the questions! Doing so could get you tossed out of the test.

Using Relaxation Techniques

Feeling a bit of stress before taking the GED tests is normal. A little bit of stress can actually help you function better, but you don't want to become so stressed that you can't think.

You need to find some ways to relax. Here are some techniques that may work for you:

- **Think positively.** Instead of listing all the negative things that may happen, start listing the positive things. You can pass the GED tests. You can go on to college. You can get a great job. You can win the lottery — well, maybe that's going too far. Don't be greedy. Just be positive!

- **Breathe deeply.** The first thing to remember during a stressful situation is to breathe. The second thing is to breathe deeply. You can do so by following these steps:

   1. **Find your diaphragm.**

      Not a diagram, although you could use a diagram to find your diaphragm. Your diaphragm is that flat muscle under your ribcage that fills your lungs with air. It's above your navel.

   2. **Breathe in and make your diaphragm rise as much as you can.**

   3. **Exhale slowly.**

   4. **Repeat, making your diaphragm rise higher each time.**

   After you see how this process relaxes you, try it before each test.

- **Count backward from ten (in your head).** You can do this before any test, not just the math one. Start to count backward from ten with no thoughts in your mind. If a thought, even a teeny one, enters your mind, you have to start over. See how many times it takes to count from ten to one without a single thought entering your mind.

   Don't do this *during* the tests, only *before*. This exercise could eat up precious time if you tried it during one of the tests.

✔ **Clench and unclench your fists.** This simple relaxation technique involves your hands and reminds your mind to relax:

1. **Sit with your hands in front of you.**

2. **Inhale deeply as you slowly clench your fists.**

3. **After they're clenched, slowly exhale as you unclench them.**

You may have to repeat this process several times, but within a couple of repetitions, you'll begin to feel relaxed.

✔ **Stare out a window.** Stare out a window, far into the distance. Try to see a point beyond the horizon. As you do, feel your eyes relax. Let your eyes relax until the feeling spreads to every part of your body. Enjoy the feeling long enough to let go of all the stress that has built up. When you're calm and full of energy, return to the test.

If your testing room doesn't have a window, stare at a blank wall and envision your favorite relaxing scene. Don't be tempted, however, to close your eyes. If you're the least bit tired or stressed, you may fall asleep and not wake up until the test is over.

Chapter 30

Ten Ways to Be Successful on the GED Tests

In This Chapter

▶ Doing what you can to prepare before the test

▶ Avoiding common mistakes on test day

▶ Weeding out some bad habits so that you can succeed

You want to be successful on the GED tests. If you didn't, you wouldn't have this book in your hands and spend all your spare time preparing for the tests, right? For your benefit, we present ten quick and easy ways to help you achieve your goal in this chapter.

Selecting the Best-Possible Test Date

Why plan to take your GED tests when you have a million other things to do? Sure, you probably live a busy life all the time, but do your best to find a period in that busy life when you can concentrate on preparing for and passing the tests. Choose the test date wisely. If you have enough time to prepare, you'll do well. It's just that simple. Select a date that gives you enough time to prepare but not one that's so far in the distance that you'll retire before you take the tests. Check out Chapter 1 for information on scheduling the test.

Preparing, Preparing, and Then Preparing Some More

If you're thinking of just signing up for the test, waiting until the test day comes, and walking in to take it — without ever preparing or studying — you'll likely be disappointed at your test results. You wouldn't start to build a house by arriving at the construction site with nothing but your good looks and a smile, right? A successful completion — of any goal — requires careful and complete planning. Check out Chapter 3 to read about some general tips for preparing for the tests. Also spend some time reviewing Chapters 4, 9, 14, 19, and 24, which give you specific tips and hints for preparing for each individual test.

Being confident is great. Being overconfident can cause problems. If you think you may be overestimating your knowledge, take as many practice tests as you can, and take them under the same time conditions as the actual tests. If your confidence exceeds the results you get on the practice tests, don't knock the practice tests. Consider yourself lucky to know in which areas you need more practice. Then start seriously preparing for what may turn out to be a life-changing situation. Preparation is never wasted, and time wasted is never preparation.

Remaining Realistic

When you take the test, you need to keep a level head. Preparing (see the preceding section) is the best way to accomplish this goal. Optimism alone won't assure success. But an optimistic attitude combined with realistic preparation will get you far in this world. Your mental attitude can steer you in that direction. Look at the bright side, but be realistic.

To help, make a list of all the things you could worry about. If you find it easier, make a series of lists: personal, family, community, state, country, region, world, ecological, environmental, financial, governmental, and so on. Make the list as long and complete as you can. Leave it for a day, and try to add more items later. When your list is as complete as possible, read it, toss it, and promise not to worry about anything on the list until after you finish taking the GED tests. Worrying distracts you from the one and only thing that should be on your worry list: passing the GED tests. On the other hand, if you make a list of the changes that could come about in your life after you pass the GED tests, you can look toward the future. Realistic preparation can help you accomplish your goals.

Being on Time for When the Tests Start

If you're late to the test site, you probably won't be allowed to enter and you'll have to take the tests on another date. Not to mention, you'll probably have to pay again to take the tests. Who needs all this grief? All you have to do to prevent this tragedy is to be early for the tests, which, contrary to popular belief, isn't as difficult as it may seem. You can prepare for your route and arrival the way you prepare for the tests. Check out some route maps on the Internet. Look into the schedules for your local public transportation services. Do your research, leave extra time for unforeseen situations, and arrive on time and ready for the tests.

Keeping Your Comments to Yourself

A little bit of stress is normal when you walk into a test. The last thing you want, though, is to increase your stress level. Although it may seem antisocial, keep your serious conversations to a minimum just before the tests. If you want to exchange pleasantries about the weather, go ahead. If you want to arrange to go for coffee after the tests, plan away. If you want to get into a serious conversation about how everything you've done to this point will only guarantee failure, run away as fast as you can and don't talk to anyone! People hanging around the test center or walking into the tests who have a hundred hints to tell everybody are guaranteed to increase your stress level. If you've prepared, you're ready. Listen to the voice in your head that says you're ready. Don't listen to the sidewalk experts who are going into the tests with you. If they were so smart, they'd already have their GED.

Staying Focused on the Task at Hand

An archer who wants to hit the bull's-eye keeps all his mental faculties focused on the goal at hand. Nobody ever hit the center of the target daydreaming about the next social gathering. For this reason, put your mind on a leash; don't let it wander during the test. Letting your mind wander back to the greatest vacation you ever had can be very relaxing, but letting it wander during a test can be a disaster. You want your mind sharp, keen, and focused before and during the tests, so concentrate on the task at hand — doing your best and passing the GED.

Be sure to get plenty of sleep in the nights and weeks before the test. If you're well rested, you'll have an easier time focusing on each question and answering it correctly.

Looking at Only Your Test

If there were a Biggest Mistake Award for test takers, it would be awarded to someone who looks at his or her neighbor's paper during the test. This action is called cheating and is a very serious matter. Not only will you be asked to leave the testing center, but you may have to wait from several months to a year before you're allowed to schedule another test. Look at only your test. For the duration of the tests, your test and answer booklets are the most beautiful, fascinating items in the world. Thus, it's impossible not to spend all your time looking at them. More than likely, your neighbor will have a different test.

Don't even give the slightest hint that you may, possibly, be looking at someone else's paper. The test proctor probably won't care about what you were actually doing; what he saw was you looking in the general direction of another person's paper, which, as you know, is considered cheating.

Writing Clearly and Carefully

The GED has only one test that allows you to write out an answer (as opposed to filling in circles). For the essay in Part II of the Language Arts, Writing Test (see Part II of this book), make sure you write clearly and carefully. Two test graders have to read it, and if they misread it because the writing is impossible to read, you'll lose marks. If your writing is naturally sloppy, spend some time improving it or figure out how to speed print. Be kind to your test graders — write clearly. You may write in cursive or print. Just be neat. Check out Chapter 4 for more advice.

Thinking Positive

Young children often inform their parents that they're in charge of themselves. Although this idea may not be true for a 4-year-old child, it's certainly true for an adult. You're in charge of your thoughts. You can think positive thoughts, or you can think negative thoughts. All we can say is that positive thoughts will make you happier, more productive, and more confident, all of which can help you do your best on the GED tests.

Doing Your Best, No Matter What

Not everyone passes the GED tests the first time. If you've taken the tests before, don't see yourself as a failure for not passing them — see the situation as a learning experience. Use your last test as motivation to discover your academic weaknesses. Sometimes you can gain more from not succeeding than from succeeding. Whether you're taking the tests for the first time or not, focus on doing your best.

Life is full of ups and downs. Although you may do your best on the test, unfortunately, fate may scheme against you. You may be a bit under the weather, or your children may have gotten on your last nerve right before you left the house. Regardless, don't worry. You can always retake the tests. Keep in mind that doing your best can build your confidence to achieve more at the next opportunity.

You can retake the tests up to three times a year and over several years, if needed. Failing once isn't a permanent condition, but not doing your best can become one.

You only have to retake the tests that you didn't pass. *Note:* There is an additional fee to retake individual tests. The prices may vary, so consult your local administrator.

Chapter 31

Ten Ways to Use Your GED After You Pass the Tests

In This Chapter

▶ Getting the most out of your diploma in your work life

▶ Reaping a few more personal benefits from your diploma

*P*assing the GED tests makes life more rewarding because it opens doors that you may not have even known were closed before you passed the tests. You've probably already figured out why you want your GED; if not, this chapter shares ten great advantages the GED diploma can give you.

Getting a Job

Many employers want to see a high school diploma or its equivalent before they even think about giving you a job. In fact, a high school diploma or its equivalent is often used as a screening tool for interviews. A GED allows you to jump this hurdle. It shows potential employers that you've mastered skills equal to most high school graduates. This accomplishment can help you get an interview, and, when the interviewer sees how brilliant you are, it can help you get a job.

The U.S. government, one of the country's largest employers, accepts a GED as being equivalent to a high school diploma. Who's going to argue with Uncle Sam?

Being Promoted

If you're already working, you want to show your supervisor that you're ready for a promotion. The GED says, "I worked hard for this diploma and achieved something special!" Passing the GED helps you show your employer that you're ready to do the same — that is, work hard — on the job. It also shows that you've taken responsibility for your life and are ready to take on additional responsibility at work. Earning a GED gives you a document that shows you've mastered skills and are ready to master some more. You've solved problems and read charts and diagrams, and you're ready to do the same at work.

Showing Others What You Can Achieve

When you earn your GED, you show the world that you accomplished — on your own — what most other high school students needed a building, teachers, counselors, principals, and at least four years to accomplish. Now's the time to visit old teachers and go to reunions to show your past acquaintances what you've accomplished on your own. Sometimes we even think you should get to wear a badge that says, "GED — I Did It!" After all, being able to show others that you've accomplished something major thanks to your own hard work is important — in both your personal and professional lives.

Including Your GED in Your College Portfolio

Your college portfolio is a binder that lists all your skills and experiences in an organized manner. Many colleges have a particular format they want you to use for your portfolio; if yours doesn't, employment counselors can suggest generic formats. You can also make up a format. The important thing is to have a place where you list all your skills and experiences that you can take to college and job interviews.

Your GED is the centerpiece of your portfolio. The diploma is a stamp of approval on all your prior learning. It shows that you officially know what high school graduates comprehend.

Proving You're Ready for Further Education

After you master the skills equal to most high school graduates, you're ready to go on to the next step: college. Most colleges accept the GED as proof of the equivalency to high school graduation. If your goal is further education, remind the registrars at the colleges you want to attend that you're a mature student who has worked hard to get where you are. Emphasize the real-world skills you've mastered by working in the real world, and explain how those skills make you a great candidate for college.

In an address to a joint session of Congress on February 24, 2009, President Obama asserted the need to graduate more high school students and to support their entrance into postsecondary institutions. Passing the GED tests proves that you're ready to be one of these students who is ready to enter college.

Setting an Example for Your Kids

If you're like most people, you want your kids (or grandchildren) to be better educated and more successful than you were. As soon as you pass the GED tests, you set the bar a little higher for them. Your accomplishment also reminds your kids that education is important — for you and them.

Enhancing Your Wall Décor

You may already have interesting mementos of your life hanging on your wall, but what could be more exciting than your very own framed GED diploma? A diploma looks great on your wall because it represents all the hard work you put in to passing the tests — not to mention your accomplishment in doing so.

If you plan to frame your GED diploma, make a couple of copies for prospective employers and colleges before you do so. Make copies of the transcript of your test results, as well. That way, you're ready to include these copies with your job and college applications (as soon as you finish the rest of them).

Making You Feel like Part of a Select Group

Earning the GED means that you've outperformed 40 percent of high school seniors, which in itself is impressive. It also places you among great company. Comedian Bill Cosby and Dave Thomas, the late founder of Wendy's, are GED graduates. Although no one can promise that passing the GED tests will make you a show-business star or help you start a fast-food chain, it will make you feel very special. Who knows when you'll become famous enough to be listed in this section of a future edition?

Motivating Yourself

One thing about challenging tests is that you have to face the challenges they throw at you on your own. You can use the fact that you overcame those challenges thanks to your hard work and determination to motivate yourself in your future endeavors. If you successfully passed the GED tests through rigid preparation and planning, nothing can stop you. After all, you've accomplished something not everyone can do. Enjoy the feeling you get from passing the GED, and use it in the future as you go on to bigger and better pursuits.

Improving Your Self-Esteem

When you pass the GED tests, you're essentially a high school graduate and can prove it (thanks to the handy diploma and transcript you receive upon passing the test). But the piece of paper is only concrete proof of your accomplishment. The real results are in your brain and in your own feelings about yourself. You need to remember that you passed the tests by yourself, with a little help from preparation texts, perhaps — but the real work was yours. Enjoy the feeling of accomplishment you feel after passing the tests, and use it to feel better about yourself.

Index

• A •

academic material, 119
accommodations for test taking, 17, 18
The ACT For Dummies, 4th ed. (Gilman, Saydak, Vlk), 393
Adams, Scott (author)
  CliffsQuickReview Physics, 393
age requirement for taking the GED test, 22
Alcamo, I. Edward (author)
  CliffsQuickReview Biology, 393
algebra
  Mathematics Test, 14, 296–297, 314–318
  sample problems, 314–318
Algebra For Dummies (Sterling), 391
Algebra II For Dummies (Sterling), 391
Algebra Workbook For Dummies (Sterling), 391
alternate-format grid, Mathematics Test, 14–16, 298–299
American history, 10, 118
analysis skills
  GED questions, 35
  Language Arts, Reading Test, 244
  Social Studies Test, 119–120
answers
  checking on practice tests, 25
  eliminating incorrect, 36
  not counting incorrect on the GED, 19, 37
  reviewing at the end of the test, 28, 37
anthology, defined, 243
AP English Literature & Composition For Dummies (Woods), 36
apostrophes, 43
application skills
  GED questions, 35
  Language Arts, Reading Test, 243–244
  Social Studies Test, 119–120
apprenticeships, opportunities for, 23
arrival (early) at the test, 31–32, 395–396, 400

• B •

bar graphs, 179–180
Basic Math and Pre-Algebra For Dummies (Zegarelli), 300
Basic Math and Pre-Algebra Workbook For Dummies (Zegarelli), 300
Biggs, Emily Dotson (author)
  CliffsQuickReview Writing, Grammar, Usage, and Style, 393
Biology For Dummies (Siegfried), 391
blogs, using as writing practice, 45
Bobrow, Jerry (author)
  Cliffs Math Review for Standardized Tests, 392
  CliffsQuickReview Algebra I, 392
  CliffsQuickReview Basic Math and Pre-Algebra, 393
Bobrow Test Preparation Services
  CliffsAP Chemistry, 4th ed., 392
body of an essay, 52, 53
books, not bringing to the GED, 33
brainstorming, 51
breakfast, eating before the test, 31
breathing deeply, 28, 31, 396
Browning, William (author)
  Cliffs Memory Power for Exams, 392

• C •

calculators
  Mathematics Test, Part I, 13, 296, 299–300, 357
  Mathematics Test, Part II, 300
  not bringing to the GED, 33
Canada, GED test recognition in, 22
capitalization, 43
Casio FX-260 solar calculator, 299
Casson, Allan (author)
  CliffsAP English Literature and Composition, 2nd ed., 392
causal relationships, 35, 310
cell phones, not bringing to the GED, 33
cells, 177
charts
  Science Test, 180
  Social Studies Test, 121, 123
chemistry, 11, 177, 185
circle graphs, 179–180
civics, 10, 118
The Civil War For Dummies (Dickson), 391
clenching and unclenching fists, for relaxation, 397
Cliffs Math Review for Standardized Tests (Bobrow), 392
Cliffs Memory Power for Exams (Browning), 392
Cliffs Verbal Review for Standardized Tests (Covino, Orton), 392
CliffsAP Biology, 3rd ed. (Pack), 392
CliffsAP Chemistry, 4th ed. (Bobrow Test Preparation Services), 392
CliffsAP English Language and Composition, 3rd ed. (Swovelin), 392
CliffsAP English Literature and Composition, 2nd ed. (Casson), 392
CliffsAP series, 392
CliffsAP United States History, 3rd ed. (Soifer, Hoffman), 392
CliffsNotes, Web site for, 392
CliffsNotes Literature series, 392
CliffsQuickReview Algebra I (Bobrow), 392
CliffsQuickReview Algebra II (Kohn, Herzog), 393
CliffsQuickReview American Government (Soifer, Hoffman, Voss), 393

CliffsQuickReview Anatomy and Physiology (Pack), 393
CliffsQuickReview Astronomy (Peterson), 393
CliffsQuickReview Basic Math and Pre-Algebra (Bobrow), 393
CliffsQuickReview Biology (Alcamo, Schweitzer), 393
CliffsQuickReview Chemistry (Nathan, Henrickson), 393
CliffsQuickReview Economics (Duffy), 393
CliffsQuickReview Geometry (Kohn), 393
CliffsQuickReview Linear Algebra (Leduc), 393
CliffsQuickReview Physical Geology (Crawford), 393
CliffsQuickReview Physics (Huetinck, Adams), 393
CliffsQuickReview Psychology (Sonderegger), 393
CliffsQuickReview series, 392–393
CliffsQuickReview U.S. History I (Soifer, Hoffman), 393
CliffsQuickReview U.S. History II (Soifer, Hoffman), 393
CliffsQuickReview Writing, Grammar, Usage, and Style (Eggenschwiler, Biggs), 393
cognitive skills for questions, 36
college portfolio, 404
column graphs, 179–180
commas, 43
community documents, 12, 246–247
comparing, defined, 35
comprehension skills
  GED questions, 35–36
  Language Arts, Reading Test, 243
  Social Studies Test, 119–120
concluding sentence of an essay, 52, 53
Congress For Dummies (Silverberg), 391
construction shift, type of question, 8
contractions, 43
contrasting, defined, 35
conventions used in the book, 1
coordinate-plane grid, 14–16, 299, 306, 310–311
correction, type of question, 8

correlating relationship, 310
Cosby, Bill (comedian), 405
counting backward as relaxation technique, 396
Covino, William (author)
  Cliffs Verbal Review for Standardized Tests, 392
Crawford, Mark J. (author)
  CliffsQuickReview Physical Geology, 393
critical reviews of visual and performing arts, 12, 246

• D •

data analysis, 14, 296, 309–314
decimals, 298
deep breathing, 28, 31, 396
DeLaney, Ann (author)
  Politics For Dummies, 2nd ed., 392
details in an essay, 49
development in an essay, 49
diagrams
  components of, 181
  defined, 180
  Science Test, questions based on, 180–181
Dickson, Keith D. (author)
  The Civil War For Dummies, 391
  World War II For Dummies, 392
dictionaries
  creating own for Science Test, 182
  reading to prepare for Language Arts, Reading Test, 247
disabilities, 17, 18
doing your best on the test, 401–402
Doyle, John (author)
  Shakespeare For Dummies, 392
drafting an essay, 52–53
drama, 12, 245
dressing comfortably for the GED Tests, 395
driving to the GED Test, 395
Duffy, John (author)
  CliffsQuickReview Economics, 393
For Dummies subject-matter books, 391–392
For Dummies test-preparation books, 36
For Dummies travel books, 392

For Dummies Web site, 392
For Dummies workplace books, 392

• E •

early arrival at the test, 31–32, 395–396, 400
earth science, 11, 177, 185
economics, 10, 119
edited American English, using appropriately, 49
editing an essay, 50, 53
educational opportunities, 22, 23, 29, 404
Eggenschwiler, Jean (author)
  CliffsQuickReview Writing, Grammar, Usage, and Style, 393
eligibility for GED tests, 17
emotional disabilities, 17
employee behavior rules, 246
employment opportunities, 22, 23, 29, 403
English as a second language, 18–19, 22
English Grammar For Dummies, 2nd ed. (Woods), 42, 45, 391
environmental conditions, 119
equations, 14
erosion, 177
essays. *See* Language Arts, Writing Test, Part II
evaluation skills
  GED questions, 36
  Social Studies Test, 119–120
Everyday Math For Dummies (Seiter), 391
evolution, 177
examiner, defined, 33

• F •

facts, separating from opinions, 35
fees for the test, 32
fiction passages, 12, 245–246
focusing on the test, 400–401
forces, 176
formula sheet for Mathematics Test, 296, 329, 365
fractions, 298
French, 18, 22
functions, mathematical, 296–297, 314–318

• G •

The GED (General Educational Development) test. *See also* specific tests
accommodations for, 17–18
analysis questions, 35, 119–120, 244
application questions, 35, 119–120, 243–244
arrival (early) at the test, 31–32, 395–396, 400
cognitive skills questions, 36
comprehension questions, 35–36, 119–120, 243
eligibility for, 17
English as a second language, 18–19, 22
evaluation questions, 36, 119, 120
GED Testing Service, 19
glancing around during, 33, 38, 401
instructions, reading carefully, 24
intelligent guessing, 37
knowing when to take the test, 17
Language Arts, Reading Test, 12–13
Language Arts, Writing Test, 7–9
Mathematics Test, Parts I and II, 13–16
mental preparation, 38, 394
people who take, 21–22
practice tests, using to prepare for, 23–24
practice tests, working through, 24–26
preparation, list of needs for, 26–28
preparation class, taking, 393–394
question types, identifying, 35–36
questions, addressing and answering, 36
questions, reviewing, on practice tests, 25–26
reasons for taking, 22–23, 29, 403–405
relaxation techniques, 28, 38, 396–397
retaking, 20, 402
reviewing at the end of the test, 28, 37
sample questions, Web site for, 26
scheduling the test, 16–18, 399
Science Test, 11–12
scores, determining, 19
scores, maximizing, 391–397
scores, poor, 20
scoring of, 19–20
signing up for, 18
Social Studies Test, 10–11
special circumstances, 18
synthesis questions, 36, 244
test, before, 31–32
test sections, 7–16
test-taking strategies, 34–37
time management, before the tests, 26–28
time management, during the tests, 24, 28, 34
unusual circumstances, 18
Web site for test, 16, 19, 26
what not to bring, 32–33
what to bring, 32
what to expect, 33
GED achievement, uses for
college portfolio, 404
education, furthering, 404
as example for children, 404
job, getting, 403
personal motivation, 405
promotions at work, 403
select group, part of, 405
self-esteem, 405
showing your achievements, 404
GED Test success
being on time, 400
being realistic, 400
doing your best, 401–402
looking only at your test, 401
not listening to other test takers, 400
preparing for, 399
selecting date for, 399
staying focused, 400–401
thinking positively, 401
writing clearly and carefully, 401
geography, 10, 119
Geography For Dummies (Heatwole), 391
geology, 177
geometry, 14, 296, 299, 304–308
Geometry For Dummies, 2nd ed. (Ryan), 391
Gilman, Michelle Rose (author)
The ACT For Dummies, 4th ed., 393
glancing around during GED test, 33, 38, 401
goal statements, 246
government, 10, 118

grammar
defined, 41
practice in everyday speaking, 45
rules, mastering, 44
usage, 43
graphical conventions, 128
graphs
components of, 180
defined, 179
Science Test, 179–180
Social Studies Test, 121–122, 128
types of, 179–180
guessing strategies, 37

• H •

Haugen, Peter (author)
World History For Dummies, 2nd ed., 392
Heads Up icon, explained, 4
Heatwole, Charles (author)
Geography For Dummies, 391
Henrickson, Charles (author)
CliffsQuickReview Chemistry, 393
heredity, 177
Herzog, Alan (author)
CliffsQuickReview Algebra II, 393
history test. *See* Social Studies Test
Hoffman, Abraham (author)
CliffsAP United States History, 3rd ed., 392
CliffsQuickReview American Government, 393
CliffsQuickReview U.S. History I, 393
CliffsQuickReview U.S. History II, 393
homonyms, 43, 45
horizontal axis on graphs, 180
how-to books, 8, 44
Huetinck, Linda (author)
CliffsQuickReview Physics, 393
hypotenuse of a triangle, 306

• I •

icons, explained, 4
identification, proper, 32, 395
immigrants, 22
implications, defined, 121
improper fractions, 298
inert chemicals, defined, 176

inferring, defined, 35
informational works, 8, 44
intersection of two lines, 304
introduction for an essay,
    51, 52
introductory sentences in para-
    graphs, 53
intuition, 36

• *J* •

journals, using for writing
    practice, 45

• *K* •

Kohn, Edward (author)
    CliffsQuickReview Algebra II,
    393
    CliffsQuickReview Geometry,
    393

• *L* •

labels on visual material
    diagrams, 181
    graphs, 180
    maps, 181
Language Arts, Reading Test
    answer keys, 270, 292
    answer sheets, 253, 273
    answers and explanations,
        267–270, 289–292
    community documents,
        12, 246–247
    critical reviews of visual and
        performing arts, 12, 246
    dictionaries, using, 247
    drama, 12, 245
    examples of questions, 12–13
    helpful pointers, 250
    instructions, 251, 255, 271, 275
    literary passages, 245–246
    multiple-choice questions,
        12, 244
    nonfiction passages, 12,
        246–247
    poetry, 12, 245
    practice tests, 247–248,
        256–266, 276–287
    practicing, 247–248
    preparation strategies,
        247–248
    prose fiction, 12, 245–246
    purpose questions, 244, 250
    question types, 245–247

sample problems, 248–250
skills required, 243–244
test format, 244
time management, 248
workplace documents,
    12, 246–247
Language Arts, Writing Test,
    Part I
    answer keys, 87, 114
    answer sheets, 59, 91
    answers and explanations,
        81–85, 109–112
    capitalization, 43
    construction shift questions, 8
    contractions, 43
    correction questions, 8
    examples, 8–9
    format of, 7–9, 41–42
    grammar, 41, 43–45
    helpful pointers, 48
    how-to books, 8, 44
    informational works, 8
    instructions for tests,
        57, 61, 89, 93
    mechanics of writing, 42–43
    multiple-choice questions,
        8, 42, 45, 57, 89
    organization, 43
    passages, questions based
        on, 44
    possessives, 43
    practice tests, 45, 61–76,
        93–104
    preparation for, 44–45
    punctuation, 43, 45
    question types, 8
    reading and writing,
        practicing, 45
    reading before, 44
    revision questions, 8
    sample problems, 46–48
    sentence structure, 43
    skills covered, 42–44
    speed-reading, 46
    spelling, 43, 45
    time management, 45–46
    usage, 43
    workplace materials, 8, 44
Language Arts, Writing Test,
    Part II
    answer sheets, 79–80, 107–108
    criteria, Web site for, 49
    details, 49
    development, 49
    drafting, 52–53
    edited written English, using
        appropriately, 49
    editing, 50, 53
    essay, writing, 9, 42
    examples, using, 50

format of, 7, 9, 41, 42
grading of essay, 49
helpful pointers, 55–56
instructions, 57, 77–78, 89,
    105–106
main points, 51–53, 55
organization, 49
passing, 49
planning, 50, 51–52
practice essays, writing, 51
practice tests, essays for,
    85–87, 113–114
preparation for, 50–51
reading to improve writing, 50
revising, 53
rewriting the essay, 54
sample essays, practicing
    with, 54–55
time management, 51–54
topic, writing about, 49–50
word choice, 49
writing, practicing, 50–51
writing neatly, 9, 50
writing skills, 49
laptop computers, not bringing
    to the GED, 33
learning disabilities, 17, 18
Leduc, Steven A. (author)
    *CliffsQuickReview Linear
    Algebra,* 393
legal documents, 246
legends on visual materials
    graphs, 180
    maps, 181
letters, 247
life sciences, 11, 177, 185
line graphs, 179–180
Lischner, Ray (author)
    Shakespeare For Dummies, 392
literary passages, 245–246

• *M* •

main points in an essay,
    51–53, 55
manuals, 247
maps
    components of, 181
    defined, 181
    Science Test, 181
    Social Studies Test, 119,
        121–123, 128
Maran, Stephen P. (author)
    Astronomy For Dummies,
    2nd ed., 391
*Math Word Problems For
    Dummies* (Sterling),
    299, 300

Mathematics Test
  algebra, 14, 296–297, 314–318
  alternate-format grids, 14–16, 298–299
  coordinate-plane grid, 14–16, 299, 306, 310–311
  data analysis, 14, 296, 309–314
  equations, 14
  examples of questions, 14–16
  formula sheet, 296, 329, 365
  functions, 296–297, 314–318
  geometry, 14, 296, 304–308
  helpful pointers, 319–320
  measurement, 14, 296, 304–308
  multiple-choice questions, 14, 297–298
  number operations, 14, 296, 302–304
  number sense, 296, 302–304
  patterns, 14, 296–297, 314–318
  preparation strategies, 300–301
  pretest, 318–319
  probability, 14, 296, 309–314
  questions, types of, 297–300
  sample problems, 302–319
  skills for, 295
  standard grid, 14–15, 298–299
  statistics, 14, 296, 309–314
  test format, 296–297
  time management, 301–302
Mathematics Test, Part I
  answer keys, 355, 387
  answer sheets, 323, 359
  answers and explanations, 347–351, 379–383
  calculators, 13, 299–300
  instructions, 321, 357
  practice tests, 325–335, 361–369
Mathematics Test, Part II
  answer keys, 356, 388
  answer sheets, 324, 360
  answers and explanations, 352–354, 384–387
  calculators, not using, 13, 300
  instructions, 321, 357
  practice tests, 336–345, 370–378
measurement, 14, 296, 304–308
mechanics of writing, 42–43
medical disabilities, 17, 18
meditation, 28
mental preparation for the test, 38, 394
mission statements, 246
mixed numbers, 298

mobile phones, not bringing to the GED, 33
motivation, personal, after passing the GED, 405
MP3 players, not bringing to the GED, 33
multiple-choice questions
  Language Arts, Reading Test, 12, 244
  Language Arts, Writing Test, Part I, 8, 42, 45, 57, 89
  Mathematics Test, 14, 297–298
  Science Test, 11, 176
  Social Studies Test, 10, 118

• N •

Nathan, Harold D. (author)
  CliffsQuickReview Chemistry, 393
National Science Education Standards, Web site for, 177
negative numbers, 299
nervousness, 33, 38. *See also* relaxation techniques
nonfiction prose, 12, 246–247
not-enough-information questions, 297, 300
notes, not bringing to the GED, 33
number operations, 14, 296, 302–304
number sense, 296, 302–304

• O •

older people taking the GED, 18
opinions, separating from facts, 35
organization
  Language Arts, Writing Test, Part I, 43
  Language Arts, Writing Test, Part II, 49
Orton, Peter (author)
  Cliffs Verbal Review for Standardized Tests, 392
overconfidence, 399

• P •

Pack, Phillip (author)
  CliffsAP Biology, 3rd ed., 392
  CliffsQuickReview Anatomy and Physiology, 393

Paddock, Lisa (author)
  Supreme Court For Dummies, 392
paragraphs, writing clear and effective, 53, 55–56
passages
  Language Arts, Writing Test, Part I, 44
  Science Test, 178, 182
  Social Studies Test, 120–121
patterns, mathematical, 14, 296–297, 314–318
pencils, bringing to the test, 32
perception, 36
personal satisfaction in taking the GED, 23
Peterson, Charles (author)
  CliffsQuickReview Astronomy, 393
photographs, 123
physical science, 11, 176–177
physics, 11, 177, 185
pie charts, 179–180
pie graphs, 179–180
planning an essay, 51–52
poetry, 12, 245
The Poetry Center
  Poetry For Dummies, 392
Poetry For Dummies (The Poetry Center, Timpane, and Watts), 392
political cartoons, 123
Politics For Dummies, 2nd ed. (DeLaney), 392
positive thinking, 396, 401
possessives, 43
practice tests
  defined, 23
  GED, preparing for, 23–24
  working through, 24–26
prayer, as a way to focus, 28
preparation strategies
  Language Arts, Reading Test, 247–248
  Mathematics Test, 300–301
  Science Test, 182
  Social Studies Test, 124
pretest, defined, 23
primary sources, 119
probability, 14, 296, 309–314
proctors, 33
promotions at work, after passing the GED, 403
prose fiction, 12, 245–246
punctuation, 43, 45, 55
purpose questions, 244, 250
Pythagorean relationship (theorem), 296, 305–306

• Q •

questions
  addressing and answering, 36
  analysis, type of, 35,
    119–120, 244
  application, type of, 35,
    119–120, 243–244
  cognitive skills for questions,
    36
  comprehension, type of,
    35–36, 119–120, 243
  easy, answering first,
    25, 28, 396
  evaluation, type of, 36, 119–120
  Language Arts, Reading Test,
    245–247
  Language Arts, Writing Test,
    Part I, 8
  Mathematics Test, 297–300
  Science Test, 177–181
  Social Studies Test, 119–123
  synthesis, type of, 36, 244
  time allowed per question, 34
  types of, 35–36

• R •

reactions, chemical, 176
reading as test preparation
  Language Arts, Reading Test,
    247
  Language Arts, Writing Test,
    Part I, 44, 45
  Language Arts, Writing Test,
    Part II, 50
  Science Test, 182
  Social Studies Test, 121, 123–124
Reading Test. *See* Language
  Arts, Reading Test
realistic expectations about the
  test, 400
reasoning skills, 36
registration confirmation, 32
registration fees, 32
relationships, graphs showing,
  180
relaxation techniques
  breathing deeply, 28, 31, 396
  clenching and unclenching
    fists, 397
  counting backward, 396
  meditation, 28
  positive thinking, 396, 401
  prayer, 28
  staring out a window, 397
  taking time for, 38

Remember icon, explained, 4
rest and sleep before the test,
  31, 394
retaking tests, 20, 402
reviewing answers at the end of
  the test, 28, 37
revising an essay, 53
revision, type of question, 8
rewriting an essay, 54
Rozakis, Laurie E. (author)
  Vocabulary For Dummies, 392
rules of the test, 38
Ryan, Mark (author)
  Geometry For Dummies,
    2nd ed., 391

• S •

The SAT I For Dummies, 6th ed.
  (Woods), 393
Saydak, Veronica (author)
  The ACT For Dummies, 4th ed.,
    393
scale on maps, 181
scheduling
  GED tests, 16–18, 399
  studying, time for, 394
school attendance, and GED eligibility, 22
Schweitzer, Kelly (author)
  CliffsQuickReview Biology, 393
Science Test
  answer keys, 212, 239
  answer sheets, 189, 215
  answers and explanations,
    207–211, 235–238
  astronomy, 177
  chemistry, 11, 177, 185
  diagrams, 180–181
  dictionaries, creating own, 182
  earth science, 11, 177, 185
  examples of questions, 11–12
  format of, 176–177
  geology, 177
  graphs, 179–180
  helpful pointers, 184–185
  instructions, 187, 191, 213, 217
  Internet sites on science
    subjects, 185
  life sciences, 11, 177, 185
  maps, 181
  multiple-choice questions,
    11, 176
  passages, 178, 182
  physical science, 11, 176–177
  physics, 11, 177, 185
  practice tests, 182, 192–206,
    218–234

preparation strategies, 182
  questions, types of, 177–181
  sample problems, 183–184
  skills for, 175–176
  space science, 11, 177, 185
  tables, 179, 180
  time management, 182
  visual materials, 179–181
  weather, 177
  Web sites for studying, 185
scientific method
  defined, 176
  steps of, 176
scores
  determining, 19
  not counting incorrect
    answers, 19, 37
  maximizing, 391–397
  receiving poor, 20
scratch paper
  Language Arts, Writing Test,
    Part II, 55
  Mathematics Test, 296
  not bringing to the GED, 33
secondary sources, 119
self-esteem, 405
sentence structure, 43
sentence types, using a variety
  of, 56
Seiter, Charles (author)
  Everyday Math For Dummies,
    391
set-up questions, Mathematics
  Test, 297
Shakespeare For Dummies
  (Doyle, Lischner), 392
Siegfried, Donna Rae (author)
  Biology For Dummies, 391
Silverberg, David (author)
  Congress For Dummies, 391
sleep and rest before the test,
  31, 394
slope of a line, 304
Social Studies Test
  academic material, 119
  American history, 10, 118
  answer keys, 150, 172
  answer sheets, 131, 153
  answers and explanations,
    147–150, 169–172
  assumptions, 121, 128
  civics, 10, 118
  economics, 10, 119
  environmental conditions, 119
  examples of questions, 10–11
  geography, 10, 119
  government, 10, 118
  graphical conventions, 128
  graphs, 121, 122, 128

helpful pointers, 128
instructions, 129, 133, 151, 155
maps, 119, 121–123, 128
multiple-choice questions, 10, 118
passages, questions about, 119, 120–121
practice tests, 124, 134–145, 156–168
preparation strategies, 124
primary sources, 119
questions, types of, 119–120
sample problems, 125–128
secondary sources, 119
skills, 117–118
test format, 118–119
time management, 125
visual materials, questions about, 121–123
weather, 119
workplace material, 119
world history, 10, 118
Soifer, Paul (author)
  CliffsAP United States History, 3rd ed., 392
  CliffsQuickReview American Government, 393
  CliffsQuickReview U.S. History I, 393
  CliffsQuickReview U.S. History II, 393
Sonderegger, Theo (author)
  CliffsQuickReview Psychology, 393
space science, 11, 177, 185
Spanish, 18, 22
Speed Reading For Dummies (Sutz, with Weverka), 46, 250, 302
speed-reading
  Language Arts, Writing Test, Part I, 46
  Mathematics Test, 302
spelling, 43, 45, 55
standard grid, 14–15, 298–299
staring out a window as relaxation technique, 397
statistics, 14, 296, 309–314
Sterling, Mary Jane (author)
  Algebra For Dummies, 391
  Algebra II For Dummies, 391
  Algebra Workbook For Dummies, 391
  Math Word Problems For Dummies, 299, 300
studying
  scheduling time for, 394
  using subject-matter books, 391–393

subject-matter books, studying, 391–393
Supreme Court For Dummies (Paddock), 392
Sutz, Richard (author)
  Speed Reading For Dummies, 46, 250, 302
Swovelin, Barbara (author)
  CliffsAP English Language and Composition, 3rd ed., 392
synthesis skills
  GED questions, 36
  Language Arts, Reading Test, 244

• T •

tables
  defined, 179
  Science Test, 179–180
  Social Studies Test, 123
Technical Stuff icon, explained, 4
Test of English as a Foreign Language (TOEFL), 19
test success, GED
  being on time, 400
  being realistic, 400
  doing your best, 401–402
  looking only at your test, 401
  not listening to other test takers, 400
  preparing for, 399
  selecting date for, 399
  staying focused, 400–401
  thinking positively, 401
  writing clearly and carefully, 401
tests
  history. *See* Social Studies Test
  math. *See* Mathematics Test
  reading. *See* Language Arts, Reading Test
  science. *See* Science Test
  writing. *See* Language Arts, Writing Test, Part I and Part II
test-taking strategies
  addressing and answering questions, 36
  identifying question types, 35–36
  intelligent guessing, 37
  leaving time for review, 37
  watching the clock, 34
Thomas, Dave (businessman), 405

time management
  Language Arts, Reading Test, 248
  Language Arts, Writing Test, Part I, 45–46
  Language Arts, Writing Test, Part II, 51–54
  Mathematics Test, 301–302
  Science Test, 182
  Social Studies Test, 125
  test, before, 26–28
  test, during, 24, 28, 34
Timpane, John (author)
  Poetry For Dummies, 392
Tip icon, explained, 4
titles on visual materials
  diagrams, 181
  graphs, 180
  maps, 181
  tables, 179
TOEFL (Test of English as a Foreign Language), 19
topic, writing about, 49–50
transition sentences in paragraphs, 53, 55

• U •

U.S. History For Dummies, 2nd ed. (Wiegand), 392
usage questions, 43

• V •

vertical axis on graphs, 180
Vlk, Suzee (author)
  The ACT For Dummies, 4th ed., 393
vision statements, 246
visual impairment, 18
visual materials
  defined, 179
  Science Test, 179–181, 182
  Social Studies Test, 121–123
vocabulary
  Language Arts, Reading Test, 247, 250
  Language Arts, Writing Test, Part II, 49, 55
Vocabulary For Dummies (Rozakis), 392
Voss, D. Stephen (author)
  CliffsQuickReview American Government, 393

• W •

water, 177
Watts, Maureen (author)
  Poetry For Dummies, 392
weather
  Science Test, 177
  Social Studies Test, 119
Weverka, Peter (author)
  Speed Reading For Dummies,
    250
Wiegand, Steve (author)
  U.S. History For Dummies,
    2nd ed., 392
Woods, Geraldine (author)
  AP English Literature &
    Composition For
    Dummies, 36
  English Grammar For
    Dummies, 2nd ed.,
    42, 45, 391
  The SAT I For Dummies,
    6th ed., 393
words. *See* vocabulary

workplace documents
  Language Arts, Reading Test,
    12, 246–247
  Language Arts, Writing Test,
    Part I, 8, 44
  Social Studies Test, 119
works of art, 123
world history, 10, 118
World History For Dummies,
    2nd ed. (Haugen), 392
World War II For Dummies
    (Dickson), 392
wristwatch, bringing to the
    test, 32
writing
  Language Arts, Writing Test,
    Part I, 45
  Language Arts, Writing Test,
    Part II, 50–51
  mechanics of, 42–43
  neatness, 9, 50
Writing Test. *See* Language
    Arts, Writing Test,
    Part I and Part II

• X •

x-axis, 299, 306, 310–311

• Y •

y-axis, 299, 306, 310–311
y-intercept of a line, 304

• Z •

Zegarelli, Mark (author)
  Basic Math and Pre-Algebra For
    Dummies, 300
  Basic Math and Pre-Algebra
    Workbook For Dummies,
    300

Business/Accounting & Bookkeeping

Bookkeeping For Dummies
978-0-7645-9848-7

eBay Business
All-in-One For Dummies,
2nd Edition
978-0-470-38536-4

Job Interviews
For Dummies,
3rd Edition
978-0-470-17748-8

Resumes For Dummies,
5th Edition
978-0-470-08037-5

Stock Investing
For Dummies,
3rd Edition
978-0-470-40114-9

Successful Time
Management
For Dummies
978-0-470-29034-7

Computer Hardware

BlackBerry For Dummies,
3rd Edition
978-0-470-45762-7

Computers For Seniors
For Dummies
978-0-470-24055-7

iPhone For Dummies,
2nd Edition
978-0-470-42342-4

Laptops For Dummies,
3rd Edition
978-0-470-27759-1

Macs For Dummies,
10th Edition
978-0-470-27817-8

Cooking & Entertaining

Cooking Basics
For Dummies,
3rd Edition
978-0-7645-7206-7

Wine For Dummies,
4th Edition
978-0-470-04579-4

Diet & Nutrition

Dieting For Dummies,
2nd Edition
978-0-7645-4149-0

Nutrition For Dummies,
4th Edition
978-0-471-79868-2

Weight Training
For Dummies,
3rd Edition
978-0-471-76845-6

Digital Photography

Digital Photography
For Dummies,
6th Edition
978-0-470-25074-7

Photoshop Elements 7
For Dummies
978-0-470-39700-8

Gardening

Gardening Basics
For Dummies
978-0-470-03749-2

Organic Gardening
For Dummies,
2nd Edition
978-0-470-43067-5

Green/Sustainable

Green Building
& Remodeling
For Dummies
978-0-4710-17559-0

Green Cleaning
For Dummies
978-0-470-39106-8

Green IT For Dummies
978-0-470-38688-0

Health

Diabetes For Dummies,
3rd Edition
978-0-470-27086-8

Food Allergies
For Dummies
978-0-470-09584-3

Living Gluten-Free
For Dummies
978-0-471-77383-2

Hobbies/General

Chess For Dummies,
2nd Edition
978-0-7645-8404-6

Drawing For Dummies
978-0-7645-5476-6

Knitting For Dummies,
2nd Edition
978-0-470-28747-7

Organizing For Dummies
978-0-7645-5300-4

SuDoku For Dummies
978-0-470-01892-7

Home Improvement

Energy Efficient Homes
For Dummies
978-0-470-37602-7

Home Theater
For Dummies,
3rd Edition
978-0-470-41189-6

Living the Country Lifestyle
All-in-One For Dummies
978-0-470-43061-3

Solar Power Your Home
For Dummies
978-0-470-17569-9

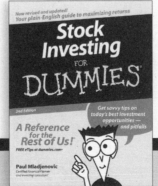

Internet

Blogging For Dummies,
2nd Edition
978-0-470-23017-6

eBay For Dummies,
6th Edition
978-0-470-49741-8

Facebook For Dummies
978-0-470-26273-3

Google Blogger
For Dummies
978-0-470-40742-4

Web Marketing
For Dummies,
2nd Edition
978-0-470-37181-7

WordPress For Dummies,
2nd Edition
978-0-470-40296-2

Language & Foreign Language

French For Dummies
978-0-7645-5193-2

Italian Phrases
For Dummies
978-0-7645-7203-6

Spanish For Dummies
978-0-7645-5194-9

Spanish For Dummies,
Audio Set
978-0-470-09585-0

Macintosh

Mac OS X Snow Leopard
For Dummies
978-0-470-43543-4

Math & Science

Algebra I For Dummies
978-0-7645-5325-7

Biology For Dummies
978-0-7645-5326-4

Calculus For Dummies
978-0-7645-2498-1

Chemistry For Dummies
978-0-7645-5430-8

Microsoft Office

Excel 2007 For Dummies
978-0-470-03737-9

Office 2007 All-in-One
Desk Reference
For Dummies
978-0-471-78279-7

Music

Guitar For Dummies,
2nd Edition
978-0-7645-9904-0

iPod & iTunes
For Dummies,
6th Edition
978-0-470-39062-7

Piano Exercises
For Dummies
978-0-470-38765-8

Parenting & Education

Parenting For Dummies,
2nd Edition
978-0-7645-5418-6

Type 1 Diabetes
For Dummies
978-0-470-17811-9

Pets

Cats For Dummies,
2nd Edition
978-0-7645-5275-5

Dog Training For Dummies,
2nd Edition
978-0-7645-8418-3

Puppies For Dummies,
2nd Edition
978-0-470-03717-1

Religion & Inspiration

The Bible For Dummies
978-0-7645-5296-0

Catholicism For Dummies
978-0-7645-5391-2

Women in the Bible
For Dummies
978-0-7645-8475-6

Self-Help & Relationship

Anger Management
For Dummies
978-0-470-03715-7

Overcoming Anxiety
For Dummies
978-0-7645-5447-6

Sports

Baseball For Dummies,
3rd Edition
978-0-7645-7537-2

Basketball For Dummies,
2nd Edition
978-0-7645-5248-9

Golf For Dummies,
3rd Edition
978-0-471-76871-5

Web Development

Web Design All-in-One
For Dummies
978-0-470-41796-6

Windows Vista

Windows Vista
For Dummies
978-0-471-75421-3